# Disordered Personalities and Crime

*Disordered Personalities and Crime* seeks to understand better how we respond to those individuals who have been labelled at various points in time as 'morally insane', 'psychopathic' or 'personality disordered'. Individuals whose behaviour is consistent with these diagnoses present challenges to both the criminal justice system and mental health systems, because the people who come to have such diagnoses seem to have a rational and realistic understanding of the world around them but can behave in ways that suggest they have little understanding of either the meaning or the consequences of their actions.

This book argues that an analysis of the history of these diagnoses will help to provide a better understanding of contemporary dilemmas. These are categories that have been shaped not only by the needs of criminal justice and the claims of expertise by professionals, but also by the fears, anxieties and demands of the wider public. In this book, David W. Jones demonstrates how important these diagnoses have been to the history of psychiatry and its claims for professional expertise, and also sheds light on the evolution of the insanity defence and helps explain why it remains a problematic and controversial issue even today.

This book will be key reading for students, researchers and academics who are interested in crime and its relationship to mental disorder and also for those interested in psychiatry and abnormal psychology.

**David W. Jones** is Reader in Psychosocial Studies at the University of East London and is the author of *Understanding Criminal Behaviour: Psychosocial Approaches to Criminality* (Willan, 2008) and, on mental illness, *Myths, Madness and the Family* (Palgrave, 2002).

This thoughtful, scholarly and readable work by David Jones explores the concepts of antisocial personality disorder (ASPD) and psychopathy, from their roots in the nineteenth-century notion of 'moral insanity' to the present day. His thesis, which is closely argued, is that ASPD is a construction of ideas located between different worlds: especially the social, the cultural and the psychological. Jones makes a clear case that the current focus on the neurophysiological and neuroanatomical accounts of ASPD miss the social dimension and that the social dimension is crucial to understanding the problems of those with ASPD, and the development of possible interventions. This is a highly readable and thought-provoking book and I recommend it to anyone working in the field of ASPD and the psychology of crime.

**Gwen Adshead**, *currently Consultant Forensic Psychiatrist at Ravenswood House, Medium Secure Unit and formerly Broadmoor High Security Hospital, UK*

This is a scholarly, instructive and insightful book. It is a fascinating read and a must for criminal justice professionals, particularly those working in clinical, criminal and legal contexts.

**Monica Lloyd**, *Senior Lecturer in Forensic Psychology, University of Birmingham, UK; formerly Forensic Psychologist in the Prison Service, HM Inspectorate of Prisons and National Offender Management Service*

The 'psychopath' haunts western culture. But does this figure really exist? David Jones's richly-documented history strikes a welcome sceptical note. Tracing the evolution of psychopathy from early nineteenth-century 'moral insanity' through to present-day 'antisocial personality disorder', Jones dissects the political and cultural forces shaping these diagnostic categories. An important and provocative book which deserves to be widely read and discussed.

**Barbara Gold Taylor**, *Professor of Humanities, Queen Mary University of London, UK*

# Disordered Personalities and Crime

An analysis of the history of moral insanity

David W. Jones

Routledge
Taylor & Francis Group
LONDON AND NEW YORK

First published 2016
by Routledge
2 Park Square, Milton Park, Abingdon, Oxon, OX14 4RN

and by Routledge
711 Third Avenue, New York, NY 10017

*Routledge is an imprint of the Taylor & Francis Group, an informa business*

© 2016 David W. Jones

The right of David W. Jones to be identified as author of this work has been asserted by him in accordance with sections 77 and 78 of the Copyright, Designs and Patents Act 1988.

All rights reserved. No part of this book may be reprinted or reproduced or utilised in any form or by any electronic, mechanical, or other means, now known or hereafter invented, including photocopying and recording, or in any information storage or retrieval system, without permission in writing from the publishers.

*Trademark notice:* Product or corporate names may be trademarks or registered trademarks, and are used only for identification and explanation without intent to infringe.

*British Library Cataloguing in Publication Data*
A catalogue record for this book is available from the British Library

*Library of Congress Cataloging-in-Publication Data*
Jones, David W. (David Wyn), 1964–.
  Disordered personalities and crime: an analysis of the history of moral insanity/ David W. Jones.
  pages cm
  Includes bibliographical references.
  1. People with mental disabilities and crime. 2. Personality disorders.
  3. Psychopaths. 4. Mentally ill offenders. 5. Criminals – Mental health.
  I. Title.
  HV6133.J66 2015
  364.3'8 – dc23
  2015004376

ISBN: 978-0-415-50206-1 (hbk)
ISBN: 978-0-415-50217-7 (pbk)
ISBN: 978-0-203-49374-8 (ebk)

Typeset in Bembo and Gill Sans
by Florence Production Ltd, Stoodleigh, Devon, UK
Printed and bound in Great Britain by Ashford Colour Press Ltd, Gosport, Hampshire

# Contents

*List of illustrations* vii
*Preface* ix
*Acknowledgements* xi

Introduction: excavating moral insanity 1

1 Informal insanity in the eighteenth-century court 21

   *1.1 The Old Bailey, the public sphere and new forms of insanity 22*
   *1.2 The state and the informalisation of control 33*

2 The medical discourse of 'moral insanity' 49

   *2.1 The beginning of psychiatry: the entrepreneurs of the moral world 50*
   *2.2 Medics, moral insanity and the law 61*

3 The rise of psychiatry in the post-M'Naghten years 79

   *3.1 The professionalisation of psychiatry 81*
   *3.2 The Townley case and the crisis of confidence (1863) 84*
   *3.3 Psychiatry, biology and the prison population 91*

4 Culture and moral insanity: selfhood and social degeneration 99

   *4.1 The novel, industrialisation and moral insanity 101*
   *4.2 Degeneracy: psychiatry and culture 109*

5 Moral imbecility: feeblemindedness and the road to eugenics 121

   *5.1 German psychiatry and constitutional psychopathy 123*
   *5.2 Criminal feeblemindedness and eugenics in the USA 128*
   *5.3 The new Municipal Court, Chicago: the 'Psychopathic Laboratory' 136*
   *5.4 Feeblemindedness in the UK 140*

6 Psychopathy in the US: psychiatry, psychoanalysis and
   sexual selves                                                          147

   6.1 Sexual psychopath laws in the United States   148
   6.2 Sexuality, civilisation and psychoanalysis in the USA   152

7 Social formulations of psychopathy and therapeutic communities   165

   7.1 Criminology, radical thinking and planned environments   167
   7.2 The development of the social diagnosis: Henderson's
       Psychopathic States   171
   7.3 The Second World War and the rise of community therapy   175
   7.4 Psychopathy as a legal category   182

8 DSM and the proliferation of personality disorders                     191

   8.1 Hervey Cleckley and The Mask of Sanity   193
   8.2 Personality disorder and the Diagnostic and Statistical
       Manual   197

9 Shifting grounds: the mass media and the insanity defence              213

   9.1 Liberalisation in the US: Durham, the ALI and the insanity
       defence   215
   9.2 The trial of John Hinckley (1982): the end of the insanity defence
       in the US?   218
   9.3 The invention of 'dangerous and severe personality disorder'
       in the UK   226

10 Concluding discussion: the contemporary debates: policy,
   theory and treatment                                                   235

   10.1 What is the future for moral insanity?   240

   References                                                             253
   Subject index                                                          283
   Author index                                                           289

# Illustrations

**Boxes**

| | | |
|---|---|---|
| 8.1 | Cleckley's clinical profile | 195 |
| 8.2 | DSM-III (APA 1980) criteria for 307.70 antisocial personality disorder | 205 |
| 8.3 | APA (DSM-IV) criteria for antisocial personality disorder | 208 |

**Table**

| | | |
|---|---|---|
| 10.1 | The Psychopathy Checklist – Revised | 248 |

# Preface

*[handwritten annotations at top: perhaps they're not necessarily trying to convince the doctors that they're not "morally insane" may be it's just that insanity traditionally & socially was connected to morality either through religious beliefs or through media & literary representations. The zeitgeist thus structured madness around one's ability to control everything about oneself but with most pressure on morality]*

This book takes a broadly historical and transdisciplinary approach to understanding the problem of what has been known at various times as 'moral insanity', 'psychopathy' or 'antisocial personality disorder'. The older term of 'moral insanity' has been used in the subtitle of the book not only because this underscores the historical nature of the approach taken here, but also because the phrase perhaps does some justice to the complexity of the problem. This is a legal and medical problem, but also a profoundly social and philosophical one; it has every bit as much to do with reflection on the nature of virtue as with 'medical science'.

A key argument of this book is that moral insanity can only be understood as a series of phenomena that have been constructed within and between social, cultural, medical and psychological domains. It does not exist in any separate realm but lives within a psychosocial space inextricably linked to the development of the 'public sphere' and processes of industrialisation, urbanisation and state formation. It reflects our concerns not only about violence and mechanisms of control but also debates about how we understand ourselves.

It is inevitable that the book must be partly about the history of the medical specialism of psychiatry, indeed it is argued here that the story of moral insanity is far more important to the history and purpose of psychiatry than is often acknowledged. The book also strays well beyond the medical texts that have defined the diagnoses and further afield than the trial testimonies that have tested those definitions, for it is in our wider culture that notions of moral insanity have been forged and shaped. This book is premised on the idea that debate about the nature of the relationship between sanity, partial insanity, offending and criminal culpability has been highly problematic because it not only crosses conceptual boundaries, but is also embedded in unresolved questions about the nature of virtue and how order and relationships can be managed between individuals in modern, industrialised, urbanised societies. It involves difficult questions about how we understand ourselves as beings who are defined or guided by emotion or rationality and whether we are best regarded simply as individuals or as creatures who can only be understood fully in terms of our relationships with others. The rapid social changes over this

*[right margin handwritten: morality is a historical term — in this period morality related to one's ability to fulfil their duties or responsibilities, both to their few dependents & to society at large.]*

period have meant that the various diagnoses have meant very different things at different times and places. At times the story is a heartening one that involves genuine curiosity about ourselves and human weakness, at others it is a dismal tale of what happens when frailty and the capacity for harm are seen as existing in 'other' kinds of people. This book is written in the hope of encouraging broader cross-disciplinary dialogue rather than in the belief of providing any surer answers.

# Acknowledgements

I am grateful to the University of East London where it has still been possible to pursue a cross-disciplinary topic like this. I must acknowledge the support of my colleagues and students in Psychosocial Studies.

I must also thank Brian Willan for going with this idea in the first place, and for the patience of Heidi Lee, and colleagues, at Routledge in seeing this through. The comments of a number of anonymous reviewers have been very helpful.

I am also grateful for an Economic and Social Research Council (ESRC) grant (ES/L000911/1) which has partially supported this work and in particular has paid the fee that allows me to quote from the American Psychiatric Association's *Diagnostic and Statistical Manual*. The image of Edward Oxford on the cover has been made available by the State Library of Victoria. Thanks also to the Old Bailey archives, Simon Wessely and the APA for their kind permission to reproduce previously published material in this book.

As ever, I am entirely in the debt of Helen, Izzie and Ben, who have put up with a lot of absence for this book to be written.

I am aware that there might have been some recklessness in trying to tell as complex a tale as this. I can only hope that I have done some justice to the lives touched by this painful and sometimes tragic topic.

> Folly is an endless maze;
> Tangled roots perplex her ways;
> How many have fallen there!
> They stumble all night over bones of the dead;
> And feel – they know not what but care;
> And wish to lead others, when they should be led
> (William Blake: *Songs of Innocence and Experience*,
> 'The Voice of the Ancient Bard', 1789)

# Introduction
Excavating moral insanity

In November 2012 Stephen Farrow was convicted, at Bristol Crown Court in England, of the cruel murder of two people he seemed to have picked, fairly randomly, to kill in a very sadistic fashion. There was no obvious motive for the crimes against these individuals. His first victim was a woman in her seventies whose home he broke into before hitting her with a walking stick 'with such force that it splintered'. He then put a pillow under her head and stabbed her four times. In his sentencing statement the judge described the manner of killing as 'an act of absolute sadism' and declared to Farrow: 'You did that because you wanted to'. Six weeks after that killing Farrow broke into the home of a clergyman, and stabbed him seven times. According to Farrow's own report, given to psychiatrists, he told his victim as he lay wounded to 'fucking die then and hurry up'. Farrow then spent the night in the vicarage helping himself to food; he drank some beer and watched an Indiana Jones DVD before leaving (*The Independent* 2 November 2012).

Farrow was well known to the mental health services, and had been given a diagnosis of 'dangerous and severe personality disorder'. He admitted that he had killed the clergyman but claimed that he was not guilty of murder as his responsibility for the crimes was diminished by the presence of such a mental disorder. The jury found him guilty, having heard psychiatric evidence that suggested that Farrow's mental disorder did not interfere with his ability to know what he was doing and that what he had done was wrong. Farrow seemed not to be hearing voices telling him what to do, nor was he deluded. He had planned and carried out his attacks and had then attempted to escape.

While the verdict of 'guilty' seemed to have been broadly approved of at the time, there was some disquiet. As the popular tabloid newspaper *The Sun* (3 November 2012) pithily put it: 'Why was psycho Stephen Farrow free to kill?'. In the immediate aftermath of the trial, the sister of one of the victims used more measured tones to ask:

> Do we, as a country, do enough to ensure that psychopaths with a known history of violence and criminal offences are not left roaming around at

large, ready to attack someone? Do we perhaps need to think again about how we might better monitor those people in our communities who present a real risk to society?

(*Daily Telegraph* 2 November 2012)

The conundrum this case illustrates is that if Stephen Farrow was indeed sane enough to be found guilty of murder, what grounds could there be for the state to intervene and perhaps detain him before he committed such offences? Was he suffering from a disorder that suggested he should be dealt with differently by the law? Can this disorder be treated or cured?

This book sets out to tell a story about the development of ideas and practices over the past two centuries or so that emerged from an assumption that there are such individuals who might be suffering from a disorder of which the principal symptoms are that they behave with indifference, recklessness, callousness, cruelty or even violence towards others. Such individuals are also characterised by the possession of a largely rational and clear understanding of the world around them. They seem not to be generally deluded, they are not suffering hallucinations and yet behave in ways that suggest they may have an abnormal ability to ignore the hurt and suffering they might inflict on others, or a limited capacity to comprehend those experiences in others, or perhaps simply little facility for restraining themselves from behaving in such ways. Controversy has raged over whether it is proper, or helpful, to categorise individuals who exhibit such behaviour as suffering from a disorder. The question that has most poignantly been asked within the criminal justice system concerns whether the recognition and identification of such a disorder ought to allow the 'sufferer' to be excused their 'criminal' behaviour on the grounds of insanity. At different times these disorders have been variously called moral insanity, moral imbecility, feeblemindedness, psychopathy, sociopathy and antisocial personality disorder. Some conceptualisations of the problem have envisaged only a small number of such disordered individuals; at other times whole classes of people have been viewed as disordered.

One of the initial sparks for this book came from the observation that the categories of psychopathy, personality disorder and moral insanity have always been highly contested, if not sometimes forthrightly disparaged, within the legal and psychiatric professions. And yet, despite the frequent criticism of and lack of support for these diagnoses from within the key professional groups, these disparaged categories have survived, albeit in evolving forms, for over 200 years. They therefore do not seem to fit with Hacking's (1998) categories of 'transient mental illnesses' that only emerged at the vertices of particular historical circumstances. There seem to have been some consistent forces that have maintained these categories over a period of time. Nevertheless, the disparagement of the categories has certainly continued. A typical example is provided by Phil Bean, who in his 2008 book *Madness and Crime* explained why he did

Introduction: excavating moral insanity 3

not include exploration of 'psychopathy' or 'personality disorder'. To him the psychopath 'is not mad'; instead the diagnosis is simply 'a moral judgement masquerading as a diagnosis' that is not properly defined or treatable – 'and that' as he concludes 'ought to be the end of the matter' (Bean 2008: 127). While this is not an uncommon view, the problem is that 'the matter' does not seem to have come to an end. At the time that Bean's book was published, the UK government was about nine years into a series of policy initiatives aimed at treating serious offenders who were deemed to be suffering from 'antisocial personality disorder'. Indeed, approximately £0.5 billion was spent on treating those categorised as suffering from 'dangerous and severe personality disorder' (Duggan 2011). After the programme was judged not to be a success (e.g. Barrett and Byford 2012), a somewhat different strategy was then proposed, projected to cost a further £0.5 billion until 2015 (DoH 2011). Meanwhile conflict over the status of the personality disorders is widely agreed to have derailed attempts to draft a new Mental Health Act in the UK despite widespread agreement that the 1983 Act (itself a re-draft of the 1959 Mental Health Act) needed to be replaced. Instead a mere amendment of the 1983 Act was passed by the UK Parliament in 2007, which included a very loose definition of mental disorder that allowed personality disorder to be included, in line with government intention (Brown 2006; DoH 2007).

The premise of this book is that there is something important here and that the significance goes beyond that of how we deal with 'difficult' people like Stephen Farrow. As Michel Foucault argued in the mid 1970s, the topic of how categories of mental disorder have been drawn to include such dangerous people was not only very important in 'the history of criminal psychiatry, but also for the history of psychiatry *tout court* and ultimately for the human sciences' (Foucault 2003: 113). It will be argued that the responses of psychiatry to these issues have been very directly important to the development of the psychiatric profession in ways that are not often acknowledged. Beyond that, as Foucault suggested, our responses to these difficulties have also shaped how we view and govern ourselves.

Crudely put, the story can be told in terms of the three diagnoses of 'moral insanity', 'psychopathy' and 'antisocial personality disorder'. The first of those arose in the early decades of the nineteenth century; the second began to emerge in the latter decades of the nineteenth century, but came to prominence in the middle of the twentieth century. Debates about the latter categories of 'personality disorder' became more distinct in the latter half of the twentieth century and are currently commonly used. The first significant definition of the problem is widely considered to be that given by the French medic Philippe Pinel who defined the category of *manie sans délire*, which he described as being marked by 'no sensible change in the functions of the understanding but a perversion of the active faculties, marked by sanguinary fury, with a blind propensity to acts of violence' (Pinel 1806: 151). The diagnosis of 'moral insanity' came to formal recognition in the early decades of the nineteenth century, defined by one of its clearest advocates in English as:

> A form of mental derangement in which the intellectual faculties appear to have sustained little or no injury, while the disorder is manifested principally or alone, in the state of the feelings, temper, or habits.
>
> (Prichard 1835a: 4)

This mental derangement could lead to the failure of an individual to conduct themselves 'with decency and propriety in the business of life'. The work of Pinel and Prichard will be discussed in more detail in Chapter 2. Suffice to say here that this was a view of insanity that was a considerable challenge to the one that had dominated constructions of madness for centuries: that madness was a state characterised by an absence of reason.

This is not the first attempt to write a history of these diagnoses. Previous histories tend to have in common a telling of the emergence of the diagnosis that has typically involved summaries of the work of Pinel and Esquirol (in France), Rush (in America) and Prichard (in England) before jumping to the more biological theories of German psychiatry (Koch, Kraepelin and Zehen, for example) and late nineteenth-century British psychiatry (exemplified by Henry Maudsley), and Hervey Cleckley's work on 'psychopathy', with more recent perspectives moving on to the developments of the *Diagnostic and Statistical Manual* produced by the American Psychiatric Association (e.g. Arrigo and Shipley 2001). While there is not the space to review those previous histories fully here, a number of points can be made from a brief sketch. Carlson and Dain (1962) give particular credit to the English medic Prichard for his concept of 'moral insanity' and the challenge that gave to many centuries of consensus that insanity could only really be understood as a loss of reason. The conclusion of their review of largely medical works was that 'moral insanity as a term and a concept is dead' (Carlson and Dain 1962: 139), although they go on to note that the concept was probably surviving within debates about 'sociopathic personality disturbance antisocial types' (which was to adopt the language of the day). They were writing before the scale of the popularity of the 'personality disorders' was to become apparent in the later twentieth century and the links between 'moral insanity' and aspects of the personality disorders grew clearer. Henry Werlinder presented an extremely thorough documentation of the medical and psychiatric work on psychopathy up until the mid 1970s (Werlinder 1978). Although Werlinder (1978) briefly puts the beginning of his story into the context of the shifting thinking in the eighteenth century, his story also truly starts with the early 'psychiatric' writings of Pinel and Esquirol. The detail of Werlinder's work on the medical texts is laudable and it has made a considerable contribution to scholarship in this area. Little attempt, however, is made to link the medical work to the social contexts in which the ideas were being formed. It is also worth noting that Werlinder, like Carlson and

Dain, published before the explosion of publication and concern about 'personality disorder' that occurred from the 1970s, when the possible links between some of the early work on moral insanity and more contemporary notions of personality disorder had become fully apparent. Berrios (1993), writing some years later, did present a sketch of the whole history of the 'personality disorders' and assumed that the roots of the concepts were in the work of the psychiatric pioneers of nineteenth century. While he concluded by arguing that 'intellectual context and historical fashion' have determined the particular model that has dominated at different periods (Berrios 1993: 26), he left the field open to establish the detail about these issues. Livesley (2000: 1–2, 2001: 6–7) also adopted a historical approach to an analysis of this topic but suggested that the chronological field could be marked by its relationship to the *Diagnostic and Statistical Manual* (published by the American Psychiatric Association). So Livesley discussed a 'pre-DSM-III stage' (ranging from the '19th century and earlier' until the publication of DSM-III in 1980); a DSM III phase; and the 'post DSM III/IV' stage. There is no doubt that the influence of DSM and debates surrounding its definitions are very important, and its development and significance is discussed in some detail in Chapter 8. This book, however, is taking a rather different perspective by investigating the earlier periods in more detail. A premise of this book is that a better understanding of the past can help us understand current conundrums. Other historical work has focused on particular periods and issues. For example, Goldstein (1987, 1998) examines the significance of concepts of monomania in the development of French psychiatry in the nineteenth century. Ramon (1986) examined the emergence of 'psychopathy' in the UK in the middle of the twentieth century. Rafter's historical work is exemplary in putting some of the early work on moral insanity into a historical context, and importantly pointing to some of the influences that debate about moral insanity had on early criminological thought (e.g. Rafter 2004). Pickersgill (2010, 2013) has presented detailed analyses of the history of ideas and the influences on DSM definitions of personality disorder in the latter half of the twentieth century.

It is worth making the point that this book is not a review of the various psychological and biological investigations of psychopathy or moral insanity. Nor is it a review of the philosophical debates that have been constructed around the issues of legal responsibility and psychopathy (Elliott and Gillett 1992; Glannon 1997, for example). This book makes a unique contribution by using a wider focus on the history and the shifting social context of the diagnosis. This helps to excavate a more helpful understanding of moral insanity and our current dilemmas. What emerges from such a perspective is that too narrow a focus on one facet of the problem, whether that be on the psychological or the biological characteristics of individuals, is to dangerously limit our understanding of something that can only be understood as a concept that lives in the psychological, social, physical and cultural realms.

## The methodological approach: excavating moral insanity

There are two distinct features of the approach adopted in this book. There is first the broad sweep of the historical approach from the eighteenth century to the twenty-first, and second the transdisciplinary approach (Frosh 2013). Both of these are important and necessary, since it is by examining the evolution of the related diagnoses and their reception that important lessons emerge about the variety of forces that have been constructing our responses to the problems associated with the diagnoses. The traversal of disciplinary boundaries demonstrates that moral insanity can only be fully understood as a phenomenon that is crucially constructed within social, cultural and psychological domains. It does not exist in any domain separately, but lives within a psychosocial space that has emerged at a particular period of human history. This book is premised on the idea that debate about the nature of the relationship between sanity, partial insanity, offending and criminal culpability has been highly problematic because it not only crosses conceptual boundaries, but is also embedded in unresolved questions about the nature of virtue and how order can be established between individuals in modern, industrialised and urbanised societies. It involves difficult questions about how we understand ourselves contrarily as emotional *and* rational beings, and as individualised *and* relational beings.

There is some attention given (in this introduction and in Chapter 1) to establishing something of the pre-history of the diagnosis of moral insanity in debates about the assumed relationship between the mind, brain and body, and in the practical concerns of courts in the eighteenth century. This helps us to understand some of the problematic debates about the emergence of concepts such as 'partial insanity', 'monomania' and 'affective insanity'. Simply put, the first two concepts refer to the idea that someone might only be partially mad, perhaps in one particular area of their 'mind' or their thinking, and the third to the idea that someone might be insane in regard to their feelings, or emotions (as opposed to their 'reason'). These categories are highly relevant to understanding conceptualisations of 'moral insanity'. As Werlinder (1978: 19) noted such concepts 'have a long past' despite not achieving any serious, formal development until the 1800s, when members of the nascent psychiatric profession began to formulate their categories of madness. Understanding that there was this past, and that there was engagement with such concepts before there was any recognisable group of experts in psychiatry, is important. Of course, to state that in order to understand the history of psychiatric concepts we will need to look beyond the psychiatric texts themselves is to evoke the influence of Michel Foucault who advocated an archaeological approach to knowledge (Foucault 1974). It is probably very difficult even to think about any aspect of the history of psychiatry without doing so within the *épistème* that surrounds the work of Foucault. The obvious linkages here between the

Introduction: excavating moral insanity 7

development of psychiatry (in terms of both its own 'disciplinary' theoretical base and practice), and more generally through the discipline and regulation of individuals through criminal justice systems (Foucault 1977) and the relationship of psychiatry to everyday practices, most notably concerning relationships and sexuality (Foucault 1979), mean that Foucault's work is simply unavoidable. It is perhaps the influence of Foucault which has made it seem obvious that this story had to range over a broad and diverse terrain.

The need to think in cross-disciplinary ways in considering insanity is hardly controversial. It would be no more than a commonplace observation to suggest that our definitions of, and responses to, madness are shaped by two key institutions: the legal and criminal justice system and the various systems of health and welfare. Legal systems have long been concerned with the boundary between sanity and madness. Courts and lawyers are involved when decisions about the allocation of criminal responsibility are to be made, and also when issues of legal capacity are to be decided in relation to property (e.g. Houston 2001). While there is clearly some overlap between these two issues, this book is concerned with the first one: the question of individual responsibility for criminal offences. It is this issue, particularly when concerning violence and 'antisocial' behaviour, that has brought the diagnostic dilemmas to prominence. The second institutional framework that is so important to our conceptions of madness is that of the various systems of health and welfare that provided for the care, support and confinement of those deemed to be insane. As a number of writers who take critical perspectives have noted, the distinction between notions of care and control might be argued to be rather fine (e.g. Foucault 1967; Scull 1979b). Nevertheless it is, in part, from the direct heat of the collision between the two worlds of the criminal justice system and the health and welfare services that we see ideas such as 'moral insanity', 'criminal lunacy', 'psychopathy', 'feeblemindedness' and 'antisocial personality disorder' being forged. An important premise of this book, however, is that beyond the concerns that have driven the development of the criminal justice and health systems there is yet another force that has powerfully shaped our beliefs about insanity, and these diagnoses in particular. This third force is the social and cultural milieu in which those ideas are born, reflected upon and further shaped. It is this third force that has been so crucial to understanding the problematic emergence of 'moral insanity'. It is the reaction of 'the public', the hopes, fears and anxieties that 'we' have that have shaped theory, practice and policy. Ideas that stem from Jürgen Habermas's discussion of the development of a 'bourgeois public sphere' are relevant to this issue. The meaningful existence of a 'public sphere' that could discuss and reflect upon ideas of madness only became possible on a large scale through the eighteenth century as the spread of the written word and of literacy meant that ideas could be discussed, spread and refined (Habermas 1989).[1] It will be argued that it is the 'public sphere' that has been crucial to understanding the development of 'moral insanity', and it therefore merits further discussion. In keeping with Habermas's historical analysis this book is most concerned with developments in theory and practice in England, with some attention being paid to the importance of French psychiatry in the nineteenth century and German psychiatry in the latter half of the nineteenth and the early twentieth century. There is then a strong focus on American developments in the twentieth century. While linguistic limitation and cultural parochialism have played their part in shaping the book, there is arguably some justification in this since Habermas describes the emergence of a 'public sphere' in Britain, France and Germany, and more precisely locates its emergence in Great Britain at the turn of the eighteenth century in the growing city of London.

## The development of the public sphere

Habermas precisely located the origins of a 'public sphere' in Britain at the beginning of the eighteenth century. Key factors were the political settlement that allowed and followed the Glorious Revolution (Miller 1983), the development of capitalism and the unique liberty enjoyed by the press (Holmes 1969). The pace of change during the eighteenth century in England, and especially London (Sheppard 1998), was enormous. Key characteristics of what was to become known as 'modernity' emerged during these times (Giddens 1990; Ogborn 1998; Porter 2000). By the end of the eighteenth century some form of urban living was increasingly regarded as a norm. The economy was on the one hand to become industrialised and globalised, and on the other to be driven by consumption. The commercial enterprises of the developing British Empire were funded largely through the use of the newly emerging international finance markets that grew up in the City of London (Dugaw 1998). The power of the church in both public and private life was to have waned considerably while government was moving away from autocratic rule. In addition, there were political and social forces that were playing their part in ushering in an increasingly secular understanding of the human world (MacDonald 1981). Aided by the relaxation of press censorship and the availability of the printed word, a growing bourgeoisie relatively free from domination by any particular agency (whether that be government, aristocracy, church or commercial interest) could discuss and shape the ideas of the day. This, Habermas argues, brought about a fundamental transformation in the way people could think about their world and themselves. It is fair to say that there was certainly a lot to think about. The social and cultural fabric was to be entirely altered by the flows of global capital, and spoils of Empire, that fuelled the development of an increasingly secular society that was to organise its economy, society and culture around consumption (Berg 2005). Such degrees of change were not surprisingly accompanied by a degree of anxiety: McKeon (1985) suggests the eighteenth century was a time that could lay claim to levels of flux, uncertainty and thus anxiety as high as those of any 'post-modern' era. No doubt the anxiety was to manifest in various ways, but this book is particularly concerned with how these anxieties were manifest in theories and practices surrounding the conduct of individuals. It will be argued that over the past 300 years different understandings of the relationship between the individual and the social world emerged, and two related developments are of particular interest. There was first a reframing of the relationship between the individual and the social world, as the domains of emotion and feeling began to assume a more central 'social' role. Second, and part of this reconceptualisation, was the 'discovery' and exploration of 'the mind' as an object of study that had depth and hidden facets that could themselves be subject to disorder. This opened the door to more nuanced theories of insanity, one of which was that of moral insanity.

The use of the ambiguous term 'moral' in relation to insanity is instructive. By the end of the eighteenth century, it referred on the one hand to ethical dimensions of human behaviour. On the other, it was used to imply what we would now think of as a psychological domain – or perhaps more particularly the world of feeling and affect. The term 'moral insanity' points firmly to its appearance at the fulcrum of debate and battle between the emergent world of modern secularism and more traditional, religious orders. The apparent ambiguity thus indicates the problem of how virtue could be defined and maintained in a world where religious assumptions were losing their power to maintain order. The state was to assume an ever more prominent role in the maintenance of order and authority. Norbert Elias (1994) has prominently argued that the development of the modern state demanded new forms of individual psychology and relationship to the social order.

## Emotions, the mind and the social order

It will be argued that the idea that states have become increasingly interested in the conduct of individuals and in the way that individuals relate to the wider social body is important to understanding moral insanity. According to Norbert Elias (in his epic work *The Civilizing Process*), the story of the past several hundred years of human conduct in the West has crucially been one that has been marked by social processes that have demanded an ever increasing internalisation of the control of behaviour and the expression of feeling. Significantly, these social processes have been connected to the development of the state and the monopolisation of violence by states as violence becomes increasingly discouraged among the general population. Elias's work has been subject to much debate, criticism and counter-criticism (Wouters and Mennell 2013). A shift in the way that 'the passions' were viewed becomes discernible in the eighteenth century as the passions themselves begin to be accorded a new social significance. Bernard Mandeville's playful yet controversial thesis *The Fable of the Bees* (published initially in 1705 as a verse, *The Grumbling Hive*) captures the awareness and anxiety experienced within a society that was witnessing the falling away of its traditional moral structures (Hundert 1994; Hutcheson 1725). In Mandeville's satirical verse a thriving and industrious hive of bees decides to eliminate all individual vice such as greed and selfishness. Mandeville suggests that without such individual passion, there was nothing to drive the wheels of industry and commerce and 'the hive' would fall into poverty, chaos and ruin. His serious point was: as society came to be driven by individual passions many considered immoral, how could the 'public good' be maintained (Mandeville 1732)? It was just this paradox of how selfish individualism could be reconciled within a civil order that apparently demanded high levels of virtue that David Hume (1738) and Adam Smith (1759) were, to widespread acclaim, to direct themselves (Hurtado Prieto 2004). Hume's work in particular puts great stress on the social importance of the human capacity for feeling as being crucial to the social good.

Allied to the development of ideas about the social significance of emotion is the emergence of the concept of 'the mind' or 'the imagination' as an object of debate and study, which George Rousseau boldly claimed was discovered 'precisely in the second half of the seventeenth century in Western Europe, particularly in England and France' (1969: 110). This 'discovery' was, he argues, to have massive implications for the development of western societies through the subsequent eighteenth century and beyond. Rousseau based his claim on the fact that the anatomy of the brain was being explored and mapped and that consequently the brain itself was being privileged as the organ of the body that housed thought, feelings and the imagination. The pioneer of this exploration was the English physician Thomas Willis (Green 2003; O'Connor 2003) who applied the methods used so successfully by William Harvey to examine the human body (most notably his work on the circulation of blood). The other, related, shift to occur was exemplified by the philosophical work of another English physician, John Locke, who studied with Willis and promoted the significance of individual subjectivity, and was to have some influence on thought about the nature of insanity. As Rousseau explains, Locke argued that the evidence for the existence of the *imagination* was very clear. No two people would describe and perceive the same tree in the same way, and so:

> [W]hilst the tree exists, it is not existential in the sense the imagination is; the tree can exist only in the eye and imaginative faculty of the beholder. So important is the formation of this 'mind', its impressions and ideas, Locke asserted, that it deserves more attention than the tree.
> 
> (Rousseau 1969: 114)

It logically followed that if 'the mind' were responsible for the construction of reality it could itself be doing this in ways that might be more or less healthy. Madness, Locke was to suggest, emerged 'not in the want of reason' (Locke, from King 1830: 171), but was better viewed as 'a disorder of the imagination' (Locke, from King 1830: 173). While there was thus a discernible development in thinking that the mind could be disordered, there was still a strong belief that the source of disease was in the body, although it was the brain, as host to the mind, that came more and more to be the centre of attention. It was the 'discovery' and exploration of the mind that was to provide new perspectives on the nature of insanity and most particularly a challenge to the dominant view of insanity that perceived it as simply the loss of reason.

As already discussed, these conceptual developments were being made at a time when the development of the 'public sphere' was creating the capacity to spread and discuss ideas. Shifts in the way that human beings could begin to think about themselves and the place and role of the mind and imagination in human life were not confined to the anatomy laboratories or the debating rooms of the Royal Society. These notions were to be aired in the newly emerging public sphere (Habermas 1989; MacDonald 1989). Indeed, while Rousseau (1969) draws attention to the significant role that advances in physiological exploration of the brain and nervous system had prompted, he argues that it was literature that was significant in leading the exploration of 'the mind' in the eighteenth century. Reed (1997) similarly argues that many important debates about the nature of human psychology were taking place outside of the circle of the narrow band of scholars whose work is now recognised, rather teleologically, within standard histories of psychology and philosophy. Indeed, Reed argues, a great deal of thinking about the mind, consciousness and the relationship of the body, brain, mind and the social world was going on outside of what are now seen as the official boundaries of the disciplines. This was especially true since those in 'official' posts in universities and medical schools had still, even in the second half of the nineteenth century, to be careful about appearing to be too secular (Dixon 2001). It was therefore the development of ideas in literature and the press, and public debate of those issues, that was to be so important to the construction of new ideas.

## Madness and the public sphere: the role of 'the media'

Though Habermas (1989) went on to argue that 'the public sphere' had, by the middle of the twentieth century, become too dominated by commercial interests that used the various channels of mass communication, the various forms of media communications have also formed significant aspects of the 'public sphere' itself. The varieties of what have become known as the mass media have, it is argued in this book, played an important role in the construction of these related diagnoses. Thus the reporting in the press of trials and of debates about the status of insanity has directly influenced policy and practice. It will also be argued that other forms of literature such as the novel have been important for encouraging and spreading ideas about how human beings understand each other and each other's motives and responsibilities. Most conspicuously, the development of the novel from the middle of the eighteenth century encouraged the exploration of individual 'interiority', which suggested models of 'the mind' that allowed courts to consider quite subtle distinctions between sanity and madness. While the novel was to remain a largely middle class vehicle for reflection on the nature of human society until well into the nineteenth century, it was the popular news press that was to unleash the power of the printed work to transform, stimulate and construct ideas among the mass of the population, helping to create what has been termed the 'plebeian public sphere' (Calhoun 1992: 38). The rise of literacy levels (Stone 1969) and the proliferation of newspapers, books and broadsides through the eighteenth and nineteenth centuries were dramatic (Black 1987). This helped to ensure that debates and ideas about physiology, madness and the nature of criminal responsibility were increasingly available within almost every echelon of society. MacDonald (1988: 41) reports estimates of newspaper sales in Britain as 15,000 in 1704, 7.4 million by 1754 and more than 15 million by 1792. As MacDonald explains, the advent of newspaper readership was to broaden the geographical and social horizons of the population. Newspapers carried stories from all over the country, particularly London, and thus they 'publicized new attitudes and ideas far more effectively than pamphlets or the pulpit. It helped form political consciousness and exposed provincial readers of every social rank to the values and opinions current in London society' (1988: 37).

May (2003) suggests that by 1782 newspaper readership levels in London had reached as many as half a million out of a total population of 750,000. Newspapers were, of course, commercial ventures and stories were designed to attract readers as much as inform them. The salacious details of crimes, particularly those involving scandal, sex and violence were always going to be prominent and as May notes newspapers also provided public forums that allowed discussion about the operation of the criminal justice system and the understanding of criminality. MacDonald (1988) presents a convincing example of the spread of ideas about insanity and its relationship to criminal responsibility being communicated through the press in the eighteenth century. He argues that an evident sea change in attitudes towards suicide during the eighteenth century was quite directly brought about through the influence of press reports of coroners' court judgments that were to become available to the general population of this period. A coroner's judgment of non compos mentis, which meant that the unfortunate individual was not guilty of 'self-murder' and could thus be buried with dignity, without their family suffering disinheritance, was rare at the beginning of the century, but virtually ubiquitous by the end of the nineteenth century.

In addition to newspapers the availability of affordable printing and the associated expansion of literacy also allowed the novel to flourish as a significant cultural vehicle that allowed for innovative ways of understanding individual psychology. There are good reasons to believe that the social conditions of London in the eighteenth century were of particular significance, as Ian Watt (1987) argued in his influential work *The Rise of the Novel*. The rampant urbanisation of London in the eighteenth century encouraged large scale interest in notions of interiority; the development of the novel was both feeding on and responding to this. Watt argued that urbanisation created a number of opportunities for new kinds of anxiety to arise, all of which led to a popular desire to reach more systematically an understanding of the interior worlds of others. London, Watt suggests, presented its inhabitants with the opportunity to observe 'an infinite variety of ways of life' that were often 'utterly alien to any one individual's personal experience' (Watt 1987: 179). Poverty and wealth were significant sources of alienation. The poor were very much visible on the streets with their chaotic lives which threatened to unbalance the ordered lives of the more wealthy. Understanding 'them' and controlling 'them' was to become an ever increasing preoccupation of the wealthier classes throughout the eighteenth century and then in more pronounced ways during the following century. Watt also makes the point that these pioneering dwellers of the modern city would have been aware of a degree of fragmentation in their lives. Individuals would have been conscious that they belonged to many social groups, whether in the workplace, church, home or spaces of leisure; no single other person could know them in all of those roles, and correlatively nor could 'he know anyone else in theirs' (Watt 1987: 185). One way of contending with any sense of anxiety or alienation that might stem from these feelings of uncertainty was to develop means of understanding and categorising other people. Watt argues that the development of the novel was in part due to this interest in understanding the interior worlds of others.[2] The popularity of the works of Daniel Defoe, Henry Fielding and Samuel Richardson in the eighteenth century signalled the emergence of a public who were aware of and fascinated by individual agency and its relation to fortune and virtue. Driven by the pen of Henry Fielding, the personality, adventures, whims and flaws of a character like Tom Jones (eponymous hero of *The History of Tom Jones: a Foundling*, first published in 1749) could sustain a whole novel. Cohan (1976: 164) boldly suggests that Samuel Richardson's *Clarissa*, first published in London in 1748, was 'the first fully conceived' example of the English novel to 'explore the difficulties in understanding a complex human personality'. It was complex because the character had depth, had feelings and impulses that were not clearly known to the individual herself and could also be in conflict with outward appearances and social convention. Subtle shifts in the significance laid upon outward appearance in the eighteenth century are emphasised in Arditi's (1994) account of the popular rise and significance of etiquette[3] as explored through the publication of Lord Chesterfield's *Letters to His Son on the Art of Becoming a Man of the World and Gentleman*, written between around 1738 and 1768, but published posthumously in 1774 as a guide to manners and etiquette. They were a major best seller, reprinted five times in the first year alone and copied many times over in subsequent years. Arditi (1994: 180) notes that they were 'the most influential treatise on manners in the late eighteenth and early nineteenth centuries in both Britain and the U.S.A.', and suggests that the significance of these rules was that they implied that on the one hand there might well be a considerable distinction between the individual self and the presentation of that self, but that on the other, convention with group norms, rather than the adoption of moral absolutes (as dictated by the church, for example), becomes essential for social success and acceptance. In Chesterfield's own words:

> A man of the world must, like the chameleon, be able to take every different hue, which is by no means a criminal or abject, but a necessary complaisance, for it relates only to manners, and not to morals.
> (Chesterfield 52–53, quoted in Arditi 1994: 183)

Thus there is the understanding that what is apparent on the surface of an individual might not be entirely consistent with the personality underneath that presentation, and second there is recognition of the fact that 'social success' is dependent upon the degree of approval found within the group. It is the recognition of this 'psychosocial' space that is vital to the development of ideas about 'moral insanity'. The diagnosis emerges on the one hand through the increasing interest in the exploration of the complexity of the internal psyche and on the other through the growing stress on the ability of individuals to engage appropriately with their increasingly complex, social milieu, which itself also becomes an object of study. Shifts in the form of the diagnosis occur over the following centuries in response to changing conceptualisations of the individual and of the nature, perceptions and expectations of the social world around us.

It is surely of considerable interest that Henry Fielding, one of the most popular authors of the eighteenth century, was also a significant figure in the criminal justice system. He was Chief Magistrate in London and was one of the founders of the 'Bow Street Runners', a forerunner of an organised police force, which took to the streets of London in 1749, the same year that *Tom Jones* was published. The criminological significance of Tom Jones bears some scrutiny. Fielding directs the reader to awareness that Tom is indeed a heroic figure, despite (or perhaps even because of) the fact that Tom pays little attention to the superficial expression of politeness and mannered etiquette of the gentry. Tom instead allows fairly cheerful and honest engagement with his own appetites (including love and sexual desire) which lead him at times to relationships with the less respectable members of society and a series of scrapes with the law. Ultimately, however, Tom's actions in his life are presented as truly virtuous rather than simply appearing to be so. Fielding's moral message might well be almost the reverse of that espoused by Lord Chesterfield, but they have in common the distinction they are making between outward appearance, and the internal world of the individual's 'heart and mind'. Fielding also points the reader towards an understanding of how the public reception of those behaviours and virtues could be powerful. It is, of course, during the nineteenth century that the novel begins to achieve pre-eminence as the medium through which an ever growing and literate population is able to think and reflect on itself and where ideas about the nature of consciousness and sanity and madness could be explored. It is in this century that we witness an explosion of ideas about the nature of consciousness, and this is when notions of moral insanity are formally formulated. The interaction between fictional and medical literature will be discussed in later chapters. The outputs of the popular press increased greatly in the nineteenth century as well. The invention of the steam press and the reduction of printing taxation 'produced almost an embarrassment of accounts of more serious trials' (Wiener 1999: 471). By the middle of the twentieth century film makers also became interested in portraying 'dangerous' individuals and their relationship to their social world. The filmic portrayal of the outsider killer Travis Bickle in the film *Taxi Driver* itself became part of the 1982 trial of John Hinckley, who was accused of the attempted murder of the US President (as discussed in Chapter 9).

Thus the diagnosis of moral insanity and its various forms needs to be understood as being shaped by a world that was witnessing key changes in people's relationships to each other, to the social body and to systems of governance. Questions about individual conduct and what might be expected from people were becoming of paramount concern. There was growing interest in the identification and study of 'mind', and the subsequent proliferation of psychological theory helped to nurture the growth of psychiatry. Ideas within psychiatry have themselves been shaped by the social and cultural forces that have surrounded its development. It is the story of moral insanity within these forces with which this book is concerned. This is a distinctly non-linear story, which involves travel down a number of very different roads. At times over the past two centuries the investigation of moral insanity has led to some of the most subtle investigations of the interior worlds of individuals. At others it has also been grappling with sophisticated conceptualisations of the mind as existing not only within the body but also within a social milieu. In short, some of these explorations have achieved an elevating exploration of the human condition. In other instances the story has been a much darker one involving the labelling, incarceration and extermination of individuals for no better reason than that they were viewed as different, a threat, or even just a little 'feebleminded'.

## Overview of the book

The first chapter examines how relatively subtle notions of insanity were becoming evident in court at the Old Bailey during the eighteenth century before the advent of medical experts on insanity. Examination of a number of the trials suggests that verdicts of 'not guilty on the grounds of insanity' were being returned in relation to circumstances and mental states that appeared to be quite a long way from the commonly held view that excuse for criminality should only be made in cases where insanity was clearly manifest and such individuals had clearly lost all reason and were 'like brutes'. It is also evident that these decisions were not being made on the basis of consideration of individual psychology alone but were embedded in understandings of the relationships that individuals had with those close to them and with the communities and institutions that surrounded them. It is here that we see the emergence of strain in the longstanding belief in the association between insanity and reason. The second chapter is concerned with the development of formal ideas of moral insanity in the first half of the nineteenth century that directly challenge that association. This is the period that sees the birth of the discipline of psychiatry (which was to become a professional body, recognised across Europe and North America, in the middle of the century). It will be argued that the promotion of the concept of moral insanity (and the related ones of monomania and partial insanity) was an important step for the budding profession. By claiming expertise in the detection of forms of insanity that damaged the capacity for affective, or moral, understanding the 'asylum keepers' donned the cloak of professional expertise and claimed their place in the relatively high status and high profile world of the criminal court. For some decades, most particularly in England, it appeared that the medical experts were, as evidenced by a series of trial verdicts, successful in their promotion of versions of monomania and moral insanity. This apparent triumph was short lived, however, since the aftermath of the inquiry into the verdict at the famous trial of Daniel M'Naghten in 1843 was to have lasting implications for the status of such diagnoses for many decades. As Chapter 3 explores, the scale of the setback for psychiatry became clear through another high profile case involving the murder of Elizabeth Goodwin by her spurned lover George Victor Townley in 1863. In the cases of M'Naghten and Townley the weight of public opinion, as promulgated and gauged by press responses, is crucial to the medics' abandonment of the concept of moral insanity in the courtroom. The medical men did not give up their interest in criminality but they turned instead to the measurement and classification of the mass of offenders beginning to accumulate in the burgeoning prison system in the latter decades of the nineteenth century. The professional gaze thus turned away from the attempt to study and understand the individual mind of the offender and towards the classification of cases and of criminal types accumulating in the growing systems of asylums and prisons.

Although the medical men had left moral insanity in the courtroom, the idea took on life in the wider culture. Chapter 4 focuses on the development of ideas of mind and sanity that were occurring in the wider cultural realm in the nineteenth century. It is developments in this realm that become so important in laying the ground for the very different paths that the medical men were to take over the following decades, well into the twentieth century. A number of examples of the use of concepts such as partial insanity and monomania can be traced within significant work of nineteenth-century fiction – in the novels of George Eliot, Emily Brontë and Joseph Conrad, for example. This emphasises the significance of the exploration of consciousness and interiority that was taking place in literature and draws attention to the interaction between fiction and medical texts. This cross-fertilisation was most evident, it will be argued, in the development of theories of 'degeneracy'. This was a theory that formally emerged from French psychiatry in the middle of the nineteenth century but was to retain a grip on western imagination well into the twentieth century. It was a sprawling and amorphous theory that promoted the gloomy image of western culture and people as being in moral and physical decline. Its success was dependent on very active dialogue between medical and biological texts and the Gothic literature of the late nineteenth century, which drew attention to the animalistic or 'primitive' traits within human beings. Charles Darwin's work *On the Origin of Species* (1859), which located the human species as only one among many categories of 'animal', was an important influence here. Interpretations of Darwinian theory gave strength to the view that there were some individuals whose genetic inheritance would predetermine their propensity towards immorality and crime. Other interpretations of Darwin would question the extent to which such dangerous and violent traits might be understood as existing only within particular individuals or within 'types' of individuals; instead perhaps they were better understood as existing within all of us. Such ideas were to have very different implications.

Chapter 5 takes up the story of what happened when notions of moral insanity became entwined with biological thinking. Ideas which had been brewing in German psychiatry for some time and which placed psychopathology in the biological realm came to the fore in the latter decades of the nineteenth century. This chapter will examine how some of the key ideas of German psychiatry gave nurturance not only to a biological orientation in psychiatry, but also to ideas about the significance of character and more 'psychodynamic' theories about the nature of character (which will be examined in Chapter 6). It was the biological theories that were to have the earliest impact on psychiatry in Europe and North America. In the first part of the twentieth century the United States was to witness the most remarkable use of ideas that supposed that moral weaknesses of character could be explained in terms of genetic characteristics. The American child psychologist Henry Goddard imported Alfred Binet's intelligence test from France and used it to identify the 'feebleminded' whose low level of cognitive performance rendered them susceptible to moral depravity and criminality. As described in the chapter, Goddard's proposed eugenical solutions were taken up with some enthusiasm within parts of the criminal justice system in the United States, most strikingly perhaps in the municipal court system in Chicago, which embraced the identification and segregation of those considered to be 'feebleminded' and thus a threat to the health of the social body. Such eugenical solutions were being given sympathetic hearings in Europe. Indeed it was the attention given to the full blown consequences of eugenical policies in Nazi Germany that was to put a brake on the development of policies that demanded the incarceration and sterilisation of 'the feebleminded'. The human and moral catastrophe of the Second World War was to encourage moves away from biological theories and back towards the exploration of the mind as a psychological entity and of the social conditions that were producing different mental states. One body of theory that provided a route away from biological determinism was that of psychoanalysis.

Chapter 6 traces the further development of ideas about psychopathy in the United States as they began to steer away from the strictly biological. The anxiety about sexuality and reproduction was still in evidence as a series of 'sexual psychopath' laws appeared in a number of states in the middle of the twentieth century. While the anxiety about sexuality is apparent, the emphasis moves away from the concern with the biological causes of such states. Indeed the influence of psychoanalysis now becomes very clear. While psychoanalysis strongly emphasised the significance of sexuality and was itself arguably emerging from some of the same anxieties about the nature of society that had nurtured degeneration theory, it also offered a clear course away from the organic determinism that had led to eugenical solutions. Psychoanalysis again put the study of the mind at the centre of psychiatry's concerns. In addition to examining some of the factors that prompted these legislative developments this chapter provides an introduction to the elements of psychoanalytic thought (particularly those concerned with theories of narcissism) that were to have an impact on concepts of psychopathy and personality disorder in the latter half of the twentieth century.

Chapters 7 and 8 explore the impact of the Second World War on the development of ideas and policies in psychiatry that were to give the topic of 'psychopathy' remarkable prominence in Britain and the US. World War Two encouraged considerable government interest in the advantages that might be gained by the systematic study of the psychic world of the individual. The professions of psychiatry and psychology were to benefit from high levels of government funding and respect. It will be argued that the war itself was also to have a crucial impact on general understanding of the notion of violence, and even of the nature of evil. The scale of the events of the Second World War rendered untenable the idea that violence could simply be located within a small number of bad individuals. Instead, violence had to be understood as something that was a part of all us, and could be conceived as existing within a group. Chapter 7 examines the acceptance of notions of psychopathy in Britain in the middle of the twentieth century and some of the remarkable therapeutic work initiated by psychoanalytically informed military psychiatrists during the Second World War. This work assumed that the problem of psychopathy was not one that simply resided within individuals, but was better viewed as belonging to the group. Some of these developments were to have an impact on government policy: the category of 'psychopathy' was included in the 1959 Mental Health Act in England and Wales. Other developments that grew from this brew were to have an influence on the institutional development of criminology in Britain. A key founding member of the British Society of Criminology, for example, was Edward Glover, a psychoanalyst with a strong interest in the links between delinquency and psychopathy.

Chapter 8 shifts to the United States, where the Second World War was also to spur a considerable expansion in the scope of psychiatry. Perhaps the most obvious legacy of this was the development of the *Diagnostic and Statistical Manual* (DSM) by the American Psychiatric Association as psychiatrists found that their previous diagnostic categories, honed on the study of the residents of the asylums, were not adequate for the categorisation of the much wider spectrum of the population that they were now seeing as they worked with the large section of the population who were conscripted into the military. An important category to appear was that of 'sociopathy'. The chapter goes on to trace the development of psychopathy concerning the various personality disorders through successive editions of DSM.

Chapter 9 ('Shifting grounds: the mass media and the insanity defence') examines key shifts in terms of legal practice and goverment policy developments that occurred in both the US and the UK. Many states in the US witnessed considerable liberalisation of the insanity defence in the wake of the Durham rule (1954) and ALI (American Law Institute) guidelines (published in 1962). These were to be more or less entirely overhauled following the public furore over the trial of John Hinckley, who attempted to assassinate President Reagan in 1981. In the UK the government response to one particular murder case in 1996 has had lasting implications for penal and health policy in this area. In conclusion, Chapter 10 will sum up where we are now in terms of understanding these diagnostic categories and briefly explore some possible trajectories that might follow from particular understandings.

## Notes

1 The tensions and overlaps between the work of Habermas and Foucault have been the subject of a great deal of debate and commentary, for example Flyvbjerg (1998).
2 Watt (1987: 195), for example, suggests that Richardson's 'Clarissa offers us the first recorded usage of the word "personalities" meaning "individual traits" long before its modern usage in the singular form was established'. See also Cohan (1976).
3 Elias (1994) makes considerable use of guides to etiquette in mapping significant historical changes in relation to expectations of individual conduct.

## Chapter 1

# Informal insanity in the eighteenth-century court

## Introduction

While notions of insanity have been accepted in legal systems for many centuries (Porter 2002), it was not until the beginning of the nineteenth century that courts were to see the entry of witnesses who were claiming expertise in insanity (Eigen and Andoll 1986; Smith 1981). As we shall see in the next chapter, the issue of moral insanity (and its various associated categories, such as monomania and partial insanity) was to be an important component of the claims made by the new profession of psychiatry as they staked out the territory of their expertise. This chapter makes the case that to understand the rise of these new experts we need to appreciate something of the demand that they were trying to fulfil. As will be discussed later in this chapter, Matthew Hale's statement on criminal culpability and insanity, spelled out in seventeenth-century England but itself built on centuries of belief, seemed to demand very starkly that the accused might be excused only when 'totally deprived of the use of reason', and 'their actions are in effect in the condition of brutes' (Matthew Hale: *The History of the Pleas of the Crown* 1736: 31). The hypothesis behind this chapter is that the definitions of the new disorders of monomania and moral insanity that provided a challenge to this assertion were not simply conjured from thin air when they were described in the medical texts of the nineteenth century. Instead it is assumed that there would be evidence of similar thinking appearing earlier. In order to explore this pre-history a number of criminal trials from the latter half of the eighteenth century will be examined, in which the insanity of the accused was used as a defence but where that insanity was not obviously manifest and could not be simply characterised as an absence of reason.

The first part of the chapter will introduce the Old Bailey Sessions Papers as a significant historical record and present an analysis of a small number of cases tried at the Old Bailey in the second half of the eighteenth century. All of the cases emerged from a search of Old Bailey cases before the beginning of the nineteenth century where the insanity defence was used, but the insanity described seemed to challenge Hale's definition. It is argued that there is considerable value in examining cases that were occurring before the language and assumptions of psychiatry had begun to obscure the view of some of the wider social processes that were troubling the courts. Cases of female offenders committing infanticide did appear in this trawl but have not been considered here. The specific case of female infanticide (mothers killing their own young children) is a particular issue that has its own history and has been extensively discussed elsewhere (e.g. Kramar and Watson 2006; Walker 1968: Chapter 7; Ward 1999; Zedner 1991). The remaining cases all concern male perpetrators directing fatal violence towards their wives. The gendered nature of these cases needs to be noted and carried through to the second part of this chapter which will be devoted to outlining some of the forces that were helping to shape the events taking place in the court. It will be argued that these cases are reflecting some important aspects of state formation. Most obviously they are occurring in a more centralised and specialised legal system that experienced pressure to intervene in crime, particularly in relation to male violence, and to provide solutions beyond capital punishment or deportation. At the same time, this was occurring in a society where there was greater interest in the emotional facets of relationships, which was prompting new ideas about the nature of insanity. This is an important period where the ground was being laid for the birth of psychiatry and the explosion of interest in monomania and moral insanity that was to take place in the first half of the nineteenth century; an interest that has continued (albeit in different guises) well into the twenty-first century.

## 1.1 The Old Bailey, the public sphere and new forms of insanity

The Old Bailey, situated in central London, was the court that hosted criminal trials for felony offences in the City of London and the surrounding county of Middlesex. Sessions were held eight times a year (Langbein 1983). The location of this court, which oversaw the dispensation of justice in the city that was experiencing the birth of the modern world (McKeon 1985; Ogborn 1998; Porter 2000) and the development of a modern legal system, was always going to give the Old Bailey a historical resonance (Langbein 1983). The fact that from 1674 a public record of the proceedings was made available reinforces the significance of the institution. What have become known as the Old Bailey Sessions Papers (OBSP) began to be published at this point in order to serve the general public's appetite for details about crime and its punishment. The publication of the OBSP provided 'one of the most widely read accounts of the criminal trial in eighteenth-century London' and its influence was spread as it was plundered by other publications (Devereaux 2003: 57). They were published under licence of the Lord Mayor purely as a commercial and entrepreneurial exercise until 1775 when, given some alarm at the accuracy of the accounts, the Common Council for the City of London began to oversee their production and demand higher levels of detail and accuracy. From 1778 the OBSP were printed under the authority of the chief at the Old Bailey

(Shoemaker 2008). The regulation of the OBSP was, Devereaux argues, in part driven by anxiety about rising crime levels and the subsequent 'desire to reconfirm the legitimacy of the law in the eyes of the public, whilst simultaneously holding out the promise of the severest possible punishment to convicted criminals' (Devereaux 2003: 59). Nevertheless, as with any historical account, care needs to be taken not to assume that the OBSP represent a straightforwardly accurate record of events in the courtroom (Shoemaker 2008). Produced to make a profit, the records needed to provide a certain amount of entertainment. They were often brief and selective in what they reported, particularly before being brought under tighter regulation in 1775. Despite the accuracy and detail increasing considerably after this point, Shoemaker still cautions that they were serving the two purposes of reassuring the public that crime was being controlled and getting the message to 'the criminal classes' that their crimes would be punished. The picture painted by the OBSP for much of the time is 'of incorrigible offenders who met their just deserts after a substantial career' (Lemmings 2012: 27). Most of the use of the OBSP made here and in the following chapter is with those trials occurring after 1775. While the detail provided gives some reason to be assured of a measure of accuracy, it might also be argued that in another sense the absolute accuracy of the OBSP is not a major concern for us here. The papers themselves are both symptomatic and constituent of the public sphere (as discussed in the Introduction) that was to become so important in shaping the modern world (Habermas 1989). The rhetorical message and purpose of the accounts of trials where sanity was the subject of debate is perhaps precisely what is most interesting about them. Even after it had the Old Bailey's official approval, and needed to be viewed as an accurate account, it was still an entrepreneurial project that needed to pander to popular taste to an extent (see Devereaux 2003 for details of how the publication was put together and the methods of recording). By the late eighteenth century newspapers were also independently producing detailed accounts and getting them to the public far more quickly. The bias towards salacious and violent offences was very clear in newspapers (King 2009). Four different trials, taking place over a 32-year period, will now be reviewed. They all involve male violence fatal to female partners, and in each case the sanity of the perpetrator was in question in the court. None of the trials involved expert medical witnesses commenting on insanity.

### 1.1.1 Robert Finch (1754): motive, reason and ostensive madness

Robert Finch stood trial at the Old Bailey[1] in 1754 for the murder of his wife in Ludgate debtors' prison, where he had been an inmate on a number of occasions. Most inmates of debtors' prisons were there because a creditor had applied to have them locked up until they had paid their debt. At this point in history, before prison was the mainstay of the punishment system, such prisoners typically formed a significant proportion of the prison population (Woodfine 2006). Conditions were not pleasant, but inmates were allowed to buy their own provisions and visitors were freely allowed. It was during such a visit from his wife that Finch killed her with a knife, cutting her throat in such a way that her head was almost removed. The account of the trial itself is quite brief, as this was in the years before the OBSP were professionalised (Shoemaker 2008). It was easy for the court to establish that Finch killed his wife; he made a full confession at the time and did not retract it. He was very distressed and had tried to hang himself repeatedly that night. Witnesses in the prison testified that Finch himself claimed the motive of jealousy, saying that 'he would do it, was it to do again, sooner than any man should enjoy his wife' (OBSP 17 July 1754). It was also testified that Finch had, during his stay in prison, never seemed 'to be disordered in his mind, there were no signs of lunacy ... he appeared as a man in his senses; and that he was very well respected by the whole house'. Finch 'said nothing in his own defence' but called a number of male witnesses who knew him from a career on sailing ships as character witnesses. They testified that 'he went by the name of *mad Finch* or *crazy Finch*, and was looked upon as a lunatick or frensical man on board'. There is more detail in the Ordinary's account[2] published after the trial, which tells of a 35-year-old man who had a somewhat unstable life and career and at times had been 'out of his mind'. On that night, according to Finch himself, Elizabeth was there to tell him that she was going away and this 'worked him up to such a pitch of anger (which is by some justly defined by the expression of A short madness) as cost them both their lives'. He loved his wife 'to distraction, but that fiend of hell, jealousy, had also taken possession of his mind, by which means he was hurried to the atrocious act of murdering her, on whom he owns he chiefly depended for support' (OBSP Ordinary's account).[3] So although language like 'possession' or 'fiend of hell', and even 'short madness' is used, these are not words of mitigation at all. They are perhaps quite the reverse for, far from excusing the crime, the emphasis on the 'pitch of anger', or the strength of the feeling of jealousy involved, provided an explanation as to why he did it. As Eigen (1998) notes, using the crime of infanticide (which had a long history of being excused) as a common example, it was the absence of motive that itself was seen as providing crucial evidence of the insanity. In this case the Ordinary's account describes 'his hand, impelled by a passion, which, when once entertained, requir's vigilant care to prevent, and guard against the furies by which it is haunted'.[4] Finch's failure to control his extreme passion was effectively an explanation for the crime and his failure to control his passion sent him to the gallows. The case emphasises a number of connected issues concerning gender, passion, violence and sanity. This male violence directed at his partner is condemned by the court. The claims, from friends and colleagues, of signals of insanity in the life of the accused are set aside. Instead what seems to drive the verdict is an ancient model of the relationship between sanity, reason and passion. As discussed later in this chapter (see pp. 41–44), the assumption that if a person has their reason then they are accountable for their acts, no matter the strength of the feelings they have that drive them to action, is an ancient one that can be traced back to Plato at least (Robinson 1971).

Another case where a man killed his wife was tried a few years later, in 1761, at the Old Bailey. In this case the motive appears to be less clear. While the lack of clarity about the motive does not save him from the gallows, there appears to be considerable unease about the verdict. This unease is fully revealed in the Ordinary's account[5] which seems to play a role far removed from that of a corrective morality tale; instead the Ordinary seems to be using the publication to raise awareness and perhaps promote discussion about the nature of insanity and criminal culpability.

### 1.1.2 Richard Parrott (1761):[6] the 'subtilty and craft' of insanity?

Richard Parrott was an elderly, rather deaf, man who was accused of murdering his wife of thirty years, with whom he shared the parentage of seven children (*Whitehall Evening Post* 22 October 1761). They lived in the parish of Harmansworth (now Harmondsworth, part of the outer London Borough of Hillingdon), then a small town outside London, although it was well connected, being just off the 'Bath Road'. It was not disputed that on the morning of 20 September, Richard Parrott attacked his wife. He told the arresting constable that 'she had told a great many lies of him, and he took a piece of her tongue off, that she should tell no more'. In court his only defence was that he was scared of her and that she had threatened to shoot him. There were two issues for the court to decide: did Anne Parrott die of the injuries inflicted by her husband, and was he sane and therefore responsible? The case was reported in the press in such a way that suggested little hesitation and was brutal in its conclusion:

> Yesterday morning about, Nine o'clock, the Trial of Richard Parrott, for the murder of his wife, by partly cutting out her tongue, came on at the Old Bailey; It lasted upwards of three hours, when the jury brought him in guilty. He immediately received Sentence to be executed next Monday at Tyburn, and his body hung in chains. On Hounslow Heath, near where the Fact was committed. He had been married upwards of 30 years, and had by her seven children, which are all living.
> (*Whitehall Evening Post* 22 October 1761)

The report provides a salutary and very public warning of the evil of this act. Richard Parrott had cruelly killed his wife, and for this crime he was to be executed and his body publicly hanged in chains near to where the couple had lived, until it had decayed. The press report has no space for any of the doubt and even sorrow that surrounded the case, as revealed by the detailed account in the OBSP. There was witness evidence that Richard Parrott's mind was disturbed. Parrott's son, who lived some miles away in Richmond (to the south west of London), reported to the court that two months earlier he had been called to visit his parents and his mother had told him: 'your father is out of his mind, and I am frightened out of my wits, fearing something should happen'. Parrott's son went on to report:

> My father seemed to be concerned about something, he told me people came after him to kill him; and my mother told me he ran away, and hid himself in a grove ... my father told me my mother had poisoned him, and that she had dressed his cloaths with poison; my mother said he had cut his cloaths to pieces, and buried them.[7]

A witness to these conversations confirmed that 'she was almost afraid to live with him, he got up at odd hours, and ran about, and conceited people were coming to kill him, and seemed out of his mind'. Despite this evidence of the presence of madness and the lack of clear motive, Parrott was found guilty. A number of factors might help us understand the guilty verdict. The court may well have been swayed by the fact that the attack was a very brutal and sustained one. The unfortunate Anne suffered an agonising death, taking seventeen days to die. It might also be significant that the last witness statements that are reported in the OBSP before the verdict present the view that Richard Parrott did 'know right from wrong':

Q. Have you heard what Cox the witness and the son have said?
*Haines* (the local Constable[8] who had arrested Parrott): I have, but I know nothing of it; I never saw the prisoner do any act of lunacy.
Q. How did he behave under your care?
Haines: He behaved very sensibly and well.
Q. Did you ever hear from the neighbours that he was out of his senses?
*Haines*: There was some talk of what this young man speaks of; but as to the truth of it, I can say nothing to that.
Q. Was the prisoner capable of knowing good from evil while under your care?
*Haines*: He was.
Q. to West (a neighbour): Do you think he was capable of knowing good from evil?
*West*: I believe at the time he did it, he did not think he should be hanged for it; but he knew what he did.

In many ways this verdict is consistent with the view that it is the complete absence of reason that is crucial to the defence of insanity. The emphasis that the neighbour puts on 'knowing good from evil' suggests a cognitive view of insanity, a view that was to be so thoroughly contested in the next century (as discussed in detail in the following chapter). It may also be that in 1761, madness was still expected to be something that was observable and manifest, 'evident to the untrained eye' (Loughnan 2007: 387). The absence of any credible motive for the crime, beyond Parrott's own statement about his wife telling lies and nagging him, is striking and perhaps might have given the court some grounds for concern. Indeed, such concern does emerge after the trial: the most significant historical point about this case is that there is a long and detailed account from the Ordinary[9] (Chaplain Stephen Roe) at Newgate prison, who had spent time with Parrott before his execution. It is generally understood that the Ordinary's accounts were there to provide contextual information on the more significant and serious cases, and it is argued that their fairly blatant rhetorical purpose was to make the moral lessons very plain to the public (McKenzie 2005). The dangers of poor choices, bad company and lascivious lifestyles were rendered as transparent warnings to the rest of the population. As Langbein summarises:

> Written in a moralizing tone purporting to instruct the reader by example in order that he might avoid the fate of the criminals condemned to death at the Old Bailey, these accounts dwell on the backgrounds and criminal careers of the convicts, their behavior in prison as they awaited death, and their executions.
> (Langbein 1978: 270)

In the case of Richard Parrott, however, the Ordinary does not dwell on the moral flaws of the perpetrator but instead very clearly indicates that insanity was very likely. This suggests that by the middle of the eighteenth century the Ordinary's accounts were not simply fulfilling a crude propagandist function. Instead perhaps there was a looser discursive role being played by the account, a point that King (2009) makes about the press generally in the latter decades of the eighteenth century. Chaplain Roe notes that there was abundant evidence that Parrott had carried out a brutal and very deliberate attack on his wife, yet 'these circumstances put together don't remove the probability of the prisoner's being insane when the fact was done'. Roe goes on to provide a perspective on the nature of insanity that is far removed from one that relies on the notion of being understood as a total loss of reason. Parrott could have 'an understanding that was far from totally eclipsed', but Roe suggests that the insanity was manifest in disturbed 'imagination', reinforcing Rousseau's point that the imagination was discovered in the eighteenth century and that Locke's view of insanity (see Introduction p.10) was part of the landscape of this educated chaplain at least:

The account he gave me of himself at several interviews and conversations with him, both before and after his trial, were consonant to this supposed [distempered] state of his mind; they shewed an imagination disturbed and agitated more or less at intervals, though the understanding was far from being totally eclipsed or obscured, but struggling between light and darkness; and this to the best of my discerning was neither put on, nor feigned with a view to palliate his crime: for he seemed to speak with all the sense and coherence he was master of.[10]

Roe also makes it clear that in his view, insanity ('this unaccountable distemper') could well impact upon the 'affections', particularly those concerned with domestic relationships:

Subtilty and craft are known to attend this unaccountable distemper, in carrying on any mischief or outrage. The affections are generally inverted; love is turned into hatred, suspicion, jealousy, and rage; and the dearest object of love, is doomed to be the first victim of the perverted passions.

So here is a representation of insanity that is conceived as not leading to 'total eclipse' of the understanding, but instead could impact upon the affections and could manifest in violence. This is the territory that was to be fully, and more formally, opened up by Pinel through his description of *manie sans délire* some forty years later (as discussed in some detail in the following chapter). Having made it clear that he thinks Richard Parrott was insane, Roe goes on to cast the blame for the tragic events on the local community for not taking care of him and thus preventing the attack:

Happy had it been for his family, his friends, his neighbours, and parishioners, had they secured and put him under care for this fatal malady; they might have prevented this sad event to the deceased, this reproach to the survivors, who are in any degree blameable for this gross and dangerous neglect.

While Roe holds the local community culpable, he also goes on to prefigure what was going to happen over the following one hundred years or so, arguing that the law needs to take more account of the 'physics' view of distemper:

Perhaps law and physic do not look on this distemper with the same eyes; and the former may now and then neglect or over-look the assistance of the latter in distinguishing it; and discerning its effects, when it may be of the least importance to some individuals to distinguish and discern it in all its monstrous shapes and manifold symptoms.[11]

It would be wrong to impute any straightforward shift in legal thinking over time, but there does seem to be a clear case to argue that Roe's plea was responded to and that there was considerable movement towards taking into account 'the subtilty and craft' that might underlie a variety of manifestations of insanity. Two further cases that occurred just over twenty years later will be examined. They both involve men who have killed their wives, but both are found not guilty on the grounds of insanity, under the direction of Judge Baron Eyre, in 1784 and 1786. As was typical of the time, there is no expert witness evidence on insanity in the court, but instead it is clear that the jury, under very firm direction from the judge, are being asked to take into account the fact that insanity might be present even when not manifestly obvious. It is perhaps not insignificant that Walker's trial took place just one year after the authorities had finally stopped the tradition of the often riotous procession of the condemned from Newgate prison to the gallows at Tyburn where they met their end in front of large crowds. The procession from Newgate and the very public executions were supposed to be a salutary warning to all about where crime would lead. There had been a long running debate about the impact of this tradition, with some very prominent writers, such as Henry Fielding (1751) and Bernard Mandeville (1725), arguing that instead the hanging days often seemed more like carnival, as the common people of London came out to drink and celebrate. The ending of the procession was perhaps a signal of a new sensibility towards crime (Foucault 1977), a turning away from the very crude exercise of power that could be witnessed by the public gallows. Similarly, there was perhaps a lessening of the insistence that insanity had to be visibly manifest and rendering the sufferer 'a brute' before it could be taken into account.

### 1.1.3 William Walker (1784):[12] failed by the community?

In April 1784 in a trial at the Old Bailey, William Walker,[13] following clear direction by the Judge Baron Eyre, is found not guilty of the murder of his wife on the grounds of insanity.[14] The judge appears to take up two important themes that had been raised by Roe following the execution of Richard Parrott over twenty years earlier. Eyre emphasises that the heart of the accused appeared to be 'free from guilt', but also points to the deficiencies in the system of care within the community. William Walker worked as a 'day labourer' and was accused of killing his wife with a knife in Harefield, Middlesex. This was then a village some way out in the outskirts of London. There was some considerable settlement there and a workhouse had been built in 1782, the parish Overseer of which featured in the trial. Overseers were introduced by the Elizabethan Poor Laws, appointed by each parish to take responsibility for raising funds from local taxation and for the distribution of welfare and the supervision of the workhouses built for the local poor (see Brundage 2002).

There is no medical evidence at the trial, and in this case none of the witnesses could point to any significant history of insanity. There was no counsel working for either the prosecution or the defence; this was still in an era where even counsel for the prosecution were rare (Langbein 1978). Yet the judge points the jury towards insanity, despite the fact that there was no report of any known history of insanity proffered by any witness, apart from the accounts of his wife being concerned about his behaviour. On the night of the killing, Ann Walker has asked for help and two neighbours have been asked to attend. It is not quite clear whether this is simply out of neighbourliness; it is perhaps more likely that they are being paid for their duty by the Overseer. Their presence downstairs, however, is not sufficient to prevent a violent attack by William on his wife upstairs in their bedroom. The grounds for Walker being found guilty appear straightforward: he evidently committed the act of killing and there were no outward signs of insanity (Loughnan 2012). Walker, as the judge explains,[15] does not seem insane since otherwise he appeared to be behaving normally, was quite aware of what he had done and attempted to justify his actions:

> [T]he general tranquillity of his behaviour, his conversing with the people like another man, and eating and drinking, and appearing to be conscious of what he had done, endeavouring to justify it, and accusing her of having behaved ill to him; these are all of them circumstances that seem to denote that he was in possession of himself, that he knew what he was doing, that he meant to do it, and that he did it on motives of malice urging him to revenge, for some injury that he had received, or was to receive from her.

The evidence pointing towards Walker's innocence, on the other hand, was the lack of motive, owing to his wife's behaviour and her goodness, his apparent lack of temper and the apparently good relationship that they enjoyed:

> [H]owever, they [witnesses] all agree in his favour, that she was a very extraordinary good kind of a woman, not likely to give him any cause of a quarrel, and he not a quarrelsome man, and that they lived in a state of good understanding together; this leads one to expect to find, that this unfortunate event did arise from something singular and extraordinary, and not to be accounted for in any way in which people ordinarily account for those dreadful acts of violence, which are committed either from deep malice, or revenge for injuries supposed to be received, or at least from some sudden transports of revenge, for some ill usage received.

The judge also points to the fact that Ann had been seeking help from the Overseer, and that although she was worried about his behaviour, she still had 'tenderness to him' and had stayed with him:

> [I]t is a fact that is beyond all contradiction I think, that the woman was conscious that there was something amiss with him, that she had made complaints to the Overseer that there was something wrong, that it was dangerous for her to be in the house with him; and these were not

complaints expressive of resentment for ill-usage offered by him to her, for brutality, or anything for which he should be punished; for she seemed to have tenderness to him to the last; she chose on the last night to go to him, to sleep with him, but if he had treated her as brutal men do women that they have in their power, one would have thought, having men in the house, she would not have gone to bed to him[.]

In the above passage the judge clearly draws a distinction between Walker's behaviour and those 'brutal men' who are violent to those women 'they have in their power'. It is difficult to see an attempt to trivialise or normalise male, 'domestic' violence towards women in this judge's direction. Indeed what seems to be significant to the judge is that the violence of the act appears to be incompatible with the relationship between the couple. The judge summarises the evidence given by Constable Tromper, who had reported that he had gone to talk with William, having been advised by Ann that something was wrong:

Tromper spoke to him and found him in a condition which should have alarmed him; he complained he was troubled in his mind, he did not know why, but he was, he could not tell what was the matter, but he was troubled and uneasy[.]

The judge notes at this point that surely there would have been some kind of physical manifestation of any illness:

I am satisfied that if at that time the state of the man's body had been examined into, he would have been found to have had a fever upon him; I have not a doubt but it was a nervous fever that had seized his spirits.

In the final summing up, the judge first makes the point that 'Where men suffer their passions to get the better of their reasons, and do in transports of rage commit this crime, they must answer for the consequences'. He goes on, however, to suggest that perhaps this was a rage brought on by a 'distemper of mind', that may be viewed as an 'act of God', and therefore Walker may not bear responsibility:

Gentlemen, upon the result of as careful an examination as I could make, it appears to me, that this was the unhappy effect of rage against this woman, conceived in consequence of distemper of mind, brought on by disease, and that under that impression the violence was committed. The man's afterwards coming to his senses will not alter the nature of the case, if it was committed under the impression of insanity, and the mind disturbed and deprived of its powers of governing the man: he is not answerable, and you must find your verdict, Not Guilty[.][16]

Like the chaplain in the Parrott case over twenty years earlier, Baron Eyre seems to be using a concept of insanity that was to be formalised by Pinel's account of *manie sans délire* at the dawn of the nineteenth century. Also, as with Roe's concerns about the Parrott case, an important aspect of the Walker trial is that the judge is clearly frustrated at the inadequacy of the community and welfarism in the village. The evidence given by neighbours at the trial seemed to suggest rather private lives; they do not seem to know the accused at all. Ann Walker had asked for help from the parish Overseer (Morton), who did not even appear in court. Most frustration is directed at the Overseer.[17] The judge thinks he should have gone straight to see Walker himself and should have got a 'person of skill' (it is worth noting that there seems not to have been any assumption that it ought to have been a doctor) to look at him:

> I am sorry to observe that the overseer did his duty very ill, for after these alarms he ought to have done more a great deal than leaving a blind message with the governor of the work-house; his duty would have been to have gone instantly to have seen the man; his duty would have been to have employed a person of skill to have looked at him; the man might have been saved, the woman might have been saved, and all this mischief prevented.[18]

The jury, strongly directed by the judge, agree with the verdict of 'not guilty' and the report concludes: 'This man must not be discharged, unless the parish officers, to save the expences, come and take him away; he must be carried before a magistrate, confined, and taken proper care of.'

### 1.1.4 John Simpson (1786):[19] 'an innocent heart'?

Two years later in 1786 John Simpson (OBSP) is also found not guilty under strong direction from the same judge. He stabbed his wife with a pocket knife at their home in 'the parish of St. Leonard, Shoreditch'. The judge suggests a 'temporary insanity' to explain what otherwise appears to be a motiveless crime and one that Simpson makes no attempt to conceal. Simpson and his wife are described as being of good character. A comment from a neighbour is typical: 'I always took him to be a very good natured, kind, benevolent man, and a good neighbour, that was his general character.' In this case there are witness accounts telling how he is not always in his right mind. A fishmonger of his acquaintance described Simpson being in an agitated state in the local public house, some 'five or six' years earlier. He had, apparently falsely, believed that he had been bitten by a 'black hog' and that he could see people hiding behind a curtain. The witness took this 'to be his illness, a kind of light headedness, or insanity'. There is no medical or expert witness in evidence, going by the account. Judge Baron Eyre points towards ideas about the physiological causes of insanity, making much of the fact that the accused had – he suggests unwisely – eaten a pork meal despite having been unwell for a number of days.

The judge set out the grounds for conviction; it seemed clear that the prisoner was not in 'a confirmed habit or state of lunacy', and that he was not 'like an idiot, but has sufficient sense to govern himself, and to be answerable for his conduct . . . generally speaking, he has been in possession of his right mind'. Thus, the judge suggests his behaviour can only be excused if he was understood to be suffering from an 'insanity, temporary in its nature'. Baron Eyre indicates the significance of the capacity of the accused to distinguish right from wrong, but also gestures to the importance of the capacity to recognise 'the affection that was due to an affectionate wife'. In doing this Eyre seems to propose the possibility of an understanding of insanity connected to affect rather than reason and raises the distinction that was to be so crucial to debate about the status on 'moral insanity' in the following decades. He offers two possibilities for how this insanity might have operated. Perhaps there was some partition between the act and the sentiment of the perpetrator: 'though his hand was guilty, his heart was free', or perhaps Simpson was suffering an insanity 'temporary in its nature':

> [Y]ou must be satisfied, at the time this fact was committed, his mind was in such a state of distraction, that he could no longer be sensible of the internal distinction between right and wrong, and more especially the distinction between the affection that was due to an affectionate wife, and this savage outrage he committed upon her; and that though his hand was guilty, his heart was free from that act which the guilt of his hand would otherwise impute to him and that if there be any foundation to excuse him from the guilt of this homicide, in consequence of his being insane at the time, it is the ground of an insanity, temporary in its nature, which arose in consequence of a particular circumstance taking effect only during a particular period.[20]

The jury agreed with the direction of the judge and John Simpson was acquitted. It is worth noting that the jury's verdict itself was inseparable from the idea that something needed to be done. In giving their verdict the jury added the caveat that 'this man should be taken care of' and the judge agreed: 'I will order he shall not be discharged at present, but that he shall be examined before the Lord Mayor; and his friends will, I hope, appear, and settle some method to take care of him.'

## 1.2 The state and the informalisation of control

In order to understand how this court might have been willing to entertain rather different forms of insanity towards the end of the eighteenth century it will be argued that the events need to be understood within the frameworks created by the emergence of the modern state. The cases examined in the previous section suggest that the nature of masculine violence, the quality of social (notably marital) relationships (insofar as this signified sanity or otherwise) and the lack of provision for those deemed insane were issues upon which courts were now having to reflect. This period was witnessing not only the creation of the modern legal system but also a fundamental shift in the understanding of the relationship between individuals and their social world. This reworking crucially involved a different understanding of the importance of emotion in the social realm. The cases of Walker, Simpson and Parrott each involved violence towards their wives that was inexplicable without some recourse to notions of insanity (that was not otherwise manifest). There is also a sense of frustration with the systems of welfare at the same time as recognition that family, friends and neighbours had failed to intervene and prevent the tragedies. Each of these points is significant and will be discussed in the following sections, which describe some of the key changes occurring in those systems within the newly emerging modern state that were concerned with criminal justice and mental health. This second part of the chapter will therefore consist of discussion of three connected issues in the later eighteenth century that were crucial to the emergence of moral insanity at the beginning of the nineteenth century:

1.2.1 The development of the legal system;
1.2.2 Gender, violence and the state;
1.2.3 The institutionalisation and theorisation of madness.

## 1.2.1 The development of the legal system

The development of a formalised legal system is an obvious manifestation of relationships of power within the emergent modern state. Laws are invented, enacted and enforced according to the wishes and interests of groups of people who wish to ensure that certain modes of conduct are rendered illegal and therefore subject to censure and punishment (O'Malley 1987). The links between the emergence of modern systems of justice and the development of the state are quite clear, and so a focus on the latter decades of the eighteenth century is therefore not merely happenstance. It was over this century, as Langbein (1983: 2) notes, that the 'fundamental attributes' of modern criminal legal procedures were put in place: 'the law of evidence, the adversary system, the privilege against self-incrimination, and the main ground rules for the relationship of judge and jury'. Both Langbein (1983) and Hay (1980: 47) argue that England, and London in particular, was at the forefront of this process, with the speed of industrialisation driving 'the rapid and pervasive transformation of England's economy and society'. These changes in the criminal justice system were essential to the construction of the nation state as it shifted during the eighteenth century from being a largely privately organised system to one that was publicly administered (Hay 1980). The most remarkable change took place in the system of prosecution, since at the beginning of the eighteenth century the organisation of policing was largely informal, with 'parish householders' taking turns as 'constables' who 'did little more than assist the private citizen who was the victim of a theft or other crime and who himself paid for the prosecution and largely organised it' (Hay 1980: 48). Within the courts it is hardly surprising, given the costs involved, that prosecution counsel, although allowed, tended not to be employed. Meanwhile, defendants were denied even the right to employ legal counsel until the 1730s (May 2003). The next century and a half was to witness transformation. By the middle of the nineteenth century a public police force was formed and the duty of prosecution was to be taken over more or less entirely by the state (Godfrey and Lawrence 2005). Eventually most trials of more serious offences would feature the consideration of the arguments put forward by prosecution and defence lawyers. On one level these moves represented a centralisation of power as policing and prosecution were taken over directly by the state. At the same time as this, the systems of justice, and indeed trials themselves, were becoming increasingly subject to public discussion and debate in the newly developing public sphere (Lemmings 2012), as the OBSP testify, and public anxiety about social change and disorder was a part of that discourse. As many have noted, the development of London as a mercantile, manufacturing and financial centre was making many people very rich, while the presence of such wealth drew in the very poor (e.g. May 2003; Ogborn 1998). With its booming population of poor, rootless and often starving individuals and families, major problems of disorder were being posed and it was no wonder that '[c]rime, criminals, and the criminal justice system' became topics that 'increasingly occupied the attention of private individuals, local officials, and the state' (May 2003: 14).

Before the nineteenth century courts were typically made up of five key groups: judges, jurors, prosecutors, witnesses and defendants. The judges held considerable power and they came from the upper echelons of society. As we have seen in the cases discussed, they directed proceedings, they led the questioning of the defendant and witnesses and they directed juries towards their verdicts. The selection of jurors was not systematic or particularly transparent, but they were all men and generally came from the middle rank: 'gentleman, merchant, professionals, and wealthier shopkeepers, tradesmen, and artisans'.[21] The existence of jury trials (most trials considered in this book were before juries) is at the very least symptomatic of some complexity in the relationship between privilege and judicial decision making. The history of trial by jury is a long one (dating back to pre-Norman England at least). In the earlier centuries the jury often functioned in an investigative role and it was their local knowledge of the area and its inhabitants that was crucial to their decision making. There was a gradual shift over the centuries towards taking on a more 'objective' stance as they weighed the evidence attached to the opposing stories of guilt or innocence that were put before them. However, even by the late eighteenth century courts were usually more investigative than adversarial (Loughnan 2012: 139), with the operating belief being that the truth should in some way be evident (May 2003). Cases were generally brought by a prosecutor (the victim of the alleged offence) who could question defendants and bring in witnesses. Prosecutors were allowed to instruct lawyers, but in reality rarely did so; it was not the norm and was no doubt prohibitively expensive. Defendants had no such right in felony trials until the 1730s and the presence of lawyers was very rare until well into the nineteenth century. Defendants could also call their own witnesses and they were allowed to question other witnesses. Witnesses called by the prosecutors were often the direct witnesses of the alleged offence itself. Questioning of these witnesses was not often very detailed and they were given space in the court to speak in their own terms. No sense of witnesses being routinely challenged or cross-examined emerges from the Old Bailey reports, certainly until well into the nineteenth century. Neither were expert witnesses with professional expertise, such as medical men, present in court in any numbers before this period. The involvement of those with expertise in insanity will be dealt with in the third section here.

The trials of William Walker and John Simpson in the 1780s are clearly examples which took place before courts were professionalised through the presence of prosecution and defence lawyers or medical expertise. At this time, as May argues, the criminal justice system in Britain was under some strain and public scrutiny as matters of crime and justice had become central concerns of the newly emerging press (see also McGowan 2005). Prosecution rates were soaring, and at the same time the failure of the war with America made the transportation of convicted felons more difficult. The city of London continued to show faith in the impact of the deterrent effect of public hangings, despite fairly widespread scepticism. May quotes *The Times* expressing extreme alarm at a state of affairs suggesting that England was executing more people than 'all the cities in Europe put together' (May 2003: 120; *The Times* 31 January 1785). The interest in crime was also strongly evident in the popular genres of novels in the eighteenth century (Faller 1987; Pepper 2011). It is worth noting that Henry Fielding, author of *Tom Jones* (first published in 1749), also enjoyed a significant career in the criminal justice system as Chief Justice of the Peace in London, where he founded the 'Bow Street Runners', the prelude to an organised police force. As Gladfelder (2001: 5) suggests, fictional crime narratives raised very directly 'the problem of relations between the individual and a community which was coming to define itself more and more through the discourses and institutions of secular law'. Most significantly this allowed the exploration of the offender:

> In the open endedness of their plots, their violence, multiplicity of voices, obsession with detail, underpinnings of social conflict, and concentration on moral and psychological disturbance, the fictions that Defoe and Fielding constructed from the corpus of criminal narrative articulate a[n] ... ambivalence about the pleasures and dangers of individual desire.
> (Gladfelder 2001: 6)

This sense of a need for greater understanding of individuals so that order could be facilitated was to assist the birth of systems of welfare (of which the care and control of the insane was a particularly important manifestation). A number of writers have noted that the criminal justice system focused ever more closely on male misconduct, most particularly that involving violence. It is worth noting that Defoe's description of the delinquent and feminine life of *Moll Flanders* was published in 1722, nearer the beginning of the eighteenth century before women had begun to vanish from the courts as offenders (Feeley and Little 1991). The next section will discuss this shift towards the control of masculine violence and it will be argued that the move was of considerable significance as it signalled wider changes in social relations of which gender formed an important part.

### 1.2.2 Gender, violence and the state

A number of historians have observed that courts became more focused on male offenders during the eighteenth and nineteenth centuries. Feeley and Little (1991) used the Old Bailey records to make the case that women effectively 'vanished' as a significant presence in the courtroom over a 150-year period from the beginning of the eighteenth century to near contemporary levels (where male offenders dominate in terms of numbers). They focused their discussion of the possible explanations for this decline on the reduction in female participation in the public labour market and the increasing social control of women as their place become more and more confined to the private world of the home (an argument that is used to explain contemporary gender difference, Heidensohn 1996, for example). Shoemaker (2001) took a rather a different tack and argued that the measurable and significant decline in the homicide rate over the eighteenth century in London could be accounted for in terms of modification of the expectations of male public behaviour. Shoemaker also used Old Bailey records to suggest that the evident decline in the murder rate can be accounted for by a reduction in what has been termed, in contemporary criminological literature, 'confrontational homicide' (e.g. Polk 1994). This occurs when men kill each other as the result of a public dispute, commonly taking place over what are often perceived by outsiders to be largely trivial matters of apparent 'honour'. The drop in such killings was not matched by such a fall in the rate of domestic killings in the private realm. Thus by the end of the eighteenth century marital disputes leading to murder accounted for as many as 29 per cent of homicide cases at the Old Bailey (whereas they accounted for 8 per cent a century earlier). This, Shoemaker suggests, is part of a 'long-term trend in which homicides involving family members increased from only a few percent in the Middle Ages to about half of all homicides in modern England' (2001: 206). Lacour (2001) makes the same observation about German homicide records: that as general homicide rates fell during the eighteenth century, domestic homicides made up a higher proportion of the total. Such shifts in gender expectations were symptomatic of the emergence of the modern state. As Liddle (1996) noted, although 'technological changes and consequent shifts in economic relations' made state formation possible it was also associated with 'a correlative ferment in the constitution of gender' (Liddle 1996: 362). This ferment, Liddle argues, cannot simply be understood in terms of an assertion of masculine hegemony, despite the fact that industrialisation and state building did for the most part centralise power in the hands of relatively few men and involved a deepening of sex role division. Instead, there was also a quite intense 'differentiation of masculinities', not only between aristocratic and bourgeois masculinities, but also between 'warrior masculinities' and more rational/calculative identities. It would thus be wrong to think that the developing criminal justice system represented and implemented an assertion of masculinity over femininity; it was rather an assertion of particular types of masculinity over other ways of being, that might be viewed in terms of social class (Messerschmidt 1993). Wiener (2001) has made a very similar point: that the disappearance of women from the courtroom and from the public imagination of violence cannot simply be understood in terms of the marginalisation and pacification of women, since such a view 'overlooks the necessarily entwined character of gender' (Wiener 2001: 186). There were thus reciprocal processes in play just as 'women became perceived as less dangerous and more in need of protection, and men, complementarily, became perceived as more dangerous and more in need of control'. One expression of these processes was in the criminal justice system that meted out more lenient treatment towards women and harsher treatment to men (Wiener 2001: 187). The sources of such changes are hard to pin down precisely, but Wiener points towards industrialisation and urbanisation. The emergent market for labour gave people freedom to move from town to town, and from job to job, but it was men, unencumbered by pregnancy and children, who were freer to take those opportunities, while women were more likely to be left holding the responsibilities. As local communities became more fragmented and temporary, so the informal means of controlling men became less viable and they were replaced by more formal methods of control. Over the same period, the expectations of marriage were also rising and the ideal of the 'companionate marriage', which would provide emotional sustenance to both parties, was becoming more commonplace (e.g. Stone 1990). This latter point about the social significance of feelings and passion begins to open up rather different lines of thought and enquiry. The view of passion, particularly between men and women, as something to be valued rather than simply controlled, contained or disciplined, is eventually to have a profound influence on culture and indeed upon psychological theory (most notably signalled by the emergence of psychoanalysis in the late nineteenth century). This recognition of the more complex role that the passions played in the structuring of human affairs – most prominently raised by Foucault (1979) in relation to the nineteenth century in the first volume of his study *The History of Sexuality* – begins to be felt in the court system, as we have seen in the cases of Walker and Simpson, where the consideration of individual motive was to be subjected to greater scrutiny. A change of focus away from the idea that courts were simply concerning themselves with the control of overt violence to the notion that courts were part of a discursive network that was debating the expectations of modes of conduct allows us to consider that they were becoming involved in more subtle evaluations of human conduct and feeling, including reflection on how people engaged with others. In the nineteenth century such interest was to be manifest not only in the emergence of psychiatry but also through explorations of interiority and relationships in fictional literature (as explored in Chapter 4). What we have seen in the cases discussed in this chapter is not only a certain rumination on the nature of masculinity, but also an emerging dissatisfaction with the institutions and ideas surrounding the understanding of insanity in the final decades of the eighteenth century.

### 1.2.3 The institutionalisation and theorisation of madness

There is no doubt that the medical specialism that came to be known as 'psychiatry' only really began to become visible on an institutional level during the nineteenth century. While there were certainly individuals at the beginning of that century who specialised in the identification and treatment of 'insanity', it was not to be until well into the nineteenth century that they had a discernible professional body, public visibility or voice (Bynum 1964; Porter 1987; Scull 1979b). It is not surprising therefore that histories of psychiatry focus their attention on the nineteenth century. Indeed, the next two chapters of the book will focus on the development of thinking about 'moral insanity' within the recognisable psychiatric groupings though the 1800s. However, as Porter (1987: 2) significantly noted, although the infancy of the profession of psychiatry might be contained within the nineteenth century, the story of madness cannot be so limited. One reason for this is simply that for centuries madness has been discussed and theorised; 'lunatics' were identified and there were the various social and cultural responses to insanity (e.g., see Midelfort 1981; Overholder 1959). There are, however, more specific reasons to be interested in the shifts in thought and practice that were occurring in the eighteenth century in England, as these were to lay the ground for the very rapid development of psychiatry and related practices in the nineteenth century.

It is very clear from the cases discussed in the first part of this chapter that the facilities and networks that were available to take care of ill, dependent or problematic individuals is relevant for understanding how madness was being treated in court. In the cases of Parrott and Walker the judge expressed considerable frustration with the inadequate systems of welfare and the rather insulated lives of those surrounding the victims and perpetrators, and suggested that they had some culpability. Better intervention might have stopped the tragedies from occurring. The acquittals of Simpson and Walker did not lead to simple discharges from the court; the men were released into the care of 'parish officers' (Walker) and 'the Lord Mayor and his friends' (Simpson). As we shall see in Chapter 2, this idea of an acquittal leading inevitably to confinement for care was to be formalised in 1800 through the case of James Hadfield. There are some reasons to believe that such problems were more prominent in England, which was, as Porter pointed out, 'singularly ill endowed with civic and pious institutions for unfortunates' owing to Henry VIII's disengagement with the Catholic church and the subsequent dissolution of the monasteries and chantries. This 'left little of the medieval fabric of hospices, almshouses and refuges' (Porter 2004: 128) but cleared the path for the appearance, particularly during the eighteenth century, of unregulated, entrepreneurial madhouses, of which the provision was often poor and decidedly patchy (MacKenzie 1992; Scull 1979b). While the market in insanity in England was quite precocious (Scull 1979b), the asylum movement was soon an international one (Castel 1988; Dörner 1981; Rothman 1971; Tomes 1994), and as we will see in the following chapter, the international nature of psychiatry was to be a feature of its development.

While a recognisable group of medics began to identify themselves as experts in insanity thanks to their work in private asylums during the eighteenth century, they were a long way from official status and it was still rare to see an expert on insanity in the court. Indeed, even when compulsory admission to the asylums was brought under state control in England through the 1744 Vagrancy Act (Section 20), which gave local magistrates the power to detain anyone who was considered to be a lunatic and who 'may be dangerous to be abroad', it gave the power of judgment on the sanity and liberty of an individual to the 'gaoler and local magistrate'; no medical expertise was required (Bynum 1964). In criminal cases, Eigen (1995) estimates that even by the late eighteenth century less than 10 per cent of trials involved a medical witness where the sanity of the accused was at question. It was not only 'psychiatric' expertise that was not being called upon in courts; experts, in the form of lawyers or medical men, were not present until the last decades of the eighteenth century. Even when medics began to appear in courts, as Landsman (1998) notes, they were often 'modest and constrained' in their approach, and this was the case until well into the nineteenth century. Landsman suggests that this reflected the rather fragmented and low status of the medical profession in general. At this time the profession lacked a coherent voice. Medics in Britain were likely to come from three different backgrounds: first there were the physicians who would have a degree from Oxford or Cambridge and could then 'acquire an MD degree by expounding a book of Galen in three written or six spoken lectures'; second there were the surgeons, who were still considered barber-surgeons and acquired their status through a system of apprenticeship until the nineteenth century; third there was the body of apothecaries, which 'licensed its own men' (Jones 1972: 6). None of the groupings had any substantial 'governing body that could effectively police practice or regulate the profession' (Landsman 1998: 484).

Individual practitioners were essentially medical entrepreneurs who were fighting for business and recognition: 'Since cure was beyond his control, a successful doctor's stock in trade was an unblemished reputation and reassuring manner' (Landsman 1998: 486). Thus the avoidance of controversy and public accusations of quackery in court, and the maintenance of good relations with judges and lawyers, were fairly common sense pathways to professional survival. It was not until well into the nineteenth century that psychiatrists made confident claims to expertise in court, and this, as we shall see in Chapter 3, was to be a controversial move for the profession.

Eigen (2004) and Walker (1968: 58) agree that the 'earliest recorded instance of "psychiatric testimony"' being put forward in a criminal trial occurred during the trial of Earl Ferrers in 1760, during which the hapless Earl attempted to defend himself against a charge of murder. He brought Dr John Munro, physician at Bethlem Hospital, to serve as witness on how insanity in general could impact on responsibility (Eigen 2004: 37; Walker 1968: 58–63). Ferrers' conviction and execution following Munro's intervention might partly explain the slow progress of expert testimony in trials involving insanity. Eigen analysed Old Bailey Sessions Papers and found that between 1760 and 1815 some form of insanity plea was used in 165 cases. It is worth noting that 60 per cent of these involved prosecution for theft (which provided by far the largest volume of work at the Old Bailey). Acquittal rates in these trials involving insanity remained fairly constant at around 45 per cent. Walker (1968: 67) uses Old Bailey records to show similarly consistent rates. While the acquittal rate may not have altered much over the time period the terms of debate over insanity were to be subject to considerable change and the emergent profession of psychiatry was highly involved in these changes. Connected issues concerning the relationship between reason, emotions (passions or feelings), insanity and criminal responsibility were to be increasingly debated. The historically dominant belief about the nature of human sanity and its relationship to reason and passion began to be questioned. This was to involve a conceptualisation of the mind as consisting of distinct faculties, and a connected re-evaluation of the role of passion within both the individual and the social realm. While these issues will be expanded upon in subsequent chapters, a brief historical sketch can usefully be made here.

Longstanding beliefs, clear from Plato at least, have held that reason needed to reign over the passions, which were untrustworthy and likely to lead individuals into vice and sin. The Roman philosopher and Stoic Seneca believed that the passions were dangerous to mental balance and contentment:

> Reason herself, to whom the reins of power have been entrusted, remains mistress only so long as she is kept apart from the passions: if once she mingles with them and is contaminated, she becomes unable to hold back those whom she might have cleared from her path.
> (Seneca 1928: Vol. 1, *On Anger* I, vii, i–viii)

The wise person should therefore steer clear of all passion, and all provocation of such passion. This notion that the provocation of the passions was detrimental to health was a strong theme in a great deal of sixteenth- and seventeenth-century writing, as is abundantly clear in Robert Burton's seventeenth-century classic *Anatomy of Melancholy*. Systems of law have been equally suspicious of passion, assuming that reason was the hallmark of human civilisation. Madness was popularly understood as occurring when reason was lost, and those unfortunates who had lost their reason were therefore left like mere 'brute animals'. Such a view underpinned legal tests of insanity for some centuries. Bracton, for example, the influential English jurist of the thirteenth century, refers to the so-called 'wild beast test' in relation to the question of the criminality of suicide (as MacDonald 1989 suggests, discussions of culpability in the case of suicide were a key arena for debates about mental disorder and responsibility).

> But what shall we say of a madman bereft of reason? And of the deranged, the delirious and the mentally retarded? or if one labouring under a high fever drowns himself or kills himself? *Quaere* whether such a one commits felony *de se*. It is submitted that he does not, nor do such persons forfeit their inheritance or their chattels, since they are without sense and reason and can no more commit an *injuria* or a felony than a brute animal, since they are not far removed from brutes, as is evident in the case of a minor, for if he should kill another while under age he would not suffer judgment.
> (Bracton *c*.1250: 244)

Thus the standard test of criminal responsibility and insanity was taken, well into the nineteenth century, to be the so-called 'wild beast test' (Scull 1979a). Thomas Arnold's discussion of the moral 'insanities' of nymphomania and satyriasis is instructive. While the immediate cause was some 'disordered states of the womb, ovaries, and spermatic vessel', such propensities might be created either by 'immodest, and unseasonable, indulgence in lascivious ideas' or by 'merely corporeal causes' (Arnold 1786: 262). Even at this point, Arnold sees insanity as a manifestation of the defeat of reason: 'the moral sense [has] been much impaired by the almost total derangement of reason'. This conception that reason sat over and controlled the passions, and that insanity could be understood only in terms of a disruption of this relationship (e.g., Perfect 1987), was to be contested on a number of different fronts, which will be discussed further in this and subsequent chapters. The challenge to the legal understanding of insanity as an absence of reason was manifest in claims about various versions of 'partial insanity' and the idea that individuals could suffer from an insanity that affected only part of their thinking, feeling or 'mind' is crucial to the beginning of the story of 'moral insanity'. The idea of 'partial insanity' actually has a long history apparent to an extent in both medical and legal writing. As Jackson (1983) points out, descriptions of melancholia have often implied that an individual could function perfectly well outside of their particular suffering. Robert Burton's seventeenth-century text on melancholy includes a section listing various afflictions and delusions that were associated with melancholia, with the comment 'Yet for all this, . . . in all other things they are wise, staid, discreet, & do nothing unbeseeming their dignity, person, or place' (quoted in Jackson 1983: 176). Significantly the seventeenth-century neurological pioneer Thomas Willis distinguished between melancholia of a *universal* type, which meant the sufferer was 'Delirious as to all things, or at least as to the most; so that they judge truly almost of no subject' and the *particular* type, in which they 'imagine amiss in one or two particular cases, but for the most part in other things they have their notions not very incongruous' (Jackson 1983: 176). This notion of partial insanity, based on clinical observation, also achieved some recognition in legal discussions dating back at least to Sir Matthew Hale's remarkably influential work as Lord Chief Justice of England (Cromartie 1995). This was published in about 1736 as *The History of the Pleas of the Crown*, some years after Hale's death in 1676, and had, Walker argues, 'more influence on lawyers of the 18th and 19th centuries than any other single work on the subject' (Walker 1968: 35). Hale's often quoted definition of the insanity defence seems very clearly to point towards the complete absence of reason, a definition going back to Bracton in the thirteenth century at least:

> [I]f they are totally deprived of the use of reason, they cannot be guilty ordinarily of capital offences, for they have not the use of understanding, and act not as reasonable creatures, but their actions are in effect in the condition of brutes.
>
> (Hale 1736: 31)

This point about being 'in the condition of brutes' was already well established by the time of Hale's writing but he was very clear that he was also aware that more subtle forms of insanity, including partial insanity, were to be found (see quotation below). This interest in partial insanity is less surprising when it is borne in mind that Hale attended Thomas Willis' lectures (Jackson 1983: 180). On the one hand Hale notes that partial insanity 'seems not to excuse them' for committing any serious offence, but he does go on to observe that in reality it can be difficult to define exactly where perfect and partial insanity begin and end, and that ultimately it is for courts to decide:

> Some persons, that have a competent use of reason in respect of some subjects, are yet under a particular *dementia* in respect of some particular discourses, subjects, or applications; or else it is partial in respect of degrees: and this is the condition of very many, especially melancholy persons, who for the most part discover their defect in excessive fears and griefs, and yet are not wholly destitute of the use of any reason; and this partial insanity seems not to excuse them in the committing of any offence for its matter

capital; for doubtless most persons that are felons of themselves, and others are under a degree of partial insanity, when they commit these offences: it is very difficult to define the indivisible line that divides the perfect and partial insanity; but it must rest upon circumstances duly to be weighed and considered both by judge and jury.

Hale goes on to observe that the decision can be difficult, and he suggests that the test should be whether the guilty have at least the understanding of a 14-year-old child:

Left on the one side there be a kind of inhumanity towards the defects of human nature, or on the other side too great an indulgence given to the great crimes; the best measure that I can think of is this; such a person as laboring under melancholy distempers has yet ordinarily a great understanding, as ordinarily a child of fourteen years hath, is such a person as may be guilty of treason or felony.

Again, a total alienation of the mind or perfect madness; this excutheth from the guilt of felony and treason.

Thus, although Hale's position is clearly not entirely consistent with a wild beast test, and despite Walker's wry observation that Hale's 'notion of "partial insanity" was to exercise the minds of lawyers, psychiatrists, and Royal Commissions for the next three centuries' (Walker 1968: 38), it was not until the beginning of the nineteenth century that there would be significant overt debate over how partial insanity might be understood and accepted in the courts.

## Conclusion

As discussed earlier in the chapter, the gendered nature of the violence, and the subsequent acquittals, in the cases of both Walker and Simpson clearly needs to be noted and considered. As Shoemaker (2001) has observed, domestic murders were making up a higher proportion of murder cases heard at the Old Bailey by the end of the eighteenth century (this was, he argues, a function of the reduction in the rate of public confrontational violence involving male victims and offenders). The fact that both of these trials seem to be allowing for more subtle forms of insanity to be thought about does point perhaps to the entwinement of ideas about affections and sanity. These were not crimes of passion, they were not motivated by jealousy or control, but the fact that they occurred within relationships that seemed to be stable and affectionate seems to point towards the insanity of the acts. Any explanation in terms of the leniency and 'sympathy' being extended towards these acts of male violence might be construed as a symptom of a patriarchal society and needs to be seriously considered. It must be said, however, that this is not what comes across from the notes from the trials in these two cases. The innocence of the victims and the apparently good relationship between the killer and victim in each case are seen as part of the evidence that the sanity of the perpetrator could be legitimately brought into question. The detail given of these accounts (amounting to over 13,000 and 14,000 words respectively) suggests that they were thought to be of considerable public interest. Perhaps the visibility of these cases and Eyre's strong direction towards insanity are signals of the significance that is being put upon conjugal relationships. The attention being paid to them is a sign that there is a concern to puzzle over such violence.[22]

An examination of ideas about insanity, as they were being played out through discussions in court, reveals a number of very important themes. First, there are ideas about the nature of insanity that suggest that forms of insanity far removed from the wild beast test are having serious influence in the courts in the latter decades of the eighteenth century. It is certainly noteworthy that it is being assumed that these more subtle forms of insanity were manifest within domestic familial relationships. William Walker is found not guilty of murder, partly it would seem because the violence was so inexplicable in what was otherwise a peaceful marital relationship. It does seem that reference is being made to a form of what was to be known as 'moral insanity' or 'monomania'. Second, it is apparent that the social context of these ideas is also important. In the Walker case, the judge expresses considerable displeasure at what he sees as the neglect of the Overseer to intervene more. Richard Parrott, some two decades earlier, had received no such mercy, despite his crime also being an otherwise inexplicable attack on his wife and the fact that there were some indications of previously aberrant behaviour. The remarkable account from the Newgate 'Ordinary' gives notice of some considerable disquiet at that verdict. In part he thinks the law needs to take account of more subtle views of insanity, but also he is concerned at the lack of intervention by the community surrounding the unfortunate Parrotts.

Despite some degree of fluctuation and uncertainty, there is clearly something major happening in the final decades of the eighteenth Century. A very different kind of insanity is being allowed in the court, and yet it was not being carried there by medical experts. It was there perhaps as the 'common knowledge of "madness"' which developed as 'part of a broader knowledge landscape, encompassing knowledge of a defendant's character, family and social status, each of which might have been an ingredient in any particular decision' (Loughnan 2012: 142). It is also evident that a very different kind of welfare system is being contemplated and expected. As will become clearer through the book, the argument being made here is that these two things – the philosophy of mind that underpinned ideas about insanity and the expectations of 'society' – were inseparable. The next chapter will examine the emergence of professional discourses on insanity in the courts. One of the striking differences seen in the cases considered so far is that it was to be a series of highly public cases that would bring about major public debate on the issues. It might be interesting to speculate as to why the hints of the acceptance of a new kind of insanity in the cases of Walker and Simpson, who were lethally violent to their wives, was not carried through into similar cases in the nineteenth century. Wiener (1999: 477) suggests that the Victorian era was characterised by a crackdown on male violence, particularly in relation to 'women, children or the elderly'. Whatever the truth of that, the highly public nature of the crimes of violence aimed at members of the establishment was surely to have a major influence on the practice of the new experts in insanity.

## Notes

1. Old Bailey Proceedings Online (www.oldbaileyonline.org, version 7.0, 31 January 2014), July 1754, trial of Robert Finch (t17540717-43).
2. This is the account written by the prison chaplain; the role of these accounts is discussed in more detail in the next section.
3. Old Bailey Proceedings Online (www.oldbaileyonline.org, version 7.0, 31 January 2014), Ordinary of Newgate's Account, August 1754 (OA17540805).
4. OBP, Ordinary of Newgate's Account, August 1754 (OA17540805).
5. An account of the trial and the circumstances surrounding the offence and often the execution written by the chaplain, discussed by McKenzie (2005).
6. Old Bailey Proceedings Online (www.oldbaileyonline.org, version 7.0, 31 January 2014), October 1761, trial of Richard Parrott (t17611021-34).
7. OBP, October 1761, trial of Richard Parrott (t17611021-34).
8. This is very likely to be a local householder taking his turn in this community role (Godfrey and Lawrence 2005).
9. That is, the prison chaplain: Old Bailey Proceedings Online (www.oldbaileyonline.org, version 7.0, 31 January 2014), Ordinary of Newgate's Account, October 1761 (OA17611005).
10. OBP, Ordinary of Newgate's Account, October 1761 (OA17611005).
11. OBP, Ordinary of Newgate's Account, October 1761 (OA17611005).
12. Old Bailey Proceedings Online (www.oldbaileyonline.org, version 7.0, 31 January 2014), April 1784, trial of William Walker (t17840421-13).
13. Walker (1968: 64) discusses this case briefly, noting its apparently anomalous outcome.
14. The press reports of the trial actually point towards his conviction for manslaughter and say that he was sentenced to be branded (burnt on the hand): 'when after a trial of three hours and a half, the jury brought him in guilty of manslaughter, to be burnt on the hand next Monday, and then discharged' (*Morning Herald and Daily Advertiser* 24 April 1784: issue 1090).
15. OBP, April 1784, trial of William Walker (t17840421-13).
16. OBP, April 1784, trial of William Walker (t17840421-13).
17. The post of 'Overseer of the Poor' was created by the Poor Law of 1597 – Justices of the Peace were once more authorised and empowered to raise compulsory funds for the relief of the poor and the post of 'Overseer of the Poor' was created.
18. OBP, April 1784, trial of William Walker (t17840421-13).
19. Old Bailey Proceedings Online (www.oldbaileyonline.org, version 7.0, 31 January 2014), April 1786, trial of John Simpson (t17860426-42).
20. OBP, April 1786, trial of John Simpson (t17860426-42).
21. www.oldbaileyonline.org/static/Judges-and- juries.jsp#reading
22. Perhaps there is useful contrast to be made with the case of James Carse (OBSP 1787) who was found guilty of the killing of a young women (identified as a lady

of the City, a prostitute). Carse is found guilty despite witnesses (including Captain Horatio Nelson) stating that he was believed to have exhibited signs of insanity and was a changed person. Though the jury (and judge) recommend that further enquiries ought to be made before the sentence (that he be executed by hanging, followed by dissection) is carried out, it has not been possible to ascertain whether he was pardoned.

Chapter 2

# The medical discourse of 'moral insanity'

## Introduction

At its narrowest the story of the 'moral insanity' diagnosis might be posed as one that charts the fortunes of a number of psychiatric ideas and their proponents over the past two hundred plus years as they have fought to be taken seriously within the criminal justice system. The previous chapter has made the point that the struggles of particular professional groups need to be understood within wider historical and social contexts. The cases of William Walker (pp. 29–32) and John Simpson (pp. 32–33) demonstrated that quite subtle notions of insanity were being considered some time before medical experts were formally promoting new kinds of diagnosis. As these cases suggest, the wider social context had to be understood partly in terms of the rather frayed welfare provisions of parishes that seemed ill equipped, in the rapidly growing urban environment, to comprehend and control the local population. A number of writers have argued that courts were ever less tolerant of male violence (e.g. Liddle 1996; Shoemaker 2001; Wiener 2001), and the case was put in the previous chapter that a part of the motivation for thinking differently about insanity was the greater stress that was being put on the capacity for emotionally coherent intimate relationships. William Walker and John Simpson were both acquitted of murder on the grounds of insanity despite the lack of medical evidence and of any overt signals of insanity. Their violence, occurring in the context of good relationships and their apparently good character, was construed in terms of an insanity that was only manifest in terms of the violence they perpetrated. This idea that there was a form of insanity that was manifest only in violence, that meanwhile left the rest of the character and reason of the individual apparently intact, was to be formulated by those whose names are now associated with the birth of the profession of psychiatry. It was from the beginning of the nineteenth century that a field of expertise and a language that can describe these new forms of insanity developed. The structure of the chapter reflects two separate, but related, issues. The first part of the chapter will trace the development of the concept of 'moral insanity' and associated notions such as 'monomania', or 'lesions of will', which, it will be argued here, have considerable connection to 'moral insanity' since they appeared within the work of those who advocated for the diagnoses, such as Pinel, Esquirol and Prichard in the first decades of the nineteenth century. This was a key period in the development of the profession of psychiatry. It is during this era that significant numbers of medical men began to identify themselves and others as experts in the study and treatment of mental disorder.

The second part of the chapter will explore a number of criminal cases where the mental state of the accused was an issue of debate for the courts and medical expertise became essential to the courts' deliberations. Medical witnesses generally began to play more of a role at all levels of the court system in England from around 1790 (Smith 1981: 3), and in the first half of the nineteenth century a number of cases that involved the insanity defence were to have long term implications for future policy. The cases examined are those of James Hadfield (1800), Edward Oxford (1840) and Daniel M'Naghten (1843), which all involved an attempted assassination of the Prime Minister or monarch. The highly public nature of the cases is a point of contrast with those looked at in the previous chapter and meant that these issues of insanity were not only contested in the courts, but they were aired and debated in the rapidly expanding public media; this in itself has implications for the development and spread of ideas of insanity (Wiener 1999). The stories themselves become a part of the social fabric in which madness and its relation to criminality become understood. The issue of the relationship between expectations of conduct and the development of the state, which had a stake in curbing the violence of individual men, was raised in the previous chapter. The relationship between the state, notions of insanity and criminal culpability becomes very clear now in the nineteenth century, as we see significant legal discussion and precedent being set, based upon direct threats towards individuals at the very head of the establishment in Britain.

## 2.1 The beginning of psychiatry: the entrepreneurs of the moral world

Accounts of the history of psychiatry[1] place its origins at the very end of the eighteenth century (Porter 2002; Scull 1979b). This is the period when a number of physicians and surgeons began to identify themselves as a group of specialists who had expertise in the recognition and treatment of 'mental illness'. The task of establishing a respectable profession was considerable. As Boime (1991) expresses it, the 'mad doctors' who ran the 'madhouses' in the eighteenth century 'occupied a niche slightly above a witch doctor in the public imagination'. By the end of the nineteenth century 'the resident psychiatrist, or alienist, of the asylum was more closely identified with the medical practitioner' (Boime 1991: 79). There were two innovations that were critical to this transformation. First, the development of ideas of 'moral treatment' gave a significant boost to the standing of 'psychiatry', since they were used to justify and shape the large scale asylum building projects across many parts of Europe and North America

(Scull 1979b). The second issue is that of moral insanity, which was less well remembered by the twentieth century but has, in rather different forms, continued to cause debate and controversy well into the twenty-first century. The first initiative was to give psychiatry a rationale, a claim for expertise and ultimately an institutional base. This was to prove crucial as western states developed large scale welfare policies from the beginning of the nineteenth century. The construction of a network of asylums, justified by the promise of moral treatment, not only provided paid positions for the medical experts but gave them access to men and women whose difficulties and disorders provided the material for the further exploration of insanity. The second issue of 'moral insanity' was to give psychiatry a claim to expertise in the legal system, and thus status in the developing state. Following initial successes in the nineteenth century, this was to prove a much rockier road towards professional recognition, but it is crucial to the longer story of the various manifestations of moral insanity, and indeed of psychiatry itself.

The relationship between 'moral insanity' and 'moral treatment' is grounded in more than linguistic coincidence. The complex and ambiguous meaning of the word 'moral' is an important part of the story. As Rimke and Hunt (2002) note, the word had much wider scope in the early part of the nineteenth century than it was to enjoy by the twentieth century, and it effectively had three rather different meanings. First, the term referred to the emotional and interior depth of an individual, which might manifest as a driving appetite or passion. Second, the term indicated concern with the ethical conduct of citizens. Benjamin Rush, a leading innovator in the treatment of mental disorder in the United States before the end of the eighteenth century, had already stressed the ethical dimension of the term, at the same time proposing it as a psychological capacity. He referred to 'the moral faculty' as the 'power in the human mind of distinguishing and choosing good and evil, or in other words, virtue and vice' (Rush 1793: 2). Third, Rimke and Hunt (2002: 71) note that 'moral' also 'referred to the inherent sociality of the self', so that 'the moral being was synonymous with the social being' since 'individuals were conceived as inherently constituted in and through social relations and ties'. The moral status of an individual could be measured by 'one's loyalty, cooperativeness and dutifulness on the ethical plane of social conduct'. Ultimately, although its meaning to twenty-first-century minds can appear confused, the ambiguity of the term is a very important aspect of the power of the phenomenon, since it points to a field of thought that 'problematizes the link between personal character and conduct and potential social harm, disturbance and disorder' (Rimke and Hunt 2002: 61).

### 2.1.1 Moral treatment of the mind

The 'invention' of moral treatment at the beginning of the nineteenth century has assumed a prominent role in the history of psychiatry. This might be mainly thanks to Foucault's (1967) seminal work *Madness and Civilization*, in which he argued that the 'medicine of the mind' was born through the emphasis in moral treatment on the significance of the healing power of the demeanour and being of the asylum keeper, rather than any physiological intervention (Foucault 1967: 274–275). Although it can be argued that there was a longer history of the consideration of moral philosophy alongside mental disorder (Schmidt 2004), it is also the case that before this point, as Bynum (1964: 319) noted, credible historical accounts of formalised treatments that look much like moral treatment are actually 'rather meagre'. Certainly, within decades of the formal accounts of moral treatment, psychiatry was achieving institutional recognition across Europe and North America. This recognition arrived alongside the widespread construction of asylums and through the activities of the emergent profession of psychiatry, as practitioners promoted their own work through newly founded professional journals and professional associations (to be discussed in more detail in Chapter 3). It was the promise of moral treatment within those asylums that gave the rationale for such building programmes and helped put some distance between the asylum and the gaols and workhouses of the public imagination, thus endowing the asylum with a modicum of respectability.

One of the significant names associated with the propagation of moral treatment is that of the French *aliéniste* Philippe Pinel. Although the facts might be somewhat contested, Pinel's rhetorical place at the heart of the story of western psychiatry cannot be denied. It is, for example, the benevolent figure of Pinel who is seen in the well known painting by Robert-Fleury (1876) as he orders the inmates of the Salpêtrière to be freed from their chains. Pinel, who argued for the humane treatment of individuals in states of distress and often living in abject circumstances, can be seen as capturing the ideals of the *liberté, égalité, fraternité* of post-revolutionary France (Werlinder 1978: 27). As physician in charge at the Salpêtrière and Bicêtre, Pinel put in place policies that saw the insane inmates released from their chains and subject to regimes of moral treatment.[2] A number of names are also notable in the story of 'moral treatment', particularly the Florentine physician Chiarugi and the Tukes in England (Gerard 1997). In Germany, Reil also recommended moral treatment although, as discussed in Chapter 5, there were some important differences in German practice and theory. In many respects the Tukes' experiments in moral treatment at the York Retreat (opened in 1796) presented the more coherent prescription for moral treatment. Pinel, however, even in Britain, was often the favoured reference point for psychiatry, in part because he coined the term 'moral treatment' and in part, perhaps, because Pinel was a medic and the Tukes were not.

Pinel had genuine medical clout; his *Traité Médico-Philosophique sur l'Aliénation Mentale, ou La Manie*, published in 1801 (and published in English as *Treatise on Insanity* in 1806), presented a remarkably modern looking nosology of insanity. Pinel, true to his medical roots and background, was interested in the anatomy of the brain, reproducing pictures of brains in his *Treatise* to illustrate his points. He did associate some conditions, such as 'ideocy', for example, with malformations of the cranium. He also used drawing of skulls to make the negative case 'that intense mental affections . . . the most ordinary cases of insanity' were 'not characterised by any peculiarity of conformation that are not to be met with in other heads' (Pinel 1806: 122–123). It is clear that Pinel, while maintaining an eclectic perspective, viewed forms of 'moral treatment' as having a considerable place in the treatment of insanity. The case study material that Pinel used makes it clear that this was a 'psychological' treatment being offered in his asylum, claiming that 'maniacs' who in a 'furious and dangerous' state were transferred from the 'infirmary' to the asylum were treated 'with affability, soothed by consolation and sympathy, and encouraged to expect a happier lot', which returned them to 'placid calmness' and 'a rapid convalescence' (Pinel 1806: 67). Meanwhile, in England, the non-medically trained Tukes at the York Retreat were entirely clear that they were advocating a treatment of 'the mind' rather than the body: 'If we adopt the opinion, that the disease originates in the mind, applications made immediately to it, are obviously the most natural; and the most likely to be attended with success' (Tuke 1813: 131).

In addition to the assumption that moral treatment operated on the mind and not the body of the patient, it was also reliant on the notion that the mind could be divided into different faculties. As Samuel Tuke explained, a key assumption of moral treatment was that 'most insane persons, have a considerable degree of self command'. That is, alongside the insane aspects of the mind, there were also sane parts that could be persuaded to take control of the individual. Such was the nature of this division that the insanity of many people admitted to the Retreat would not be immediately detectable and patients could at first impression 'conceal all marks of mental aberration' (Tuke 1813: 139). It was this assumption that was to have major implications for the presentation of notions of insanity in the courts.

Pinel's formulation of 'moral treatment' also had a clear theoretical rationale based on his assumption that 'the mind' could be divided into different faculties. It is worth noting that this idea that the mind could be so divided was to achieve very widespread acceptance over the first half of the nineteenth century through the theories of phrenology. Originally proposed through the work of Gall and Spurzheim, phrenology (Simpson 2005) proposed that different parts of the brain were responsible for different functions of the mind, or character, of an individual. The differential sizes of the various faculties within an individual's brain would be reflected not only in the characteristic behaviours and dispositions of each individual, but in the bumps in their cranium. Phrenology became highly popular, with over 300,000 copies of *The Constitution of Man* (1828) by George Combe (the chief advocate of phrenology in Britain) being sold. This made it the fourth most widely read book of its time at this point, behind the Bible, *The Pilgrim's Progress* and *Robinson Crusoe* (Tomlinson

1997: 1–2). The popular marketing of phrenology as a technique for reading the bumps of an individual's skull to divine their character and provide advice on their future was to lead to the status of phrenology being downgraded to that of fortune telling by the middle of the nineteenth century.[3] Nevertheless, the notion that the mind could be divided into different characteristics was widely accepted, certainly within French and British psychiatry.[4] One of the distinctive faculties was taken by Pinel to be 'the intellect', which held the rational capacity of the mind. This part of the mind was itself certainly subject to 'lesion', resulting in 'mania' or insanity. Pinel was, however, insistent that 'the active faculties' could also be 'subject to serious lesions and changes'. Such lesions might well occur concurrently with those of the intellect, but 'At other times, however, the understanding is perfectly free in every department of its exercise' (Pinel 1806: 151). It was this distinction that allowed Pinel to define different categories of madness, including, importantly, one that did not affect the sufferer's capacity to reason: *manie sans délire*. In contrast there was also *manie avec délire*. The former might be translated as 'mania without delirium' and the latter 'mania with delirium', although perhaps the word 'delusion' might be a slightly better translation (Werlinder 1978). This issue will be discussed below in more detail, but in brief, *manie sans délire* referred to a capacity for seemingly irrational fury and violence that could appear in an individual who otherwise had a full and undamaged capacity to reason. It is thus frequently cited as being the first formal definition of 'moral insanity' or 'psychopathy',[5] as he is proposing that insanity might not simply be a result of the loss of reason, but instead a disorder of the 'active faculties' (Pinel 1806: 150).

Pinel makes clear through his discussion of 'mania without delirium' that he arrived at the category 'through observation', which challenged his previous acceptance of Locke's view that insanity was caused by the faulty association of ideas. Pinel admitted that he was 'surprized to find many maniacs who at no period gave evidence of any lesion of the understanding, but who were under the dominion of instinctive and abstract fury, as if the active faculties alone sustained the injury' (Pinel 1806: 150). He then goes on to give a succinct definition of *manie sans délire*: 'It may be either continued or intermittent. No sensible change in the functions of the understanding; but perversion of the active faculties, marked by sanguinary fury, with a blind propensity to acts of violence' (Pinel 1806: 151).

Pinel's influence was immense; the treatise was translated quickly into German in 1801, and English in 1806. Despite the fact that the differences between French and German psychiatry were considerable (Augstein 1996), the major figure in German psychiatry, Reil (whose work is discussed in Chapter 5), was influenced by Pinel's case studies (Hansen 1998). Pinel made an undoubted contribution to the argument for moral treatment, which was to have a significant impact on asylum building policies throughout the nineteenth century. Whatever the result of intellectual argument about whether other writers, such as Benjamin Rush, deserve to be placed alongside Pinel in the history of psychiatry (others were scoping out the terrain of psychiatry perhaps even before Pinel), it does seem very clear that Pinel very directly spawned a French school of *aliénistes* that was to have immense and unparalleled influence on psychiatry and its place in the courtroom until the middle of the nineteenth century (Werlinder 1978: 31), chiefly through its promotion of the diagnosis of 'monomania'.

## 2.1.2 Esquirol, Georget and 'monomania'

It was the work of the French school of *aliénistes*, dominated by Esquirol, who, following Pinel's path, were to formalise and to an extent popularise the idea that it was possible for acts of violence to be carried out by people who had all outwards signs of normality but were driven by some flawed belief or impulse. Jean-Étienne Esquirol, Pinel's most influential pupil, was the central member of the group, which was determined to establish the legitimacy and influence of its ideas and practice. Esquirol established the term *aliénation mentale* in place of the ancient term *folie*, and he skilfully steered French psychiatry (the *aliénistes*) into a position of some esteem (Goldstein 1987). A key vehicle for this manoeuvre was the concept of 'monomania', which Esquirol developed in his article for the *Dictionnaire des Sciences Médicales* in 1819. By the 1820s the concept was to have widespread cognisance within a French intelligentsia (Boime 1991); it was being favourably reported on in English medical journals, and was to make celebrated appearances in a number trials in England (as discussed in the second part of this chapter). It was also to have a significant life in some of the most influential fictional literature of the nineteenth century (as will be discussed in Chapter 4). The notion of monomania had a highly generative impact on the nascent professional groupings of psychiatry. As Goldstein (1987, 1998) observed, it was important because, emerging from the concept of Pinel's *manie sans délire*, it developed through the careful observational work of Esquirol and encouraged the scientific understanding of the mind as if it were constructed of various faculties open to the exploration of trained experts. It was also, and ultimately controversially, to be 'the linchpin in the effort made by the Esquirol circle from the 1820s to the 1840s to gain public recognition for psychiatry by carving a place for expert psychiatric testimony in the courts of law' (Goldstein 1998: 389). The concept of monomania provided an excellent vehicle for this project precisely because it was by its nature quite subtle in its manifestation and it therefore required the professional expertise of the medical practitioner to detect. It is remarkable that Esquirol and Étienne-Jean Georget also commissioned drawings, paintings and sculptures of their case studies, including a particularly striking series of paintings of monomaniacs (said to be commissioned by Georget) by the renowned artist Géricault. The faces, of a kleptomaniac and a child snatcher for example, though expressive are most obviously marked by an ordinariness that, as Browne (2004: 156) observes, is suggestive of an understanding of monomania 'not in terms of behaviour, nor in terms of a disease category that transcends the individual, but as a state of mind which, though disordered and clinically classifiable, emphasised rather than obliterated individuality'.[6] They were, Boime (1991: 88) suggests, 'designed to exemplify the concealable traits of the monomaniacal type', and thus promote the expertise of the alienists who could detect and understand the hidden insanity.

As Goldstein's detailed account makes clear, there was plenty of disagreement and unease among the French school about the extent to which monomania could be used as defence against ordinary responsibility for criminality. It was Georget who did the most to publicise the contribution that the *aliénistes* might make to the legal system. He produced a number of publications on the topic (Georget 1820, 1826, 1827), which argued that the new knowledge of insanity could help understand serious criminality (Boime 1991: 88). He provided commentary on a number of notorious cases, including that of Léger, for example, who was accused of murdering a young girl and drinking her blood, but who, according to Georget, should not be considered 'a great criminal' or 'a monster' but 'an unhappy imbecile . . . who ought to have been shut up in Bicêtre' (Goldstein 1987: 165). The most significant case was that of Henriette Cornier, a 25-year-old woman who in 1825 decapitated a 19-month-old infant in her charge (Georget 1826). This case was to prove very important in promoting the role that *aliénistes* might play in making judgments on sanity and establishing the case for the existence of 'monomania'. It was a case that not only stimulated debate (and indeed dispute) between the leading lights of French psychiatry, but its spectacular nature ensured that those debates were enacted 'on a stage lit by the full glare of publicity' (During 1988: 87). The newly established *Gazette des Tribunaux*, which brought court reports into the public arena, gave the case a full account (Appignanesi 2009). This apparently motiveless crime was, Foucault (2003) argued, a perfect one for nineteenth-century psychiatry, which had, he suggests, long been interested in 'the problem of criminality and criminal madness', in particular the 'madness that kills'. Psychiatry needed to 'advance its claim as a power and knowledge of protection within society' (Foucault 2003: 121), 'for if one gets to identify and analyze this kind of crime it will be the test of the strength and knowledge of psychiatry and the justification of its power'. Indeed, the case 'was to leave traces across nineteenth-century society and culture and not just in France or on the psychiatrists and lawyers to whom Henriette was at once delivered' (During 1988: 86). In 1827 in Britain, nearly four pages of the 'Quarterly Periscope' section of the *Medico-Chirurgical Review*[7] was devoted to a discussion of the case (although they did report her name as being 'Harriet'). In the US, Isaac Ray gave Georget's accounts of the case considerable space in the various editions of his *Treatise on the Medical Jurisprudence of Insanity* (first published in 1838; see Ray 1853, and Beck and Beck 1860).

Henriette Cornier was a servant who was described as having had a 'cheerful and rather gay disposition' until around June of 1825, when she became somewhat 'taciturn and melancholy', which in turn perhaps led to her being sacked by her employers. This seemed to increase her melancholic state and in September she tried to drown herself in the river Seine, but was saved by some bystanders. Later that year on 4 November she visited her local grocer and there persuaded the shopkeeper, of her acquaintance, to allow her to look after her 19-month-old daughter Fanny. According to the *Medico-Chirurgical Review* (1827: 483):

> Cornier hastened home to her master's house with the child and laying it on the bed, instantaneously severed its head from its body with a large kitchen knife! This bloody deed was done with such rapidity, that the infant had not time to utter a single cry! On a subsequent examination this infatuated creature declared that, during the murder, she felt no particular emotion – neither a sense of horror, of joy, or of fear.

When Fanny's mother arrives at the house to fetch her child back, Henriette tells her bluntly that her child is dead. When the disbelieving mother finds the corpse, Henriette picks up the child's head and throws it out of the window, where it lies in the path of the child's father, who is rushing to the scene. Amidst these scenes of horror:

> All this time the murderer was coolly seated on a chair in the room near the body of the child, and making no attempt to escape. . . . She denied no part of the act, but detailed all the circumstances – even the premeditation of the murder, and the arts, which she had used to lull the suspicions of the mother, and enveigle from her the devoted victim of her bloody design.
> (*Medico-Chirurgical Review* 1827: 484)

To all demands for an explanation Henriette would only say 'J'ai voulu le tuer!' ('I meant to kill the child'). When the case was first tried the medical expertise of Esquirol, Adelon and Léveillé was sought. They declared that although they could not detect insanity, neither could they rule it out, so the accused was sent to the Salpêtrière asylum for further observation and reports. At the second trial in June 1826, the prosecution detailed the planning of the killing as evidence of Cornier's guilt. The case of the defence was that her own detailed confession of the plan to kill the child, alongside a lack of motive or any appearance of remorse and the knowledge of the change in her typical behaviour some months before the killing, was evidence of monomania. As Georget summarised, 'Un acte atroce, si contraire à la nature humaine, commis sans motif, sans intérêt, sans passion, opposé au caractère naturel d'un individu, est évidemment un acte de démence'[8] (*Medico-Chirurgical Review* 1827: 486).

The court found her guilty of murder, but not of premeditated murder, so she was sentenced, not to death, but to be branded with the letters TP ('travaux [forcés à] perpétuité', Dauge-Roth 2005: 133), followed by a lifetime of hard labour. As Ray approvingly reported some years later, Georget condemned the verdict, which seemed to blur the issue of responsibility: 'if the accused was mad she ought to have been acquitted; and if not mad she acted from premeditation, and should have suffered the punishment of death' (Ray 1853: 223). The writer in the *Medico* was adamant that the court had been wrong to find her guilty at all:

> The jury ought to have acquitted her on the plea of insanity – and the punishment should have been imprisonment, not hard labour, for life. We are convinced that this would have been the case had the prisoner been tried in an English court.
> (*Medico-Chirurgical Review* 1827: 486)

To Foucault, the Cornier case is exemplary in representing a transformation 'that has still not come to an end; the process that enabled psychiatric power, centred on illness within the mental asylum to exercise a general jurisdiction, both within and outside the asylum, not over madness, but over the abnormal and all abnormal conduct' (Foucault 2003: 134). Indeed, Goldstein (1987) argues that Esquirol was actually rather sceptical about the existence of *manie sans délire* (and Prichard's 'moral insanity'), but by the time of the publication of his treatise in 1838 (translated into English in 1845) he had reached an accommodation that was driven by an appreciation of the need for psychiatry to gain a significant foothold in French society by demonstrating expertise in matters of criminality. As part of a whole chapter on monomania he discussed the existence of 'affective monomania' (Esquirol 1845: 320), suggesting that such monomaniacs 'are not deprived of the use of their reason, but their affections and dispositions are perverted'. At the same time he suggests that in criminal cases the 'understanding is more or less at fault' because otherwise they would recognise that their acts were 'unusual and strange'. Nevertheless, the 'lesion of the understanding is not the controlling cause of their acts' (Esquirol 1845: 321). He does go on to describe 'homicidal mania', but here he includes a range of monomanias, and asks:

> But does a form of mania really exist, in which those who are affected by it, preserve the integrity of their reason, whilst they abandon themselves to the commission of acts the most reprehensible? Is that a pathological condition, in which man is irresistibly led on, to the commission of an act which his conscience condemns?

He answers positively: 'I think it is. I have seen a great many insane persons, who appeared to enjoy the use of their understanding, and who deplored the determinations towards the execution of which, they were powerfully drawn' (Esquirol 1845: 362).

By the time he was writing his treatise in 1838 the issue of monomania had been taken up very seriously in Britain, and one writer in particular, James Cowles Prichard, was to shift the terms of debate quite significantly by formally introducing the concept of 'moral insanity'.[9]

## 2.1.3 Prichard and moral insanity

James Cowles Prichard's engagement with French psychiatry is quite explicit: his *Treatise*, published in 1835, is dedicated to Esquirol, and he credits Pinel for describing 'madness without delirium', although he argues that the examples were unfortunately of just one kind of insanity – that marked by an outburst of 'anger or rage'. Indeed, as we will see, it was Prichard's engagement with elements of German psychiatry that proved of some significance. Crucially, to Prichard, moral insanity was not simply a version of 'monomania' or 'partial insanity'. With hindsight Prichard's work looks remarkable; a number of his case studies concerning those whom he believed to be suffering from 'moral insanity' seem to have much in common with descriptions of personality disorders that appeared in the latter half of the twentieth century. Yet, beyond his being credited with the use of the term, his work is not frequently examined.[10] Prichard described three broad categories of insanity: 'moral insanity'; 'Monomania or partial insanity'; and 'Mania and Incoherence or dementia'. He gives considerable prominence to the separate category of 'moral insanity' in his *Treatise on Insanity*, and makes the distinction from the French 'monomania' quite clear:

> Most of the French writers by whom this affection has been recognised, particularly Messrs. Esquirol, Georget, Marc and Michu, have termed it *'monomanie homicide'*, which is assuredly an erroneous designation. . . . That term is always used to express *partial illusion*, or intellectual derangement affecting only a certain train of ideas; whereas, in connection with the homicidal impulse now under consideration, there is confessedly no delusive opinion impressed on the belief, and the intellectual faculties are wholly unaffected.
>
> (Prichard 1835a: 397)

The case studies he uses are quite distinct from the violent cases of Pinel and the homicidal examples used by Esquirol, and a number at least seem to have far more in common with descriptions of 'personality disorder' that appeared in the twentieth century (as discussed in detail in Chapter 8). In a famous and often quoted passage Prichard (1835a) described 'moral insanity' in the following terms:

> A form of mental derangement in which the intellectual faculties appear to have sustained little or no injury, while the disorder is manifested

principally or alone, in the state of the feelings, temper, or habits. In cases of this description the moral and active principles of the mind are strangely perverted and depraved; the power of self government is lost or greatly impaired; and the individual is found to be incapable, not of talking or reasoning upon any subject proposed to him, for this he will often do with great shrewdness and volubility, but of conducting himself with decency and propriety in the business of life. His wishes and inclinations, his attachments, his likings and dislikings have all undergone a morbid change, and this change appears to be the originating cause, or to lie at the foundation of any disturbance.

(Prichard 1835a: 4)

Augstein (1996) observes that in some respects it appears odd that Prichard should produce such a radical theory, which suggests that a form of insanity could quite subtly debilitate an individual's ability to behave with decency. He was after all a pious man who took the Christian scriptures as quite literal truth. To others who were anxious to promote the spiritual dimension of the human mind, the category of 'moral insanity' was itself problematic (Waldinger 1979) since it appeared to minimise the significance of individual responsibility and guilt. Prichard was also a confirmed Tory who believed that the French Revolution and the subsequent tumult presented solid evidence of the importance of clear social hierarchy and authority. Augstein (1996) compellingly argues that Prichard was influenced by elements of German psychiatry (to be discussed in more detail in Chapter 5) that were shaped by a Romantic tradition that not only emphasised the holism of the body, mind and brain, but also the spiritual dimensions of the relationship between individual imagination and the works of nature that could certainly countenance a relationship with deity. This would have appealed enormously to Prichard, who had struggled to accept the materialism that was evident in the phrenological theories that were so influential on French and British psychiatry. Prichard's rejection of phrenological ideas meant that his ideas were somewhat out of step, and despite general interest in the concept of 'moral insanity' there was not that much engagement with the specifics of his theories. Augstein argues, however, that Prichard was sufficiently aware, however much he resisted the work of the phrenologists, to know he could not deny that the scientific and anatomical progress that those such as Georget and Esquirol were promoting was clearly indicating that mental processes were at the very least associated with physiological processes. He still wanted to avoid the implication that it would be possible to locate the 'mind' or soul entirely within the cerebral structures of the brain. Elements of German 'psychiatry', despite a materialist outlook, also rejected this cerebral location of the mind and instead took a more holistic view of the relationship between mind and body. Here the 'mind' was thought of as being a consequence of interactions between the organs of the viscera as well as the brain (e.g. Hansen 1998). This move preserved the possibility of an immaterial psyche, or even soul, that was not simply the function of the material brain; nor was it the result of the association of ideas within the mind, as followers of Locke's associationism supposed. This more holistic German notion of the psyche, which foregrounded forms of insanity that might involve the 'character' or personality of the individual, was to become widely held towards the end of the nineteenth century. It was this combination of the idea of a moral insanity that might link to the character of an individual rather than as a limited monomania, confined to just one facet of an individual's psyche, that was so prescient in Prichard's work. By the beginning of the twentieth century the idea that moral insanity could be located within the whole body of the individual was to become highly influential. Any notion, however, that this might have a psychological, let alone spiritual, dimension had by then been dropped. Such a reductionist and organic view was not what Prichard had in mind at all. Prichard seemed to have some influence on Esquirol; although in his 1838 treatise Esquirol explicitly distanced himself from Prichard's 'moral insanity' by arguing that such conditions were marked by 'partial delirium', he went on to say that this partial delirium might well have considerable impact on an individual, and more particularly on their relationships with others:

> [S]ome are turbulent, unsociable and commit ridiculous and blame-worthy acts, contrary to their former affections and true interests . . . They both speak and do ill through malice, from a want of employment, and from wickedness. Incapable of application, and averse to labor, they overturn, break and destroy. The perversion of their disposition renders them exceedingly troublesome to their families, and in those establishments to which they are brought.
> 
> (Esquirol 1845: 351)

## 2.2 Medics, moral insanity and the law

While it is clear that in France and Britain there were groups of medical men in the early decades of the nineteenth century who were very keen to constitute the profession of psychiatry by making claims to expertise on legal matters (and 'moral insanity' was an important weapon in this campaign), this process was not at all smooth. In reality, the relationship between the longer established legal profession and the emerging medical profession was not an equal one and 'medical men experienced condescension and even contempt, from lawyers and journalists' (Smith 1981: 7). Debate over the insanity plea became highly emotive, even within the emerging profession of psychiatry. Some medics who were already alarmed enough at their association with highly stigmatised work with the insane and pauper lunatics were wary of redoubling 'their unpopularity when defending the repellently aggressive' (Smith 1981: 7). Others – in Britain (Smith 1981), France (Goldstein 1987) and the United States (Ray 1853) –

saw the insanity defence as an area where they could stake their claim to expertise. The related issues of moral insanity, partial insanity, monomania, delusion and lesions of will presented themselves as important opportunities for the newly coalescing profession of psychiatry. Here were disorders that did not lend themselves to easy observation or common sense notions of sanity. The detection of such disorders required the expertise of the professionals, and was therefore regarded as a key step in the public recognition of the psychiatric profession. This was no easy manoeuvre to make and resistance within the law and in other parts of society was considerable. As Eigen (1999: 437) argues, the concept of moral insanity provided a very direct challenge to the legal notion of knowing criminal intention, and furthermore:

> This direct assault on the common law's conception of guilt came at a time when concern with the will had particular social and political significance. The bedrock centrality of the self-control to the maintenance of civilization resonated with all manner of cultural thought and expression for the Victorians.

The following section will examine a number of prominent legal cases tried at the Old Bailey in London over the first half of the nineteenth century. This is a crucial period in the construction of the profession of psychiatry. By the middle of the nineteenth century the formal birth of the new profession was marked by the inauguration of various professional societies in Europe and America (as discussed in Chapter 3). The trials of James Hadfield (1800), Edward Oxford (1840) and Daniel M'Naghten (1843) each involved very literal attacks on prominent figures in the establishment. They all therefore provided the developing state with the challenge of how to respond appropriately. The trials of Oxford and M'Naghten involved the very elite of the new psychiatric profession and their appearance, during which they steered the courts towards acceptance of their theories about the nature of insanity, was a triumph. The longer term legacy of these apparent successes turned out to be rather unexpected. As will be explained, the public backlash against the verdict of M'Naghten was to have a lasting impact on the shape of the profession.

### 2.2.1 James Hadfield (1800) and the 'special verdict'

The trial of James Hadfield (described by Walker 1968: 74–79) occurred a year before Pinel published his treatise, which publicised his definition of *manie sans délire*, and some years before monomania was to be found in regular medical parlance. He was successfully defended on the grounds of insanity, chiefly by his lawyer, who argued that he was driven by insane ideas (delusions) that allowed other parts of his mind to be unaffected. The case was also backed by medical men testifying about the significance of damage to his brain. The arguments presented by his defence counsel sounded rather like those of monomania. Hadfield made an attempt on the life of George III on 15 May 1800, as the King was attending Drury Lane theatre in London's West End. Just as the orchestra finished playing the national anthem, Hadfield stood on a seat and fired a pistol at the King, who was taking a bow in the royal box (*American Law Register* 1856; Anonymous 1800; Moran 1985). Not surprisingly, given the distance and relatively crude design of the weapon, the shot missed the King and harmed no one. The 28-year-old Hadfield was seized by members of the orchestra and the audience and bundled into custody. Following a chorus of 'God Save the King', the show continued.

Hadfield was tried for treason, which meant that the trial was far more thorough than it would have been had he been charged with attempted murder. Had the latter occurred, Hadfield would have appeared at the Old Bailey within days and, if found guilty, would perhaps have been dispatched at the gallows soon after. There were, however, political protections in place for those charged with treason, introduced in the wake of the Glorious Revolution (Claydon 1996), as safeguards against the abuse of government power. Defendants had to be served notice of the evidence against them. They were allowed to challenge jurors and, most crucially, were permitted a defence team of lawyers and counsellors. Among his team, Hadfield requested the appointment of Thomas Erskine, one of the most distinguished lawyers of his time. Hadfield appeared for trial at Westminster Hall before the Bar of the Court of King's Bench, on 26 June 1800. As O'Reilly-Fleming (1992) points out, these were not the only unusual circumstances of this case. It was well known that the victim of the assassination attempt, George III, had suffered from insanity himself (Jones 1996), and was sympathetic to the plight of the insane.[11] His brother, the Duke of York, who knew the King's condition well, was a member of the Privy Council that heard the case. He had also commanded Hadfield's battalion in the war, where Hadfield had sustained his injuries. In anticipation of the defence's case the prosecution raised the traditional standard of the insanity plea, referring back to Mathew Hale's arguments (see Chapter 1, pp. 43–44) that if the accused had the level of reasoning of a 14-year-old, then they should be considered to be in control of their actions. Hadfield's conduct in committing the offence was pointed to as evidence of his capacity to reason: he had bought the pistols, gained admission to the theatre and had (as witnesses attested) aimed and fired at the King. When arrested, Hadfield was apparently aware of what he had done and knew the likely consequences for himself. He was quoted as saying that he was tired of life and hoped to be executed. These facts were presented by the prosecution as evidence of knowing intent (Moran 1985).

Before embarking on the specifics of the defence, Thomas Erskine artfully argued that the fact that this trial was taking place as it was, with such care taken to ensure a proper defence for a man who had tried to kill the King, was 'one of the greatest monuments of justice' and 'placed the Government of this country and the wisdom and administrations of its laws upon the highest pinnacle of human estimation' (Anonymous 1800: 17). Thus Erskine cleared the way for the court to demonstrate the strength and power of the state, not by brutal retribution, but by showing mercy to a man who had tried to kill the head of state. Erskine then moved on to argue that the restriction of the concept of insanity to someone who was totally without reason was impractical; that very rarely would any 'madmen' be found who were so totally without reason. He argued instead that individuals might 'be called a lunatic, who proceeded on grounds that had no truth, whose mind the Almighty had been pleased to attack in its citadel, filling it with delusions which had not foundation in the actual state of things' (Anonymous 1800: 19). Erskine then set about arguing that it could not be proven that Hadfield acted on any malice he bore towards the King (as he had none) and therefore it could only be that his violence stemmed from insanity, albeit a condition that allowed him 'to converse as rationally on other matters' and left his memory as 'perfect as ever' but still made him believe that he needed to sacrifice himself by killing the King as part of a wider theological scheme (Anonymous 1800: 21). Erskine went on to argue that Hadfield's insanity began when his brain had been damaged during his military service in the 'Napoleonic' wars with France. The wounds to Hadfield's head were obvious and disfiguring (Walker 1968: 76). Witness evidence was sought from Henry Cline and Mr Lidderdale (both surgeons) and, most significantly, Dr Creighton, a physician with claims to expertise in matters of insanity.[12] Creighton's presence is significant because, unlike the other medics, he had not seen Hadfield until after the offence – a fact which emphasises his presence as an expert witness. Between them the medics testified that the severe head injury that Hadfield had acquired in battle would undoubtedly lead to insanity and had directly led to his discharge from the army (Moran 1985: 506).

Eigen (1991) argues that this trial introduced the term 'delusion' in court, and represented a major leap in the acceptability of a more subtle and psychological understanding of insanity. The term, as Eigen argues (supported by the evidence of Creighton), 'suggested a state of partial derangement – "total" to be sure when the subject of delusory fear or belief was touched upon – but absent when any other subject was invoked' (Eigen 1999: 428). Aware, perhaps, that his own fine phenomenological arguments, even when accompanied by medical testimony, would not necessarily sway the court, Erskine proceeded to call numerous witnesses from different parts of Hadfield's life, who all in various ways were able to testify as to the peculiarity and aberrance of Hadfield's behaviour. After a number of such witnesses the Judge Lord Kenyon interrupted and asked whether the prosecution were going to call any 'evidence to contradict all this?' (Anonymous 1800: 28). Hearing the Attorney General suggest not, Lord Kenyon argued that there was no point in continuing since the trial was heading for acquittal. The prosecution agreed and thus a verdict of 'not guilty' was agreed. The verdict did not create a public stir because there was undoubtedly widespread sympathy for Hadfield, with the war wounds on his face very visible (Moran 1985). There was, however, judicial concern about the implications of the verdict. Judge Kenyon wanted Hadfield confined on the grounds of public safety but was aware that this would normally mean being sent to the local asylum (in this case Bethlem Hospital). The lack of security and the potential threat to the King's safety caused some anxiety.[13] With the Attorney General's agreement, Kenyon 'uttered the words that were to echo throughout the ages. "The prisoner, for his own sake, and for the sake of society at large, must not be discharged"' (Moran 1985: 508).

As Allderidge (1974: 899) notes, this verdict 'caused an immediate change in the law, paving the way for all the subsequent 19th century legislation on criminal lunacy'. The 'Act for the safe custody of insane persons charged with offences' was passed within a month of the trial (and its use allowed retrospectively to cover Hadfield himself). The Act opened the way for the 'special' verdict of 'not guilty by reason of insanity', which would oblige the court to dispose of the defendant to a suitable place 'until his Majesty's pleasure be known'. This change to criminal law meant that subsequently anyone found not guilty of a serious offence on the grounds of insanity had to be considered under the Criminal Lunatics Act: 'the court before whom such trial be had, shall order such person to be kept in strict custody, in such place and in such manner as to the court shall seem fit, until his Majesty's pleasure be known (Criminal Lunatics Act: Section 1).

The Act did not attempt to define insanity, but in creating the category of 'criminal lunatic' clearly brought insanity within the purview of the criminal law. Moran (1985) suggests that, contrary to many accounts of the trial and the subsequent Act, which portray the trial as originating the insanity defence, the result of this trial was effectively to abolish the insanity defence. Henceforward, any successful use of the insanity defence would also put the defendant at risk of being confined for life. From this point on in England consideration of insanity in the court was not only a plea for mitigation; it also involved an assessment of risk. Indeed, Hadfield himself was to spend the rest of his life as an inmate of Bethlem until his death in 1841 (Walker 1968).

The Criminal Lunatics Act drew attention to the apparent problem of the large numbers of people who were being found 'not guilty' due to insanity and who were being sent to hospitals and workhouses. Thus a plan emerged to create a special hospital that could accommodate the growing numbers of 'criminal lunatics'. When Bethlem was rebuilt in 1815 it was designed to include two 'criminal blocks' that would accommodate 45 men and 15 women. The wards become problematically overcrowded, despite the fact that considerable numbers of 'criminal lunatics' were elsewhere. According to Walker and McCabe (1973: 5) a survey of criminal lunatics in 1837 identified 178 criminal lunatics, only 55 of whom were in Bethlem, while the rest were scattered in various county asylums and private madhouses. The notion of a state asylum specifically for 'criminal lunatics' began to be discussed by the 1850s; this eventually led to the construction of Broadmoor in the Berkshire countryside.

The network of 'special hospitals' of Rampton and Ashworth was to become a notable feature, representing a physical manifestation of the interface of the criminal justice system and the health system.

Eigen (1995: 51) suggests that Thomas Erskine had, alongside his erudite defence of James Hadfield, ushered in a whole new psychological dimension to the courtroom. He had 'asked jurors to expand their search beyond signs of histrionic, beastly antics to include a consideration of the prisoner's *ideas*'. Despite this apparent leap towards the acceptance of more subtle forms of insanity, it is important to note that there is no straightforward story of progress (as Walker 1968: 81–83 emphasises). In the years following Hadfield's trial there were cases that achieved some notoriety because of the way in which insanity pleas were ignored and the accused were executed. One example was the lesser known case of Thomas Bowler,[14] executed for murder in 1812 despite documented evidence concerning insanity before the offence. A much higher profile case was that of John Bellingham, who in 1812 shot Spencer Perceval (the Tory Prime Minister, and the only British Prime Minister to be assassinated while in office). Bellingham had experienced ill-treatment while in Russia on business and had felt aggrieved that the British government did not come to his aid. Frustrated that he received neither apology nor compensation, Bellingham became 'obsessed' (Eigen 1995: 52) with his grievance and shot Perceval at the House of Commons. The trial was very short and no postponement of the trial was allowed by the judge, despite pleas by the defence team for more time (Junius 1812). He was tried for murder rather than treason (Bellingham's own assurance that it was a personal rather than political matter presumably helped to account for this decision). Two physicians were asked to see him but did not do so. A number of witnesses were called from Liverpool to testify, but the postponement necessary to allow them to attend was not allowed. He was tried on Friday 15 May, only five days after he killed Perceval, and then he was executed on the following Monday. The prosecution successfully sought to establish that Bellingham was quite rational in planning the assassination. He had ordered a tailor to make an ordinary coat, and had then had this coat altered so that it could disguise a gun. Judge Mansfield at the trial directed the jury to the question of whether Bellingham 'possessed a sufficient degree of understanding to distinguish good from evil, right from wrong' (Goddard 2004: 12). The outcome of the trial came to be regarded as notorious. Even at the time there were many voices of protest, including that of Henry Brougham (later Lord Chancellor between 1830 and 1834, and one of the Lords involved in the Lords debate that followed the M'Naghten trial), who referred to the case as 'the greatest disgrace to English justice' (Goddard 2004: 19).

There were two trials in the 1840s, both held at the Old Bailey, that at first glance seem to represent the establishment of the insanity defence in cases where some version of monomania was held responsible. They are both worth dwelling on in some detail. The trial of Daniel M'Naghten was to become one of the most significant in legal history, marking the way insanity would be discussed in courts across the globe. Just three years before the famous trial of Daniel M'Naghten, the trial of Edward Oxford has significance, since it seemed to open the door to new psychiatric expertise. Thus in many respects the M'Naghten verdict was itself not that surprising, despite the fact that its reception and impact were to be exceptional.

### 2.2.2 The trial of Edward Oxford (1840)

Like Hadfield, Oxford was tried for treason, having fired shots at the young Queen Victoria. The subsequent high profile trial involved many witnesses, and most importantly a number of expert medical witnesses. Much of the trial was clearly concerned with exploring and reaching a conclusion about the mental state of the 18-year-old Edward Oxford. The trial took place over two days and resulted in over 30,000 words of description in the Old Bailey Sessions Papers.[15] Some considerable attention is paid to establishing the facts of the act itself. Much the greater part of the trial is however taken up with enquiry into the sanity of Edward Oxford. The verdict of 'not guilty' might be considered to be a triumph of nineteenth-century psychiatry; this field was well represented by experts at the trial, including John Conolly, who went on to become one of the most significant figures in the formal birth and development of British psychiatry (Scull 1984). The psychiatric ideas used in the court were eclectic, but there was clear reliance on notions of moral insanity. Perhaps prompted by Oxford's relative youth, there was emphasis on his childhood.

Hannah Oxford, Edward's mother, gave evidence about the strange and eccentric behaviour of his father and grandfather. Reference is made to 'hereditary insanity', but she particularly dwells on her husband's behaviour during her pregnancy, the (Lamarckian) assumption being that this behaviour had somehow informed the character of the unborn baby. This surely relates not just to simple theories of heredity but also the more complex idea of 'degeneracy'. This latter issue will be discussed in more detail in Chapter 4 (pp. 109–113), although it is worth noting that it appears that the concept is being used in the trial some 17 years before Morel (1857) was to formalise the theory. Hannah Oxford was asked directly about her son: had she observed anything remarkable about him from his infancy? She suggested that she was always aware that Edward was different:

> Yes, he would burst out crying when there was no one near him, and no one speaking to him, and he was always very troublesome – it was different to the mere waywardness of childhood – if he sat still or stood still, he would burst out crying – that was after he had learned to walk as well as before – all children cry, but this was when he was three or four years old, and he has continued to do so through life, to cry without any apparent cause.[16]

Despite the space given to the family witnesses the OBSP account is most interesting in relation to the number of expert medical witnesses who clearly claimed an expertise in insanity. The first medical witness was Dr John Birt Davis, who had had attended Hannah Oxford before and had been aware of the eccentric behaviour of Edward's father. More remarkable was the fact that Davis was questioned about whether he had 'formed any opinion of the sanity or insanity of the prisoner' through his observations of the trial. Admitting that he had, he is strongly directed to explore the issue of 'moral insanity'. Davis's response is to try to open up the (possibly safer) territory of hallucination (Eigen 1991).

Q. Supposing a person in the middle of the day, without any suggested motive, to fire a loaded pistol at Her Majesty, passing along the road in a carriage, to remain on the spot, to declare he was the person who did it – to take pains to have that known, and afterwards to enter freely into discussion, and answer any questions put to him on the subject, would you refer such conduct to a sound or unsound state of mind?

A. If to that hypothesis were added what I deem a proof of hallucination—

Bodkin (counsel for the defence) waved away this attempt to introduce the notion of delusion and maintained focus on the question of whether a judgment of sanity could be made upon consideration of reckless and perhaps 'amoral' behaviour:

COURT. Q. The question is, whether upon those facts alone you should judge a person to be insane?
A. I should judge him to be insane upon those facts alone, but I should be stronger in that opinion if I was permitted—
Q. You mean to state, upon your oath, that if you heard those facts stated, you should conclude that the party must be mad?
A. I do.
Q. Without making any other inquiry?
A. Yes – taking this into consideration, the absence of motive, the absence of precaution, the deliberate owning, and the free discussion afterwards, of his own conduct, criminating himself in that way immediately afterwards, with the danger staring him in the face.[17]

This was returned to later, as Sir F. Pollock cross-examined Davis and raised the question as to the grounding of his expertise on insanity. Davis was clear that he was claiming expertise as a physician:

Q. You have answered some hypothetical questions put by my learned friend opposite, (Mr. Bodkin)[.] I beg to ask you whether you give that

answer from your knowledge, as a physician, or from your experience as a Coroner, or as a Magistrate, or merely as a member of society?
A. I answer as a physician – I think the circumstances which have been supposed, have, medically speaking, a tendency to prove insanity.
COURT. Q. We do not exactly understand what you mean when you say medically?
A. If, as a physician, I was employed to ascertain whether an individual was sane or insane, in whom I found those facts, I should undoubtedly give my opinion that he was insane.

Pollock then moved on to draw attention to the danger of the circularity of Davis's definition, but Davis responded by emphasising the detail of the particular case:

Q. As a physician, you think every crime that is plainly committed to be committed by a mad man?
A. Nothing of the kind; but a crime committed under all the circumstances of the hypothesis.
Q. What are the circumstances in the crime itself, which you think show madness?
A. The crime is committed in open day, it being obviously of great magnitude and danger; of great atrocity; it is committed without any precaution, without any looking out for the means of escape; it is afterwards spoken of openly, so far from concealing the criminating facts; facts which might afford a chance of escape; the existence of the balls is acknowledged, the free discussion of the circumstances, the absence of motive – by the free discussion, I mean a free respondence to the questions put to him immediately afterwards in the cell – the questions which Lord Uxbridge stated yesterday he did put – he said, on Lord Uxbridge entering the door, 'I did it.'[18]

In addition to this medical evidence there was a series of expert witnesses, Drs Hodgkin, Conolly, Chowne and Ferdinand Clarke. Perhaps the most notable name was that of John Conolly, one of the most celebrated men in British psychiatry (Scull 1984). By the time of this trial, the age of the expert witness had clearly come. Conolly, as part of an expert delegation, had visited Oxford in Newgate the day before the trial began in order to assess his mental state. He introduced himself to the court as 'physician to the Hanwell Lunatic Asylum' where he cared for '850 patients' and therefore 'had some experience in the treatment of disorders of the mind'. He reported that he had interviewed the prisoner with a view to being a witness, had observed the witness and evidence at the trial and was of the opinion that Oxford was 'of unsound mind'. The notes from the interview were read out in court and they began with some brief phrenological observations that were widespread and popular at the time:

'A deficient understanding; shape of the anterior part of the head, that which is generally seen when there has been some disease of the brain in the early period of life.'

Conolly moved on to make brief reference to reason, but there is much more attention on Oxford's failure to grasp the meaning and significance of the act, and here Conolly seems to be alluding strongly to the description of 'moral insanity' as described by Prichard: an 'insensibility as regards the affections', and 'incapacity to comprehend moral obligations':

> [A]n occasional appearance of acuteness, but a total inability to reason – a singular insensibility as regards the affections – an apparent incapacity to comprehend moral obligations, to distinguish right from wrong – an absolute insensibility to the heinousness of his offence, and to the peril of his situation – a total indifference to the issue of the trial; acquittal will give him no particular pleasure, and he seems unable to comprehend the alternative of his condemnation and execution; his offence, like that of other imbeciles who set fire to buildings, &c, without motive, except a vague pleasure in mischief – appears unable to conceive anything of future responsibility.[19]

The next witness, Dr Chowne, physician at Charing Cross Hospital and lecturer 'on medical jurisprudence', was asked a hypothetical question about the sanity of someone who commits a crime without apparent motive and who also appears oblivious to the consequences. Chowne argued that such behaviour is indeed a strong indicator of insanity and that it has been called lesion of will, but also 'moral insanity'.

> Q. If you heard of a person committing a crime without the ordinary inducements to crime, either revenge or interest, and that crime exposes him to loss of life, and he seems reckless of consequences, and delivers himself into the hands of justice, and appears wholly exempt from any thing like consciousness of responsibility for the act, what opinion should you form of that state of mind?
> A. I should consider it an exceedingly strong indication of his being in an unsound state of mind – a propensity to commit acts without an apparent or adequate motive under such circumstances is recognized as a particular species of insanity, called in medical jurisprudence, *lesion of the will* – I do not know a better term – it is an old term – it has been called moral insanity.[20]

With the weight of expert testimony, the conclusion to the trial is given bluntly in OBSP: 'NOT GUILTY, being Insane[.] To be detained during Her Majesty's pleasure.' Thus Oxford received the special verdict and was transferred to Bethlem and then Broadmoor Hospital, where he stayed until 1868 when he was allowed to emigrate to Australia (Walker and McCabe 1973: 5), no longer to be a threat to Her Majesty's peace of mind. Oxford had taken upon himself to achieve an education and earned a living as a housepainter under the name of John Freeman.

### 2.2.3 The trial of Daniel M'Naghten (1843)

The trial of Daniel M'Naghten in 1843 was arguably to become one of the most renowned trials in legal history. It also featured an attempted assassination; this time the attempt was on the life of the Prime Minister, Robert Peel. The assassin was not successful because, in a case of mistaken identity, he shot Peel's secretary Edward Drummond instead. When arrested, he explained that 'The Tories in my native city have compelled me to do this. They follow me and persecute me wherever I go, and have entirely destroyed my peace of mind' (Memon 2006: 235). Since Drummond died three days later M'Naghten was put on trial for murder, but was fortunate that this trial took place after the right to defence counsel had been extended to a far wider range of offences beyond treason (Walker 1968: 84). The prosecution produced a number of witnesses who were acquainted with M'Naghten and testified as to the fact that he was a functioning adult and had not seemed to them to be insane. His landlady Eliza Dutton, for example, described him as rather quiet and reserved but of regular and sober habits. She could not recall seeing anything that made her think that 'he was not right in his mind'. There were a number of witnesses from his home town of Glasgow, all testifying that they had not been aware of his mind being in any way unsound. William M'Lellan, a blacksmith, had known M'Naghten for some 15 or 16 years, but could not recall anything peculiar in his habits or manner. He had appeared to have made his living, albeit not in a very straightforward way. He had attended night classes, borrowed books, applied for jobs, kept his banking in order, all in a very unremarkable fashion. At his arrest at the scene, he appeared to know what he had done – despite the obvious confusion about whether he had shot Peel or his secretary. Overall, the picture that emerged from the prosecution account was that M'Naghten was a regular man, perhaps rather quiet and reserved or even eccentric. Moran (1981) has commented that the prosecution might have made more of his connections with Scottish nationalism and suggestions made that he might have been paid to kill Peel, but as they did not pursue this, they were left to stress his hatred of Peel and the Tories as his motivation. In pursuit of his goal, he had planned the attack, he had aimed the gun and killed Drummond. This was therefore knowing, intentional murder.

The defence produced an array of acquaintances and family members as witnesses to bolster their case that M'Naghten was not of sound mind. M'Naghten's father gave a clear account of his belief that his son's mind was unsound only upon the subject of his persecutions. On other topics he was quite rational, however. Just as in the Oxford trial, a number of medical witnesses were called. Indeed, the luminaries of British psychiatry were there to give evidence. While there are some differences in the language they use and the emphasis that they place upon different concepts, there is agreement that M'Naghten is of unsound mind. Edward Thomas Monro, Esq. MD was one of the group who visited the accused in Newgate in order to make an assessment. Monro, the last in line of a four generation dynasty who had been in charge at Bethlem Royal Hospital, was clear that he could detect the insanity through the interview alone, and that he was detecting the presence of delusion:

> I believe I am able to discriminate between a case where a man is labouring under delusion, and where a man feigns delusion – I am quite satisfied that the prisoner entertained the delusions he was giving utterance to – I have not the slightest shadow of a doubt on the subject – if I had heard nothing of his past history, nor the evidence given to-day, my examination in the prison would certainly have led me to the conclusion that he was insane – coupling that with the history of the two last years of his life, I have not the remotest doubt of his insanity – I am quite satisfied of it.[21]

In order to counter the prosecution case that M'Naghten was capable of managing the affairs of everyday life and therefore could not be considered to be without reason, the defence were keen to advance the case for the existence of a 'partial delusion' or 'monomania' as distinct from general mania and to assert that the monomania may exist despite the 'appearance of sanity in all other respects'.

> Q. Is it now an established principle in the pathology of insanity that there may exist a partial delusion sufficient to overcome a man's moral sense and self-control, and render him irresponsible for his actions, exciting a partial insanity only, although the rest of the faculties of the mind may remain in all their ordinary state of operation?
> A. Yes, it is quite recognised – the distinction between monomania and general mania is quite recognised – I apprehend that monomania can exist distinct from general mania – it can sometimes unquestionably exist to the extent of overcoming a man's self control – I have no doubt that this partial insanity may exist, and the faculty that it affects may be impaired and destroyed, and yet the monomaniac exhibit all the appearance of sanity, in all other respects – the acutest reasoners on many points, good arithmeticians, good artists, and good architects – I have known great ability on those points, co-exist with disease in others – I have heard the evidence on the part of the prosecution as to his pecuniary transactions, and heard the letter read which answered the advertisement – that does not at all impair my conviction as to

> his insanity – I have known many lunatics keep accounts with great accuracy – persons affected on one point, where their intelligence is clear on others – it is quite manifest that such persons carry out their designs, with great ingenuity and contrivance; and afterwards, when they have done the act, they are very frequently alive to the consequences of it – they have shown great cunning in endeavouring to escape from the consequences – I have observed it every day.

Monro was careful to show that his understanding of insanity was that its influence could be very circumscribed. The focus on 'monomania' makes the influence of French psychiatry quite clear. Indeed, defence counsel drew attention to recent work and cited that by 'Monsieur Marcs', who had given evidence at the infamous trial of Henriette Cornier in 1825 (During 1988). The next witness was Sir Alexander Morison, who was consulting physician at Bethlem. Morison had been responsible for the first medical lectures on insanity (Eigen 2004: 43) and published *The Physiognomy of Mental Diseases* in 1843. Morison also attended the interview with M'Naghten and agreed that he was suffering from a delusion that would 'deprive him of the exercise of all restraint against the act to which it impelled him – I do not speak with the slightest doubt on the subject'. William M'Clewer, a surgeon based in Harley Street, was also a member of the company who visited the prisoner in Newgate and reported that he believed that M'Naghten was suffering such delusions of persecution and that they 'were really felt by him'. He gave the opinion 'that in the commission of the act, he was not under the ordinary restraint by which persons in general are bound in their conduct; his moral liberty was destroyed'. William Hutchinson, a physician at the Royal Lunatic Asylum at Glasgow, also gave confident evidence that M'Naghten was suffering from a delusion and that the impulse to kill would be too powerful to resist. John Crawford, 'lecturer on medical jurisprudence at Andersonian University' in Glasgow, seemed to add nothing more than his agreement with Hutchinson. Gilbert M'Murdo was a potentially more challenging witness for the defence. He was well known for his appearances at the Old Bailey, where he had given his views on the sanity, or otherwise, of various defendants whom he had been able to observe in his position as surgeon at Newgate. He had a certain infamy for denying insanity and sending people to the gallows (Eigen 2010: 449). On this occasion, however, his message was consistent with that of the other medics at the trial. Forbes Winslow, who was to be the chief expert witness in the trial of George Townley some years later (discussed in some detail in Chapter 3) and had just published his book *The Plea of Insanity in Criminal Cases* (1843), also gave evidence based only on witnessing the proceedings of the trial and concluded that he 'had not the least doubt of the existence of the prisoner's insanity'.

For the defence, Alexander Cockburn summed up (at extreme length according to Walker 1968), but concluded with this:

> I trust that I have satisfied you by these authorities that the disease of partial insanity can exist and that it can lead to a partial or total aberration of the moral senses and affections; which may render the wretched patient incapable of resisting the delusion, and lead him to commit crimes for which morally he cannot be held responsible.
>
> (Walker 1968: 94)

The judge (Lord Justice Tindal) summed up the arguments rather briefly. On the prosecution side the issue for the jury was that if the prisoner had been 'capable of distinguishing right and wrong, then he was a responsible agent and liable to all the penalties the law imposes'. On the defence side was all the medical evidence, which he did not review, since it had all been consistently emphasising insanity (Walker 1968: 95). With apparently little hesitation the jury brought in the special verdict, 'not guilty, being insane', and M'Naghten was taken directly to Bethlem Hospital.

### 2.2.3.1 The storm after the trial

Although, as we have seen, this verdict was not unique, it did cause some heated public debate. Famously, Queen Victoria expressed her frustration, writing to Prime Minister Peel:

> We have seen the trials of Oxford and MacNaughten conducted by the ablest lawyers of the day – and they allow and advise the Jury to pronounce the verdict of not guilty on account of insanity. Whilst everybody is morally convinced that both malefectors were perfectly conscious and aware of what they did.
>
> (quoted in Walker 1968: 188)

The press responses to the verdict suggested that the Queen was not alone in questioning the verdicts. A leader in *The Standard* (6 March) was scathing:

> On Saturday, indeed, the whole process of a criminal trial appeared to have been inverted. The mad doctors, who attended in the modest character of witnesses, were really the persons who charged the Court and the jury, laying down the law of moral responsibility to both, and the judge it was who returned the verdict, under the direction of the mad doctors. . . . If the mad doctor's evidence upon the existence and degree of insanity is to be received with suspicion, we respectfully submit that upon the question of responsibility, his evidence is not received at all. That is a question for the law, and the law was clear until the *verdict* of Saturday.

The *Morning Post* on 14 March 1843 continued the assault upon the quacks of the madhouses and denounced the whole notion of 'partial insanity':

> [P]artial madness (considering madness as an active physical disease) is impossible. Since the creation, there has not been an instance of it, whatever the quack keepers of madhouses, who, of course, try to exalt their craft, may say upon the subject; and even supposing such as thing as partial madness to exist in M'Naughten's case, what connection was there between the surmised partial madness and the murderous act of the villain.[22]

*The Times* on 6 March used a more sarcastic tone to beg leave,

> in a spirit of humble and honest earnestness, of hesitating and admiring uncertainty, and of almost painful dubitation, [to] ask those learned and philosophic gentlemen to define, for the edification of common-place people like ourselves, where sanity ends and madness begins, and what are the outward and palpable signs of the one or the other.
> (Walker 1968: 95)

The public furore led to a debate in the House of Lords, which resulted in a decision by the House to question a panel of judges on how issues of insanity should be handled in court. It was the answers to questions about how jurors should consider the state of mind of the accused that came to be regarded as 'the M'Naghten rules'. These suggest that in order 'to establish a defence on the ground of insanity':

> [I]t must be clearly proved that, at the time of the committing of the act, the party accused was labouring under such a defect of reason, from disease of the mind, as not to know the nature and quality of the act he was doing; or, if he did know it, that he did not know he was doing what was wrong.
> (Walker 1968: 100)

When unpacked these rather dense phrases amount to a formulation that narrowly restricts the defence of insanity, putting the focus firmly on whether the accused knew and understood that they were doing an act that was wrong. That is certainly the way 'the rules' came to be largely interpreted, although the use of the words 'nature and quality' of the act might have suggested a little more subjectivity. This might explain why the medical experts in insanity seemed quite slow to take up the challenge that was being posed by 'the rules' to what were becoming quite accepted doctrines about the nature of insanity within the emerging profession. As we will see in the next chapter, at this very point in time the mad-doctors were busy founding their professional bodies and the associated journals. The conception of moral insanity was an important plank in their claim for legal expertise. It was only when a number of trials occurred in the glare of publicity that the scale of the reversal for psychiatry became clear.

## Conclusion

The first half of the nineteenth century appeared to be something of a triumph for the new profession of psychiatry. From a position of some obscurity at the beginning of the century they were to appear, as we will see in more detail in the following chapter, as a professional body with some coherent claims to expertise and a body of knowledge. These claims were made in relation to their ability to treat insanity with new 'psychological' therapy in the form of moral treatment and through their capacity to offer expertise on the nature of insanity in the courts. Thus both moral treatment and moral insanity were crucial to the development of the profession. A transnational body of scholarship about insanity was built and this was to form the basis of the new profession in the middle of the nineteenth century.

The trials of Oxford and M'Naghten in the 1840s demonstrated the potential power of this new professional group. The luminaries appeared at the Old Bailey and successfully claimed insanity for men who were clearly not raving mad, but were suffering from some hidden insanity – whether it were called monomania, partial insanity or moral insanity. The trained eye of the medical expert in insanity could be called upon to identify the presence of such disorders. The next half a century was to be one of somewhat ambiguous progress for psychiatry. It was to achieve official recognition as a professional grouping, and its members were put in charge of large scale asylum building projects across Europe and North America. The scale, however, of the reversal represented by the emergence and acceptance of the M'Naghten rules, which seemed to deem these subtle hidden forms of insanity to be illegitimate, took some years to become fully evident. It was to mean that psychiatry lost its footing in the court system and needed to look elsewhere if it were to establish an expertise in the area of criminal justice. The next chapter will explore these two issues concerning the developmental paths of psychiatry over the second half of the nineteenth century. It will be argued that the development of psychiatry was deeply affected by the rejection in court and turned its gaze on the classification of population rather than the exploration of individual psychology.

## Notes

1 The term is a convenient short-hand to use when referring to those who identified themselves as having medical expertise in the treatment of insanity, even before they would have used the term themselves. The term 'psychiatry' itself can be traced to the work of the German medic Johann Christian Reil around the beginning of the nineteenth century. The phrase began to be used quite extensively in Germany by the middle of the nineteenth century; in France this happened more gradually, while in Britain the term was not used much before the latter decades of the nineteenth century (Werlinder 1978: 15).
2 As Bynum summarises: '"Moral therapy" was simultaneously a triumph of humanism and of therapy, a recognition that kindness, reason, and tactful manipulation were

more effective in dealing with the inmates of asylums than were fear, brutal coercion and restraint, and medical therapy' (Bynum 1964: 318).
3 By the middle of the nineteenth century the claims made by phrenology were largely discredited and yet had been influential; notably Conolly: *On the Characters of Insanity: a Lecture Delivered at the Royal Institution of Great Britain* 17 February 1854:

> Although the doctrines of the phrenologists have met with little favour, and the pretensions of recent professors of occult methods of acting upon the nervous system have thrown an air of absurdity even over the truths of what is called phrenology, no person not altogether devoid of the power of observation can affect to overlook the general importance of the shape and even of the size of the brain in relation to the development of the mental faculties.

4 As discussed in Chapter 5, psychiatry in Germany was quite resistant to this notion.
5 Benjamin Rush had independently on the other side of the Atlantic put forward notions of 'moral derangement'. Discussed by Werlinder 1978: 24–26).
6 See also Ben Pollitt: http://smarthistory.khanacademy.org/gericaults-portraits-of-the-insane.html, accessed 14 April 2015.
7 Medical Jurisprudence: Homicide-suicide-infanticide: The Trial of Harriet Cornier: *The Medico-Chirurgical Review* 1 January 1827, vi (11), 482–486.
8 'An atrocious act, so contrary to human nature, committed without motive, without gain, without passion, opposed to the natural character of an individual, is evidently an act of madness.'
9 The term 'moral insanity' was used by both Thomas Arnold and Benjamin Rush in the eighteenth century. They were referring to 'the perversion of the moral sense as a result of madness' (Augstein 1996: 314), and not, as Prichard was, to a specific disorder that might be defined by the perversion of moral behaviour.
10 Augstein (1996) argues that in many respects Prichard was out of time with medical work of the day – the French particularly were influenced by phrenology, which saw the faculties of the mind being linked to different parts of the brain. To the deeply religious Prichard this was problematic. He addresses phrenology directly: 'the real ground on which so many have become converts to phrenology has not been the evidence of facts, but the plausible and specious nature of the theory and the ready explanation which *seems to* afford of a great number of phenomena in natural history and psychology' Prichard 1835a: 469).
11 His sympathetic intervention in the case of Margaret Nicholson, who had threatened to stab him in 1786, was believed to have played a part in her being transported to Bethlem rather than put on trial.
12 Walker (1968: 76) assumes that this is Alexander Crichton, who had published in 1798 *Inquiry into the Nature and Origin of Mental Derangement*.
13 Indeed, Hadfield did manage to escape from Bethlem, and so he was kept at Newgate prison until secure accommodation for 'criminal lunatics' was built at Bethlem in 1816 (O'Reilly-Fleming 1992).
14 An interesting case tried at the Old Bailey in 1812. Bowler was sent to the gallows despite the fact that he had previously been diagnosed as insane and had medical experts support the claim of insanity. It certainly makes the point that the courts were not easily swayed by claims of insanity.
15 Old Bailey Proceedings Online (www.oldbaileyonline.org, version 7.0, 26 January 2015), July 1840, trial of Edward Oxford (t18400706–1877).
16 OBP, July 1840, trial of Edward Oxford (t18400706–1877).
17 OBP, July 1840, trial of Edward Oxford (t18400706–1877).
18 OBP, July 1840, trial of Edward Oxford (t18400706–1877).
19 OBP, July 1840, trial of Edward Oxford (t18400706–1877).

20 OBP, July 1840, trial of Edward Oxford (t18400706–1877).
21 Old Bailey Proceedings Online (www.oldbaileyonline.org, version 7.0, 26 January 2015), February 1843, trial of Daniel M'Naghten (t18430227–874).
22 The *Morning Post* (London, England), Tuesday 14 March 1843; Issue 22512:2.

Chapter 3

# The rise of psychiatry in the post-M'Naghten years

## Introduction

While it was taking place, the trial of Daniel M'Naghten in 1843 might have appeared to be a triumphant landmark in the development of the profession of psychiatry. As we have seen in Chapter 2, the 'psychiatric' witnesses, including figures like John Conolly, who have a significant place in the history of British psychiatry, were confident of themselves and their knowledge. The court seemed to listen respectfully to what they had to say and the jury were persuaded to a return a not guilty verdict; the medical experts on insanity had been relatively free to put forward their ideas about what constituted insanity: it might not be visible, it could arise in different forms, and it could be very restricted in its manifestation. Notions of 'lesions of will' and 'moral insanity' were embraced by defence attorneys and accepted by juries (Eigen 1999; Wiener 1999). The public storm after the M'Naghten trial and the subsequent inquiry seemed to rule against such expertise being taken so seriously in court. Subsequent to the M'Naghten rules medical witnesses, 'regardless of whatever else they had to contribute to the court's understanding of the defendant's mental state', were generally pinned down to one question: 'Did the prisoner, in your opinion, know right from wrong?' (Eigen 1999: 441–442).

Since this happened at a time when the British Empire was at a peak of its influence, this narrowing of the legal definition had influence on legal systems across the globe. Thus in the wake of the M'Naghten rules it might have appeared that a certain kind of order had been re-established. The 'rules' seem to confirm the privilege of reason as the seat of virtue. The 'mad-doctors' were firmly put in their place, some steps behind the legal profession (Smith 1981). This tale of the subjugation of psychiatry would be far too great a simplification, however. On the contrary, the decades following the trial were to witness the establishment of the profession of psychiatry which, over the next century in Europe and North America, would develop and eventually hold some considerable sway over legal discussions on the nature of insanity. Furthermore, psychiatric discourse of one kind or another was arguably to exert influence over every aspect of cultural life and on the systems of welfare that were developing in the industrial world. Some of the notions of insanity that were to have such cultural impact were those that would be met with scepticism in court: that insanity could take many different forms, could be difficult to detect and be restricted to only very particular aspects of people's mental lives. The interaction of such ideas with wider social and cultural currents will be the subject of the next chapter, as the ideas emerging from that interaction themselves become significant. Psychiatry did not lose its interest in the issue of crime. It was too key an issue to the state to be ignored by the profession, who were still keen to declare their expertise. It was on offenders within the prison system, itself a development of nineteenth-century efforts to cope with the problem of crime, that psychiatrists were to turn their expert gaze, but they were now formulating far more biological models of moral insanity.

This chapter will first describe the institutional establishment of psychiatry in the middle of the nineteenth century, just around the time of the M'Naghten trial. It is clear that at this point British psychiatrists, although eclectic, and in many ways thoroughly rooted in the world of physical medicine, had a distinctly 'psychological' claim to expertise as 'doctors of the mind'. The new profession enthusiastically pursued an assertion of professional expertise in the criminal courts. This latter claim was to become severely dented, however, as the ramifications of the M'Naghten rules became clearer. The second part of the chapter will look in some detail at one murder trial that garnered a vast amount of largely negative publicity for psychiatry. This was the trial in 1863 of Victor George Townley, who had murdered the young woman who had just broken off an engagement with him. The killing was arguably inspired by jealousy and so was not unmotivated, but Townley's behaviour afterwards certainly gave some credence to the notion that he was suffering from an insanity that was impacting on his sense of morality. While medical opinion on the case was divided, the public derision of the 'mad-doctors', who argued for Townley's acquittal on the grounds of insanity, was overwhelming. This case powerfully illustrates how deep the reversal for psychiatry had been since the apparent legal triumphs of the 1840s, and why psychiatry had to move away from this claim for expertise in moral insanity. The third section of the chapter will trace the shift of psychiatry's attention away from this exploration of the minds of individuals, trying to gauge finely the moral culpability of individual offenders, and instead towards the categorisation of the larger population of offenders accumulating in the newly developed state prisons. This move towards the classification of the mass of offenders in the offending population was to give succour to those interested in theories of degeneration and of the biological roots of mental disorder. To understand this fully, the cultural significance of degeneracy theory will be discussed in Chapter 4. It helped to promote a distinct turn back towards organic theories of mental disease. This organic turn became a powerful force when notions of 'moral insanity' collided with notions of 'the criminal man' coming from the criminal anthropologists (led by Cesare Lombroso) and ideas from German psychiatry on congenital states marked by 'moral imbecility' and 'moral idiocy'.

## 3.1 The professionalisation of psychiatry

The first forty years of the nineteenth century in England had witnessed growing acceptance of the forensic expertise of medical witnesses. Eigen reports that by the beginning of the 1840s around three quarters of the homicide trials in London were informed by at least one medical witness; by the late 1840s this figure was as high as 90 per cent. There also was a growing trend for witnesses in insanity trials, so that by the middle of the nineteenth century nearly one half of trials in which insanity was being raised featured a medical witness (Eigen 1999: 430). The confidence, and the numbers, of the 'asylum doctors' who took a specialist interest in insanity had been growing for some time; there was a number of key steps in the middle of the nineteenth century that consolidated the profession in Europe and the United States. In Great Britain the Association of Medical Officers of Asylums and Hospitals for the Insane was founded in 1841. It changed its name to the Medico-Psychological Association in 1865, and to the Medico-Psychological Association of Great Britain and Ireland in 1887.[1] In the United States the Association of Medical Superintendents of American Institutions for the Insane (AMSAII) was formally set up in 1844 in Philadelphia. This became the American Medico-Psychological Association in 1892 and finally the American Psychiatric Association in 1921. The equivalent development in German psychiatry took place in 1842 with the inaugural meeting of the German Association for Psychiatry and Psychotherapy (DGPPN). In 1844, the first issue of the *Allgemeine Zeitschrift für Psychiatrie und Psychisch-Gerichtliche Medizin* ('General Journal for Psychiatry and Mental-Forensic Medicine') was published.

In France, a national asylum system, to be staffed by full time medical doctors who would be funded to support the training of students, was established following legislation in 1838 (Goldstein 1987). The journal *Annales Médico-Psychologiques* was first published in 1843 and reflected the growing confidence of the *aliénistes*. In Britain the professional confidence of the asylum doctors was also matched by important policy initiatives, with the 1845 Asylum Act mandating all local authorities to build an asylum. The self-assurance of the asylum doctors led to the creation of their own professional journal, called *The Asylum Journal*, which was launched in 1853, changing its name to the *Journal of Mental Science* in 1858, before eventually becoming the *The British Journal of Psychiatry* in 1963. The original name of the journal draws attention to the key factor in the development of psychiatry: the large scale government support for the construction and maintenance of a national network of asylums. It is worth dwelling on the content of the very first edition of *The Asylum Journal* as an indicator of how the profession saw itself at this time. It includes an, unsurprisingly, celebratory 'prospectus' that clearly tries to establish the ownership of the field of mental science. It is notable how the claim for professional status is being made on the grounds of psychological expertise and specifically in relation to forensic matters. The claim for psychological expertise is made through reference to the work of Pinel and Conolly as advocates of moral treatment and this 'new school of special medicine' (*The Asylum Journal* 1853 Prospectus: 1). The work of the Austrian Ernst von Feuchtersleben (see Burns 1954 for a review of this medic's work) is then quoted in some detail. Part of the justification for the development of a specialist medical profession was that particular talents were required: 'in the so called psychical mode of cure, one personality has to act upon another', and he must

> be able by his personal demeanour to obtain influence over the minds of other men, which, though in fact an essential part of a physician's mode of cure, is a gift that nature often refuses to the most distinguished men, and yet without which mental diseases, however thoroughly understood, cannot be successfully treated.
> (*The Asylum Journal* 1853 Prospectus: 2)

The reference to Feuchtersleben is striking for a number of reasons. First, because he was a professor of psychiatry in Austria his presence reinforces Rimke and Hunt's (2002: 63) point about psychiatric knowledge, particularly in relation to moral insanity, being 'shared by a transcontinental psycho-medical community'. Second, Feuchtersleben took a distinctly 'psychological' view of psychiatry. His notable work *The Principles of Medical Psychology* was published in 1845 in German and translated into English in 1847. As Parkin (1975) notes, he might be regarded as a forerunner to Freud, for while he makes the case for the fundamental interdependence of Psyche and Soma, he also uses the term 'ego' and alludes to the significance of dreams and of 'sensations with dormant consciousness', for example.[2] In addition to the commitment to working in the psychological domain, it is also apparent that forensic matters are regarded as of some significance, as indicated by the fact that one of the papers in this very first edition is called 'On Monomania, in a Psychological and Legal Point of View' by Dr Delastauve (Physician of the Bicêtre).[3] This paper reinforced the view that insanity fell into two fundamental categories depending on whether the 'malady has an intellectual or sentimental (emotional) origin', and the article concludes by emphasising the legal significance of the fact that 'monomania – or better, *emotional madness* – may be compatible with the exercise of the intellectual function' (Delastauve, *The Asylum Journal* 1853: 9).

Overall, it is important to recognise that although there are very different strains of psychiatric thought – and this continues to be the case – the claim that British psychiatry was making in the middle of the nineteenth century at the birth of the profession was that it offered to be both a 'science of the mind' and a treatment for that 'mind'. It was also apparent that the conceptualisation of monomanias, and of forms of insanity that could impact upon someone's 'morals' and emotions, was still an important line of thought within psychiatry, despite the M'Naghten rulings of 1843. This latter matter was to be undermined as the implications of the M'Naghten ruling became clear in the decades that followed. This realisation took some years, despite clear indications that psychiatric expertise would meet a far less comfortable arena in the immediate post-M'Naghten era. In 1847, for example, William Allnutt[4] was accused of poisoning his grandfather, and was defended on the grounds of insanity. According to the OBSP[5] one Frederick Duesbury ('Doctor of medicine at Clapton') reported treating Allnutt for indigestion and scrofula, and indicated some form of moral deficit:

> I think he would understand that he was poisoning his grandfather, if explained to him, but at the time the sense of right and wrong was not acting with sufficient power to control him – I mean a morbid state of the moral feelings, of the sense of right and wrong – I think he knew what the act was that he was doing, but that he did not feel it as being wrong – I am speaking of moral feeling.

No less a figure than John Conolly also spoke for the defence, having visited Allnutt in prison and listened to the evidence in court. He offered an opinion that, while circumspect, gestures towards a disorder of conduct rather than intellect:

> [H]e is imperfectly organized; and taking the word 'mind' in the sense in which it is used by all writers, I should say he is of unsound mind – I believe, from the various circumstances which have been mentioned, that his brain is either diseased, or in that excitable state in which disease is most probable to ensue, that it is not a healthy brain – I should think him very likely to become insane, but that the future character of his insanity would be more in the derangement of his conduct than in the confusion of his intellect – that is conjecture.[6]

Conolly's and Duesbury's evidence was ignored by judge and jury, and Allnutt – despite being only 12 years old – was duly sentenced to death.[7] Further evidence of the impact of the M'Naghten rules was to be provided ten years later through the higher profile trial of William Dove, who was accused of poisoning his wife (Davies 2005). The defence of moral insanity was raised by Caleb Williams, who was an experienced medical officer to the Friends' Retreat in York. The fact that Dove had administered the strychnine was largely not contested. The defence was focused on Dove's state of mind and much was made of his history of eccentric and often cruel behaviour, with strong reference to Prichard's definition of moral insanity. This expert testimony was put down in no uncertain terms by Judge Baron Branwell as part of a detailed six hour summing up of the evidence:

> Experts in madness! Mad doctors! Gentlemen, I will read you the evidence of these medical witnesses – these 'experts in madness' – And if you can

make sane evidence out of what they say, do so; but I confess it's more than I can do'.

(Williams 1856: lxxxvii)

Perhaps not surprisingly, given the tone of the summing up, the jury agreed with the judge and returned a verdict of 'guilty' with less than 20 minutes' deliberation, although they did recommend 'mercy on the ground of defective intellect' (Williams 1856: cxv). This was ignored by both judge and authorities, and Dove was hanged on 9 August 1856. By this time psychiatry had a form of 'professional' voice and the case was given nine pages of comment by John Bucknill in *The Asylum Journal of Mental Science*, where the judgment of 'guilty' was largely supported (Bucknill 1857), despite the supportive intervention post-trial of Dr Forbes Winslow, who argued that Dove was constitutionally defective. Forbes Winslow was a prominent member of the new profession, and was to be centrally involved as the chief medical witness for the defence in the trial of George Victor Townley. Coming seven years after the trial of Dove, this was to receive a huge amount of publicity and would provide the decisive twist of the rope for the acceptance in the courts of moral insanity as a form of psychological disorder. The scale of the impact of the case means it is worth paying some attention to the detail.

## 3.2 The Townley case and the crisis of confidence (1863)

The trial of Townley was arguably to have considerable practical implications for the development of psychiatric practice in England in the latter decades of the nineteenth century. As Walker (1968: 208) notes, the case was accompanied at the time by almost as great a public debate as the M'Naghten trial, and it was one that was to bring 'mad-doctors' into very public disrepute (Forshaw 2008). There were once again derogatory discussions of the business of 'mad-doctors' and in particular their views of such conditions as moral insanity. The *Journal of Mental Science* devoted a special pamphlet to discussion of the case (which largely distanced itself from the defence of 'moral insanity').[8] The debate was noted in the United States (see *American Law Register* 1864), and Francis Galton used the case in his series of papers that was effectively a rallying call for eugenics. To Galton, Townley was a born 'moral monster' (Galton 1865: 324) and it was 'notable' that such a man without conscience should have been 'able to mix in English society for years, just like other people', before his acts had revealed his nature. Galton's interest in the case was to prefigure what was to become of the medical profession's interest in such dangerous individuals. The case was in some ways an exemplary test of the notion of moral insanity and the public outcry about its use was to prove decisive in shifting the attention of the young psychiatric profession away from the courts.

George Victor Townley was 25 years old and had been engaged to 22-year-old Miss Elizabeth Goodwin for four years. She was of a well-to-do and respected family from Chester in the north west of England, but was living at the time with her grandfather, Captain Goodwin, in Wigwell Grange in Derbyshire. For reasons that might have been simply to do with her own heart, or perhaps the wishes of her family, she broke off the engagement and declared her intention to marry another man. Distraught, Townley (who lived some miles away near Manchester) insisted on visiting her in order to hear her views for himself. He arrived at Wigwell Grange on Friday 22 August. He and 'Bessie' spent some hours together and went out for a walk, during which he stabbed her at least twice in the throat and neck. The deep wounds were sufficient to sever her carotid vein and arteries, and she died soon after. The story was reported widely over national and local newspapers. There was doubtless a salacious fascination with a story that involved young members of the gentry, sexual intrigue and a fatal knife attack on a young woman by her spurned lover. Townley's subsequent behaviour added to the intrigue since he stayed with her as she died, and even tried to save her. He made no attempt to escape and boldly told everyone around that he had killed and showed no remorse.

Detailed accounts from witnesses were quickly available in the press, even before the trial. A passing labourer, Reuben Conway, came upon the distressed and bleeding Miss Goodwin, who was able to ask him to help her home and to identify her attacker, who had not fled. Townley introduced himself and was forthright in claiming: 'I have stabbed her, she has proven false to me . . . and I shall be hanged.' Nevertheless he helped Conway carry his dying sweetheart back to the house, and attempted to stem the bleeding from the terrible wounds as he instructed Conway to fetch help. Two other witnesses joined the rescue party and Miss Goodwin was carried back to her grandfather's house. Townley also told the new witnesses that he had 'done it and that he would be hanged for it'. Meanwhile he kissed his victim several times, saying 'Poor Betsy'.[9] At the house the group was met by Captain Goodwin, who was informed by Townley himself that he had killed his granddaughter. Townley explained: 'She has deceived me and the woman that deceives me shall die . . . I told her I would kill her. She knew my temper.' The summoned doctor could do nothing but report on the mortal wounds. Townley, meanwhile, took a cup of tea and a brandy and soda with Captain Goodwin (who explained this bizarrely unruffled behaviour in terms of his concern for his own safety and that of his staff). As Townley was escorted into custody he remarked to the policeman: 'I feel far more happy now that I have done it than I was before, and I trust she is.' Aside from this he chatted of inconsequential matters, including the weather (Anonymous 1864: 16).

At the trial Dr Forbes Winslow himself defended Townley on the grounds of insanity. Forbes Winslow was a prominent and respected member of the new profession. He had been elected President of the Association of Medical Officers of Asylums and Hospitals for the Insane in 1857–8 and he had strong parliamentary connections.[10] He could also claim some expertise in this area since he had been an expert witness in the M'Naghten trial, and had published *The Plea of Insanity in Criminal Cases* twenty years earlier in 1843. Witnesses were called from Townley's family to testify as to the existence of insanity in his own family. Evidence was also presented on the sincerity of the feelings between Townley and Miss Goodwin and the distress that the withdrawal of the promise of engagement had created. Of course, jealousy was likely to be no defence at all. The evidence of Forbes Winslow himself was therefore the main plank of the case for the defence. Forbes Winslow saw Townley on two occasions, the first for nearly two hours on 18 November (that is, two months after the killing) and the second for three quarters of an hour, the day before the trial. Forbes Winslow argued that the fact that Townley showed no remorse or contrition was itself a significant symptom. Townley had persisted in arguing that he was right to do as he did; that Miss Goodwin was effectively his property and that by killing her he was reclaiming that property and no others had the right to judge him. He also believed that he was the victim of a conspiracy, with her relatives seeking to undermine the proposed marriage. On the tricky issue of knowing right from wrong, Forbes Winslow had to concede that 'he knew he had done a thing contrary to law' but said:

> I found his moral sense to be more vitiated than in any man I ever saw. He had no ideas of duty either towards God or towards man. He seemed incapable of reasoning upon any moral question that I brought before him. And he made the unaccountable assertion that he was not responsible to God or to man . . . He clenched his fists and his eyes started from his head, and as I thought he was going to have a paroxysm of maniacal fury – he said 'I have done no murder, I am not a murderer'; I thought it would be unsafe to continue the investigation and I stopped.[11]

The facts marshalled in defence of Townley were that he made no attempt to escape and he was entirely candid in telling everyone that he had murdered Bessie Goodwin. He then showed no remorse and indeed continued to insist, even months after the crime, that he was entirely justified and would do the same again. Such wanton behaviour in the shadow of the gallows had been taken as evidence of innocence in the trials of M'Naghten, Hadfield and Oxford (as described in Chapter 2). Townley's defence would have been unexceptional as judged by the evidence used in the M'Naghten trial. Forbes Winslow's perspective here was consistent with that of his 1843 book, which identified forms of insanity which promote 'a morbid desire to sacrifice human life' despite the fact that 'no intellectual delusion is perceptible' (1843: 60). In summing up the case, the judge was on one level sympathetic to Townley, believing that the breaking of the engagement brought him 'as much agony of mind as it was almost possible for any man to suffer', but he also made it clear that the criteria to be used to reach a conclusion of insanity were those of the M'Naghten rules:

> If he knew when he did the act likely to cause death, and it did cause death, and he did it for that purpose; if he did it purposively, and knew that in doing it he was doing what the law of God declares to be a bad act, a wrong act, contrary to the sixth commandment; that it was also an act that he knew to be contrary to the law ... in my opinion he is guilty of murder and your duty will be to find him guilty.[12]

After a mere five minutes' deliberation, the jury returned a verdict of 'guilty' and Townley was duly sentenced to be executed. Press reports finished with the dramatic paragraph which suggests that feelings were running high, and may go some way to explaining some of the subsequent events:

> Mr Baron Martin, whose lips quivered with emotion, put on the black cap, and the usual awful proclamation having been made, the learned judge said – George Victor Townley, after everything that could possibly be urged in defence of your crime has been done with an ability never excelled, the jury have found you guilty of murder, and I am bound to say that in that verdict I entirely concur, for if that defence that has been set up in your behalf was allowed to have prevailed, it seems to me it might have been attended with the most disastrous consequences to the country; and if it did become instilled into the minds of young men that they were justified in taking away the life of a young woman who transferred her affections to another, the consequences indeed would be dreadful.

As Baron Martin completed his duty of ministering sentence, it was reported: 'The heartrending scene in the court will never be forgotten by those who witnessed it; the miserable criminal, however[,] bowed to the learned judge, and left the dock apparently unmoved by the result.'[13]

Judging by the copious press coverage of this case, there was general approval of the guilty verdict (despite there being by this time some rumblings of discontent about the continuation of capital punishment). A leader in the *Daily Telegraph* is typical in approving of the way that the court had set aside the medical evidence:

> If Dr Winslow's theories had been accepted, and if this unhappy Townley had been spared, no one would have been safe.... Dr Winslow's name is widely and deservedly respected; but it is clear enough that his diagnosis of Townley's mental condition was feeble and imperfect.... Had the evidence of the eminent psychologist swayed the Court, one man might have been saved from the gibbet; but hundreds might have qualified for admission to the madhouse or the gaol.[14]

In the days and weeks after the sentence, events descended into farce. The judge, Baron Martin, wrote to the Home Secretary (Sir George Grey) to say that although he thought that the verdict was just, the medical witnesses had testified to Townley's insanity at the point he was interviewed. Since this raised the question of the propriety of the execution, the Home Secretary decided he needed assurance that Townley was not 'now' insane and so he was examined by Lunacy Commissioners in Derby Gaol on 28 December. While they found him to have an 'extraordinarily perverted moral sense', which, coupled with the evidence of hereditary insanity, meant that they could not find him of 'sound mind', they also saw that he was responsible within 'the law as laid down by Mr Baron Martin' (Anonymous 1864: 52). This ambivalent statement seemed to stress the division between the M'Naghten ruling and the psychiatric views of insanity. Meanwhile, Townley's family employed lawyers and their own medical witnesses who certified that Townley was insane. In addition, a series of petitions was raised[15] and nine of the jurors from the trial wrote to the Home Secretary requesting clemency:

> We believe the verdict to be perfectly legal and just, but owing to an absence of premeditation on the part of the prisoner, his previous good character, and the state of his mind as described by the medical evidence, we venture to suggest that the extreme penalty of the law should not be carried into effect without further consideration being given to the case.
> (Anonymous 1864: 39)

The Home Secretary, just 48 hours before the planned execution, ordered that Townley should be sent to an asylum for further examination, and he was consequently taken by train to 'Bethlem' Hospital in London on 5 January. The announcement of the respite led to a huge public outcry. To many of those writing in the newspapers (journalists, leader writers or correspondents), the case was an example of a wealthy family being allowed to buy justice. The *Caledonian Mercury*,[16] for example, was scathing and sarcastic, pointing out that the prosecution's case was very straightforward (given Townley did not deny killing Miss Goodwin):

> When in such circumstances, the worst comes to the worst, there are, thank goodness, the 'mad doctors'. Accordingly, the attempt was made to prove Townley insane. With a felicitious ease only known to theorists, Dr Forbes Winslow proceeded to his demonstrations. . . . Here is something like the Doctor's allegation: – If, he says, a man kills another under the belief that he is responsible to the laws of neither God nor man, there is no murder, because a man who holds these opinions is insane.

The *Lloyd's Weekly Newspaper* was equally condemnatory in suggesting that the only reason for the rethink was that 'Gentility shuddered at the idea of seeing "one of us" hanged'. Townley's wealthy supporters 'spared neither gold nor exertion in his behalf' and 'Medical evidence . . . was bought in hard cash'.[17]

At Bethlem Hospital Townley was examined by other doctors, including Meyer of Broadmoor and Hood of Bethlem (Walker 1968: 208), who declared him to be of sound mind. He was transferred back to Pentonville prison to serve a sentence of a lifetime of hard labour. Here, 'he put an end to the tragic-comedy' (Walker 1968: 208) by throwing himself over the balcony after leaving the prison chapel, where he had loudly sung the last two verses of 'Abide with Me'. In a final twist, at the Coroner's inquest he was assumed to be 'morally insane' and the jury returned the verdict that he killed himself 'whilst in an unsound state of mind'.[18]

The profession of psychiatry moved to protect itself from the negative onslaught and so a considerable portion of the first edition of *The Journal of Mental Science* in 1864 was devoted to the Townley case and a special Commentary on the case was produced by 'The Editors of the *Journal of Mental Science*' (Editors 1864). Leading members of the profession explored the grounds that might have justified leniency towards Townley through discussions of the trial and the diagnostic categories of 'partial insanity', monomania and moral insanity which are here described as 'ill chosen and objectionable'. There is a detectable move to distance themselves from the more psychological notions of 'moral insanity' that had held sway 20 years earlier at the birth of the profession. *The commentary* argued that moral insanity was usually caused by 'hereditary taint' represented in the form of 'nervous disease' (Editors 1864: 25). John Hitchman was given a considerable amount of space (Hitchman 1864: 21–34) to describe his own interview with George Victor Townley and implied that Forbes Winslow was in error (Smith 1981). His account of Townley's behaviour was similar to that of Winslow but there is far more detail given here compared with what is available in the accounts of the trial. Despite the fact that Townley's behaviour and attitudes appear consistent with descriptions of moral insanity as given by Prichard (and others subsequently), Hitchman baulked at arguing that Townley should be regarded as insane before the eyes of the law. He had written to Townley's defence attorney, Mr Leech, that his client 'possessed a feeble intellect associated with strong emotions; that these conditions, aided by a hereditary predisposition to mental disease, may at no distant day cause him to become insane, but that at the present time, he was a rational and responsible person' (Hitchman 1864: 28). He concluded his report: 'I allege that Mr Townley is not now insane, in the legal sense of that term, because he is under no hallucination; because absurd as are his dogmas, in reference to man's responsibility . . . they are theories entertained by hundreds of persons who are capable of all duties of social life'[19] (Hitchman 1864: 28).

Formal interest in moral insanity within British psychiatry declined through the latter half of the century. Indeed, it is striking that just a few years later, in 1867, the very well publicised and brutal murder of 8-year-old Fanny Adams did not seem to raise any serious debate about the sanity of the murderer. Frederick Baker, the 24-year-old office clerk who was hanged for the offence, had somehow kidnapped, killed and very thoroughly dismembered the little girl during his working day. He made no attempt to escape, despite having blood on his clothes and having written in his own diary 'Killed a little girl; it was fine and hot'. Although the issue of insanity, and 'homicidal mania' in particular, was raised in the court, it did not appear to be taken that seriously. The judge argued that the magnitude of the crime should never be taken as evidence of insanity, and a comment piece in the *Journal of Mental Science* did not demur from this point of view, admitting: 'It is not possible, we fear, to call him actually insane, unless we are content to give up all exact notions of insanity.' Nevertheless, as the comment continued, there were grounds to doubt his sanity:

> but there is little doubt that had his life been prolonged, he would have become insane. The evidence at the trial showed that a near relative of his father was in confinement suffering from homicidal mania and that his father had an attack of acute mania. Moreover, it was proved in evidence by independent witnesses that he himself had been unlike other people, that he had been prone to weep frequently without evident reason, that he had exhibited singular caprices of conduct, and that it had been necessary to watch him from the fear that he might commit suicide.
> (*Journal of Mental Science* 1868 Vol XIII: 38)

Had Baker been brought to trial before the M'Naghten trial the outcome might well have been very different, and certainly the issue of insanity would very probably have been raised far more prominently. Indeed, Henry Maudsley himself referred to the case and invoked ideas of homicidal insanity (as a form of monomania or affective insanity) in order to explain the crime: 'the impulsive character of the crime, the quiet and determined ferocity of it, the savage mutilation, his equanimity immediately afterwards, and his complete indifference to his fate – all these indicated an insane organisation' (Maudsley 1874: 163).

The acquiescence of psychiatry to this verdict following the problems of the Townley affair is striking. This is not to say that versions of the insanity defence were not used in the late nineteenth century (a number of interesting cases are discussed by Wiener 1999, for example), but that the specific defences of 'moral insanity' or 'monomania' were not used. It can also be noted that Ainsley (2000) suggests that juries often did put aside the M'Naghten rules when dealing with female defendants, consistent with the longer history of leniency in cases of infanticide. Cases of female homicides were still dwarfed by those committed by men, however.

The special edition of the *Journal of Mental Science* (1864) concluded its discussions of the Townley affair with two substantial recommendations. These can be summarised as, first, advocating the scrapping of the narrow legal maxims of responsibility that were in place since the introduction of the M'Naghten 'rules', and, second, making the case for the professionalisation of the system of expert witnesses so that they would be appointed by the court rather than by either the defence or prosecution.[20] The fact that neither proposal was taken up did not stop the British medical and psychiatric journals from engaging with issues concerning insanity and the law. They were to do this not through the promotion of moral insanity as a defence in court but instead by taking a growing interest in the study of the characteristics of the criminal classes and a very distinct turn back to biological theories of mental disorder.

## 3.3 Psychiatry, biology and the prison population

In the year following the murder of Fanny Adams, Thomas Laycock (1868), Professor of Medicine and Medical Psychology at the University of Edinburgh and President elect of the Medico-Psychological Association at this point, used an address given to the Association[21] to argue that the legal system was poorly adjusted to cope with the growing knowledge of medical matters of insanity. In strongly defending the forensic consequences of medical expertise, he set out a series of ideas that made little claim for expertise in the exploration of individual minds, but far more significant claims to expertise in the disposal of the sections of the population who might be classified as dangerous. Laycock was well known for his work on the physiology of consciousness and had translated German works on psychiatry (Pearce 2002) that were to play an increasing role in the development of psychiatry across Europe and North America (as discussed in some detail in Chapter 5). He followed an explanation of the difficulty of establishing insanity in court and providing appropriate punishments for those who might know that murder was wrong but still be drawn to such acts, with a discussion of the much wider problem of the '*classes dangereuses*' (which he translated into English as 'known to the police') and the larger number of 'incorrigible vagabonds, drunkards, mendicants' who in their tens of thousands are

> so constituted corporally that they possess no self-control beyond that of an ordinary brute animal – nay less than a well-bred horse or dog. They are, for the most part, immoral imbeciles, so that however frequently they may have been subjected to prison or other discipline, the moment they are set free, they resume their vicious and criminal course. . . . They are all the mere weeds of society, but, like weeds they multiply their kind, and thus continually keep up the breed.
> (Laycock 1868: 342–343)

The solution that Laycock indicated was that 'means be taken to restrict their personal liberty during the fertile period of life' in order to counter an otherwise inevitable 'continual increase in the insane, imbecile, vicious, and degraded part of our population' (1868: 344). Laycock, as signalled by his being elected President of the Medico-Psychological Association, was not a lone voice in arguing for a more organic perspective on mental disorder. Henry Maudsley, one of the most influential figures in British psychiatry in the latter half of the nineteenth century, thundered:

> For at least two thousand years, mind has been studied from a psychological point of view, and how vain and fruitless are the results! Assuredly the time has come for studying it, as every other department of nature is studied – inductively, for entering on the investigation of its phenomena from a physiological and pathological basis. Then the results will not fail.
> (Maudsley 1868: 162)[22]

### 3.3.1 Psychiatry in the Victorian prison

As it is clear, the still developing psychiatric profession had found that the courtrooms, and perhaps more especially the surrounding 'public sphere', had not provided a very accommodating arena for the presentation of their expertise in the decades that followed the M'Naghten ruling. There were efforts to establish an expertise in providing testimony on various forms of 'extraordinary states of consciousness' that were linked, for example, to 'peculiar variation(s) of epilepsy' (Eigen 2010: 438) and thus might carry some physiological respectability, but these were not successful. The interest in the relationship between insanity and crime did not go away, however. Instead, as signalled by Thomas Laycock's paper to the Medico-Psychological Society, attention turned away from the defence of individuals in courts and towards the contribution that medical expertise might make to controlling the more general population of criminal offenders. During the nineteenth century there had been a growing interest in, and reliance upon, prison as a means of control, punishment and rehabilitation (Garland 1985). Urgent pressure for a national prison system had come from the sheer weight of the numbers of offenders being sent to prisons. The prison population was growing, first because of the withdrawal of the use of execution (in all but the most serious of crimes) and other forms of physical punishment (such as whipping and branding), and second (and more importantly, in terms of the numbers of people involved), there was the need to find an alternative to transportation (Thomson 1870). Up until the middle of the nineteenth century transportation was still a very important means for British society to get rid of its unwanted members, and the very last transportation ship to Australia sailed in 1868. The first state built prison, for 860 inmates, had been erected at Millbank in 1816. In 1842 Pentonville was built to house 540 inmates. This was modelled on the 'panopticon' and was designed to house inmates in solitary confinement. Over the next six years, 54 prisons were built on this model (Howard League 2014).

The extent to which the move to imprisonment as the cornerstone of the justice system was motivated by the urge to reform individuals or simply to punish them is subject to much debate (Bailey 1997; Garland 1985). It is certainly the case that there was recognition that a large proportion of the prison population was suffering from some form of illness or disability. Contemporary figures compiled by Guy (1869: 169, Table VI) suggest that just over 40 per cent of the convict population were categorised as 'weak minded', insane, epileptic or subject to scrofula, chronic disease or some other deformity or defect. One argument in favour of the reform thesis is that medical practice did become institutionally linked to the prison system. The Act for the Better Government of Convict Prisons in 1850 and the subsequent creation of a central 'Directorate of Convict Prisons' led to the organisation of a prison medical service. It was the formation of a prison medical professional grouping that Davie (2010b: 1) argues led to the 'systematic scientific study of the Criminal in Britain'. The turn of British psychiatry towards the prison system is well represented by the appearance of two articles in the *Journal of Mental Science*, both written by Scottish prison doctor James Bruce Thomson. The first article appears, as the title suggests, to have a clear focus on the hereditary nature of crime (1869), but is heavily influenced by degeneracy theory (which will be discussed in some detail in Chapter 4) to make the case that there was an identifiable 'criminal class'. The more substantial article appeared later in the same year as 'The Psychology of Criminals' (1870). A great deal of the article consists of an engagement with the French theorist Prosper Despine, whose *Psychologie Naturelle*, published in 1868, drew on degeneracy theory (Rafter 2009; Verplaetse 2002). Thomson also considers the various categories of offenders in prisons. He is clear that there are forms of insanity that affect the 'moral faculties', resulting in forms of 'moral insanity'. The focus, however, is still on the fact that criminal types could be regarded as a distinct class, visible as physical types: 'puny, sickly, scrofulous, often deformed, with shabby heads unnaturally developed, sluggish, stupid' (Thomson 1870: 328). The idea of a criminal type was to become highly galvanising, as will be explored in Chapter 5. In the short term, the idea stimulated the Home Office to fund Francis Galton in a project to look at how photography might be used to identify criminal types (Davie 2010b). This project did not succeed, but the interest in classification remained strong, and Galton's attention to the measurement and study of individual characteristics was to have a decisive influence; he went on to found the Eugenics Education Society (later the Eugenics Society). The notion of criminal types was to be taken up and made famous by the advocates of 'criminal anthropology', which came to be virtually synonymous with the work directly influenced by the ideas of Cesare Lombroso. This was an Italian medic who argued that criminality could be explained in terms of the inherited characteristics of the offenders (e.g. Lombroso 2006 [1876]). The publications of Lombroso and colleagues, which enthusiastically put forward the claims made about the genetic faults of miscreants, were adorned with drawings of offenders that illustrated their physiological characteristics. As Rafter and Ystehede (2010) observe, the writing style of Lombroso and followers had more in common with the popular Gothic horror genre of the nineteenth century than with more sober empirical analysis of the facts. Indeed, despite the appeals to scientific rhetoric it quickly became evident that most of Lombroso's claims were simply not sustainable when subjected to empirical review (Goring 1913). This point about the significance of popular imagery of horror and the Gothic is not a trivial one. The following chapter will explore the significance of literary and fictional explorations of the nature of human society and the individual psyche, and argue that the interplay between such fictional narratives and the professional and scientific models was of considerable importance and impacted very directly upon the various ways that theories of moral insanity were to evolve.

Davie (2010a) argues that the British medical and psychological staff never fully embraced the idea that criminal types were simply born that way, and the reasons for this were quite subtle. The accusation of abstract theorising that emerged so strongly in the aftermath of the Townley trial had struck strongly home to British psychiatry. While this applied to such concepts as 'moral insanity', it also applied to such ideas as the 'criminal type' and atavism. Also, the rise of the prison doctors in the late nineteenth century – another plank through which psychiatry could establish its claim to expertise – was predicated on a belief that they could categorise a variety of offenders and make assessment of the rehabilitative potential or incorrigibility of individual offenders. Too great an emphasis on the hopeless diagnosis of 'the criminal type' would undermine the argument for the reformatory nature of the prison and the professional role of medical staff. The category of 'weak minded', Davie (2010b) suggests, was nevertheless a useful one for prison medical staff since it could help explain the poor success of rehabilitative programmes. At the same time there were strong incentives for the case to be made that it was only a proportion of individuals who fitted into these categories and might be identified through psychiatric expertise. The interest in categorisation is evident in Thomson's (1870) work 'The Psychology of Criminals', so although the criminal classes are described and reference made to Laycock's comparison to 'weeds' whose multiplication needed to be controlled by law, there were also descriptions of 'dypsomaniac murderers' who were 'often from the better ranks of society', but whose 'callousness and insensibility' could still astonish, and 'puerperal maniacs' (Thomson 1870: 341).

Not surprisingly, given the drubbing the diagnosis of 'moral insanity' had received in the Townley case, it was almost to disappear from the courtroom (Eigen 2010) and it was to be far less frequently referenced in the psychiatric journals. As Rafter notes (Rafter 2004), the first mention of moral insanity for a decade, following Thomson's use of the term (Thomson 1870), appeared in the July 1881 edition of the *Journal of Mental Science*, but even then it is in a form that is marked by biological considerations. The original article by George Savage, who was Medical Superintendent of Bethlem Hospital, was simply entitled 'Moral Insanity'. The issue was returned to in the same journal in April 1885 in an article by Daniel Hack Tuke. Both accounts maintain that, however 'reviled' the term moral insanity might be (Tuke 1885: 176), there was a worthwhile distinction to be made between disorders that might separately affect the intellectual faculties and the moral, or emotional, faculties. In many respects the descriptions would be considered consistent with many of the case studies in Prichard's classic text. Tuke makes it clear that he is discussing a form of disorder that is not just found in the asylums or criminal courts but: 'They may be the plague of life, the thorn in the flesh, the skeleton in the cupboard' (Tuke 1885: 175). What is striking, however, is that both accounts are now putting their observations within biological frameworks; many cases Tuke suggests are those 'in which there was a constitutional defect' (Tuke 1885: 181). The concern with the hereditary perhaps makes the association with matters of sexuality inevitable, but this was to become an increasing preoccupation. Tuke (1885: 176) notes that in some patients 'uncontrollable sexual proclivities dominated the mind from infancy upwards'. The issue of sexuality and moral insanity caught the attention of Havelock Ellis, whose name was to become associated with studies of sexuality and eugenics, and he argued that the term 'moral insanity' was 'an unfortunate one; the condition described by no means falls in easily as a subdivision of insanity, and it is moreover frequently of a congenital character'. He felt that 'moral imbecility' had thus become the preferable term (Ellis 1890: 229–230). Although Ellis was clearly interested in the physiological bases of insanity and urged British researchers to become more involved in the newly emerging discipline of 'criminal anthropology', there is also a distinct ambivalence and restraint apparent. He notes that 'greater importance was formerly attributed to the shape and measurements of the head than we can now accord to them' (1890: 49). Studies of physiognomy seemed more promising, since '[t]he beard in criminals is usually scanty.... On the head the hair is usually, on the contrary, abundant' (1890: 72–73) and '[b]eautiful faces, it is well known, are rarely found among criminals. The prejudice against the ugly and also against the deformed is not without sound foundation' (1890: 86–87). Ultimately, however, Havelock Ellis is quite restrained in his conclusions about the significance of hereditary factors; in matters of 'criminal heredity' there is an 'element of innate disposition and there is the element of contagion from social environment', and the two were usually difficult to disentangle (Ellis 1890: 91–92). The links between ideas of criminality, heredity and sexuality were to open new and important chapters in the story of moral insanity, which will be explored in the following chapters.

## Conclusion

By the end of the nineteenth century psychiatry was established as a *relatively* respectable profession, and three factors could be identified as accounting for this. The first of these was the establishment of public asylums. The asylums gave psychiatrists a role and an income and a regular source of 'cases' to study. Second, there was the expert contribution of psychiatry to the criminal justice system and to the developing discipline of criminology. The respectability here was precarious, however. The first decades of the nineteenth century had witnessed the triumphant entry of the medical men into the courtroom as experts of the mind. The reversal of fortune suffered in the wake of the establishment of the M'Naghten rules was on one level considerable. The public relations disaster of the Townley affair surely affected psychiatry's confidence in the courts in Britain. By the final decades of the nineteenth century British psychiatry had taken a turn back towards its biological roots. The interest in professing expertise on matters concerning offending had, however, not diminished. The concept of criminal anthropology and explanations of offending entirely in terms of the constitution of the offender were becoming more popular. There was an ambivalence in Britain about these ideas. In part this ambivalence was born through the role assigned to prison psychiatrists, who had little to gain from such blanket pessimism about the capacity for rehabilitation of prison inmates. In other parts of the world there was to be less ambivalence about these ideas.

The third road that psychiatry was to take towards acceptance was through the adoption of the profession's ideas in the public realm. In the end the public and cultural fascination with the mind and with reaching new understandings of the interior world of individuals was to prove of decisive importance to the success of psychiatry. The interaction of ideas born in psychiatry with those of the wider culture of the nineteenth century will be the subject of the next chapter. It will be argued that moral insanity had a life outside the medical texts and clinics, and this was to give the concept very different forms and means of influence. More nuanced forms of insanity were to have a life in fictional literature, where the influence of psychiatric models of monomania and moral insanity was to be evident in the work of some of the most influential novelists of the nineteenth century. It was here that the notions of insanity as hidden and subtle disorders were to be more fully explored even as mainstream psychiatry moved towards blunter models of biological and hereditary disorder. These latter psychiatric theories of degeneration were also to become embroiled with a widespread culture of pessimism and anxiety. It is these two issues that will be explored further in the following chapter.

In terms of theoretical claims, there were two clear pathways for psychiatry to follow. It could become more reliant on biological explanations of behaviour and 'the mind'. This had the major advantage of offering scientific respectability, and it was clearly the route chosen by mainstream psychiatry – well represented by the views of the leaders of the profession, such as Charles Lockhart Robertson and Henry Maudsley, for example, in the last few decades of the nineteenth century.

The second route was to take the road to further exploration of the interior world of the individual psyche. Psychoanalysis was to become the most significant vehicle to take this road and its influence on thinking in psychiatry was to be immense. This latter aspect is taken up further in Chapter 6 particularly, but its influence has continued. Meanwhile, the organic turn in Germany and the United States was even more pronounced in the early decades of the twentieth century. It is this organic turn that will be explored in Chapter 5; ideas about the constitutional basis of moral insanity were to be pursued in the courts and clinics in the United States.

## Notes

1 The organisation received a royal charter in 1926 and thus became the Royal Medico-Psychological Association. It was not until 1971 that it became a medical Royal College.
2 Feuchtersleben can also, according to Werlinder, be credited with using the term 'psychopathy' for the first time. This is significant since by the end of the nineteenth century German psychiatry (discussed in some detail in Chapter 5) was to have become dominated by somatic thinking, and the use of the word 'psychopathy' was to have assumed distinctly organic connotations.
3 Abridged from the *Annales Medico-Psychologiques* by J. T. Arlidge.
4 Old Bailey Proceedings Online (www.oldbaileyonline.org, version 7.0, 9 January 2015), December 1847, trial of William Newton Allnutt (t18471213–290).
5 This case is described by Eigen (2003), who includes the judge's summing up, which is not part of the OBSP.
6 OBP, December 1847, trial of William Newton Allnutt (t18471213–290).
7 The sentence was commuted to transportation. He died of tuberculosis in Australia in 1851, aged 18 (www.convictrecords.com.au/convicts/allnutt/william-newton/39731, accessed 20 November 2014).
8 *Insanity and Crime: A Medico-Legal Commentary on the Case of George Victor Townley*, by the editors of the *Journal of Mental Science* 1864, John Churchill and Sons: London.
9 There are detailed accounts of the inquest in various newspapers, e.g. 'The Dreadful Murder of Miss Goodwin, of Chester' (*Cheshire Observer and Chester, Birkenhead, Crewe and North Wales Times*, Friday 29 August 1863, Issue 430, p. 3).
  There is also a very full account of the events and trial in Anonymous (1864).
10 As witnessed by the notes of the meeting of the Association of Medical Officers of Asylums and Hospitals for the Insane (1857: 9), in which Forbes Winslow notes interviews with Gladstone and Palmerston on matters relating to legislation and insanity.
11 *Derby Mercury* Wednesday 16 December 1863, pp. 3–4.
12 *Derby Mercury* Wednesday 16 December 1863, pp. 3–4.
13 *Liverpool Mercury* Monday 14 December 1863.
14 *Derby Mercury* Wednesday 16 December 1863, p. 8, column 2.
15 Petitions were signed by 963 males and 584 females from Derby, 371 from Wigwell, 140 from Burton-on-Trent and the very large figure of 16,709 from Townley's home town of Manchester. There was another petition raised through immediate friends that had 7,938 signatures (3,251 of them women) (Anonymous 1864: 39).
16 *Caledonian Mercury* Friday 25 December 1863.
17 *Lloyd's Weekly Newspaper* Sunday 14 February 1864, Issue 1108.
18 'Suicide of Victor Townley, who was found guilty and sentenced to death for the murder of Miss Goodwin at Manchester' [London]: Disley (*c*.186–?) (http://pds.lib.

harvard.edu/pds/view/4788255, accessed 14 April 2015). 'Suicide of George Victor Townley'. *Wellington Independent*, Rōrahi XX, Putanga 2207, 18 Haratua 1865, p. 5.
19 Hitchman was referring to the bold godless views of the 'necessitarians', championed by Percy Shelley.
20 Dr Bucknill is quoted to give a flavour of the perception of the problem that medical witnesses could be bought:

> 'An array of medical men,' [as Dr. Bucknill observes,] 'are marshalled by the attorneys on each side according to their preconceived opinions of the case. These medical witnesses may usually be divided into two classes – those who know something of the prisoner and nothing of insanity, and those who know something about insanity and nothing of the prisoner. They generally succeed in neutralizing each other's evidence, and in bringing the medical profession into contempt, at least among lawyers' (p. 46).

21 Subsequently published in *The Asylum Journal* and *The Lancet* in September 1868.
22 Even here the ambivalence about cause needs to be noted. This strong statement is at the end of a long talk/essay on the evils of masturbation – where it is clear that the habit itself is the cause of 'moral insanity' and risks further degeneration to further generations.

# Chapter 4
# Culture and moral insanity
## Selfhood and social degeneration

### Introduction

By the end of the nineteenth century it seemed to be clear that psychiatry had turned its back on the idea that there was a legally defensible notion of moral insanity, understood as a form of monomania, or partial insanity. The doctors of the mind were no longer to be found in the courts arguing for the innocence of prisoners in the dock by claiming an expertise in the detection of such disorders. In the face of public censure and the strictures of the M'Naghten rules it was apparent that the courts were no longer willing to accommodate models of insanity that might involve the detection of hidden pockets of moral insanity in an otherwise sane mind. Therefore, it would be easy to read the story of moral insanity, understood as a product of psychiatry, as having reached an end by the close of the nineteenth century. This was, however, not the end of the story at all. Crucial to an understanding of the evolution of moral insanity is that it had, by the middle of the nineteenth century, a life outside of psychiatry. Even if the courts, under pressure from trenchant criticism in the press, were no longer receptive to these more subtle kinds of insanity that could impact in remarkable ways on people's lives, these ideas were to assume far greater importance in the wider culture of which psychiatry was a part. There should be no surprise at this, for as discussed in Chapter 1 there is evidence that rather nuanced versions of insanity were being discussed in court before there were medical experts there to propound them. In reality there was a great deal of interaction between ideas being generated within the newly formed medical profession of psychiatry and the wider culture, most notably through literature, and the novel in particular. It is here, in the expanding public sphere, that these nuanced conceptualisations of madness survived and flourished. These ideas were, however, jostling for position amidst public anxieties about the pace and direction of social change – anxieties which were to shape ideas about the nature of human society and of the characteristics of human beings. This chapter will review some of the wider social and cultural factors that were instigating and shaping psychiatric theory and practice during the nineteenth century. The themes that emerge from such a review can help us understand the developments that occurred over the following century and a half, and why the questions posed by 'moral insanity' emerged as they did, and how the very different answers to those questions were shaped.

The first section of the chapter will argue that there was a very active interchange of ideas between medical writings on 'psychiatry' and fictional literature. They were both conceiving ways of understanding the new social world emerging out of the ferment of the Industrial Revolution. As discussed in the Introduction, a driving force of the popularity of the novel was its exploration of interiority (Watt 1987); thus the belief that individuals had complex interior lives, where monomanias and moral insanity might be found, was encouraged. It is also striking that depictions of monomanias, as developed by some creative writers (such as George Eliot and Joseph Conrad), influenced by psychiatric and psychological writing of the day, emphasised not only their hidden state within mental interiors, but also their connection to the surrounding social world. This fascination with the exploration of the mind was eventually to be channelled into theories of psychoanalysis that, as will be explored in Chapter 6, were themselves to have great influence on ideas of moral insanity in the twentieth century. The public sphere was not simply a space for disinterested debate, but it was also where major social concerns and anxieties of the century were aired and would thus shape concepts of moral insanity. Shuttleworth (1996: 37) pithily suggested that shifting ideas concerning mental illness over the nineteenth century might be 'plotted directly against the changing patterns of industrial prosperity'. Thus the optimistic prescriptions of moral treatment that emerged through 'the brash confidence' of the early Victorian era were to give way to 'the increasingly pessimistic visions of inherited brain disease and social degeneration propounded by Maudsley and other post-Darwinian theorists writing in the era of economic decline in the latter part of the century'. Shuttleworth's model might well aptly explain some of the developments in the first half of the nineteenth century that saw the ideas of monomania and the new experts being taken seriously in courts.

The second part of the chapter moves to discussing the significance of some of the more 'pessimistic visions' of the latter half of the century. Most notable among these were theories of degeneracy that were themselves products of the interaction of ideas within culture and medicine. Theories of degeneracy were to hold a profound grip on the imagination of western culture in the second half of the nineteenth century. The idea of degeneracy had its roots in Esquirol's French school of psychiatry, particularly in the formal medical texts of Bénédict-Augustin Morel. However, the emergence, and power, of the theory can only be understood in terms of its entanglement with a broad set of social, cultural concerns and anxieties. These anxieties about the pace of social change and the nature of humanity were themselves evident not only in literature but also in medical texts and elements of sociological thought.

## 4.1 The novel, industrialisation and moral insanity

By the second half of the nineteenth century the impact of industrialisation and technological change was in full flow across the western world and it was arguably most evident in Britain (Rubinstein 1998). In a move that Giddens (1991: 20–21) referred to as the 'reflexivity of modernity' these changes were not only to have profound impacts on people's experience and understanding of what it meant to belong to a society (Berman 1982), but the same changes also enabled communication of feelings and ideas that fed, relatively speedily, into further processes of social change. By the end of the nineteenth century, the process of urbanisation that had begun in the eighteenth century was advanced (Perkin 1969). Literacy levels continued to grow so that by the end of the nineteenth century the vast majority of the population was literate. Even by 1840 male literacy in England has been estimated at around 66 per cent, and female around 50 per cent, but by the end of the nineteenth century virtually the whole population could read and write (Stone 1969: 119). Books and newspapers became ever more available to the mass of the population. A serviceable road and canal network developed and railways were making cross-country travel fast and affordable in a way that was unprecedented in human history (Evans 1981; Perkin 1969). Such technological advances were, like any processes of change, likely to raise new anxieties, including those about the capacity of the human body to cope with such leaps.[1]

The availability of the printed word and a population that could not only read those words but understand and respond to them meant that the size of the public sphere was ever larger. The interaction between ideas that were appearing in academic treatises and journals, and in reports of events in newspapers, and reflected upon in popular literature was becoming ever more significant. Ideas on psychology and insanity that might have been born in the formal texts and journals of psychiatry were to become accessible to a growing, and more educated, readership (King 2007; Shuttleworth 1996). As became evident through the trials of Daniel M'Naghten (described in Chapter 2) and George Victor Townley (described in Chapter 3), the expert testimony of medical witnesses in the criminal courts was to face not only the verdict of the gentlemen sitting on the juries, but the gentlemen of the press and their ever wider readerships, which most definitely included women (Donovan 1991). It was often women who, through the deployment of the novel and other popular literary forms, explored the interior worlds of the individual and the new social orders that were emerging and being imagined. The interest in the interior worlds of individuals continued to grow as people sought to understand themselves and the widening circles of people they were expected to 'know'. The spread and popularisation of the novel during the nineteenth century was on the one hand a manifestation of this desire to know more of the interior world of ourselves and others, and on the other was itself a major instigator of this interest (Kearns 1987; Watt 1987). Thus it is no surprise that during the nineteenth century imaginative fictional literature was joined in dialogue, in the public sphere, with the doctors of the mind who were then developing their own literature that sought the exploration of insanity and the mind. While there was evident influence of psychiatry on poetry, with Faas (1988) giving examples of the influence that 'psychiatric' theories had on various themes (in the work of Tennyson and Browning, for example[2]), the most fertile ground was to be found in the novel. Through the Victorian era, Shuttleworth (1996: 14) argues, novelists and physicians were sharing 'similar ground', as novelists 'took on the role of social sage, empowered to diagnose the moral and social illness of the society', while physicians meanwhile were finally winning acceptance as arbiters of 'mental and physiological health'. There were no simple territorial demarcations here as they both strayed across the terrain of the newly emerging industrialised world, fuelling the interaction between fiction and medical literature. The nature of mind explored in fictional work by the likes of Jane Austen, the Brontë sisters, Herman Melville, George Eliot and Joseph Conrad was influenced, as will be discussed, by discussion of topics like monomania that were appearing in medical treatises on insanity and in the reports of criminal trials. A striking point about the nature of the mind that was being sketched in fiction was that it had not only an interiority, but was also social in its nature and was assumed to be reflective of and connected to the social issues of the day.

While commentators on the explosion of interest in the novel at the beginning of the nineteenth century were not always respectful – novels were sometimes seen as trivial romances written by women authors for a female audience (Munday 1982; Behrendt 1994) – this was to have significantly shifted by the middle of the nineteenth century. By then there was an established body of work of literary criticism that was 'clearly in dialogue with contemporary writings on science, religion, sociology, philosophy and politics' (Regan 2001: 2). For example, critical reactions to Jane Austen's work, in the early decades of the century, emphasised the potential importance of her detailed observation of social mores and her documentation of inner dialogue. Walter Scott, who had been very critical of much that had appeared in the form of the novel, noted on reviewing *Emma* (first published 1815) that it suggests 'a knowledge of the human heart, with the power and resolution to bring that knowledge to the service of honour and virtue' (Munday 1982: 208). By mid century there were adverse criticisms of Austen's work for its relatively narrow exploration of the comparatively easily observable and conventional facets of consciousness. Kearns (1987) quotes Charlotte Brontë's criticism of Austen:

> What sees keenly, speaks aptly, moves flexibly, it suits her to study, but what throbs fast and full, though hidden, what the blood rushes through, what is the unseen seat of life and the sentient target of death – *this* Miss Austen ignores; she no more, with the mind's eye, beholds the heart of her race than each man, with bodily vision sees the heart in his heaving breast.
> (Kearns 1987: 141–142)

As Kearns suggests: 'With the word *sentient*, Brontë located emotional life outside of the relatively limited realm of consciousness and within the broader realm of sentience, which incorporates unconscious facts, those that lie outside the range of introspection' (Kearns 1987: 142). Given the interest in the nature of sentience and consciousness, it is no wonder that Charlotte Brontë was to explore the limits of consciousness and sanity in her own fiction (Cohen 2003). Despite some popular narratives that stress the Brontës' isolated lives in rural Yorkshire, they are better understood as being actively engaged in and informed by debates on the social and psychological issues of the day. There is good evidence that the Brontës were influenced by the phrenological theories that were immensely popular in the first half of the nineteenth century (Dames 1996), but perhaps the key influence on the Brontës' writing was the notion that the mind consisted of different, and perhaps warring, faculties (Shuttleworth 1996). Charlotte Brontë's portrayal of the character Bertha Mason (Mr Rochester's wife) in *Jane Eyre* (first published in 1847) has been directly linked to her awareness of Prichard's descriptions of moral insanity (Shuttleworth 1996; Small 1996). It is probably fair to conclude, however, that her use of moral insanity is not based upon close reading of Prichard's text. In some respects the description of Mrs Rochester is of insanity as a wild beast. It was Charlotte's sister Emily Brontë who was to use a far more subtle notion of insanity in her novel *Wuthering Heights* (first published in 1847) with the portrayal of the monomaniacal love of Heathcliff for Cathy Earnshaw. The intent to explore the territory of 'mind' as it existed outside the boundaries of conscious awareness is made clear by Emily Brontë through her inclusion of vivid descriptions of dreams experienced by Lockwood, the narrator (Fine 1969). These are not only suggestive of the narrator's own 'unconscious' mind, which is in touch with the gloomy aggression that surrounds the house he is staying in, but it prefigures and emphasises the passion and violence that underlie the story. It is the portrayal of Heathcliff himself, the damaged and damaging anti-hero, that is most startling and suggestive of the dialogue with psychiatric ideas of the day. In the novel itself Heathcliff is described as having 'a monomania on the subject of his departed idol' while his wits were otherwise 'sound' (Brontë 1870: Chapter 13). As a number of commentators point out, the psychological portrayal of Heathcliff is remarkable (Levy 1996; Shuttleworth 1996), with Symington (1980) specifically arguing that the novel can be read as a detailed psychological case study of 'the psychopath', much as the disorder would be understood within a psychoanalytic object relations theoretical framework that would only appear almost a century later (for discussion of these theories see Chapter 6).

Meanwhile, the concept of monomania was also prominent, and named as such in Chapter 46 of Herman Melville's classic American novel *Moby-Dick* (first published in 1851). In this case Captain Ahab's monomania, his violent obsession to hunt the whale Moby-Dick who had taken his leg some years before drives the narrative of the tale. Melville's very direct engagement with legal concepts of monomania is traced by Henry Nash Smith (2007). He observes that Melville's father-in-law was one Justice Lemuel Shaw of the Supreme Judicial Court of Massachusetts, who had written about the relevance of monomania to criminal trials in 1844. While the obsession with the whale is an entirely conscious one for Ahab, it still invades his sleep: he 'sleeps with clenched hands; and wakes with his own bloody nails in his palms' and is often driven from his hammock by the 'phrensies' whirling around his brain, so that he becomes a different person:

> yielding up all his thoughts and fancies to his one supreme purpose; that purpose, by its own sheer inveteracy of will forced itself against gods and devils into a kind of self-assumed, independent being of its own . . . the tormented spirit that glared out of bodily eyes, when what seemed Ahab rushed from his room, was for the time but a vacated thing, a formless somnambulistic being, a ray of living light, to be sure, but without an object to colour, and therefore a blankness in itself.
> (Melville 1892: Chapter 44: The Chart, 192)

To Melville this monomania is ultimately catastrophically destructive, not only of Ahab himself, but of the boat and its crew. The concept of destructive, even homicidal, monomania is explored with greater delicacy, perhaps, in two of George Eliot's later novels, *Middlemarch* (first published 1871–2) and *Daniel Deronda* (first published in 1876). They both include significant scenes where the death of another might be explained as a homicide occurring through an episode of 'monomania'. Both episodes are explored by During (1988) who locates these significant dramatic events within preoccupations of mid nineteenth-century psychological debates about monomania and its relationship to criminal responsibility. In *Middlemarch* the young doctor Lydgate, who is in Paris studying the role of electricity in muscular movement (emphasising the significance of French biological science at this time) becomes romantically involved with an actress called Laure, who *actually* kills her husband during a scene on stage where she is supposed to pretend to stab him. Lydgate is immediately sympathetic and assumes that it was a terrible accident, but Laure refuses this easy innocence and, according to During, Eliot consciously echoed the notorious case of Henriette Cornier in France (whose infamous decapitation of a 19-month-old girl was widely debated, as described in Chapter 2). When challenged later Laure declares '"The idea came to me. . . . I meant to kill him"'. Lydgate's response is to attempt to put such an act into a comprehensible narrative of an escape from brutality, but Laure denies even this and suggests her motivation was more trivial, and yet although she had not planned it, she had *meant to do it*:

> Laure paused a little and then said, slowly, '*I meant to do it.*'
> Lydgate, strong man as he was, turned pale and trembled: moments seemed to pass before he rose and stood at a distance from her.

'There was a secret, then,' he said at last, even vehemently. 'He was brutal to you: you hated him.'

'No! he wearied me; he was too fond: he would live in Paris, and not in my country; that was not agreeable to me.'

'Great God!' said Lydgate, in a groan of horror. 'And you planned to murder him?'

'I did not plan: it came to me in the play – *I meant to do it.*'

Lydgate stood mute . . . He saw this woman – the first to whom he had given his young adoration – amid the throng of stupid criminals.

(Eliot 1874: 146)

The fact that a rather similar death occurs in Eliot's last novel *Daniel Deronda* (first published in 1876), suggests that Eliot believed there was an issue of some significance here. The eponymous lead character plays the role of advisor to Gwendolen throughout the book. She has made mistakes in her life; she had been drawn to a marriage through a felt need for financial security rather than love, and is left unhappily to endure the consequences of that decision. Towards the end of the book she escapes from this painful and loveless marriage through the death of her husband Grandcourt in a sailing accident. Gwendolen is the only other person present at the incident and declares herself guilty to Daniel, who is by her side soon afterwards. In fragmented monologue she tells him that she had wished Grandcourt dead and that she remembered that as he struggled in the water she hesitated to throw a rope to him that might have saved him:

'I had the rope in my hand – no, there he was again – his face was above the water – and he cried again – and I held my hand, and my heart said, "Die!" – and he sank; and I felt "it is done – I am wicked, I am lost!" – and I had the rope in my hand – I don't know what I thought.'

(Eliot 2013: Book vii 273)

One reading of this is to suggest that Eliot was anticipating Freud in suggesting that hidden unconscious desires are being acted out (Rodensky 2003). During, however, suggests that Eliot is interested in the phenomenon of monomania, since it points to one way in which the violence of patriarchy and women's responses to that violence might be manifested. This idea that Eliot was formulating an understanding of 'monomania' that could be understood as not only a psychological state that existed within individuals but also a social phenomenon is given credence by consideration of Kearns's analysis of her attempts to describe 'mind' as a web of sentience (see Kearns 1987: 200–204 particularly). Kearns (1987: 203) points to an often used quotation from *Middlemarch* to illustrate this: 'For the first time Lydgate was feeling the hampering threadlike pressure of small social conditions, and their frustrating complexity.' The hypothesis that she was exploring how the mind was part of a social web can be given further credibility when it is noted that she and the noted intellectual polymath George Lewes lived together as man and wife. He was arguably an important figure in the spread and development of ideas about a number of topics including psychology, sociology and literature in the middle decades of the nineteenth century. His influence on psychological theorisation was particularly notable, despite his absence from text book accounts of the development of psychology written in the twentieth and twenty-first centuries (Reed 1997). Lewes took on the task of trying to integrate work from philosophy, psychology, literature, physiology and sociology and worked to popularise these ideas by writing relatively accessible texts and magazine articles. His work on physiology was known to be an influence on Pavlov, and he introduced English audiences to diverse authors such as Goethe, Hegel and Comte (Reed 1997: 145). Despite his pivotal role at the time, he now tends to be largely ignored in narrations of the history of psychology, and is often better remembered for his relationship with Eliot. To be fair, this relationship was not merely an incidental domestic relationship. It is well documented that the two were sharing readings and ideas, which perhaps helps us understand why Eliot herself was using notions of mind and consciousness, in her groundbreaking novels, that were also being explored by Lewes in his work on psychology. Eliot's interest in and engagement with contemporary psychological and social theory is well documented. Her interest in phrenology, for example, has been noted, although its appearances in her novels suggest that she became somewhat wary of the strong claims that were being made (Wright 1982). Of more significance here is her exploration of 'the mind' as an entity to be understood as a phenomenon that existed as part of the social realm, or web of sentience (Kearns 1987). This notion of mind as a social web had been formally proposed by Lewes (1879) as he scoped out the anticipated terrain of psychology:

> Man is a social animal – the unit of a collective life – and to isolate him from society is almost as great a limitation of the scope of Psychology, as to isolate him from Nature. To seek the whole data of our science in neural processes on the one hand, and revelations of Introspection on the other, is to leave inexplicable the many and profound differences which distinguish man from the animals; and these differences can be shown to depend on the operation of the Social Factor, which transforms perceptions into conceptions, and sensations into sentiments.
> 
> (Lewes 1879: 78)

Lewes's plea for psychological theorising that did not separate the individual from the social nexus was to go unheeded. By the end of the century the cleavage between social and psychological understandings of the human world was to have particular consequences for constructions of moral insanity: it came to be conceptualised as existing entirely within the body of individuals rather than having any existence within the social realm. Only in the middle of the twentieth century was the notion that such problems needed to be understood as social disorders to emerge again as a theorised concept (as will be discussed in Chapter 7).

Meanwhile, in fiction, 'moral insanity' was alive and well right at the end of the nineteenth century. It makes a prominent appearance in Joseph Conrad's *Heart of Darkness* (first published in 1899); through the portrayal of Kurtz (Bock 2002) Conrad paints a thoroughly psychosocial disorder. The story is narrated by Marlow, a ship's captain who takes a job with a shipping company which trades in the Congo. To reinforce the point that Conrad is using psychiatric discourse in the book, he describes Marlow being sent for a check up with the company's doctor before his assignment. The doctor admits he has the interests of 'an alienist' and is fascinated by the mental changes wrought in those who go 'out there'.[3] The version of 'moral insanity' that Conrad explores through his characterisation of Kurtz is one that is powerfully linked to conceptions of 'the social', but in rather a different way from that which During (1988) suggests of Eliot. Written with a sense of foreboding as European colonial adventures were finally collapsing in moral disgrace (Watt 1979), the novel describes how Kurtz is rendered morally insane because he has become free of the binds and inhibitions of a social web. As Marlow travels up the river towards Kurtz's domain he sees evidence of the cruelty and brutality of the operation being run there and starts to hear stories about Kurtz's regime. Marlow feels alarmed by the unscrupulous methods being used and then he is horrified (but fascinated) by Kurtz when he meets him. Conrad's use of psychiatric descriptions and debates about moral insanity become apparent as Kurtz's intelligence is described as 'perfectly clear' while 'his soul was mad':

> There was nothing either above or below him, and I knew it. He had kicked himself loose of the earth. Confound the man! He had kicked the very earth to pieces. He was alone, and I before him did not know whether I stood on the ground or floated in the air . . . Soul! If anybody has ever struggled with a soul, I am the man. And I wasn't arguing with a lunatic either. Believe me or not, his intelligence was perfectly clear – concentrated it is true, upon himself with horrible intensity, yet clear, . . . But his soul was mad. Being alone in the wilderness, it had looked within itself, and by heavens! I tell you it had gone mad. . . . I saw the inconceivable mystery of a soul that knew no restraint, no faith, and no fear, yet struggling blindly with itself.
> 
> (Conrad 1933: 374)

Conrad was writing right at the end of the nineteenth century, a time of *fin de siècle* tension (Marshall 2007) and change. The imperial enterprises of the past couple of centuries were looking frayed and were clearly coming to an end (Arata 1996), and Conrad was able to draw on his own experiences of witnessing the decline of the European colonial project. Conrad's portrayal of Kurtz is of someone who has 'kicked himself loose of the earth' and become an amoral husk, driven only by acquisitive desire as he acts free of the ties and restraints of civilisation. As Walcutt (1968: 100) observed, Conrad deliberately explores what happens to his characters when taken out of their conventional environment 'where they are free from the dulling confines of routine, manners and security'.

Thus the concept of monomania, particularly a violent and destructive one, as a symptom of a mind that had depth and hidden facets, continued in culture despite its decline in formal psychiatry. Nevertheless, at least through the writing of Conrad and Eliot, it was also a concept that was assumed to belong not only to the psychological but also to the social dimension. The link between internal states and the social body was to be made directly through the development of degeneracy theory, which was to become a hugely important theoretical framework in the second half of the nineteenth century (Pick 1989). Indeed, Dollimore places Conrad's *Heart of Darkness*, and particularly his portrayal of Kurtz, within a paradigm of degeneracy theory, suggesting that Kurtz might be considered what Max Nordau[4] was calling at this time a 'higher degenerate': 'excessively, dangerously, brilliant because endowed with an intelligence which has evolved *too* far, and at the expense of the other faculties, especially the ethical ones, which have become correspondingly atrophied' (Dollimore 1998: 145). It will be argued in the following section that although the concept of 'degeneracy' had its formal roots as a theory of organic, medical and 'psychiatric' deterioration, it was really an all-encompassing theory of social and cultural deterioration which emerged from a very general sense of anxiety about social change and decline. We will come back to some of the particular imagery used in *Heart of Darkness* in relation to notions of degeneracy, which was such a widespread and influential idea in the latter half of the nineteenth century. As will be discussed, Conrad also very directly, and with savage scepticism, engaged with theories of degeneracy in his novel *The Secret Agent* (Hunter 1983).

In a very important sense the metaphor of society as forming a 'social body', through the entanglement with the medical theorisation of degeneracy, was to become regarded as not simply a *mere* metaphor (see Poovey 1995, for a discussion of the significance of 'the social body' as metaphor in the mid nineteenth century). The population of human beings came to be viewed as a mass of organically connected material which could be subject to disease and was in need of treatment. The concept of moral insanity, construed as a symptom of organic decline, was to play a considerable role in the formulation of some of the most powerful forms of 'treatment' prescribed for that social body, as discussed in the next chapter. The next section will explain how connected the idea of 'moral insanity' was to this grander theory of degeneration.

## 4.2 Degeneracy: psychiatry and culture

The growing public sphere was not only an arena in which ideas about the psychology and the nature of the social world could be exchanged. It was also a space where anxiety could be fostered and might be allowed to shape those ideas. As social theorists have noted (e.g. Giddens 1991), the growing population of the modern world of the nineteenth century (of which Britain was one of the prominent examples) was indeed becoming better informed, but also arguably more anxious. There were existential anxieties to be found amidst ideas emerging from the natural sciences (notably Darwinian theories of evolution) that challenged any sense of divine or natural order and asked questions about the nature of humanity and its distance from the supposedly primitive behaviour of the animal kingdom. There were also more tangible reasons for anxiety. The better off were, often justifiably, worried about the presence of a growing class of people excluded from the spoils of Empire. Henry Mayhew's descriptions of London emphasised the

> incongrous chaos of the most astounding riches and prodigious poverty – of feverish ambition and apathetic despair – of the brightest charity and the darkest crime . . . the very best and the very worst types of civilized society are to be found . . . where there are more houses and more homeless – more feasting and more starvation.
> (Mayhew and Binny 1862: 18–19)

While Britain was not experiencing the revolutions and attempted revolutions that France and Germany were witnessing, the anxiety of such unrest was immanent for middle and upper class anxieties. It seemed clear to the Victorian bourgeoisie that the health of the mass of the population was poor, and levels of crime and other manifestations of apparent moral depravity (such a s prostitution, drunkenness and sexual incontinence) were high (Jones 1971; Pratt 1998).

As the nineteenth century trundled towards its end, a rather amorphous set of theories began to coalesce around the theme of social anxiety and the feeling that 'society' was generally deteriorating. These theories were to develop under the name of 'degeneracy', a concept that emerged formally in French psychiatry. It was not only to have very specific implications for the construction of ideas of the nature of moral insanity but was to wield considerable influence within popular culture, politics, medicine and the newly developing human and social sciences across the western world (Chamberlin and Gilman 1985). The theory of degeneration has its roots in the French school of *aliénistes* surrounding Esquirol. The theory was fleshed out by Bénédict-Augustin Morel who, though born in Vienna (of French parents), trained at the Salpêtrière in the 1830s (Harris 1989). It was not surprising therefore that Morel's initial preoccupations were typical of the time and were focused on the concept of monomania as developed by Esquirol (Goldstein 1998: 388). Esquirol's work may be best remembered for his classification of individual insanity but it was also steeped in anxiety about the newly emerging social world and the lack of moral fortitude in people's lives: 'For thirty years, the changes that have been going on in our morals in France, have produced more insanity than our political troubles. We have exchanged our ancient usages and opinions, for speculative ideas, and dangerous innovations' (Esquirol 1845: 42).

Esquirol was scathing about the behaviour of the wealthy, whose marriages were 'mere pretences, which are formed . . . either as speculation, or to gratify their self-love', as well as the lower classes, where 'corruption is most general, greatest, most hideous' and 'gives birth to almost all the evils of society; that it produces much insanity, and at the same time much more of crime than in the higher classes' (Esquirol 1845: 43). Morel's theory of *dégénérescence* emerged into this same gloomy atmosphere and his own work moved far from the idea of monomania in the sense of a disorder to be discovered hidden in the mind of an individual. Yet these ideas of degeneration were to have a powerful influence on the way different and dangerous individuals came to be perceived and treated, so Morel's theory is worth dwelling on here. Dowbiggin (2004: 191) describes his treatise as having good claim to be 'the most influential psychiatric text of the 19th century', presenting no less than 'an anthropologic-psychiatric view of European civilization'. It was not simply a theory about the hereditary transmission of disease, but was a mixture of 'religious conceptions and anthropological hypotheses, as well as theories of disease and heredity' (Werlinder 1978: 57). Morel's theory of *dégénérescence* emphasises the interconnection of mental, physical and social disorders, and it was work on degeneration that was to provide psychiatry with a rationale for a route back towards a more organic perspective. It does need to be recognised, however, that degeneration is very far from being simply a theory of the hereditary nature of mental and physical ill health. As Daniel Pick explains, even in Morel's formal definition of degeneracy, he 'pulled together a bewildering array of physical conditions, moral and social habits' that included hernias, goitres and various physical defects including deafness and blindness, as well as the impact of tobacco, opium and alcohol. Morel also explored 'disturbances of the intellectual faculties and the noxious tendencies of certain forms of romanticism which resulted in languorous desires, effeteness, reveries, impotence, suicidal tendencies, inertia, melancholy and apathy' (Pick 1989: 50).

One of the curiosities of Morel's work is that his treatise was never published in English or German. The influence of his name is all the more remarkable, but this does mean that perhaps it is the essence, or particular understandings of the essence, of this work that has been so influential. Werlinder (1978: 58) summarises Morel's theory of degeneration in terms of three central ideas:

1  Nervous and mental illnesses are in most cases passed on by hereditary means although they might be acquired in the life of an individual. There is the Lamarckian belief in the inheritance of acquired characteristics.

2  The mechanism of heredity is 'polymorphic' (meaning that the same hereditary disease could manifest in different symptoms).
3  The diseases tend to be characterised by progressive deterioration, which sometimes occurs during an individual's life span, but more ordinarily occurs from one generation to the next.

Thus, although theories of degeneration were reinforced by the popularity of Darwinian theories of evolution, this was not straightforwardly a theory of 'natural selection'. The fact that individual characteristics could be acquired during the lifetime of an individual and then passed down to the next generation opened the door to the idea that the life conditions and habits of an individual would themselves have an impact on the physique and sanity of their offspring and thus have ever growing influence on the broader social body. Morel's theorisation was steeped, like that of his tutor Esquirol, in nineteenth-century anxiety about industrialisation and social change:

> Working in dangerous or insalubrious occupations and living in unhealthy, over-populated cities, the human organism is subjected to unprecedented agents of debilitation and consequently degeneration ... Despite all the progress science has made, it is impossible that he should not be transformed by bad working conditions in the factories and mines where he is forced to spend most of his days in the bowels of the earth. Now add to these generally bad conditions the profoundly demoralizing influence of poverty, lack of education, want of thrift, abuse of alcohol, sexual excess, and inadequate nourishment, and you will have some idea of the complex circumstances which tend to modify unfavourably the temperaments of the poor classes.
> (Morel 1857: vii, quoted in Harris 1989: 54)

Nye (1985: 60) suggests that it was no coincidence that the initial ideas of degeneration sprang from France, since the recently available statistics suggested that the 'nation was suffering from a variety of internal ailments', marked by 'a birth rate [that] was dramatically lower than other European states' and which dipped below the mortality rate before the end of the nineteenth century. Rates of alcoholism, insanity and criminality were estimated to be high and growing. According to Nye, doctors estimated that 13–15 per cent of the Parisian male population had syphilis. As Harris (1989) argues, the very pessimistic view of insanity as being relentlessly created by a mix of social circumstances and the inherent weaknesses in the population had a certain utility to the fledgling profession of psychiatry in France. Even by the 1850s and 1860s it was clear enough that the triumphant claims for the curative value of their treatment methods in the asylums were proving hard to sustain. The asylum populations were growing and many of the inmates seemed not to be easily returned to their communities as rational and functioning citizens. There was similar interest in theories of degeneration elsewhere. British psychiatry had taken on a distinctly pessimistic hue well before the end of the nineteenth century. The association of degeneration with acquired characteristics was very evident in Henry Maudsley's work in Britain and Krafft-Ebing's in Germany. Werlinder (1978: 62) quotes Krafft-Ebing (from his 1875 work *Lehrbuch der gerichtlichen Psychopathologie*): 'anything that weakens the nervous system or reproductive capacity of the progenitor, whether this might be extreme youth or too advanced age, undergone debilitating illnesses (typhus, syphilis, tuberculosis), mercury cures, alcohol and sexual excesses, over-exertion, etc. can result in a neuropathic constitution and through this lead to every possible nervous disease in the progeny'. The idea of degeneracy, with its mix of eugenical zeal and anxiety about the growing urban poor, powerfully informed the work of the Scottish prison doctor James Bruce Thomson, who described a 'criminal class' as having:

> A locale and a community of their own in our great cities . . . in the midst of foul air and filthy lairs they associate and propagate a criminal population. They degenerate into a set of demi-civilized savages. . . . Regardless of the rules of consanguinity . . . they beget a depraved and criminal class hereditarily disposed to crime. . . . They are born into crime, as well as reared, nurtured and instructed in it; habit becomes a new force – a second nature, superimposed upon their original moral depravity.
> (Thomson 1869: 488)

Beyond the world of psychiatry, the idea that noxious environments and people's own immorality could seep into the individual body and could then accumulate in subsequent generations, leading to a weakened form of humanity, seems to have appealed to some who were watching the enormous social and industrial changes of the nineteenth century with trepidation.

It was not only the pace of change that was creating anxiety; new ideas were also contributing to growing uncertainty about a reliable natural order. Some of these uncertainties were to arouse profound anxieties about sexual matters (Chaperon 2010). The most obvious set of disturbing ideas was that surrounding the publication of Charles Darwin's *On the Origin of Species* in 1859, which not only had an impact on the natural sciences but was to have marked influence on literature. Hurley (1996: 10) describes the influence of Darwinism on elements of 'Gothic' literature in the latter part of the nineteenth century, which explored the felt horror of the 'intimate continuity between humans and the "lower" species'. The idea that civilised human behaviour was simply a veneer that covered up far more troubling and primitive impulses was to become something of a Victorian fascination and had important implications for the treatment of those individuals who seemed to embody these fears through their violent, criminal and deviant behaviour. Bram Stoker's *Dracula* and Stevenson's *Jekyll and Hyde*, two of the most popular and celebrated fictional works of the late nineteenth century, are good examples of a particular 'urban gothic' (Donovan 2009), born of this particular anxiety that not only 'blurred the boundaries between human and animal' (Spencer 1992: 204) but also shifted the territory of horror away from isolated rural settings and into the city. *Jekyll and Hyde* (and part of *Dracula*) is set in London, where the dangers of the erosion of traditional community roles and relationships seemed readily apparent. Both works provide a significant contrast in terms of whether moral insanity is a potential within all of us or something that only exists in other stranger creatures. Robert Louis Stevenson's *The Strange Case of Dr Jekyll and Mr Hyde* was to become perhaps the most famous portrayal of the 'primitive' element within individuals. Published in 1886, this was 'a literary sensation', selling over 40,000 copies in its first six months (Lacey 2009: 2). The story has the hard-working and largely virtuous Dr Jekyll invent a potion that turns him into the evil Mr Hyde. The stimulating horror of the novel is that Hyde, drawn with ideas related to degeneracy with a 'hardly human', 'troglodytic' appearance and 'ape-like fury' and all his venial desires unchecked by conscience, is actually a part of Dr Jekyll as well. Jekyll finds himself having to accept that man is not simply a being with one unitary consciousness, but is made up of at least two different kinds of beings, and that perhaps 'man will be ultimately known for a mere polity of multifarious, incongruous and independent denizens' (Stevenson 1886: 'Henry Jekyll's Full Statement of the Case'). The even more disturbing theme was that Jekyll, despite knowing that Hyde was not 'morally sane', found himself being drawn back to the potion again and again to live as Hyde. There was pleasure to be had as Hyde, as is evident from his first experiment with the potion:

> I felt younger, lighter, happier in body; within which I was conscious of a heady recklessness, a current of disordered sensual images running like a millrace in my fancy, a solution of the bonds of obligation, an unknown but not an innocent freedom of the soul. I know myself, at the first breath of this new life, to be more wicked, tenfold more wicked . . . and the thought in that moment, braced and delighted me like wine.
>
> (Stevenson 1886: 78)

Mighall describes how Stevenson portrays an urban version of 'going native', typical of the 'anthropological' focus of late-Victorian Gothic 'that involved a double movement: outwards to the margins of Empire, and inwards to focus on the domestic "savages" which resided in the very heart of the civilized world, and even in the ancestral memory of the modern civilized subject' (Mighall 1999: 136). Just such a 'double movement' is amply represented in Conrad's *Heart of Darkness*, already discussed for its portrayal of moral insanity in Kurtz. Conrad also has his character Marlow in *Heart of Darkness* allude to the thrill and anxiety of nineteenth-century explorers as they experienced a sense of connection with the supposedly 'primitive' tribes they encountered, who on the surface appeared so different from 'civilised' European man that they might not be the same species. They were of course 'not inhuman' at all:

> Well, you know, that was the worst of it – this suspicion of their not being inhuman. It would come slowly to one. They howled, and leaped, and spun, and made horrid faces; but what thrilled you was just the thought of their humanity – like yours – the thought of your remote kinship with this wild and passionate uproar. Ugly. Yes, it was ugly enough; but if you were man enough you would admit to yourself that there was in you just the faintest trace of a response to the terrible frankness of that noise, a dim suspicion of there being a meaning in it which you – you so remote from that night of first ages – could comprehend. And why not? The mind of man is capable of anything – because everything is in it, all the past as well as all the future.
> 
> (Conrad 1933: 187)

In the hands of thoughtful writers like Stevenson and Conrad these anxieties about the nature of humanity can be read as pleas for a more sophisticated and realistic understanding of ourselves. However, another response to the anxiety created by the sense of primitive connection, the feelings of disgust and fascination with the 'animalistic' traits that were now hypothesised to be an integral part of humanity, was to deny their existence within 'us' and instead to suggest that they lived only within particular individuals or groups. This 'othering'[5] facet of degeneracy theory is explored by Conrad in *The Secret Agent*, in which the cynical and powerful men who pull the strings of the secret service organisations and the revolutionary groups who are trying to outwit each other are both obsessed with theories of degeneration (Greenslade 1994). By having the revolutionaries guided by theories of degeneration Conrad is emphasising the detectable traces of Enlightenment utopianism amidst the sooty fog of existential gloom clinging to the industrial cityscapes of *fin de siècle* London. While theories of degeneration did on the one hand encourage nightmares of the collapse and ruin of human society, and indeed of the human species, they also opened up alternative fantasies of the potential for purity and redemption if only the right measures were taken. To adopt the language of psychoanalysis, it might be argued that this kind of 'denial' led to the projection of these feared characteristics on to other groups. Such projective processes can be fairly clearly traced within racist discourses and narratives about urban slum dwellers (Booth 1890), but also within another powerful current of thought associated with 'criminal anthropology'. As noted in Chapter 3, the similarities between the Gothic fiction of the late nineteenth century and the interest in the 'criminal anthropologists', such as Lombroso, are quite evident (Rafter and Ystehede 2010). It may be no surprise therefore to find Lombroso's work referred to in Bram Stoker's *Dracula*, published in 1897. One feature of the book is the engagement with contemporary medical debates, with particular attention being paid to Lombroso's theories.

Dracula is described as 'a criminal type' as classified by Nordau and Lombroso (Stoker 2009: 542). The obsession with sexuality and contamination in this work have drawn a great deal of comment, with many writers noting the insistent sexual themes of the threat of, and fascination with, an alien sexual presence that provokes desire in men and women alike (Davison 1997). Spencer (1992: 198) argues that the emergence and success of *Dracula* needs to be understood in terms of a culture in crisis struggling with the impact of diminishing confidence in imperialism, the somatic nature of humanity and gender conflict. The setting of the main drama in London was consistent with the view that true horror lay 'at our own doors' (Spencer 1992: 199) and the horrors that might be lurking there were to do with the blurring and questioning of sexual boundaries. Women were beginning to make demands for education and equality that not only threatened male privilege but also the social order itself. Male homosexuality had also forced its way into public consciousness with the trial of Oscar Wilde in 1895 and the Cleveland Street brothel scandal of 1889. The success of a story like *Dracula* was fuelled by its capacity to channel anxieties about corrupting influences that might lie within away from ourselves and on to 'safe' external targets (Spencer 1992).

The boundaries between such fictional accounts and work stressing the scientific credentials of the authors became blurred, and Lombroso's own work was arguably influenced by the Gothic (Rafter and Ystehede 2010). In an often quoted paragraph (e.g. Pick 1989: 122; Wolfgang 1961: 369) Lombroso describes how he himself came to his insights about the origins of criminality when performing the post-mortem examination of a particularly notorious criminal. The febrile language used here could have come straight from a Gothic horror novel:

> This was not merely an idea, but a revelation. At the sight of that skull, I seemed to see all of a sudden, lighted up as a vast plain under a flaming sky, the problem of the nature of the criminal – an atavistic being who reproduces in his person the ferocious instincts of primitive humanity and the inferior animals. Thus were explained anatomically the enormous jaws, high cheek-bones, prominent superciliary arches, solitary lines in the palms, extreme size of the orbits, handle-shaped or sessile ears found in criminals, savages, and apes, insensibility to pain, extremely acute sight, tattooing, excessive idleness, love of orgies, and the irresistible craving for evil for its own sake, the desire not only to extinguish life in the victim, but to mutilate the corpse, tear its flesh, and drink its blood.
> (Lombroso 2006: xiv–xv)

As noted in the previous chapter, while the reception of Lombroso's work among penologists in Europe was often ambivalent, there is no doubting his wider influence. It is striking that the German cultural critic Max Nordau chose to dedicate his influential book *Degeneration* (*Entartung*), published in 1892, to Lombroso. The publication and success of Nordau's work might best be regarded as degeneration theory taking a cultural turn. It is a highly polemical book that reads as a howl of protest at the direction that European society and culture was taking at the end of the nineteenth century. The dedication to Lombroso was doubtless due to Lombroso's pronouncements on the significance of physiologically based degeneration and criminality, but Nordau also mentions 'the smiling serenity with which you pursue your own way, indifferent to ingratitude, insult, and misunderstanding' (Nordau 1895: dedication). If it is possible to summarise Nordau's wide-ranging assault on the direction of culture and art, one might say that, as they shaped human consciousness, those forms of culture that Nordau judged to be inferior were themselves contributing to the further degeneration of the species. It is perhaps somewhat ironic that the notion that so-called degenerate art could have a toxic impact on culture was taken very seriously by Adolf Hitler and the Nazi Party. Hitler believed it was very important that his Third Reich should take firm control of the whole of German culture, including its art. In order to make it clear to all just which forms of art were acceptable and which were not, Hitler instructed Goebbels to organise an exhibition of 'degenerate art' in 1937 (Zalampas 1990). The exhibition was housed in the gallery of the Hofgarten arcades in Munich and included the work of 112 artists whose work had been confiscated from museums across Germany. The work was deliberately badly hung, and ridiculed. The list of the artists represented reads like an inventory of some of the most celebrated artists of the twentieth century, including Max Ernst, George Grosz, Paul Klee and Max Beckmann (Peters 2014). One of the ironies of the affair was that Max Nordau had Jewish roots and also identified German anti-Semitism as a symptom of 'hysterical' German degeneracy. Of course, the story of the exhibition might be a diverting historical footnote were it not for the fact that the notion of degeneracy was to go on to fuel the marginalisation, separation and extermination of millions of people who were seen as falling short of the Aryan ideal. The story of how degeneracy came to play a role in the Holocaust is very directly linked to the theories of moral insanity that took a distinctly organic turn in the early decades of the twentieth century as they became entangled with theories and practices of eugenics. Theories of eugenics were very widespread, with the term itself originating from Francis Galton's work in London, though (as will be explored in the following chapter) England was not to be the main site of eugenical practice. It was instead the United States that was first to see the widespread use of eugenical practice in the criminal justice system, as solutions were sought to cleanse the social body of criminal elements. The reasons why Britain did not put eugenics into practice are no doubt complex (and some are discussed in the following chapter) but it might in part be to do with the strength of ideas about the social body not simply being about organic material. A rather different conceptualisation of the social body emerging from France stressed the idea that society itself was a determining force.

While France spawned the formal theorisation of degeneracy theory, it also produced the new discipline of sociology. Themes of anxiety about social change loom large in the work of Auguste Comte (e.g. Comte 1855) and Émile Durkheim (e.g. Durkheim 1982). As a set of ideas that could categorise feelings about the growing urban spaces with their expanding populations of troublesome poor, it is perhaps not surprising that the language of degeneracy was also to be found in the texts of the nascent discipline of sociology. Pick notes how even Émile Durkheim, who so clearly enunciated the idea that social phenomena had existence outside of the individual body and mind (Durkheim 1982), was at the same time 'captivated by the medical analogy of sickness and health' (Pick 1989: 97). His *Division of Labour* (1893) most notably relied heavily on an 'organicist discourse' (Pick 1989: 98), through the concept of organic solidarity and the functional metaphor of the different facets of society being akin to the organs of a body. It is certainly only fair to say, however, that Durkheim never propagated degeneracy theory itself, as Hawkins (1999) emphasises. Indeed the insistence of the founders of the discipline of sociology that social factors were, in Durkheim's terms, *sui generis* and could thus operate quite independently of biological and psychological factors, helped steer much thought away from a focus on inferior and dangerous individuals. In Britain, Charles Booth's detailed exploration of the lives of the English working class was crucially influenced by this line of thought. His work was to have a fundamental impact not only on British sociology and social policy but also on the development of sociology in the US through its influence on the work of the Chicago School in the early twentieth century (Gidley 2000). Charles Booth is a good example of someone who was clearly concerned with the moral impact of mass urban poverty but very plainly distanced himself from eugenical conclusions. Instead he was keen to emphasise the causal impact of poverty itself. It is very notable, for example, that in the final volume (Booth 1903: 26) he goes to some lengths to argue that the relationship between poverty and high birth rates was best explained, not by the recklessness of the poor, but by the high child mortality rates. If you improved the conditions for the very poor, their children would be less likely to die and they would have fewer of them as they became less poor, was his unflappable logic. Even James Bruce Thomson, whose studies of the prison population (also discussed in Chapter 3) are shot through with the claims of degeneracy theory, notes:

> Who can doubt that the poor and the criminal classes, born and brought up amidst the foul and poisoned air of the lanes, wynds, and closes of over crowded cities, have a physical deterioration, and are a class of men and women totally different from the rich and great communities in the well ventilated streets and squares of the West End.
> (Thomson 1870: 329)

This stance towards the significance of the environment ultimately had considerable impact on the development of welfarism in Great Britain, where the eventually chosen route for assuaging anxiety about the growing urban masses was to try to improve the material conditions of the mass of the population through health, education, housing and welfare systems. Another route was clearly being proposed during the latter half of the nineteenth and early decades of the twentieth century: eugenical solutions, whether of the positive or negative varieties. It was the latter strategy that was to find a remarkable place in aspects of legal and social policies in a number of states of the USA, and of course most dramatically in the Third Reich of Germany. This story will be taken up further in Chapter 5.

## Conclusion

By the end of the nineteenth century, psychiatry had largely established itself as a profession, legitimated within the development of the state. An important stage in the process was the contribution that psychiatry could make to the workings of the criminal justice system. As described in Chapter 2, in the first half of the nineteenth century the entry of the mad-doctors into the courtroom had been quite triumphant and their claims for expertise in the body of knowledge about hidden forms of insanity in the shape of monomania, partial insanity and moral insanity achieved a degree of legal acceptance. The second half of the nineteenth century witnessed a reversal of fortune for these notions of non-manifest insanity, and the young and vulnerable profession had to adjust. Psychiatry had its base in the asylums and began to make claims to categorisation of criminal types, but it was also making major inroads into, and was firmly in interaction with, the wider culture. So while, as described in Chapter 3, psychiatrists were no longer to be found identifying 'moral insanity' in defendants in court, the ideas did take on a different life in wider cultural discourse, in particular in the burgeoning world of literature. As argued in Chapter 1, the first appearances of what looked like forms of monomania in the court seemed to emerge amidst perceptions of changing community and gender relations. These issues seem to loom larger during the nineteenth century, when psychiatry was very explicitly drawn into what was often anxious debate about the direction of social change. The pessimistic views on this were to be given full voice through theories of degeneracy that were to lead to determinedly biological views of the nature of moral insanity. By 1874 Henry Maudsley, by then a major figure in British psychiatry, was still propounding a view of 'moral insanity', whose characteristics he was content to describe as being quite consistent with those described by Prichard in 1835. Maudsley (1874: 181–182), however, unswervingly assumed that 'moral insanity is a disorder of mind produced by a disorder of brain'.

The amalgam of anxiety about degeneracy with biological psychiatry, which had strong ideas about the organic roots of 'moral insanity' (buoyed by German organicist thinking), was to make massive inroads into public policy in the US. The next chapter will focus on how ideas about the biological nature of moral insanity were to lead to the widespread implementation of eugenical policies. Of course, the more 'psychological' notions of mental health had not gone away. They were to receive a massive boost at the end of the nineteenth century, largely through the work of Sigmund Freud. We will come back to the important influence of these ideas in Chapter 5.

## Notes

1  Charcot's intervention in the debate about 'railway spine' and the danger posed by the speed of railway travel and its relation to hysteria is a particularly notable illustration of this (Keller 1995).
2  There should be little surprise about the interaction between psychology and literature here. As Rousseau (1991: 582) points out, prior to the nineteenth century the development of imaginative literature was crucial as 'the solitary beacon shaping the reader's sense of his or her Self and of the Other, and of virtually all the normal and pathological states lodged in between'.
3  As part of a general physical check up, he also takes measurements of Marlow's skull but explains that he does not see people to take the measurements again when they return; there would be little point since 'the changes take place inside'.
4  Max Nordau's work *Degeneration* (1895), published in German as *Entartung* in 1892, is a wide-ranging attack (utilising some of the 'medical' conceptualisations of degeneracy) on the direction of western culture, claiming it is degenerating.
5  As described by Blackman (2008: 48) 'Darwinistic evolutionism' was part of a process which *Othered* – that is, which considered that groups such as 'colonial subjects, people with different sexualities and the working classes' were alien, inferior and degenerate.

Chapter 5

# Moral imbecility
## Feeblemindedness and the road to eugenics

### Introduction

The previous chapter described how the notion of moral insanity had spread beyond the medical texts and courtrooms of the nineteenth century. While it often appeared in fictional literature as a hidden psychological disorder, sometimes itself assuming strong cultural dimensions, by the end of the century the concept had become became thoroughly enmeshed in medical literature with ideas of 'degeneration'. As discussed, this latter term covered an amorphous set of ideas that connected a range of anxieties prompted by the perception of the spread of disease, immorality, disorder and crime among the growing urban populations. There was also the uneasiness raised by discussion of Darwin's theories of evolution, which suggested that human beings contained within them the animalistic characteristics of 'lower' species, and the connected concern that civilisation might be blunting the impact of processes of natural selection, allowing weaker genotypes to flourish. For much of the nineteenth century these anxieties were vague enough to cling around beliefs concerning not only the biological inheritance of weaknesses, but also the social and environmental factors and the immoral habits of individuals which themselves could trigger and sustain 'degeneration'. By the end of the nineteenth century, among particular professional groups, these ideas had crystallised around a narrower belief in the genetic Mendelian inheritance of weakness, disorder and disease (Field 1911). The idea that moral insanity might be a very particular hidden psychological state, a monomania as described by the likes of Esquirol, or even one that might be connected to a social web of sentience as arguably depicted by Eliot (see During 1988) was to be set aside by groups of psychiatrists who settled instead on notions of moral insanity that were entirely bred, and existed in the body of particular categories of individual. The rejection of moral insanity as a defence in the courts (as described in Chapter 3) had not dampened the desire of the medical specialists in madness to have their say on matters of criminal justice. By the latter decades of the nineteenth century some medics in Britain were attempting to develop an expertise in 'prison psychiatry' by turning their gaze on the growing population of offenders, who were no longer executed or deported, but instead accumulated in the growing prison systems (also discussed in Chapter 3). The strategy became one of categorisation, and new categories were thus created. The category of 'feeblemindedness' was to be especially useful in allowing for the elision of moral insanity with ideas of constitutional inferiority. It was this category of feeblemindedness that was to have considerable implications for the many individuals, initially in the United States, who would be confined and/or sterilised on the grounds of the perceived weakness of their genetic material and its association with criminality. Perhaps the earliest and most systematic enactment of the eugenical belief in the constitutional nature of criminality was to occur in the United States in the Metropolitan Court system of Chicago, where minor offenders often received psychological assessment in 'psychopathic laboratories' that would lead to lifetime institutional confinement. Speaking in 1920, Chief Justice Harry Olson, who led the development of this modern system, explained that they had looked to continental European psychiatry, particularly German, as shaped by 'Kraepelin, Ziehne and Bleuler' for inspiration since these were 'fully twenty years in advance' of clinical practice in the United States or England (Olson 1920: 25). The first section of this chapter will therefore begin by discussing the developments of thought in German psychiatry that Olson saw as helpful to his cause. Some of these ideas were to be generally influential in the development of psychiatry in Europe and North America in the twentieth century, particularly in relation to questions of 'psychopathy'. The legacy of German psychiatry is complex. It had certain unique features that explain why it came to lay the ground for a fundamentally biological approach to the understanding of moral insanity. Other important strands of thought were to lead to the development of psychoanalytic thinking (which was to dominate psychiatry in the United States by the middle of the century), and to very different ideas about the nature of moral insanity.

The importation of aspects of German psychiatry, with eugenical implications, into the court system of Chicago did not occur in isolation. As the second section of the chapter describes, the idea that criminality was a largely inherited individual trait was propagated through a series of eugenical initiatives that included the work of the Eugenics Record Office (ERO), founded in Cold Spring Harbor (New York) in 1910. The task of the ERO was to coordinate research and promote the implementation of eugenical polices across the United States, and it had strong links to German psychiatry that were to be directly implicated in the operationalisation of Nazi eugenical policies. This section will also examine some of the most striking research and practice that occurred in the nearby Vineland Training School (New Jersey), which had strong links with the ERO under the leadership of the child psychologist Henry Goddard, who drove research and practice that assumed that feeblemindedness could be detected in individuals and needed to be eradicated from the population.

The third section of the chapter will move on to describe the Metropolitan Court system in Chicago itself, where these same eugenical principles strongly shaped some aspects of the work of the court, which underwent significant reorganisation in the early decades of the twentieth century and incorporated within it the 'Psychopathic Laboratory'.

The fourth section will look at how eugenical ideas that had been quite strongly promoted in Britain were rather effectively defeated by the experience of the First World War. The psychological trauma, so evident among the mass of men who served in the military, served as living proof that there were forms of insanity that were generated by the environment rather than the faulty genes of the sufferers. If the First World War planted seeds of doubt about the efficacy of eugenical policies, the Second World War instigated a sea change in attitudes towards the understanding of violence and psychopathology that was to have huge impact on notions of moral insanity in the second half of the twentieth century, as discussed in Chapters 6 and 7.

## 5.1 German psychiatry and constitutional psychopathy

German psychiatry had taken a rather different pathway from French and British psychiatry as it developed through the nineteenth century and into the twentieth, with two important trends discernible. First, there was the strong materialist belief in the physiological foundation of the mind and of any mental disorder. Second, there was the belief in the dynamic nature of mind, an assumption that its functions could not simply be broken up into individual components. The latter notion of the dynamic understanding of mind was to wield considerable influence through Freud's 'psychodynamic' theories. These were to lead back to more subtle psychological investigation of 'the mind' which had been largely abandoned by mainstream psychiatry by the end of the nineteenth century. The significance of psychoanalysis in providing a theoretical framework for understanding the development of 'psychopathy' and personality disorders is taken up in some detail in Chapter 6. The first of these trends, the belief in the organic foundation of any psychological disorder, will be discussed most substantially in this chapter. It arguably encouraged an entirely biological understanding of the nature of moral insanity that was to have considerable impact on policies, in a number of countries, which were to devastate the lives of many.

As discussed in Chapter 2, the concept of monomania was significant during the infancy of the profession of psychiatry in France and Britain. Monomania implied that the mind had depths that could be explored by those with expertise. The promotion of this concept in its various guises had been quite successful, even in the courtroom, and then later in the wider culture (as discussed in Chapter 4). German psychiatry had taken a somewhat different path, however. Crucially the theory of monomania had never been accepted (Werlinder 1978: 77). The reasons for this were quite complicated, as were the consequences. In contrast to France and Britain, German psychiatry had developed within the universities rather than the asylums. While the asylums gave the professional groups an institutional base, the efforts of the French and British to make a mark in the courts can be understood as an attempt to achieve professional respectability away from the stigma of the asylums. There were also systems of asylums in Germany, but the universities had given German psychiatry a more philosophical and research-oriented flavour. The influences were in some ways slightly paradoxical. On the one hand, philosophical arguments about the nature of mind had provided some resistance to the idea that mental functions could be precisely located in a particular part of the brain. On the other hand, the connection with medicine and physiological research had meant that particular kudos was sought by endeavouring to base the discipline within physiology, and neurology in particular.

In the early decades of the nineteenth century the leading name in German psychiatry was Johann Christian Reil (Richards 1998). His text *Rhapsodies on the Use of Psychological Treatment Methods in Mental Breakdown* was published in 1803 (soon after Pinel's treatise appeared in German). Although he was concerned with the treatment of the insane, he was largely not writing from professional experience in asylums and was quite reliant on the case studies of others, notably Pinel (Bell 2005). Reil's perspective was therefore less rooted in the reality of asylum management and more typical of a philosophical approach. His *Rhapsodies* was arguably able to claim its place as the most influential text on German psychiatry for most of the nineteenth century, perhaps in part thanks to its eclectic nature. As Hansen (1998: 397) summarises, Reil took up a number of positions in the book: in part he was, like Pinel, 'a crusader for mental health reform', but he was also 'by turns a materialist religious skeptic, a rationalist Aufklärer, Kantian philosopher, a practical physician, a would-be Prussian bureaucrat, and, finally, a Romantic singing hymns to the goddess Nature'. There were paradoxical, if not conflicting, lines of thought here. Reil was not only influenced by the Enlightenment tradition, which valued scientific and technological progress, but he was also embedded in a German Romantic tradition that emphasised the value of nature and lamented the negative effects of civilisation. To Reil, society was itself in a state of crisis (Hansen 1998: 397), and so he promoted 'moral treatment' that involved the provision of asylums away from the hectic modern world, much as envisioned by the Tukes and Pinel. He also objected to the incarceration and ill-treatment of the insane and proposed treatments that aimed to 'reform behaviour by persuasion, training, and aversion' (Bell 2005: 167). So, just like 'moral treatment', the strategies were clearly aimed at 'the mind' but, somewhat unlike the version prescribed by Pinel and the York Retreat, they also included the recommendation that shock and fear were to be included as treatment measures. Reil put emphasis on fear, arguing that 'brutal shock treatments work well', even for rather sensitive patients: 'Tender or fearful subjects can be made obedient by means of rough instructions, threats or the mere sight of a frightening science' (Reil, quoted in Bell 2005: 170). This points to a rather different model of psychology that was operating here. To Reil and his German colleagues, insanity was viewed as involving the whole personality or character of the individual. Notions of partial insanity and monomania which supposed that only one discrete part of the mind might be affected therefore made little sense. Thus the rationale of a treatment that aimed to reason with parts of the mind that remained sane and rational, which Pinel and the Tukes had assumed, was largely unsustainable to Reil. Instead, to Reil (and to generations of German thinkers) 'the mind' was understood, not as compartmentalised,[1] but as a dynamic construction which had to strive to pull together memory, sensation, feeling and thought into a coherent sense of self. Madness was the result of a failure 'in the dynamic construction and continuous reconstruction of their very selves, with the consequence that their personality crumbled' (Richards 1998: 722). It is possible to see from this why notions of monomania so important to the story of 'moral insanity' in France and Britain would be simply untenable within a German tradition that understood 'the mind' as actively constitutive: if 'it' was mad, the whole character or personality was also insane. This line of thinking was crucial to the development of theories about disorders of character and personality (as discussed in Chapter 2, German ideas had been influential on James Prichard's definition of moral insanity). Instead of searching for a particular type of partial insanity that might affect only the moral decisions or the behaviour of an individual, attention was turned to types of personality that might be prone to immoral conduct. This was to prove to be a decisive move in thinking about the issue and led to a whole nosology of character disorders, evident in the highly influential work of Julius Koch (1891) and Emil Kraepelin, for example.

Besides the perception of insanity being tied to the notion of character, an overt interest in the physiological causes of mental disorder also came to the fore of thinking in German psychiatry. There were of course exceptions to this, with Heinroth (Werlinder 1978) notably propounding the idea that disturbances of the mind could not be understood in terms of physical causation, and Feuchtersleben's (1847) work on the significance of psychological treatment being taken very seriously in Britain (as discussed in Chapter 3, pp. 81–82). Nevertheless, the hallmark of German psychiatry became an interest in the physiological bases of mental disorders. The advance of biological thought in German psychiatry was led from the middle of the nineteenth century by Griesinger, who founded the *Archiv für Psychiatrie und Nervenkrankheiten* in 1867 in order to promote a more clearly physiological psychiatry (Werlinder 1978). He took a radical materialist position to research: any notion of soul or mind could only be the product of cerebral activity. In this project he was to be joined by Meynert and Wernicke, sharing in common the firm belief that all forms of 'psychopathology' could be understood in terms of neurology. Despite this, Griesinger, and some of those who followed in his footsteps, did not dismiss the importance of psychological understanding (Marx 1975). However, in terms of psychology he was working within the German framework of understanding the function of the ego in maintaining a healthy dynamic equilibrium. Nevertheless, the idea that the character of an individual could be insane, coupled with the reliance on the constitutional basis of insanity, was to lead to some very strong and influential notions of the organic basis of moral insanity.

The work of J. L. A. Koch, it has been argued, did most to endorse the use of the term 'psychopathic' as preferable to that of 'moral insanity' (Millon et al. 1998: 8). He did a great deal of work to systematise the concepts and language of psychiatry, notably through his *Kurzgefasster Leitfaden der Psychiatrie*, published originally in 1888. His efforts to systematise the diagnosis of all mental disorders put stress on there being a range of difficulties from overt 'illnesses' to states of abnormality and led him to introduce the group of disorders called 'psychopathic inferiorities'. Although the term 'psychopathic' had been used before, it was Koch's use that was to establish the term, despite the lack of specificity (Werlinder 1978: 86). Koch defined 'psychopathic inferiority' in general terms as including 'all mental irregularities, whether congenital or acquired, that influence a man in his personal life and cause him, even in the most favorable cases, to seem not fully in possession of normal mental capacity' (Koch, quoted by Paštar et al. 2010: 466).

Werlinder (1978: 88) summarises Koch's schema as it relates to psychopathic inferiority:

### I *Permanent psychopathic inferiority*

*A Congenital states*

1  Congenital psychopathic disposition
2  Congenital psychopathic taint
3  Congenital psychopathic degeneration.

*B Acquired states*

1  Acquired psychopathic disposition
2  Acquired psychopathic taint
3  Acquired psychopathic degeneration.

### II *Temporary states of psychopathic inferiority*

In delineating 'dispositions' and 'taints' Koch was 'drawing attention to the fact that the distance was but short between the institutional cases and the character defects in the normal person' (Roback 1927: 264). Koch was also clear that those with inferiorities might well function at a higher level than average in other areas.

Other German theorists were also to have significant influence. Krafft-Ebing, for example, an important figure whose work was widely read on both sides of the Atlantic, was to make the link between theories of psychopathy and sexuality very explicit. He worked in that same German paradigm of understanding 'moral insanity', not as a form of monomania, but as 'a singular degeneration process of the mental sphere which effects the core of individuality, its emotional, ethical, and moral relations' (Krafft-Ebing, quoted in Werlinder 1978: 76). His emphasis on aggressive sexual disorders, through his publication of *Sexual Psychopathy: A Clinical Forensic Study* (*Psychopathia Sexualis: eine Klinisch-Forensische Studie*, 1886), including his introduction of the terms 'sadism' and 'masochism' into psychiatric nosology, was to signal an important direct connection between mental disorder and the world of aberrant sexuality. As we will see in the following chapter, the association between 'psychopathy' and sexual offending was to become a strong feature of clinical models and of legislative activity in the United States in the middle of the twentieth Century. A number of attempts to categorise forms of psychopathy further were made by German theorists working in this organic tradition. These include Ziehen, who drew up a list of 'psychopathic constitutions' largely determined by heredity (Werlinder 1978: 90–93); Kretschmer, who linked character types with body types (Werlinder 1978: 100–102); and Schneider, who was to be an influential name in psychiatric diagnosis in the middle of the twentieth century. Schneider's work stressed the continuity of 'normal' personality types with disordered psychopathic types, but also continued to view psychopathic types as constitutionally determined (Werlinder 1978: 104–111), much in keeping with his training under Emil Kraepelin at the Kaiser Wilhelm Institute for Psychiatry in Munich. Kraepelin was to have a lasting influence on the development of psychiatry, in part through his system of classification, which he maintained should be based on the observation of patterns of symptoms, and also because of his insistence that many disorders, including that of moral insanity, should be regarded as congenitally determined. Kraepelin, who wielded considerable influence through his directorship of the Institute, was distinctly eugenical in his views. We can see the slide from degeneracy to eugenics in this paragraph from his *Text book of Psychiatry* (1909), where he voices his concerns that

> the number of idiots, epileptics, psychopaths, criminals, prostitutes, and tramps who descend from alcoholic and syphilitic parents, and who transfer their inferiority to their offspring, is incalculable. Of course, the damage will be balanced in part by their lower viability; however, our highly developed social welfare has the sad side-effect that it operates against the natural self-cleansing of our people. We may barely hope that the degeneration-potential will be strong enough in the long term to eliminate the overflowing sources of germ lesion. . . . Nevertheless, the well-known example of the Jews, with their strong disposition towards nervous and mental disorders, teaches us that their extraordinarily advanced domestication may eventually imprint clear marks on the race.
> (translated and quoted by Brüne 2007: 5)

It was this quite overtly eugenical and racist theorisation of the origins of psychopathy and criminality that was to have such devastating influence in the first half of the twentieth century. The Kaiser Wilhelm Institute for Psychiatry was given considerable financial backing by the US-based Rockefeller Foundation and was to carry out extensive eugenical research. It was to be led by Ernst Rüdin, who would go on to formulate Hitler's 1933 sterilisation law (Weber 1996).

Despite the very clearly destructive pathway that German psychiatry was to open up, its philosophical legacy by the end of the nineteenth century was more complex. The notion that the mind, or the personality, of the individual could not simply be divided up into independent faculties, but needed to be considered as a complex dynamic whole, was to become largely accepted. Two very different paths were to lead from this point, however. On the one hand there was the idea that the character was fundamentally grounded in the whole body of the individual and could thus be *determined* by biology; on the other hand there were the 'psychodynamic' theories that were to be so influentially taken up in the psychoanalytic movement led by Sigmund Freud, who himself was a product of German psychiatry (he had a famously combative relationship with his former tutor Meynert, arch advocate for organicist psychiatry; see Sulloway 1979). It is no surprise that Freud saw his work initially in terms of neurological investigation, only later deciding that the contemporary state of neurological knowledge was too crude to allow proper investigation and turning instead to 'psychoanalytic' methods. It is, however, the influence of the theorisation of the constitutional nature of moral insanity that will be considered in the rest of this chapter. When German organic psychiatry was mixed with ideas about the significance of the hereditary nature of the psychological and moral characteristics of individuals and put forward as a solution to the perceived problem of a growing and disorderly population in the United States, the results were to be catastrophic.

## 5.2 Criminal feeblemindedness and eugenics in the USA

While eugenical movements were detectable in at least 35 countries across the globe, those of the most substantial interest occurred in Scandinavia, Great Britain, Germany, Australia, New Zealand, the United States and the Soviet Union (Adams *et al.* 2005; Dikötter 1998; Pratt 1998). In terms of the impact on government policies the longest lasting impact occurred in Scandinavian countries, while the most extreme and devastating impact was in Germany; the greatest outpourings of research occurred in the United States, where there appeared to be a thorough conflation of notions of degeneracy with eugenics. In 1907 the State of Indiana passed legislation, thought to have been the first in the world, that allowed for the forced sterilisation of individuals who were 'confirmed criminals, idiots, imbeciles and rapists'. In a pamphlet (1908) that celebrated this legislation, H. C. Sharp, who was physician to the Indiana Reformatory, uses the language of degeneracy to justify the policies:

> Most of the insane, the epileptic, the imbecile, the idiotic, the sexual perverts; many of the confirmed inebriates, prostitutes, tramps and criminals, as well as the habitual paupers found in our county poor asylums; also many of the children in our orphan homes belong to the class known as degenerates.
>
> (Sharp 1908: 1–2)

While there was certainly significant interplay between developments in British, German and American psychology in the fields of mental testing and of the promotion of eugenical policies,[2] as Rafter (1997) argues, the influence of eugenical thought, particularly 'eugenical criminology', on US penal policy in the early decades of the twentieth century was very considerable. The question can still be asked as to why the United States was to be the test bed and launch pad for eugenical social policies. One answer would be the very distinct philosophy of individualism that was prevalent in the United States and was to have influence, not only on the development of jurisprudence and the legal system in the US, but also on psychological thought. By the end of the nineteenth century, psychology in the US had 'distinguished itself as the science of individual differences', with an emphasis on the quantification of skills and capacities that equip individuals for industrial society (Haney 1982: 210). In addition, the search for systematic solutions to the problem of crime was particularly notable in the US. For example, the National Prison Association was founded in 1870, as an outgrowth of the American Social Science Association, and was made up of an eclectic grouping that included jurists, clergy, prison administrators, doctors, politicians and social reformers. Their goals were to promote the reform and rehabilitation of individual offenders. While this did demand that a certain amount of attention be paid to the conditions being met by those released from prison, Haney suggests that 'For them, the crises faced by the late nineteenth-century America were ones of personal shortcoming and irrationality rather than social structure, politics or economics' (Haney 1982: 211). Thus, in the latter decades of the nineteenth century, there was quite considerable enthusiasm for the idea that the assessment of individuals could aid the choice of the correct sentence that would lead to reform (Lindsey 1925). Efforts were made to identify individuals who were likely to cause problems and the notion of 'indeterminate sentences' was introduced. Papers given at the Association meetings suggest that there was an interest in degeneracy theory rather than straightforward eugenics. This interest in individual assessment, however, was gradually to be transformed into an interest in eugenical ideas.

### 5.2.1 The Eugenics Record Office (ERO)

The hub of eugenical activity in the US was to be the Eugenics Record Office (ERO), which was set up in 1910 under the Directorship of Charles Benedict Davenport and his Deputy Harry Hamilton Laughlin in Cold Spring Harbor, Long Island, New York. It was initially funded by Mary Harriman (widow of the railroad magnate) and then by the Carnegie Institution until its termination in 1939 (Field 1911). Laughlin devoted his career to the promotion of eugenical social policies. He had two particular interests – first, the segregation or sterilisation of those regarded as genetically inferior, and second, the 'racial' selection of suitable immigrants to the USA (Laughlin 1922). To the former end he drafted a model sterilisation bill that he actively and successfully promoted, and he published *Eugenical Sterilization in the United States*. Hitler's 'Law for the Prevention of Hereditarily Diseased Offspring', passed in 1933, was said to have been influenced by Laughlin's model bill. He was an enthusiastic supporter of Hitler's policies on eugenics,[3] was on the editorial board of a number of German academic journals devoted to eugenics and race hygiene and was awarded an Honorary Doctorate at the University of Heidelberg in 1936 for his work on 'race hygiene' (Lombardo 2008). Laughlin was not only the Deputy Director of the ERO but he was also employed by the 'Psychopathic Laboratory of the Municipal Court of Chicago' as 'Eugenics associate'. This was one facet of the considerable interaction between the ERO and the Municipal Court system in Chicago, with Harry Olson, Chief Justice of the Court, being elected President of the ERO in 1923 (Olson 1923: Editorial). The work of the court and of the 'Psychopathic Laboratory' will be discussed in the following section. Laughlin also energetically pursued research that might show that much of the crime in the US was committed by recent immigrants and aliens, and was an enthusiastic supporter of the Johnson–Reed Immigration Act of 1924 (which limited immigration by quota on 'racial' grounds). He influenced US immigration policy, bringing forth 'reams of biological data to prove the genetic inferiority of southern European, Central European and Jewish people' (Allen 1986: 247).

Under the leadership of Davenport and Laughlin, the ERO was to become 'central to the development of eugenics in the United States' (Allen 1986). It provided an institutional home and gave the appearance of scientific respectability to its two central purposes: the investigation of human hereditary factors, particularly in relation to characteristics of social significance; and the extension of the influence of eugenical ideas into key areas of social policy. It brought together scientists who were to exert discernible influence in North America and Europe through their propagandist publications and activities (Allen 1986: 226). The focus of a great deal of the work was on the gathering of case material on families who were seen as being of inferior stock. This was in keeping with a tradition of work that had investigated and described the family trees of particular families who were viewed as providing inferior genetic material to descendent generations. Richard Dugdale, for example, studied the descendants of one woman, Ada Jukes, and argued that her inferior stock was responsible, amidst poor environmental conditions, for the creation of subsequent cohorts of criminals, paupers and diseased individuals (Dugdale 1877). This work was updated and published in 1916 by Arthur Estabrook, working at the ERO, who used the data to emphasise the significance of hereditary factors, with clear eugenical propagandist intent (Estabrook 1916). Working in the same genre Henry Goddard himself, a key member of the ERO, published his study *The Kallikak Family* in 1912. The descendants of one 'feebleminded' woman were traced and polemically presented as variously deviant alcoholics, prostitutes, criminals and epileptics. Goddard was a psychologist who was also Director of the Vineland Training School, and oversaw the training of fieldworkers at the ERO. The training of 'fieldworkers' in the methods of recording information about families and genetics became an important facet of the work of the ERO. The fieldworkers' job was to go out and work in various institutions (but particularly insane asylums or almshouses), record information on the inmates and feed information back to the ERO.

### 5.2.1.1 Henry Goddard: identifying and segregating the 'feebleminded'

Henry Goddard is a remarkable figure in the history of American psychology. In 1908 he translated and adapted for use in the USA the intelligence test created by the French psychologist Alfred Binet in 1904 (Stubblefield 2007). Binet's original scale of measurement already included the categories of 'idiot' (with a mental age of 2 or below) and the 'imbecile' (with a mental age of 3 to 7). Goddard introduced the term 'moron' (drawn from the Greek word for foolish, *mōros*), which he used to describe people with a mental age of 7 to 12. Goddard uses this term fairly interchangeably with that of 'feeblemindedness', which had been subject to debate, especially in Britain (Goddard 1920: 4). Feeblemindedness was, as Willrich (1998: 89) puts it, a 'capacious nineteenth century term' used to describe a whole array of deficiencies. It is worth noting how the words 'feebleminded', 'moron' and 'defective' are often used quite interchangeably by Goddard. He refers to the Royal College of Physicians, who defined feeblemindedness as a characteristic of someone who is 'incapable from mental defect existing from birth or from an early age (a) of competing on equal terms with his normal fellows or (b) of managing himself and his affairs with ordinary prudence' (see Goddard 1911, for example). This issue of the lack of 'ordinary prudence' was to be emphasised by Goddard and the association with dangerous or risky behaviour was stressed. The first and most prominent category of social problem to be considered by Goddard was that of 'Crime'. Goddard was surely consciously echoing legalistic language in making the case for morons or the feebleminded being 'without sufficient intelligence either to know right from wrong, or those, who if they know it, have not sufficient will-power and judgment to make themselves do the right thing and flee the wrong'. Thus to Goddard, the so-called criminal type was merely a form of feeblemindedness (Goddard 1920: 8). Goddard estimates that perhaps 25 to 50 per cent of the prison population consisted of those who were 'mentally defective and incapable of managing their affairs with ordinary prudence' (Goddard 1920: 7), but points to evidence that was being gathered using the Binet tests that much higher levels of feeblemindedness were detectable among the populations resident in juvenile delinquent institutions – as high as 89 per cent in Geneva, Illinois, for example (Goddard 1920: 9).

Goddard was careful to explain that there was no point in blaming, or punishing, individuals who were not up to the demands of modern American life. His solution was that of eugenics. In 1913, Goddard, in a pithy paper called *Sterilization and Segregation*, had brought certain 'startling facts' (Goddard 1913: 3–4) to the attention of the world. These included the 'facts' that there were many so-called delinquents who were mentally deficient and unable to do well, and that large numbers of children fell into these categories and were, in the main, creations of hereditary factors. Goddard (1913: 4) rhetorically raised the question of what might be done about the fact that 'a large percentage of our criminals, paupers, prostitutes, drunkards and ne'er-do-wells are mentally defective'. He went on to suggest that it was necessary to sterilise the feebleminded and segregate them in colonies so that they would not reproduce their kind.

Goddard's book *Feeble-mindedness: Its Causes and Consequences* (published in 1920, but originally presented in 1914) records in detail the work of the Vineland Training School in New Jersey, of which he was Director between 1906 and 1918. There are a number of notable features in this work. First, there is little doubt that the presentation of very many of the numerous case studies was aimed at making the point that these were very difficult individuals who needed to be confined, and that eugenics presented a longer term solution. Second, it is also striking that the notes included seem to be written from a perspective of some disgust, or perhaps they are designed to invoke feelings of disgust. There is no sympathy, let alone empathy, here; these were people who were different: they were 'other' kinds of people. There is no doubt that very powerful processes of 'othering' have informed this work. Third, it is evident that strong professional claims to expertise are being made. To Goddard the state of feeblemindedness was not necessarily immediately obvious to the untrained eye; it could be quite hidden, but might be detected using techniques available through training in the methods of testing and observation provided by the ERO. These were to include the use of psychological testing, particularly with the Binet intelligence test, and through the study of family background. Goddard suggested that the feebleminded were particularly dangerous because they had such 'strong resemblance to the normal person' that they would be difficult to identify for those who did not possess the expertise. Properly trained people were needed, who knew not only how to identify them but also that 'they are the persons who make for us our social problems' (Goddard 1920: 4). Fourth, it is important to note how thoroughly notions of 'feeblemindedness' are conflated with immorality, delinquency and criminality. It becomes clear that it would be wrong to read feeblemindedness as equivalent to twenty-first century notions of learning disability or mental handicap, despite the linguistic and conceptual slippages apparent in the use of terms like 'moron' and 'mental defective'. It is far better to understand that feeblemindedness (to choose the word that was to have most common currency in this regard) was a particular construction that brought together notions of constitutional psychopathy (Hulbert 1939) and moral insanity, alongside the newly established technology for measuring intelligence. In considering the evidence of his case studies, Goddard is blunt in linking feeblemindedness to criminality: 'Every feebleminded person is a potential criminal. This is necessarily true since the feebleminded lacks one or other of the factors essential to a moral life – an understanding of right and wrong, and the power of control' (Goddard 1920: 514).

Goddard went on to explain that of course not all those judged to be 'feebleminded' did become criminal, but that those who were of the 'excitable, nervous and impulsive feebleminded' were 'almost sure to turn in the direction of criminality' (Goddard 1920: 515), and that hereditary factors were particularly strong among the criminal feebleminded. Goddard's presentation of the case of 24-year-old 'Kurt' exemplified these issues. He is described as having a 'mentality' of 8 years old and had been institutionalised since the age of 11. One of the specially trained fieldworkers visited the family of 'Kurt' in order to assess and describe them. They did not usually use the full scale Binet tests but the fieldworkers, trained in the observational and recording methods of the Eugenic Research Office (Stevens 1915; Vogt 2009), were sent out to gather information, and reported:

> [T]he family in all its connections is the lowest of the low, living in remote cabins that every now and then vomit forth their brood to be a pest in the land, and to finally go and fill our jail and almshouse records. Lucky the boy that finds entrance in an Institution like Vineland!

The account continues, and describes a meeting with the grandmother (Goddard 1920: 295).

> Whether the old woman was born feeble-minded or whether it is only the stupor engendered by her hideous life I do not know, for she does not belong to any category I have yet encountered. Certainly such a woman, let her condition be one way or the other, has no right to continue to exhale her renown over the land and to afford the hideous protection to vice and crime which she is certainly doing. I left her with feelings of loathing and disgust, such as human beings seldom engender in me.

Goddard's presentation of the case of Sam G. is typical in emphasising feeblemindedness which appears to emerge from hereditary factors and suggests a dangerous propensity towards criminality that justifies the institutionalising of Sam G. for the rest of his life.

> Our boy is of the type that would pass for bright and brutal. He would get into all kinds of trouble and commit any sort of crime, but having a certain shrewdness would be considered simply as an ignorant rowdy, a very dangerous person to have in any community. The probabilities are that he would spend most of his time in jail.
>
> (Goddard 1920: 76)

Sam G.'s difficulties are presented as being thoroughly embedded in his genetic inheritance. Both parents are described as feebleminded, although the father was described as 'very high grade', taking the form as being 'peculiar'. The mother was 'also sexually immoral' and the grandparents were also feebleminded, as were various siblings, including a 'half-brother' who was described as 'a low grade defective and criminalistic' (Goddard: 1920: 75). Not all those who were confined to Vineland were seen as presenting a danger in their own right, but it was their genetic material that was the problem. Florence and Byron T. are a sister and brother who are described as having mentalities of 8 and 11 years respectively, despite being 23 and 19 years old. Both are noted to be able to function quite well – indeed, Florence is described as 'good natured' and 'a willing worker'. If she were, however, 'not in the care of the Institution [she] would probably be the wife of some low grade worker and the mother of many children, probably defective like herself' (Goddard 1920: 52). Byron is portrayed as 'one of our highest grade boys . . . entirely lacking in stigmata of degeneration'. Byron, like his sister, seems to have been marked out for permanent institutionalisation. This is despite the fact that they have neither committed any crime nor presented any particular difficulties to anyone. It is the evidence of their family background that seems to have damned them. In the account of the family the powerful themes of immorality, degeneration, contamination and frank disgust are very clear: 'The parents were feeble-minded, syphilitic and sexually immoral. The father who was an alcoholic died in an almshouse. This is one of the worst histories, socially and morally that we have. . . . An older brother is sexually immoral and criminalisitic.'

The case description moves on to describe feeblemindedness and immorality in the wider family, which were assumed to go back four generations at least. Goddard notes that although neither Florence or Byron 'would be recognised as defective if out in the world', this would actually exacerbate the problem since 'both would undoubtedly go the way of their ancestors in crime and immorality as well as in the matter of marrying and reproducing defective children' (Goddard 1920: 53).

This pair were not the only ones who appeared to face confinement based on the evidence of their family background. Sixteen-year-old Gertrude E., for example, has been confined since the age of 9. She is described as being of 'relatively high intelligence in almost everything she does; does excellent work about the cottage, sews very well, is quite a musician . . . a useful pleasant girl, good tempered . . . obedient, truthful, active and affectionate . . . dances, sings and loves to appear in entertainment work'. However, it seems that her very normality is actually part of the problem since 'her beauty and attractiveness and relatively high grade would enable her to pass almost anywhere as a normal child'. She would be 'incapable of controlling herself' and would make 'so much trouble', and so Goddard concludes that it 'is fortunate for society that she is cared for as she is'. It is difficult to avoid the conclusion that Gertrude is confined because of her place in a wider eugenical plan. Goddard considers that 'a glance at her family chart will show that it is pretty clear that there must be an hereditary trait. An older sister and an older brother are both defective. . . . The father and mother were both alcoholic and may possibly have been mentally defective also' (Goddard 1920: 51). The allusion to Gertrude's 'beauty and attractiveness' and her inability to control herself starkly raises the issue of sexuality. Of course this is not surprising given the premises of eugenics, yet there is still something noteworthy here about the significance accorded to the control of sexuality, and of women in particular, and the relationship of sexuality to questions of 'race' (Stubblefield 2007). One of the specific 'social problems' addressed at the beginning of the book is that of 'Prostitution and the White Slave Traffic'. While acknowledging the scarcity of data on the subject, Goddard fully expected that it would be found that 'a large majority' of prostitutes would 'be found to be feeble-minded' (Lombardo 2008: 14). While feeblemindedness in boys was associated with criminality, with girls it was prostitution. Again, it was the fact that such women could appear normal 'to the uninitiated' that was part of the problem: their immorality existed 'in spite of their pretty faces, in spite of their often winsome ways and sometimes even a kind of shrewdness' (Zenderland 1998: 207). Goddard reasoned that one step towards the reduction of vice across the USA would be to introduce policies that demanded that such women were 'rescued' and confined. To Goddard, confinement was only a partial solution and a more preventive action in the form of sterilisation was also needed. Such logic was to be taken up across the United States, despite the fact that there was debate as to the efficacy of the whole project (Hunter 1914).

In Virginia the famous case of *Buck v. Bell* was to establish the right of the State to sterilise those who it determined fell into the category of 'feebleminded'. The test case at the Supreme Court arose following the passing of the State's 'Eugenical Sterilization Act' in 1924, and focused on 17-year-old Carrie Buck. She was institutionalised at 'the colony for epileptics and feebleminded' at Lynchburg, Virginia, having become pregnant.[4] Administrators of the colony wanted to sterilise Carrie because, they argued, she carried the related traits of feeblemindedness and promiscuity. Among the experts who gave evidence was Harry Laughlin, Deputy Director of the ERO (Lombardo 2008). He did not appear in court, but submitted a written statement which argued that there seemed to be evidence supporting the classification of Carrie as 'a moron' and broadly supported the supposition put forward by the Institution that Carrie was part of 'the shiftless, ignorant and worthless class of anti-social whites of the South' (Sprinkle 1994: 92). Justice Oliver Wendell Holmes, Jr, issued the court's verdict in favour of Virginia's right to sterilise Carrie Buck:

> It is better for all the world if, instead of waiting to execute degenerate offspring for crime or to let them starve for their imbecility, society can prevent those who are manifestly unfit from continuing their kind. The principle that sustains compulsory vaccination is broad enough to cover cutting the Fallopian tubes. . . . Three generations of imbeciles are enough.
> (Supreme Court 2 May 1927 *Buck v. Bell*)

Unsurprisingly, Laughlin and Olson were very pleased with the verdict, with Olson claiming that 'The road is now open' for the much wider application of compulsory sterilisation in order to prevent 'racial degeneracy' (Spiro 2009: 240). Harry Olson was already busy applying eugenical principles through his role in the court system in Chicago (Olson 1915), which will be discussed in the following section.

Willrich (1998: 70) argues that, although not without resistance and controversy, 'eugenic jurisprudence infused American public discourse on crime during the 1910s and 1920s' – a time when there was considerable interest in the problem of crime.

Interest in eugenical solutions was certainly widespread across the US. The chief strategies considered to be most effective were the confinement or sterilisation of the individuals concerned. Thirty US states went on to enact compulsory sterilisation laws between 1907 and 1940. Estimates suggest that between 1927 and 1957 approximately 67,000 inmates of state institutions had been sterilised by direction of state law because they were regarded as feebleminded or insane (Stubblefield 2007; Willrich 1998). Confinement was the choice of a number of areas. Rafter (1997: 188), for example, describes how Napanoch Reformatory Prison in New York became an institution devoted to the confinement of 'defective delinquents' in 1920.

## 5.3 The new Municipal Court, Chicago: the 'Psychopathic Laboratory'

Events in Chicago in the early decades of the twentieth century are worth exploring in some detail; they provide an exemplary case study in the development of the assumption of the link between moral insanity and criminality.

Chicago became the most eminent example of urban expansion in the late nineteenth century. In 1840 the population was just over 4,000; by 1870 it was nearly 300,000 and by 1910 it was well over two million. Such growth had thus far been unprecedented in human history. It is no wonder perhaps that this city was to witness the development of two institutions that were dedicated to understanding the consequences of such growth and controlling what were seen as the criminogenic costs. The first of these was focused on understanding social dynamics: the city hosted the establishment of the very first Department of Sociology in the United States at the University of Chicago (Bulmer 1984). The other institution was the groundbreaking and innovative Municipal Court, which was organised in the first two decades of the twentieth century (Willrich 1998, 2003). This innovation shared some of the anxiety about urban growth, but was more focused on the control of crime.

The creation of a coordinated criminal justice system was a response to perception that crime was a major social issue facing the city and surrounding counties and that the already extensive and yet fragmented court system trying to dispense justice and impose order over the sprawling area of Chicago was failing its tasks. It was felt that some central authority needed to be brought to bear in order to squeeze out the widespread inefficiency and corruption widely perceived to pervade the old system, which consisted of local justices of the peace and magistrates, and county and state courts. The charter that created the Municipal Court was fashioned by a coalition of businessmen, judges and attorneys. It came to represent a model of a municipal court system – a shiny example of modernist idealism, with its streamlined organisation of different departments and its capacity for the accumulation of statistics (Greene 1910). Many urban centres in the USA, including Cleveland, New York, Pittsburgh, Atlanta, Birmingham and Kansas City, adopted its model. In addition to the centralisation of facilities, part of its foundation was to provide a progressive approach to the problem of crime in the 'modern era', when societies could no longer expect the traditional authority of the community, church and family to enforce order. Thus, according to the *Oxford Handbook to United States History* (Boyes 2001: 524), 'the municipal judges' were to approach each offender 'as a social worker might, using knowledge of the person's mental abnormalities, family history, and social experiences to shape appropriate punishments'. In the case of Chicago, Harry Olson was put in overall charge, as Chief Justice, of the establishment of the court system, and as part of the reorganisation he established separate courts for 'Domestic Relations' and, in 1914, 'Boys'. This latter court was to serve justice on those between the ages of 17 and 21 who were accused of offences. Soon to be integral to the work of the court system was the work of the 'Psychopathic Laboratory', which was to become a significant vehicle for eugenical solutions to the problems of crime that were facing the city (Bisch 1916). As we have already seen, Olson was a confirmed and determined advocate of eugenical solutions, and despite the evident interest among some other groups in Chicago in the environmental causes of crime, it was eugenics that were to have a lasting and remarkable influence on the work of the court system.

The accelerated growth of Chicago and the high levels of poverty and crime strengthened both the feeling that something had to be done about crime and the belief that the problem lay within the newly urbanised populations of the problematic poor. These sentiments overrode some potential differences between the hereditarians, like Olson, and the environmentalists in the city (Willrich 1998, 2003). As Fenning (1914: 804) noted, the social and medical views at this time were actually quite 'closely allied'. This is perhaps no surprise, given the significant legacy of degeneracy theory, as described in the previous chapter. Willrich (1998) argues that there was something of an unholy alliance between the highly eugenical 'Psychopathic Laboratory' (also known as the Psychopathic Institute) and such movements as the Juvenile Protective Association (JPA), which were otherwise largely 'liberal' in their outlook. This latter group, which was instrumental in drawing in social perspectives to the activities of the juvenile courts, was inclined to blame poor environments for the criminality of the young people it came across: 'poorly clad, ill-nourished, and uneducated youth offenders from the immigrant neighbourhoods' (Willrich 1998: 79). The group's wish to see the juvenile courts take a more investigative approach was encouraged by Olson, who extended the remit of the Juvenile and Boys' court to include 21-year-olds, and focused particularly on domestic matters and sexuality. Despite this sympathetic stance towards the young people they met and engaged with, the JPA was equally inclined to admire the modernist promise of a world of 'experimentalism, empiricism and expertise' (Willrich 1998: 79). Thus the work of juvenile courts was open to being taken over by the groups interested in eugenical solutions.

The 'Psychopathic Institute' was incorporated into the work of the Boys' Court. Defendants who gave leave for their case to be taken to the Psychopathic Institute waived their right to a jury trial and thus allowed a less adversarial and more investigative approach to be taken. The investigation was led by professional judges, social workers and physicians. Ultimately, the courts, guided by the judges, had free rein to devise alternative sentences or 'treatments'. Herman Adler (1917), while director of the Illinois Juvenile Psychopathic Institute, defined the term 'psychopathic' in terms that were 'broad enough to include variations from the normal type of the severe grade of insanity or feeble-mindedness as well as those milder forms of mental disorder which often amount to little more than eccentricities of personality' (Adler 1917: 362). Adler described the work of the institute as offering 'a new affiliation between law and science' that offered the hope not only of solving various social problems but also of invigorating the discipline of criminology. According to Adler, the 'psychopathic work' carried out with the criminal courts promised two particular avenues of development. First, it allowed for the classification of individual delinquents or criminals 'according to the elements of his personality' rather than the substance of the criminal act or consequences.

Second, this classification meant that 'a plan of treatment may be devised' (Adler 1917: 365).

There is no direct reference to eugenics in this paper, but it is easy to see how the door was well ajar to such methods, and other individuals involved in the Psychopathic Institute were far more openly enthusiastic about their eugenical goals. The Psychopathic Laboratory had originally been set up by William Healy and was funded by private donation in 1909 by Mrs William Dummer (Olson 1920). When its funding was taken over by the State of Illinois in 1914, Olson reported seeking advice on the right kind of individual to put in the role of Director and was advised that since German psychiatry was 20 years ahead of the United States and England he should find someone who had 'spent at least two years studying there' (Olson 1923: 45). Conveniently, Olson was able to appoint Dr William Hickson as Director of the laboratory in 1914; he had studied with Kraepelin in Munich and Ziehen in Berlin (as well as with Bleuler in Zürich). When Olson met him Hickson was working under Henry Goddard at the Vineland Training School (Willrich 2003) and was thus thoroughly immersed in eugenical thinking. Indeed, Hickson was an extremely enthusiastic proponent of eugenics, and he stayed in this role until 1929. As early as 1915 Olson was able to declare that Hickson's work was demonstrating that 'one of the principal factors at work in bringing offenders into these courts is the abnormal mental and physical status of the accused' (Olson 1915). He chided the 'sociologists, probation officers, teachers and judges' who, he argued, were working with so little effect because they did not recognise that the causes of criminality lay in 'feeble-mindedness, insanity, light and severe grades, or a combination of both, to say nothing of the large percentage of physical defects and neurological deficiencies'. Olson claimed that over 85 per cent of the individuals coming to both the Morals and Boys' courts could be classified as feebleminded. The delinquents, both boys and girls, he argued, were:

> the victims of a society too complex for their mentality to assimilate, and being equipped with the same powerful instincts for self-preservation of the normal, and not being able, in competition with the normal, to provide food and shelter, they must take more direct methods, and so transgress the law.
>
> (Olson 1915: 62)

In 1915 Olson was part of the 'Illinois Committee on Social Legislation' which helped steer the 1915 'Commitment and Care for the Feeble-minded Persons' bill through both houses of the Illinois General Assembly. This, as House Bill 655, passed without a single dissenting voice and gave power to courts to commit anyone categorised as 'feebleminded' to an institution – permanently. The associated House Bill 654 empowered state officials to create such institutions (see Merriam 1915 for details). This was part of a state wide initiative to develop farm colonies that would permanently confine the insane, feebleminded and 'repeated juvenile delinquents' (Merriam 1915: 359). It was the very first such legislation in the US (Rembis 2002, 2003). Accurate figures on the number of Americans committed to institutions of the grounds of feeblemindedness are difficult to compile. Hickson himself reports committing as many as ten cases a day from the Municipal Court to various institutions for the feebleminded, and he assumed such confinement would be for life. It is estimated that between 1906 and 1930 'tens of thousands' were sent by the courts to the Psychopathic Laboratory, and between 68 and 87 per cent of these may have been confined (Willrich 1998: 69). The size of the populations of state institutions for the feebleminded rose dramatically in Illinois. In 1919 there were 2,400 inmates in the only institution dedicated to the feebleminded; in 1920 there were 19,000 inmates housed in ten institutions dedicated to the care and confinement of variously 'mentally ill, handicapped, dependent, and delinquent inmates'; by 1930 there were 27,000; and by 1940 there were around 39,000 (Rembis 2011: 69).

It must be acknowledged that there were critical voices, with Stevens (1915) (while Director of the Psychopathic Institute in the University of Chicago), suggesting that although the link between feeblemindedness and crime was strong, he thought that Goddard and other adherents of eugenics were ignoring other causes (see Hulbert 1939). Henry Goddard himself came to temper his views considerably, and even in 1921 he was writing more cautiously about the likely success of eugenical projects. Through the 1930s, as awareness of the reality of eugenical policies became clearer, funding for the ERO began to dry up, and in 1939 it closed, despite still having its adherents (Hulbert 1939).

## 5.4 Feeblemindedness in the UK

If the events of the Second World War were to have a major impact on the global eugenics movement, it was also the case that the experience of the First World War had arguably already curtailed the influence of eugenics in the UK. A summary of attitudes and policies directed towards the topics of feeblemindedness and eugenics within the UK presents something of a conundrum. Some of the theoretical premises of eugenics were rooted in the work of British scientists, notably Francis Galton (Galton 1904). Many of the ideas of eugenics were taken up by prominent politicians and, albeit through the notions of degeneracy, many influential cultural commentators were also keen to promote eugenical solutions. The Eugenics Education Society (later the Eugenics Society) attracted the support of prominent individuals such as John Maynard Keynes, Beatrice and Sidney Webb and H. G. Wells (e.g. Ray 1983, but also see the Eugenics Society Archive).[5] Despite this, Great Britain did not ultimately witness the enactment of any legislation that was directly eugenical in its intent. Perhaps the closest that England and Wales came to officially endorsing eugenical policies was the debate that took place around the 1908 Radnor Commission, which led to the publication of the Mental Deficiency Act of 1913. The Royal Commission on the Care and Control of the Feeble-Minded began taking evidence in 1904. Reading the report of the Royal Commission, published in 1908 and based on the evidence of 248 witnesses, it is very clear that at official levels there was anxiety about the links between mental deficiency and 'crime and misery':

> Of the gravity of the present state of things, there is no doubt. The mass of facts that we have collected, the statements of our witnesses, and our own personal visits and investigations compel the conclusion that there are numbers of mentally defective persons whose training is neglected, over whom no sufficient control is exercised, and whose wayward and irresponsible lives are productive of crime and misery, and of much injury and mischief to themselves and to others, and of much continuous expenditure wasteful to the community and to individual families.
> (Royal Commission on the Care and Control of the Feeble-Minded 1908: 3: Introduction)

The report summarises information on mental deficiency in London:

> There is thus a comparatively large class of feeble-minded persons who are not now considered as insane, but who cannot fairly be held responsible for their misdeeds, and who are the cause of great trouble and anxiety to those who deal with them. Many of them in their youth have not been kept under control by their parents. Frequently little attempt has been made to educate them. . . . They are only fit for unskilled labour and most are so wanting in the power of continued application, that they soon leave of their own accord. . . . They are greatly wanting in initiative, and are easily influenced by others. Their moral sense is defective.
> (Royal Commission on the Care and Control of the Feeble-Minded 1908: 61)

Despite the language, which is suggestive of eugenics, it is notable that the Commission observed that the parents of individuals with such mental deficiencies may be 'industrious members of the middle and working classes'. There was thus no direct link being made to a dangerous and inferior class, as had been evident in the pronouncements of the ERO in the USA. On the matter of criminal responsibility, the Commission made no move to change the relationship between mental disorder and criminal responsibility, so in effect the M'Naghten rules were left intact. The fact that an accused individual was thought to be 'mentally defective' should be kept separate from the issue of responsibility for the crime committed (Royal Commission on the Care and Control of the Feeble-Minded 1908: 10: Introduction). Nevertheless there were powerful advocates of eugenics. Notable among them was Winston Churchill, who in 1910 (as Home Secretary) went so far as to draw the attention of Home Office officials to the 'Indiana Law' (as discussed earlier in the chapter), which allowed for the sterilisation of those seen as degenerate. He asked them to investigate the practicalities in terms of the surgical operations and the legislative practicalities. The Chief Medical Advisor of Prisons, Dr Horatio Donkin, responded by suggesting that the arguments for sterilisation were 'The outcome of an arrogation of scientific knowledge by those who had no claim to it . . . It is a monument of ignorance and hopeless mental confusion' (Gilbert 2009). There was some direct lobbying for blatantly eugenic policies in Parliament, as Jackson (2000) describes, but the 1913 Mental Deficiency Act, when finally published and enacted, stopped short of overt eugenical policy. It did oblige all local authorities in England and Wales to make institutional provision for those falling into the various categories of mental deficiency, and the Act also allowed for the compulsory supervision and segregation of those deemed to be in need of such care. As Thomson (1998) emphasises, many of the drivers of the Act were to improve the lives of those who were often left to the squalor of prisons, workhouses or derelict housing. As Jackson (2000: 205) summarises, although the Act might have been influenced by 'the rhetoric of eugenics', it was also shaped 'by a complicated mix of social and political anxieties about poverty, criminality, lower class fertility, and national efficiency'.

The reasons for the failure of policies of sterilisation to become established are no doubt complex (Thomson 1998). There was, in the eugenical movement itself, always a slight ambivalence. Even Leonard Darwin, in an address as President of the Eugenics Education Society, observed that 'all human beings are the product of two factors, heredity and environment, and . . . consequently to both of them some attention should be paid'. He justified the apparent emphasis of the Eugenics Education Society on heredity 'only because so many other societies think only of the environment' (Darwin 1921: 314). A strong case can be made that by the time Darwin was making this point, the events of the First World War had already had their decisive influence in diverting thought in Britain away from eugenical plans. A number of writers have argued that the experiences of this war heralded huge changes in the orientation of psychiatry and psychology in the UK (Howorth 2000; Stone 2004). The conflict provided a severe test for those theories of degeneracy that supposed that psychological and psychiatric weaknesses were to be found hand in hand with physical and constitutional deficiencies. Many of what were perceived to have been the most healthy specimens of British masculinity were deemed to have suffered from 'shell shock', a disorder that was increasingly understood as a psychological disorder attained through the trauma of war (e.g., Rivers 1918). The psychological damage was occurring with no respect to the boundaries of social class. Indeed, army officers, almost exclusively drawn from the middle and upper classes, were, according to army statistics, almost twice as likely as lower ranks to suffer mental breakdown (Stone 2004: 249). The psychological casualties of the early days of the war were all volunteers; they were hardly likely to be malingerers or cowards. As Stone summarises: 'Heredity, the ubiquitous explanatory tool of the psychiatric profession was in deep water here – the ideological tables had been turned.'

The evident significance of the impact of the environment on psychological health was to promote the ideas of psychoanalysis in particular. Psychoanalytic ideas had their followers in Britain before the war, but the escalation of the appetite for, and the growing credibility of, those ideas through the war was remarkable. According to Stone, before the war 'there were only a handful of British doctors using psychological methods to treat nervous disorders'. By the end things had changed dramatically: 'squads of fifty RAMC [Royal Army Medical Corps] officers were given three-month courses on the techniques of "abreactive" psychotherapy – including dream analysis'; the use of psychotherapy was being promoted in army hospitals in France; and the Ministry of Pensions was encouraging general practitioners to refer cases of war-related nervous disorders to specialist psychotherapists. It is worth noting that this was a brand of psychoanalysis that de-emphasised the psychological significance of sexuality (Howorth 2000) – this was still a step too far for the conservative establishment at this point. The sheer scale of the problems created by shell shock meant that the Ministry of Pensions set up over a hundred treatment centres. This was a structural change that provided considerable challenge to the asylum psychiatrists. In addition to all this, the numbers of people who were apparently psychologically damaged by the experience of war meant that there was a great deal of public sympathy, fanned by largely compassionate press reporting of the problem. So while those in the medical and military sphere might have been reluctant to leave behind conventional beliefs and an organic approach, public thinking was becoming very different. As early as 1915 stories were regularly appearing in *The Times* on such topics as 'hysterical blindness', 'The wounded mind' and 'Wounds of Consciousness', so that by the middle of 1916 'the shell shocked soldier' had become almost a cliché within the English press (Bogacz 1989: 234).

The largely sympathetic view of the victims of shell shock was reflected in parliamentary discussions of the issue (Stone 2004: 254). Bogacz (1989) analyses the production, by parliamentary committee, of the *Report of the War Office Committee of Enquiry into 'Shell-Shock'*, published in 1922. Bogacz (1989) draws attention to the remarkable ambivalence of the report and the often fractious nature of the discussions of the committee. The investigation was proposed in the House of Lords in April 1920 by Lord Southborough, in terms that themselves signalled the sea change in attitudes of an establishment that before the war would have taken a very dim view of any attempt to blur the distinctions between sanity and madness, and between morality and immorality:

> The subject of shell-shock cannot be referred to with any pleasure. All would desire to forget it – to forget ... the roll of insanity, suicide, and death; to bury our recollections of the horrible disorder, and to keep on

the surface nothing but the cherished memory of those who were the victims of this malignity. But, my Lords, we cannot do this, because a great number of cases of those who suffer from shell-shock and its allied disorders are still upon our hands and they deserve our sympathy and care.

(Grogan 2014: 34)

Bogacz (1989) describes how the subsequent committee was highly conservative in its makeup. It was largely composed of members of the military, government and medical establishment. There was just one member, a representative of the Labour Party, who was not drawn from the upper middle or upper classes. There was particular conflict over the issue of cowardice. Military conservatives saw the threat of execution for cowardice and desertion as crucial to the maintenance of discipline and resisted the idea that men who had abandoned their posts only did so due to illness. The tension meant that the conclusions were guarded and slightly confusing. The final report still argued that 'cowardice' should be recognised as a military offence, but that 'seeming cowardice' might well be 'beyond the individual's control' and that 'experienced and specialised medical opinion is required to decide' whether someone was suffering from war neurosis or cowardice (Bogacz 1989: 246).

The report went on to recommend that the term 'shell shock' should be abolished (with its implication that this was a purely physiological phenomenon occurring through close proximity to the blast of a shell). Medical officers should have some psychological training, and although psychoanalytic ideas were rejected, simple forms of psychotherapy should be made available for the treatment of shell shock. The most significant emphasis in the conclusion, however, was given to the importance of the recruitment and selection of military personnel. This was prompted by the more conservative inclinations of the committee as they sought to cling on to the notion that the phenomenon could stem from the predispositions and inadequacies of recruits (Bogacz 1989: 248). While the purpose of this recommendation may have been to reassert theories of hereditary and constitutional insanity, it was ultimately to have a very different effect when psychiatric and psychological advice was sought at the outbreak of the Second World War in 1939. By this time psychoanalytic ideas, and theories that put stress on the social causes of psychological illness, were to be far more accepted within the psychiatric mainstream. The impact of these ideas on thought about insanity, and in particular on the development of different approaches to the problem of moral insanity, was to be considerable.

Yet again we have a clear example of a very important debate about the borderline between sanity and madness taking place in the public sphere. Individual members of the British public themselves knew people affected by shell shock; they read the sympathetic newspaper accounts and could no longer be satisfied with medical and psychiatric accounts of insanity that drew upon organic explanations. Many people had been provided with powerful evidence that events in the world could drive people 'mad'. The acceptance of 'war neurosis' was a significant cultural shift that signalled the downfall of a stance that had put great emphasis on clear divisions between the naturally healthy and the unhealthy, the worthy and the unworthy, the sane and the insane. As previous chapters have shown, public opinion could be very conservative. It was in part the hostile reaction of the public to the verdict at the trial of Daniel M'Naghten and the debacle of the Townley affair that had put a major damper on the acceptance of notions of moral or partial insanity. In this case, public opinion was more radical.

Advocates of eugenics did not stop agitating for policies that would see the sterilisation of the unfit. A Private Member's Bill which would allow for the voluntary sterilisation of those seen as deficient was put before Parliament in 1931 by Major A. G. Church. While this was defeated in Parliament, efforts to secure the policy continued. In 1932 the Brock Committee was appointed to investigate the possibilities of legislation on voluntary sterilisation, and did recommend that a Royal Commission should be established with a view to shaping such legislation. This never happened, because events in Germany entirely discredited eugenical policies, and even the Brock Committee was 'discreetly forgotten' (King 2002: 74).

## Conclusion

An array of factors and circumstances came together to shape an understanding of 'moral insanity' as a genetically determined disorder in the latter decades of the nineteenth century. While distinctly psychological notions of the nature of moral insanity and monomania had informed theory and practice in France and Britain in the first half of the nineteenth century, the reversal of the M'Naghten rules had pushed psychiatry back towards a more organic base. German psychiatry, with its more entrenched theoretical approach rooted in organicist claims, came to have decisive influence in terms of theory. Widespread anxiety about the health of the social body, fed by interest in Darwinian ideas of the survival of the fittest, led to the formulation of eugenical policies. These were to be put into action across the United States as the well funded Eugenics Record Office wielded real influence on policy and practice. The category of feebleminded – or 'moron', in Henry Goddard's terminology – was to become a new guise for moral insanity. Although precise figures are difficult to come by, it is clear that tens of thousands of Americans were confined or sterilised purely because they were viewed as falling into this new formulation of 'moral insanity'.

The interaction and cooperation between the advocates of eugenics and German psychiatry was to inform the eugenical policies of Nazi Germany (Breggin 1993). However, as the full horror of the reality of those policies became apparent, there was something of a backlash against biological determinism and theories of degeneracy. The impact of the Second World War itself, aside from the feelings engendered when the horror of the Holocaust was revealed, was to be considerable. Governments on both sides of the Atlantic became interested in funding the psychological and psychiatric disciplines as a method of guiding the war effort in a number of ways. The backlash against biological determinism meant that more psychological ideas were back in fashion. Perhaps less obvious was the interest that was to be engendered in understanding moral insanity as a social phenomenon, as experiences of war forced people to acknowledge that the potential for violence and antisocial behaviour was not confined to small numbers of dangerous individuals but was apparently widespread, perhaps lurking in all of 'us'.

## Notes

1  It is worth observing that Gall and his student Spurzheim, although originally working in Vienna, were to be based in Paris from 1807. Their work on phrenology might appear to be the clearest example of a faculty of psychology, but their work was not central to German psychiatry at all.
2  'Triangular points of support between England, Germany and the USA were to become an important cultural network, which shaped international eugenic campaigns' (Pilgrim 2008: 274).
3  The Harry H. Laughlin Papers, Truman State University, document D-2–4, *c.*1934 (www.eugenicsarchive.org/html/eugenics/static/images/1036.html, accessed 14 April 2015):

> If however, we study Hitler's methods, accept what is gold, reject the dross, we may make America Germany's successful rival. Germany plans sterilization of 400,000 low powers soon. We will not proceed with such speed. We can however, commence to think of positive eugenics, of multiplying our high power strains, while we consider working out a common-sense sterilization program.

4  It is alleged that this occurred after she was raped by a relative of one of her foster parents. University of Virginia: http://exhibits.hsl.virginia.edu/eugenics/3-buckvbell/, accessed 17 November 2014.
5  http://wellcomelibrary.org/using-the-library/subject-guides/genetics/makers-of-modern-genetics/digitised-archives/eugenics-society/, accessed 17 November 2014.

Chapter 6

# Psychopathy in the US
Psychiatry, psychoanalysis and sexual selves

## Introduction

The previous chapter traced some of the impacts of lines of thought which, at the end of the nineteenth century and into the twentieth, had located the causes of immorality within the constitution of individuals. The fledgling psychiatric profession had largely abandoned its courtroom claims to detect hidden forms of monomania and moral insanity in otherwise seemingly normal citizens. The move to focus on individual constitutional factors as the cause of antisocial behaviour led to catastrophic outcomes for individuals who were so labelled. The United States had witnessed the introduction of an array of policy initiatives, driven by eugenical ideas, that aimed to cure the problems posed by feeblemindedness or psychopathic inferiority by expunging the bad genes from the social body. Many of the atrocities of the Nazi regime in Germany followed this line of thinking. Although eugenical practices did carry on in certain countries, this was to be to a far more limited extent once the horror of Nazi programmes of racial purity became clear. Thus by the end of the 1930s public interest and state legislative attention in the United States had shifted away from notions of inherent feeblemindedness and instead towards the phenomenon of the 'sexual psychopath'. This was a very different guise for moral insanity and signalled a move away from a general concern with the reproduction of inferior and dangerous forms of humanity and towards the particular danger posed by individuals who were sexually violent and constituted a threat towards women and children in particular. In one sense this was a discernible shift back towards the search for hidden, psychological forms of insanity, since here a 'sexual psychopath' might appear to be a very ordinary citizen but contained within the capacity for violent sexual attack. The development of a series of sexual psychopath laws is significant for a number of reasons. The legislative activity in the post-Second World War period was symptomatic of a sense of crisis in gender and sexual matters and an acknowledgement of their wider social significance. This same climate that nourished the new laws also helped foster psychoanalytically informed psychiatry (Karpman 1949; Lipton 1950), which was to achieve considerable social and cultural influence. As this chapter will explore, this development needs to be understood within the context of social changes occurring in American society which foreshadowed transformations across the globe. The development of American psychiatry itself, heavily influenced by psychoanalytic thinking, was to have a profound impact, not only on the understanding of the source of moral insanity, but more generally on the way that people understood themselves and others. With its insistence that people's behaviour and distress could be understood within the context of their psychological histories, psychoanalysis provided a clear alternative to theories of biological determinism. The versions of psychoanalysis that were to have such major influence on the development of thought and practice in relation to psychopathy and personality disorder rose to prominence in the United States, but they were powerfully shaped by experiences of war and genocide that erupted in Europe. Although psychoanalysis had roots in German psychiatry, many of its founders, including Freud himself, had to flee for their lives from the eugenically inspired Holocaust. It is no wonder that psychoanalysis should have much to say about violence and its relationship to the social order. The rejection of biological determination and the belief that the potential for cruel violence was to be found not only in a minority of deviant individuals but also in many others was both a philosophical stance and, often, one born from bitter personal experience.

This chapter will first describe the development of the 'sexual psychopath' laws in the USA, which can be understood in part as a manifestation of anxiety about shifts in the relationship between the genders and of expectations of sexual relationships, and as a symptom of the growing domination of psychoanalytic ideas within American psychiatry and mainstream culture.[1] The second part of the chapter will describe developments within psychoanalytic theory, and in particular the theoretical developments shaped by experiences of war, which were to have a decisive impact on concepts of personality disorder, eventually leading to the proliferation of the diagnostic categories in the various editions of the *Diagnostic and Statistical Manual*, described in Chapter 8.

## 6.1 Sexual psychopath laws in the United States

Beginning in 1937 a number of states in America introduced a series of what became known as 'sexual psychopath laws'. While Australia and New Zealand followed a similar pattern in introducing laws aimed specifically at sex offenders (McCallum 2001), the move was most strongly initiated in the United States, which Pratt (1998: 95) suggests might be explained by the fact that the United States had 'the least developed forms of welfare' and so the laws were being used to 'compensate for the greater lack of security that was to be found elsewhere in the social fabric'. While there was in reality a variety of legislative procedures and definitions covered by this term, the purpose of the initiatives was to identify those individuals who were seen as presenting a potential danger to others through their sexually aggressive behaviour. By 1960, 26 states had enacted such laws (Swanson 1960), and the influence of ideas coming from psychiatry (Pratt 1998), and psychoanalysis in particular, appeared to be evident in the assumptions that were made: that trained professionals could distinguish a group of sexual psychopaths, even from other sex offenders; and that the disorder they suffered from was preventable and treatable (James et al. 2008: 5). Despite the influence of psychiatric thought, it is important to recognise that the sexual psychopath legislation was not driven by the clinical professions but, as Freedman (1987: 84) suggests, it was 'the media, law enforcement agencies, and private citizens' groups' which led the way in demanding that something be done. The national mass media, now in the ascendant, played a crucial role in promoting debate about sexuality (Reumann 2005).

To understand fully the significance of the sexual psychopath laws it is important to recognise that there were in fact two distinct periods of legislative activity, and that they were shaped by rather different forces. There was a pre-war phase of activity between 1937 and 1939 when just five states introduced legislation, and then a more considerable post-war wave of legislation in 25 states between 1947 and 1957 (Denno 1998). Only the state of Vermont introduced legislation during the wartime period. The pre-war interest in the sexual psychopath can be seen as emerging from similar anxieties which had motivated the attempts to halt the contagion of feeblemindedness through eugenical solutions. An important difference now was the fact that the targets of the new initiatives were most definitely men, whereas the eugenical activity in the US (described in Chapter 5) aimed to control the fertility of both men and women who were viewed as constitutionally and morally inferior. The shift back towards a focus on men is consistent with the theme of anxiety about dangerous masculinity evident from the eighteenth century (as discussed in Chapter 1). It may have been prompted now by the social impacts of the economic depression of the 1930s and the subsequent high levels of male unemployment, which meant that many poor American men were left to drift and become part of a potentially dangerous underclass. A series of harsh legislative initiatives during the 1920s and 1930s, which included 'three strike laws, mandatory minimum sentences, attacks on disparities in judicial sentencing, efforts to repeal the insanity defence, habitual sex offender laws and the expansion of vagrancy laws to cover gangs' (Nourse 2004: 926), were perhaps other symptoms of such anxieties. John Steinbeck's celebrated American novella *Of Mice and Men*, published in 1937, received popular and critical acclaim for its portrayal of wounded, flawed, dangerous and yet ultimately tragic masculinity. The lead character, George, is finally unsuccessful in his attempts to protect his mentally subnormal friend, Lennie, who kills the attractive wife of their boss's son in a clumsy attack that came about through terrible misunderstanding rather than sexual aggression. George defends Lennie from the mob, who are chasing him to bring him to justice, by killing him. Covey (2009) discusses the similarity of the depiction of the 'imbecilic criminality' of Lennie and the arguably eugenical ending of the book to the sexual psychopath laws of the time.[2]

The post-war wave of sexual psychopath legislation occurred some years later and was far more widespread and thus of greater significance. It can be seen as a response to the rather different conditions that emerged from the seismic shifts in the cultural landscape brought about by the Second World War itself, which had created a crisis of sorts in gender relationships and the expectations of family (Anderson 1981; Higonnet 1987). On the one hand the needs of war had legitimated an aggressive masculinity, and yet on the other they had also encouraged women to take on masculine roles in the workforce. The irony for many men, returning home as heroic combatants, was that life had gone on and that many women were finding they could manage without them. There was certainly a marked and significant peak in the divorce rate in the immediate post-war period (Costello 1986; Turner and Rennell 1995). Wartime necessities had liberated many people from their conventional roles and had allowed unprecedented levels of sexual freedom and expression. There was thus arguably a very public fascination with sexual behaviour. Anxiety about sexual behaviour was of course nothing new. As argued through Chapters 3, 4 and 5, anxiety about the health of the social body and the control of sexual behaviour had become firmly linked through theories of degeneration, both within medical circles and in the public sphere. In this respect the effort to focus attention on individuals whose behaviour was viewed as sexually aberrant is not at all surprising. The cultural transformations in sexual and gender relations that energised the creation of the sexual psychopath laws were not only being enacted in the public realm but were subject to great public and media discussion. Concern and anxiety grew about what appeared to some to be the threat of 'uncontrolled desires' (Freedman 1987: 87). The high profile publication of the first Kinsey Report in 1948 (focusing on male sexual behaviour) was arguably both a symptom of a fascination with sex and a stimulation to further exploration of a range of sexual behaviour. The report was a best-seller that divided experts and the public. Kinsey 'was simultaneously hailed as a liberator, denounced as a pornographer, compared to the scientific martyrs Darwin and Copernicus, and declared a Communist bent on destroying the American family' (Reumann 2005: 2). The follow-up book on female sexual behaviour was greeted with even greater interest when published in 1953. The claims that Kinsey and colleagues were making about the range of sexual behaviour evident in the population were the cause of some anxiety and backlash, and there were organised efforts by conservative groups to discredit the Kinsey Institute and starve it of funds. Whether or not it can be claimed that the panic about sex crime was similarly orchestrated by those keen to advocate for sexual restraint, it is the case that most psychiatrists were sceptical about the new laws (Freedman 1987) and that the legislation was highly politically shaped (Sutherland 1950). Guttmacher and Weihofen (1952: 153) reported at the time that an examination of the legislative initiatives confirmed that they were founded primarily upon emotional reactions. A child is sexually abused and murdered and the community calls loudly for blood and for action. Bills are impulsively rushed through the legislature with new and dire regulatory provisions dealing with the widest variety of sexual behaviour.

In support of this view, there is no evidence that the laws arose from an actual epidemic of sexual offending (Denno 1998; Lave 2009), but it does seem plausible to suggest that the US was gripped by a sex crime panic in the late 1940s. This was partly evident in the nature of the press reporting of sex crime but was also manifest in the reception of these anxieties among the wider public. In developing that argument Chauncey (1993: 161) notes that 'the gruesome details' of three sexual murder cases all occurring within the period of a week in 1949 were 'telegraphed' into the homes of ordinary Americans. Six-year-old Linda Joyce Glucoft was sexually assaulted by the relative of a friend, who then viciously attacked and killed her before burying her in a rubbish heap. A 17-month-old girl was assaulted and murdered by a farm labourer in a small town outside Fresno, and 7-year-old Glenda Brisbois was thought to have been abducted and assaulted before her body was thrown into a canal. While, with hindsight, these events may not have been statistically aberrant, the coincidence of their timing made for a sense of panic among a public who were being made aware of the dangers of aberrant sexuality from a number of quarters. The popular and serious press ran stories on the dangers of 'The Psychopathic Sex Menace' and were carrying headlines that asked 'What can we do about sex crime?' (Chauncey 1993). Most famously, J. Edgar Hoover himself penned an article in the *American Magazine* in 1947 (Morris 2002), rhetorically entitled 'How safe is your daughter?', the implication being that she was not terribly safe since 'degenerate sex offenders . . . depraved human beings, more savage than beasts, are permitted to rove America almost at will' (quoted in Lave 2009). As Chauncey (1993: 163) argues, through the publicity given to the issue, 'sex deviation' became a staple of public discourse. State governments felt obliged to respond and 15 of them established commissions to study the problem and make recommendations for action. Thus, although psychiatry had not driven the campaigns, the commissions of inquiry allowed psychiatry to wield quite direct influence not only upon public discourse but also on the shaping of the 'sexual psychopath' legislation itself.

As is clear from Chapter 5, anxiety about unregulated female sexual behaviour was very prominent in discussions of psychopathic inferiority and the work of the Eugenics Record Office (ERO) and the Chicago Municipal Court system. The concern of the sexual psychopath laws was very much with *male* sexual violence[3] and this contrasted with the anxiety about the control of female sexuality and behaviour some decades earlier, when any female sexual behaviour outside marriage had been viewed as highly deviant and could lead to labelling and confinement. Freedman (1987) suggests that new demands for the control of men grew from awareness of a new sexual order in the twentieth century, which was encouraging more sexual expression among women. The 'Victorian' era, as Foucault (1979) argued, had promoted sexuality, desire between men and women, as a part of the social fabric. This Victorian world had depended upon the bifurcation of female sexuality between madonna and whore to define the limits. Male sexuality had, in a sense, been allowed to remain 'intact' but had been defined and controlled by its relationship to these two poles of female sexuality. The acceptance of the more fully sexualised woman who was emerging through the latter nineteenth century, and then more distinctly in the twentieth century, began to present problems. If 'ordinary' women – mothers and wives – could be fully sexual beings, with desires and needs, then the question arose as to where the limits might be. Greater attention needed to be paid to the control of the behaviour of individual men. Psychiatry itself was arguably, at least in part, born of the need to investigate and regulate intimate relationships (Foucault 1980; Jones 2002). This dimension to psychiatry became quite overt by the middle of the century and, especially in the United States, came to be largely dominated by a psychoanalytic outlook. Psychoanalysis was not just influential within psychiatry, but it was also to achieve a remarkable cultural resonance; thus, as Denno (1998: 1341) expresses it, 'the sexualisation of the psychopath' perhaps had a lot to do with acceptance of Freudian concepts not only within the psychiatric profession but also within wider society. Covey (2009) argues that Hollywood films from around the mid 1940s began to be influenced by Freudianism, in that dangerous madness began to be portrayed, not only as linked very clearly to sexuality, but also as treatable. The films of Alfred Hitchcock, for example, tended to portray characters who were normal on the outside but suffering from inner turmoil. The murderous Norman Bates in the Hollywood film *Psycho* (released 1960) is his most obviously Freudian character.

Whatever the intentions of the 'propaganda' surrounding the 'sexual psychopath' laws, their overall impact was to encourage a very different perspective on the nature of the relationship between sexuality and deviance. While the acts of 'sexual psychopaths' might have been vilified as monstrous in the popular media, they were construed in professional circles as being rather like ordinary citizens who suffered from a curable disorder (e.g., Gibbens 1951–52). Psychoanalytic theory was key in shaping thought about how ordinary citizens might also be capable of acts of great cruelty and sadism. As discussed in the following section, it was psychoanalysis that was to revitalise thinking about the nature of moral insanity in the latter half of the twentieth century.

## 6.2 Sexuality, civilisation and psychoanalysis in the USA

It is arguable that there was in a sense a 'utopian' aspect to nineteenth-century theories of degeneration which suggested that 'evil' was 'out there' among the dangerous mass of 'other' people – the poor, feckless and dangerous individuals of the underclass. If only something could be done about 'them', then the mainstream of the human world would be made safer. The more gloomy decades of the twentieth century, overshadowed by the First World War, and then the further moral catastrophes of the Second World War, seemed to draw attention to the likelihood that there was evil and violence lurking inside everyone. This view is perhaps no better summed up than in Sigmund Freud's 'Civilization and Its Discontents' (a paper that has its roots in the paper 'On War', written during the First World War itself). The essential arguments of this paper are that individuals in a state of civilisation are doomed to unhappiness because such a condition inevitably involves the suppression of our baser instincts of aggression, selfishness and sexual avarice. To Freud, living with others was a strain because all of us had the capacity for violence and hatred, which had to be constantly restrained and repressed. If one of the tenets of civilisation was to 'love they neighbour', it was also, according to Freud, totally unrealistic:

> [T]heir neighbour is for them not only a potential helper or sexual object, but also someone who tempts them to satisfy their aggressiveness on him, to exploit his capacity for work without compensation, to use him sexually without his consent, to seize his possessions, to humiliate him, to cause him pain, to torture and to kill him.
> 
> (Freud 1991a: 302)

The degree of repression required to channel all of this aggression and anxiety meant that all social arrangements were inherently unstable and prone to cracks and strains, which would manifest in outbreaks of violence and disorder. This shift to viewing all individuals as capable of antisocial and violent behaviour was certainly encouraged by events during the First World War in Europe, but was to become an organising principle of various schools of psychoanalysis that were to have considerable influence on thinking about disorders of personality in the second half of the twentieth century. All individual character states came to be regarded as various contingent compromises through which we all try to square the circle of the impossible social and psychic demands being made upon us. Such Freudian ideas were to have enormous impact on psychiatric and psychological thought throughout the twentieth century, particularly in relation to how issues of what might have been considered moral insanity were thought about. To appreciate the extent of this influence, it is necessary to understand more about how psychoanalysis came to dominate psychiatric thought in the United States.

An arguably 'nodal' event in the history of American psychiatry took place in 1909, when Freud gave a series of lectures at Clark University in Worcester, Massachusetts (Hoffman 2010). He was invited by G. Stanley Hall, the father of child psychiatry in America. The lectures were attended by James Jackson Putnam, William James and Adolf Meyer. The latter was perhaps the single most influential figure in the development of US psychiatry. Trained in Switzerland and well versed in German psychiatry, he had brought the term 'constitutional inferiority' to the US (Millon et al. 1998: 8; Werlinder 1978), and as implied by this he had a strong interest in the organic basis of psychiatry. Despite this he became an influential advocate of psychoanalysis and his position in the mainstream of American psychiatry meant he was in a powerful position to draw psychoanalysis in to the heart of institutional psychiatry. James Jackson Putnam was instrumental in setting up the American Psychoanalytical Association and then became its first President. Putnam was a highly respected and pioneering neurologist who had been interested in the 'psychodynamic' ideas that were emerging from Europe (he was aware of Charcot's work, for example) but was only really won over to psychoanalytic methods and theory when he met Freud in 1909. He went on to publish many papers supporting psychoanalysis, and he was arguably an important figure in translating and propagating psychoanalysis in the US (Hale 1971). Tucker (1978) suggests that the appeal of psychoanalysis to Putnam, and like-minded colleagues, was that it provided a more optimistic path for psychiatry to follow since it offered the hope of individual cure rather than the restrictions of biological determinism. It was the seemingly impressive clinical results of psychoanalysis that overcame Putnam's initial reluctance to accept the importance of the psychological roots of many psychiatric symptoms, and in particular the sexual nature of those roots. Tucker (1978) explains that Putnam tried to weave more moralistic and ultimately optimistic goals into the Freudian project. This optimistic stance survived even as Freud's own work took a distinctly more pessimistic turn during the First World War; American psychoanalysis put more emphasis on the adjustment of the ego and the development of personality throughout the lifetime of an individual.[4] While psychoanalysis provided a very different way of understanding the development of mental disorder from those that focused only on constitutional inferiority, it was, however, still consistent with some of the narratives of nineteenth-century fears of degeneration – for example, the interconnected mass of the population whose unchecked desire threatened the social order. The relationship between the individual and the social body needed to be fundamentally understood, according to psychoanalysis, in terms of sexuality. Individuals all contained aggressive, destructive and sexual impulses which had to be adjusted to the needs of civilisation, but always threatened its destruction. This relatively gloomy view was tempered by the fact that individuals were also capable of change and development.

Overall there is perhaps a paradox in the relationship between psychoanalysis and the United States. Despite Freud's own suspicion of, and even antipathy towards America (Kaye 1993), psychoanalysis was to achieve more power and influence across the culture in the United States than in any other nation. It was to do this in a culture that was looking, not simply for a gloomy analysis of the human world, but for paths to positive change. Psychoanalysis was certainly to be accepted within the mainstream of American psychiatry in ways that it never was in Britain, and arguably more so than in Germany or France. Since all this occurred at the time in the twentieth century when America was achieving unprecedented levels of global economic and cultural dominance, it meant that psychoanalysis too was to have remarkable global reach (Zaretsky 2004). Psychoanalytic theories, as shaped in the United States, were to have considerable influence as the 'most fully conceptualised' (Millon 1981: 45) theories of personality development. From these were fashioned theories of disordered personalities that were to become the new form of moral insanity by the latter decades of the twentieth century. It is therefore important to understand some of the important themes of this work.

### 6.2.1 Psychoanalysis and character development

It would be impossible to do justice here to the array of psychoanalytic theories that have been applied to the development of character and personality, but it is important to understand how some of the assumptions of psychoanalysis were to shape ideas about personality disorders during the twentieth century, particularly in relation to understanding violence and destructiveness. Freud was born in Freiberg in Mähren (now in the Czech Republic, but at the time part of the Austro-Hungarian Empire) and trained and worked most of his life in Vienna, so it is little wonder that psychoanalytic theories themselves were initially shaped by certain assumptions of Germanic psychiatry that emphasised the physiological basis of mental processes. Indeed, Freud initially considered himself to be a student of neurology and his experience studying the work of the eminent neurologist Charcot in Paris was an important step in the foundation of psychoanalysis. Freud also clearly worked in the German tradition of understanding the mind as a very active and constitutive entity (see Chapter 5). Griesinger, for example, had used the term 'ego' in the 1840s to refer to an individual's active construction of selfhood (Verwey 1985). It was this more psychodynamic model that was to dominate Freud's development of psychoanalysis.

Freud's initial ideas of character development emerged from his early 'drive theory'; he was interested in how individuals repressed or sublimated their basic desires (or drives) in order to conform to the requirements and demands of the society and culture around them (Freud 1991b). An individual's characteristic modes of channelling their own sexual and aggressive drives determined and shaped their character. This would manifest in terms of their typical way of being and relating. Early attention in psychoanalysis was given to the idea that fixations at particular stages of psychosexual development (in the oral or anal stages of development, for example) would be associated with particular character traits. As Freud and followers developed psychoanalytic theories, there was a shift in emphasis towards incorporating an understanding of how individuals were able to sublimate and direct their more aggressive and destructive drives, and there was further interest in the structuring (or topography) of the mind (the division between the id, ego and super-ego). It was his work on melancholia and narcissism (which emerged later in Freud's career and was radically developed by others) that was to have most influence on theories of disordered personalities. Arlow (1990) argues that Freud's work on melancholia (Freud 1917) was an important step, because he argued here that aggressive feelings could be directed inwards, resulting in feelings of guilt and experiences of masochism and depression. Such thinking (see Aichhorn 1935) was extended to include individuals who might have a pathological sense of guilt owing to the internalisation of aggression and thus might seek out punishment (through criminal acts, for example). It was work on narcissism (Freud 1991c) that was eventually to open up whole fields of exploration in terms of how people related to each other; these have subsequently assumed considerable prominence in psychoanalysis, particularly in relation to the personality disorders. The influence of psychoanalysis was given a major boost by the experience of the Second World War and it took a significant role in shaping the development of theory and practice in relation to disorders of personality.

### 6.2.2 War and the psychology of fascism

The experience of both 'world wars' drew the attention of governments, on both sides of the Atlantic, to the possible benefits of investigating the psychological states of their populations (Hoffman 1992; Rose 1989; Wanke 1999). Thus both the First and the Second World War had huge impact on the development of the institutions of, and ideas connected to, psychiatry and psychology. There was continuing effort, now funded in part by government, to explore systematically the interior worlds of individuals. There were arguably at least two distinct, and considerable, drivers of governmental investment in the development of psychological knowledge. There was first the very clear interest of governments in understanding the psychology of their own armed forces. This included the development of techniques concerned with the selection and training of troops and the treatment of psychological disorders (Wanke 1999). These issues were to have considerable impact on the development of psychiatry and psychological treatment in the post-war period (as will be discussed in the next two chapters). Second, there was the interest in the mass psychology of populations as it was recognised that the 'morale' of the general population in times of mass warfare might well be the key to victory (Dunham 1942; Rose 1989). During the Second World War this interest in morale included the theorisation and analysis of the psychology and sociology of democracy versus that of 'fascism'. The latter conundrum was a key preoccupation of western governments in the wake of the rise of Hitler in Germany. Particular theoretical strains of psychoanalysis were to achieve some prominence through their apparent utility in comprehending events that surrounded the war and it is argued here that those ideas themselves were fundamentally shaped by the experience of war. The most significant psychoanalysts of the post-war years, many of whom were Jewish, had been very directly affected by Hitler's Nazi regime 'as refugees from Europe, therapists of Holocaust victims, army officers and/or contributors to wartime intelligence' (Pick 2009: 141). Freud himself had a final desperately late flight from Vienna to London in 1938, while his sisters were to die in concentration camps (Cohen 2012). Limentani (1989) observed that although the disruption of the institutional activities in the London-based Psychoanalytical Society was great, so too was the level of creativity. Pick (2009: 140) suggests that even the clinical material of psychoanalytic theorists like Melanie Klein, whose influence was to be immense but whose work focused on the internal world of young children, was marked 'by the horrors taking place in the outside world' amidst the Second World War. Key work by those such as Klein, Ronald Fairbairn, Paula Heimann, Edward Glover and John Bowlby, whose work came to define object relations thinking, was carried out during this traumatic period (King 1989; Shapiro 2013). It was this school of thought that was to become 'the dominant psychoanalytic paradigm' in Britain and North America in the second half of the twentieth century (Alford 1987: 4). It will be argued here that a number of the ideas that were forged through these experiences are highly relevant to the concerns of this book: how we understand those who do harm to others. There was an entirely comprehensible preoccupation with understanding, first, how such a high proportion of the German population came to be in thrall to the Nazi Party and Adolf Hitler, and second, how so many ordinary Germans had become active participants in the mass murder and slaughter of their fellow human beings. This was certainly an understandable concern of the psychoanalytic movement, many of whom had had to flee Germany and Austria for their lives.

The study of fascist or authoritarian states of mind – meaning states of mind that were capable not only of an unstinting allegiance to authority but also of carrying out acts of atrocious cruelty towards perceived enemies (perhaps at the same time as evincing the ordinary signals of human decency and kindness to those not considered enemies) – became a central concern of a group of thinkers in Germany itself, which was to become known as the 'Frankfurt School'. This was a loosely allied and diverse group which grew out of the Institut für Sozialforschung (Institute for Social Research).[5] Although the history of the group is somewhat contested (McLaughlin 1999), its members survived turbulent times: they themselves had to flee Germany, initially to Switzerland and then to New York, soon after Hitler became German Chancellor in 1933. Not only were prominent members Jewish, but as self-declared Marxists they would undoubtedly have been unable to survive, let alone work. The Institute was affiliated to Columbia University in New York, with some members returning to Frankfurt in 1950 and others staying in New York and California. While the work of the group was diverse (Jay 1973; McLaughlin 1999), there were strands of its work that were to have some impact on thought about personality, and it is worth focusing on the development of thinking that linked the theorisation of potentially dangerous and damaging personality types with social processes. This work was begun at the foundation of the organisation while it was still based in Germany. The problem being addressed by Erich Fromm and Max Horkheimer was how it was that Germany, a relatively industrialised economy in the midst of dire economic circumstances that might have been strongly predicted by a Marxian analysis to lead to proletarian revolution, was actually heading instead towards fascism. While Fromm (e.g. Fromm 1942; Frosh 1987) eventually moved away from traditional Freudian libido theory (and indeed became estranged from the work of the other members of the Frankfurt group), work on the developmental roots of individuals' capacities to embrace fascism was carried on, and published most famously by Theodor Adorno and colleagues. Building on Fromm's pre-war work in Germany, Adorno argued that fascist states of mind could be understood as being produced by specific child rearing practices that led to the development of certain character types. In this case the particular type was the authoritarian syndrome (Baars and Scheepers 1993), which was also associated with psychopathic personality types. Adorno and colleagues argued, using Freud's notion of super-ego development, that a rather crude, sadomasochistic resolution of the Oedipus complex would result in some variety of authoritarianism. As Pick (2009: 153) suggests, the development of ideas about the super-ego, as a potentially 'antisocial' force, was considerably shaped by the encounter between fascism and psychoanalysis. Within this formulation of the super-ego there was a mechanism for understanding how it was that individuals could internalise highly aggressive tendencies which could be directed against the self or others. It was hypothesised that children either brought up by very disciplinarian and harsh father figures, or who were subject to fantasies of masculinity focused on strength, fear and domination, would be left to internalise a very hated and aggressive object. The consequent internalisation would produce an unstable psyche that was beset by ambivalence and would be dependent upon psychological mechanisms that split off feelings of love and hate and developed a sadomasochistic identification with authority. The resultant character types would be likely to relate sadomasochistically to hierarchical social authority structures, since they could take some libidinal satisfaction in subordination, while sadistically taking pleasure in humiliating and punishing those 'below' them. The dependence on mechanisms of splitting meant that thinking would tend to be rather concrete or 'black and white'; objects in both the external and internal worlds would be crudely categorised as 'good' or 'bad'. The degree of internalised aggression meant that there was a powerful need to find external 'safe targets' for their aggression. Thus 'out' groups, such as ethnic minorities, or members of perceived degenerate underclasses, would easily become targets for prejudice since any feelings of weakness would be powerfully projected on to them and aggression and derision directed at them (see Worrell 2008). In this way Adorno and colleagues argued that they were identifying the psychosocial roots of prejudice and racial hatred. On both sides of the Atlantic such psychologically informed thinking was being used to shape policies of rebuilding in post-war Germany (Pick 2009). Once its members had fled and based themselves in the US, it is perhaps no wonder that the work of the group would have attracted the attention of the US government as it searched for insight into Nazi German society and the Nazi mindset. As Kātz (1987) notes, the involvement of members of the self-proclaimed Marxists of the Frankfurt School in American military and secret service operations might seem surprising to both sides, and yet such cooperation was driven by common purpose. The general interplay between clinicians, the military and the government over the period of the Second World War and its aftermath was remarkable. Henry Dicks, for example, served in the British Army as a psychiatrist and, thanks to his fluency in German, conducted interviews and psychological evaluations of German prisoners of war (including Rudolf Hess). He reported on the morale of German forces and towards the end of the war and in its immediate aftermath he advised Allied governments on the denazification of Germany, publishing work on fascist states of mind (Dicks 1972).[6] Later he went on to become the director of the Tavistock Clinic (discussed in Chapter 7), and his work had some considerable impact on Kernberg, who himself was to shape thought about destructive and antisocial personalities (e.g. Kernberg 1995), as we will see.

Adorno also noted that the difficulties of super-ego integration, as witnessed in the so-called 'fascist' personalities, could also become characteristic of 'psychopathic personalities'. This might occur where there is no masochistic 'transference' to authority, or where that transference is so repressed that there is 'an irrational and blind hatred of *all* authority, with strong destructive connotations, accompanied by a secret readiness to "capitulate" and to join hands with the "hated" strong' (Adorno 1950: 762).

As part of the wider study of authoritarianism, Morrow (1950) reported on studies of such 'fascist' states of mind in the prison system. Adorno (1950: 762) had described the 'rebel and psychopath' as a type of authoritarian personality. It was argued that such states of mind were indeed commonly detectable among populations of severe offenders who could be diagnosed as 'psychopathic'. Morrow argues that those who scored highly on measures of 'fascism' in the prison population were likely to be most particularly difficult to rehabilitate. It is interesting to note that among the issues that emerged from their interviews was the prevalence of defences against any sense of weakness within themselves (Morrow 1950: 856); the defence would typically be the façade of toughness that men would present to disguise any feeling of their own weakness or inadequacy. Typical in this regard is 'Robert', who declared that from an early age 'my greatest desire was to be somebody in life. . . . Every man has a certain ego that he has to satisfy. You like to be on top. If you're anybody at all, you don't like to be on the bottom' (Morrow 1950: 857). Findings such as these were to prefigure the explosion of psychoanalytic work on narcissism and related character disorders, which was to have such influence on research and clinical work on personality disorders. Indeed, a number of authors and researchers have argued that narcissism underlies many forms of antisocial behaviour (Millon 1981: 172). The strong links between theories of fascism and those of narcissism, which were to be so influential in the development of theories of personality disorder, can be understood in terms of the biographies of the some of the leading instigators. Otto Kernberg, who led a great deal of thinking on the significance of narcissism, experienced the violence of Nazism as a child in Vienna. He is quoted by Kuriloff (2014: 63–64) describing vivid memories of the rise of Nazism and the fact that normal citizens could behave with such brutality:

> I walked with my mother on a major avenue. The Nazis stopped her and made her get down on her knees and wash the street. Everyone – normal citizens, not soliders – gathered around and laughed and made fun . . . these experiences led to my being impressed by the brutality in humans that was unleashed in the group process . . . I realized the regressive, destructive potential in human beings.

The realisation of this destructive potential appeared to have some considerable impact on Kernberg's theorisation of narcissism and the prevalence of aggression and rage among the ordinary Americans he was to work with as an émigré.

### 6.2.3 Narcissism and personality disorder

Descriptions of narcissistic personality types began to emerge from psychoanalytic theorisation in the middle of the twentieth century. Freud originally postulated that all infants pass through a stage of 'primary narcissism', when they do not differentiate themselves from others and therefore invest libidinal energy in themselves. Such primary narcissism is a necessary condition for the care of self and is thus functional. As individuals develop and become aware of others they begin to invest libidinal energy in others. Freud then suggested an economic model to explain that people would, in healthy circumstances, receive love from other people in exchange for the libidinal energy they were investing elsewhere – thus maintaining the libidinal balance. An individual who did not experience this equilibrium would be in danger of retreating from relationships with others to a stage of 'secondary narcissism', where they direct love only towards themselves (Freud 1991c). According to this economic model, those who invest too much libido in themselves, like Narcissus of the myth, will be unable to form meaningful relationships with anyone else and will thus remain fixated on their own image. Later work on narcissistic personality types was prefigured by Wilhelm Reich in pre-war Vienna; he described the 'phallic-narcissist' in the 1920s (Reich 1972). Important developments in thinking about narcissism were then to come from psychoanalysts who had fled from Nazi-occupied Europe. Karen Horney (1939), for example, argued that narcissism could be seen as a form of character disorder which arose from an individual having an over-inflated sense of their own worth that was not tied to any realistic assessment of their actual abilities. It was the work of Otto Kernberg (who fled Nazi Vienna with his family) and Heinz Kohut (who also fled Austria in 1938) that was to have the biggest impact on thinking on narcissism in the second half of the twentieth century. This work was to have an influence far beyond the bounds of the psychoanalytic clinic and made its mark on mainstream psychiatric diagnosis, as can be observed from its influence on DSM[7] (DSM's development and significance to the story of 'psychopathy' and personality disorder will be discussed in Chapter 8). The narcissistic personality type only entered the DSM in its third edition in 1980, but it was then to assume some significance as the work of both Kernberg and Kohut 'carried many of their colleagues along a path that has promised a renewed vitality for psychoanalytic theory and therapy', as Millon and Davis (1995: 393) observed in discussing the significance of their work to the development of DSM categories of personality disorder. It is therefore important to try to grasp the fundamental premises of their work.

Heinz Kohut emphasised the infant's growing developmental ability to distinguish itself from its mother and thus the increasing need for the capacity to direct and focus libidinal energy on both the self and others. Kohut suggests that the infant creates the internal image of the 'idealised parent' and of the 'grandiose self' in order to recreate the sense of perfection and omnipotence experienced before the realisation of separation. The idealisation would allow an individual to cope with the inevitable anxiety created by the engagement with the real world, which will invariably be unable to meet all needs of the infant and will equally inevitably find the self of the individual unable to cope with all environmental adversity that it faces. The key maturational task then becomes to integrate and modify both the 'grandiose self' and the 'idealised parent' as the infant continues to develop and engage with reality. Healthy development will involve a series of manageable disappointments as the child realises that they do not match up to their own grandiose self and their carers do not meet the standards of the idealised parents. Events that are experienced as too traumatic or too threatening will result in a retreat back to the fantasised forms of self and parent, resulting in various narcissistic configurations – notably the apparently paradoxical exaggerated sense of self-worth, alongside remarkable vulnerability to criticism or any other threat to the fantasy of the grandiose self. Kohut's formulation of the 'narcissistic rage' that might follow from injuries to the ego of such individuals laid the ground for later work that has emphasised the role of narcissism in aggression and violence (Cartwright 2002; Gilligan 1997). While Kohut did argue that malignant forms of narcissism could be associated with an array of highly problematic behaviour, Otto Kernberg presented a gloomier view of the prevalence and consequences of narcissism. Kernberg's formulation was to push the theorisation of narcissism towards being an explanation for manifestations of antisocial personality disorder.

Kernberg (1975) also saw narcissistic character disorders as being marked by the apparent paradox of an individual having a great *need* to be loved and admired by others alongside their exaggerated belief in their own self-worth. Writing explicitly within the object relations tradition of psychoanalysis (notably influenced by Klein and Fairbairn), Kernberg saw the inner world of the narcissist as 'shot through with aggression and rage'. Narcissists were 'unsatisfied and unsatisfiable, a contradictory mix of superficial but seductive sociability, glittery fascination, and high self regard on the one hand and of restless emptiness, unempathic ruthlessness, and fragile self-esteem on the other', motivated by 'anger, resentment and envy, and animated by grandiose fantasies of triumph and revenge' (Lunbeck 2014: 60). It is not difficult to see why such formulations might be viewed as providing clues within an individual's character to the source of serious offending; Kernberg's writing is full of examples of how such people 'mistreat, exploit, and destroy one another' (Lunbeck 2014: 61). To Kernberg, antisocial and psychopathic personality disorders were on a continuum of narcissistic disorder (Kernberg 2004), with such antisocial disorders forming the more pathological end of the spectrum. Kernberg's (1975) descriptions of borderline states have also had considerable impact on psychiatric nosology (as discussed in Chapter 8). The borderline personalities are those that are considered to be neither predominantly neurotic nor psychotic, yet they feature consistent patterns of behaviour that are marked by high levels of impulsiveness, anxiety and other neurotic symptoms, and major difficulties in maintaining relationships. The kernel of ideas around narcissism has been hugely influential on theories and descriptions of personality disorder that were to achieve prominence through the publication of DSM (to be discussed in Chapter 8).

## Conclusion

The tumult of war and the rise of Nazism led to a turn away from theories that had pinned the blame for antisocial behaviour on the genes and constitutions of particular individuals. Instead there was renewed interest in more psychological theories of moral insanity. Psychoanalysis played a key role, providing a means of linking the continuing interest in the exploration of the inner worlds of individuals with anxiety about the health of the sexualised social body in the early decades of the twentieth century. The appearance of the series of sexual psychopath laws in the USA, particularly in the immediate post-Second World War period, represented this interest, encouraged by fascination with and anxiety about the new sexual liberation and the increasing dominance of psychoanalytic ideas on American psychiatry.

As Lave (2009) observes, by the 1970s it was evident that the sexual psychopath laws had not fulfilled the promises of their advocates. In 1977 the Group for the Advancement of Psychiatry (GAP) could conclude that the sexual psychopath laws had failed: 'The mere assumption that such a heterogenous legal classification ('sex psychopath' or 'sexual offender') could define treatability and make people amenable to treatment is not only fallacious; it is startling' (Lave 2009: 589).

While the particular sets of legislation were not successful, many of the premises that had legitimated some of the initiatives were to continue to have influence. The acceptance of psychiatry, then dominated by psychoanalytic ideas, at cultural and government levels was to have a remarkable impact on official responses to the problem of moral insanity, notably in the US and UK. The response in the UK is the subject of the next chapter, where the concept of 'the psychopath' was to be described and enshrined in the Mental Health Act of 1959. In the US the influence of psychoanalysis on mainstream psychiatric thought was to be immense. In particular the work of Kernberg and Kohut on the significance of narcissism for understanding antisocial personality disorders was considerable. Some of this work will be taken up in subsequent chapters, but it is worth noting the influence on the development of the categories of the *Diagnostic and Statistical Manual* (published by the American Psychiatric Association). The story of psychopathy in the USA will be returned to in Chapter 8, where the development of the role of the American Psychiatric Association's various editions of the *Diagnostic and Statistical Manual* is taken up.

## Notes

1  See Chenier 2003, for a description of the development of 'sexual psychopath' laws in Canada.
2  While Covey does acknowledge that Steinbeck's narrative is tragic, sufficient weight is not given to either the social context of the story (the economic predicament that Lennie and George are suffering) or, perhaps more importantly, the very sympathetic portrayals of both Lennie and his protector George. These considerably lessen any eugenical message.
3  Evidence from Indiana (Grannuchi and Grannuchi 1969, for example) suggests that the vast majority of those committed under the Act were male (only four out of 396 considered under the Act between 1959 and 1960 were women).
4  Such theories have been subject to a great deal of criticism. The argument is made that they have sacrificed the radical edge of psychoanalysis (e.g. Jacoby 1978). (For reviews of the significance of American psychoanalysis see Burnham 2012; Zaretsky 2004.)
5  Originally founded in 1923 by Felix Weil, a young Marxist who used his own inherited wealth to support the initiative. Based in Frankfurt, it was to be an independent academy for the development of Marxist thought in the twentieth century.
6  As part of the work of the Columbus Centre, set up in 1966 at the University of Sussex to promote understanding of the Holocaust.
7  The *Diagnostic and Statistical Manual*, published by the American Psychiatric Association.

Chapter 7

# Social formulations of psychopathy and therapeutic communities

## Introduction

The diagnosis of 'psychopathy', employed to refer to a form of moral insanity, was to receive a remarkable level of official government recognition in Britain through the introduction of a Mental Health Act in 1959 (DoH 1959). This explicitly included the category of 'psychopath' as one of four categories of mental disorder. According to the Act, 'Psychopathy' was described as referring to a: 'persistent disorder or disability of mind (whether or not including subnormality of intelligence) which results in abnormally aggressive or seriously irresponsible conduct on the part of the patient, and requires or is susceptible to medical treatment' (DoH 1959: Part 1, Point 4).

In the parliamentary debates that preceded the approval of the Act, there was general enthusiasm for the inclusion of psychopathy. Indeed it appears that the category was no mere appendage to the legislation; Dr Edith Summerskill (Member of Parliament for Warrington) went so far as to argue:

> It is the new approach to the psychopath – indeed, the official recognition of his condition – to which I attach the greatest importance in the Report and which will come to be regarded as another step forward in the evolution of our civilisation.
> 
> (Hansard 1957: c51, discussion on MHA)

The explanation for how this controversial category came to have such a central role in the Mental Health Act (MHA) lies to an extent in some of the forces that were shaping thinking in psychiatry, and particularly psychoanalysis, in the United States (discussed in the previous chapter). Governments on both sides of the Atlantic had ploughed money into psychiatry and psychology as part of the war effort. The experiences of the Second World War itself had an impact on psychiatric and psychoanalytic theories and had brought a far larger proportion of the population into contact with psychiatry. Developments in psychiatry in the United States over this period were undoubtedly very important in establishing the diagnosis of 'psychopathy', and then the various diagnoses of 'personality disorder' that were to come to play a larger role in debate in this area through the latter part of the twentieth century and into the twenty-first. Some of the important developments of psychoanalytic theory have been dealt with in Chapter 6, and the important steps in the appearance and progress of the *Diagnostic and Statistical Manual* published by the American Psychiatric Association (APA), which has provided such a focus for debate about personality disorders, will be discussed in more detail in Chapter 8. It is worth noting, however, that the Commission and the parliamentary debates that passed the MHA did not refer to American work on psychopathy and personality disorder. The development of ideas in Britain had their own particular trajectory which, while undoubtedly influenced by the same ideas, also deviated from the American scenario. The most remarkable point about the developments in Britain was the emphasis given to the social dimension of the disorder of 'psychopathy'.

The inclusion of the category in government legislation was aided by a turn towards the identification of the problem of psychopathy as something which could be understood as emerging from social conditions and therefore amenable to social solutions. Undoubtedly the differences from the United States here might well be connected to the greater emphasis on individualism in the US (Haney 1982, for example). It might also be speculated that there was disparity in the nature of the impact of the two world wars on Europe and the US. In Britain, the First World War had brought mass warfare and slaughter very close to home (Roper 2010). It would be unusual to find families and communities in Britain who were not affected quite deeply (Doyle 2012; Fountain 2014). The Second World War too brought about mass mobilisation on both sides of the Atlantic, and the large scale bombing of many populated areas brought destruction and terror to the populations of the major cities of Europe (Gardiner 2010). This helped bring about awareness of the impact that psychological trauma could have on individuals, not only through the experience of physical destruction and terror, but also through the psychological trauma brought about by the separation of families and communities as a result of evacuation programmes (Summers 2011). However, it needs to be recognised that discernible characteristics of psychiatric and criminological thought were already in place in Britain before the Second World War and these emphasised the social dimensions of problems of crime and disorder.

The first part of this chapter will consider the particular development of criminology in the UK in the middle of the twentieth century. The most prominent point here is that at this time criminology was being shaped, not by ideas about the organic and hereditary causes of delinquency, but by a mixture of psychoanalysis and radical social thought concerning the interaction between the environment and individual psychopathology. This amalgam put the concept of 'psychopathy' in a prominent position within debates about the causes of crime.

The second section will examine how some of these ideas were to be formalised by David Henderson, whose work *Psychopathic States*, published on the eve of the Second World War, was to go on to have very direct influence on government policy in the post-war period.

The third section will examine developments in military psychiatry during the Second World War, which were to feature experiments in community therapy that pointed towards an understanding of 'psychopathy' as a social disorder, and to apparently viable forms of treatment that grew out of this conceptualisation.

The fourth section will describe the debates on the legislation that introduced the term 'psychopathy' into government legislation, and the aftermath. Another significant development in legislation was the 1957 Homicide Act (Home Office 1957); this introduced the charge of 'diminished responsibility', which could reduce a murder conviction to that of manslaughter. The aim of this was to allow courts to use far less stringent criteria for the judgment of insanity than allowed by the M'Naghten rules. This, in theory at least, would allow a wider range of mental disorders to be accepted in courts.

## 7.1 Criminology, radical thinking and planned environments

As has already been discussed (in Chapter 6), experience of the First World War meant that governments in Europe and the United States were very aware of the potential significance of psychological and psychiatric services, leading to these being funded on an unprecedented scale on both sides of the Atlantic. Some of the new ideas about the formulation and treatment of psychopathy, forged in the otherwise highly conservative British military, will be discussed later in more detail. It is important to acknowledge, however, that these ideas did not emerge from a vacuum. There was already an environment in Britain that was sympathetic to the view that the social world provided important factors which determined the mental health of individuals. One facet of this sympathetic environment was the formal discipline of criminology, which only developed in Britain in the middle of the twentieth century.[1] The later development of British criminology perhaps helps explain why it was not so influenced by the biologicalism that marked much of late nineteenth-century thought. For whatever reason, British criminology was shaped in the middle of the twentieth century by interest in the social conditions of crime and more particularly the significance of conditions early in the life of individuals (Valier 1995). As Rose (1958) suggested, there were two pivotal events in the development of criminology in the UK. The first was the founding in 1931 of the Association for the Scientific Treatment of Criminals, later the Institute for the Study and Treatment of Delinquency (ISTD); the second was the fleeing of Hermann Mannheim from Nazi Germany to London in 1934 and the subsequent establishment of the formal academic discipline at the London School of Economics and Political Science. The ISTD was to play a considerable role in the emerging discipline of criminology in the UK in the years following the Second World

War (Garland 1997). It began publishing its own journal, the *British Journal of Delinquency*, in 1950 (later to become the *British Journal of Criminology*). In 1953 it initiated 'The Scientific Group for the Discussion of Delinquency Problems' as a forum for academic debate on crime and this set up independently of ISTD in 1955, adopting the title 'The British Society of Criminology' in 1961. In reality the births of a recognisable discipline of criminology and of the ISTD were entwined. Hermann Mannheim himself was also a supporter of the Q Camp experiment in the therapeutic benefits of community living at Hawkspur (Essex), which was to have direct input to the thinking of the ISTD.

### 7.1.1 The Institute for the Study of Delinquency and the Psychopathic Clinic

The founding mother of the ISTD was Grace Pailthorpe, and prominent among the founding fathers was the psychoanalyst Edward Glover, along with Emanuel Miller, Maurice Hamblin Smith and E. T. Jensen (Braggins and South 1998), while Wilfred Bion had some involvement with the work of the Institute (Harrison 2000: 70). Grace Pailthorpe (who later became a renowned Surrealist painter) trained in psychoanalysis after serving as a surgeon during the First World War, where she had helped run a field ambulance unit. She took particular interest in women's delinquency and women's experiences of prison. Her book *Studies in the Psychology of Delinquency* (1932) gave an account of her research into the mental health of female offenders. With hindsight it is her combative stance towards the work of the previous decades on criminal types that is perhaps most striking: 'it must be repeated that in England the prevailing tendency is still to regard the criminal as one of a distinctive class, a class apart, inherently and permanently evil' (Pailthorpe 1932: 10).

The data from interviews and psychological tests carried out with 100 female offenders (between the ages of 16 and 30) were used to argue that many offenders should be treated (with psychoanalysis among other forms of intervention) rather than face imprisonment and punishment. While this was 'met with some consternation in official circles' (Garland 1997: 39), it attracted the interest of others, including the psychoanalyst Edward Glover, who organised meetings to discuss the significance of her findings. This led to the inauguration of what was to become the ISTD. In order to further the group's interests in the treatment of delinquency the 'Psychopathic Clinic' was also set up in 1933 in London. This was later to be called the Portman Clinic; in 1948 it became part of the NHS, and has continued to be a well known clinic for the treatment of personality disorders as part of the Tavistock and Portman NHS Foundation Trust, still based in London (Yakely 2009). The naming of the clinic as the 'Psychopathic Clinic' reflected the belief that although they had accepted that delinquency might be associated with a range of psychological disorders, it was 'in the psychopathic group where most of the unresolved problems of delinquency lie' and, further, 'the proportion of delinquents diagnosed as psychopathic is a high one' (Glover 1947). Glover, Pailthorpe and colleagues also argued that, contrary to the expectations of many people (McCord and McCord 1964), the 'psychopathic delinquent' was proving amenable to treatment. Despite the involvement of psychoanalysts in the development of the ISTD at this point, it is very important to note that some of their work was shaped by ideas about the significance of 'community treatment' that did not come from psychological theorisation, but drew from the beliefs described below, that gained currency in the pre-war years, that the experience of living in a community could itself be therapeutic.

### 7.1.2 Q Camps and community therapy: the Hawkspur experiment

Some strong ideas about the significance of community to mental health were to come from the Quaker movement (Kraemer 2011). This influence might be less surprising when the role of the Quaker Tuke family of York in the promotion of moral treatment is borne in mind. What became known as the 'Hawkspur experiment' was triggered by a letter written by David Wills to *The Friend*, the in-house journal of the Quaker movement. Inspired by his own experience of working with 'maladjusted' boys in Quaker-sponsored resettlement houses, he called for the establishment of an experiment in group living designed specifically for young delinquents (Quakers in the World 2014). At the same time the Quaker-led British Friends' Penal Reform Committee developed the idea of having 'Q Camps' for troubled young people. Marjorie Franklin, a psychoanalyst who was also involved in ISTD, invited David Wills to be Chief of Camp as they set up the first Q Camp in 1936 at Hawkspur in the Essex countryside, which was to be just such an experiment in 'group living' (Franklin 1966). It was not explicitly set up to deal with issues of 'psychopathy' or 'moral insanity' but they were dealing with 'misfits' between the ages of 16 and 25, who were causing problems in their own communities but who had often had difficult lives (Toms 2013). For example, Wills (1941: 18–19) describes the first arrival who, as a 23-year-old, had applied for his own admission: 'Buffeted about, kicked from pillar to post since his parents deserted him as a baby, misunderstood and mishandled, he had become . . . one of society's "misfits".' They took other volunteers, but also others '"sent" by courts, probation officers, social workers, doctors, parents'.

Not only can Hawkspur be credited as being the first example of what were to become known as 'therapeutic communities' (Whiteley 2004), but it was remarkable in its direct influence on men and women who were to establish radically different ways of understanding and treating 'psychopathy' over the following decades. Hermann Mannheim (responsible, at the London School of Economics, for the first academic course in criminology in the UK) was on the Q Camp committee and was a regular visitor, having become convinced of the significance of the early experiences of offenders (he discusses Hawkspur in Mannheim 1955). The psychiatrist Dennis Carroll was also a committee member and regular visitor. He went on to become a director of the ISTD and was commanding officer at the Northfield military psychiatric hospital (Glover 1957). As we will see, this military unit was to become almost legendary for the groundbreaking work in the use of group and community treatments for mental disorders. David Wills had observed the running of Junior Republics and the work of Homer Lane, who had been involved with those schemes in the US but came to England and set up the Little Commonwealth[2] in Dorset between 1913 and 1918 (Toms 2013). However, Wills's ideas were distinct from those of the US pioneers, and these differences became quite central to the advancement of therapeutic communities for the purpose of the treatment of personality disorders. As they developed in Britain, therapeutic communities were to be questioning places, more concerned with 'the dynamic of democracy' than with establishing conformity.

In telling his own story of the Hawkspur Camp, Wills himself referred to the system of the Junior Republics in the US, the brainchild of William George (see George 1910) a wealthy philanthropist who was drawn to the idea of providing children who were already getting into trouble in the poorer districts of New York City with an experience of rural living. He envisaged and tried to create a community to be 'modelled exactly on the plan of our big Republic . . . a village conducted just exactly the same as a village of grown-ups except that it should be "of the youth, for the youth, and by the youth"' (George 1910: 65–66). Begun in 1895, it was to be based on the veneration of the American civic ideal, which these young people, George felt, were being denied in the slums of New York. While great emphasis was put on how much the boys and girls ran the community, they were doing this within firm, and conventional, frameworks. Thus the young people took on specific roles and responsibilities that emphasised order and authority. The Junior Republic had its own 'President, Vice-President, Cabinet, Comptroller, Judge, Attorney-General, lawyers, policemen and all the paraphernalia of American Democracy including a gaol' (Wills 1941: 59). Discipline was enforced by those who took on the roles of police officers, while fines and other punishments could be applied through the courts. Adult supervision and surveillance was also notable (Thurston 1910: 566). All the time great emphasis was put on the benefits of American society,[3] including the economic system, as observed by Henry Thurston, who remarks that 'the economic motive is prominent' (Thurston 1910: 566). To Wills, however, this was too much 'a slavish imitation of what is, after all, not necessarily an ideal system of government'. Wills (1941: 60) quotes Russell Hoare, who ran an experimental children's home in Lincolnshire, saying 'I am not out to make good little citizens. I am out to make rebels'. Wills explains he does not mean that he wants everyone to be 'agin the government', but that

> our aim is to develop the capacity for personal judgement so that when he goes from us the lad does not necessarily accept the standards of the

first group with which he happens to come into contact, even if that group happens to be a group of normal citizens. Criticism is the dynamic of democracy, and if its citizens have lost that capacity, we had much better have a dictatorship, which will in any rate be efficient. So we don't foist a system on them and say, 'Here's a system – work it.' So far as we have a system at all it has been built up very gradually, with much squabbling, and very often we rub it out all together and start all over again.

(Wills 1941: 61)

This concern with the 'dynamic of democracy' is an important point to note. Doubtless inspired by concern with the brutal reality of the rise of fascism, it emphasises how the initiative was not simply about the adjustment or treatment of individuals but was concerned with the health of a democratic society (Toms 2013). Wills (1941) gives examples of allowing the community to take responsibility for the running of key aspects of the camp, notably the cleaning of the latrines, which had become dirty. He and the staff did not intervene until the residents themselves took on the responsibility for organising cleaning. Matters of discipline were also dealt with by the community rather than by any pre-set rules or the intervention of authority. The fundamental point that the experience of being and living in a group offered the opportunity for therapeutic change was to be taken up by a number of military psychiatrists whose work was to play a prominent role in shaping thinking about how treatment of 'psychopathy' might be organised. The third part of this chapter (7.3) will examine some of these developments. Before this, the next section will look at the work of David Henderson, who was to have some direct influence on the parliamentary debates that saw the passing of the MHA in 1959. Henderson was significant in that he was very much a part of the medical and psychiatric establishment (Haldane 2006), but brought ideas about the development of character from American psychiatry and amalgamated those with some of the more radical thinking about the significance of community in the formation of 'psychopathy'.

## 7.2 The development of the social diagnosis: Henderson's *Psychopathic States*

While there is only brief mention of Q Camps and the work of the ISTD right at the end of David Henderson's book *Psychopathic States* (Henderson 1939: 166), these were surely significant in informing some of his belief that possible solutions to the problem of psychopathy were becoming available. Henderson much more explicitly engaged with Edward Glover's radical work as he traced out a theory that suggested that the phenomenon of 'psychopathy' was immanently social in its nature. The influences of ideas from the United States also shaped his clinical formulations, since although most of Henderson's career was based in his native Scotland, he held a number of appointments in the USA, notably under Adolf Meyer, a significant figure in American psychiatry (Werlinder 1978). The impact of Meyer might be seen in the use of the term 'psychopathic states'; Henderson was critical of the categorical approach to psychiatric diagnosis, arguing that these were not constitutionally derived peculiarities but 'dynamic processes which are much more modifiable than has been supposed' (Henderson 1939: 150–151). The published version of a series of lectures given by Henderson in the United States (Henderson 1939) was often to be cited and was of some considerable material influence in the development of legislation and mental health policy in England and Wales (Prins 1980; Ramon 1986). Henderson's definition of the problem at the beginning of the book puts him firmly in the tradition of Pinel and Prichard (whose nineteenth-century work is described in Chapter 2), outlining the existence of disorders defined by immoral, or antisocial, conduct which occurs in the absence of any psychosis or defect of reason. According to Henderson the term 'psychopathic state' might be applied to individuals who

> conform to a certain intellectual standard, sometimes high, sometimes approaching the realm of defect but yet not amounting to it, who throughout their lives, or from a comparatively early age, have exhibited disorders of conduct of an antisocial or asocial nature, usually of a recurrent or episodic nature.
>
> (Henderson 1939: 18)

Although Henderson suggested that such disorders were also marked by their resistance to change, his intention was, through defining the clinical concept more clearly, to outline a more social approach to its understanding, which pointed the way to more hopeful prognoses. Meanwhile, Henderson described a nosology that distinguished three groups: 1. Predominantly aggressive; 2. Predominantly passive or inadequate; 3. Predominantly creative. Although they could be identified by the key characteristic, Henderson suggests that they shared features such as 'instability, queerness, explosiveness, intuitiveness and egocentricity' (Henderson 1939: 119) and stressed that these were not fully separate and distinct categories, but were sketched to facilitate 'discussion' (Henderson 1939: 43). Henderson described the 'predominantly aggressive' state as one that would include people who might attempt to injure themselves or others, alcoholics and drug addicts, 'the epileptoid' and 'the sex variants' he saw as standing between the aggressive and the passive/inadequate group (Henderson 1939: 44). The aggressive states, according to Henderson, tended to be of a more intermittent or transitory nature than those of the other groups (Henderson 1939: 43). Violent acts that sprang from the aggressive state were often an attempt to impose order in the face of considerable 'mental disorganisation' (1939: 44). It is worth dwelling a little on the prominence given to Edward Glover's work in Henderson's account, particularly *The Dangers of Being Human* (Glover 1936).[4] Although a psychoanalyst, Glover was firmly convinced that it was necessary to understand the psychological world as being indivisible from the social:

> The greatest mistake the social scientist can make is to isolate the subject matter of their researches. We cannot hope to understand the criminal unless we investigate the behaviour of the law abiding citizen to see how far they play into each other's hands.
> (Glover 1936: 84)

Henderson uses and quotes from this paragraph to make the point that 'Whereas the criminal discharges his fear and aggression by attacking and punishing the peaceful citizen, the peaceable citizen discharges his fear and aggression by attacking and punishing the criminal' (Glover 1936: 84). Henderson goes on to wonder whether 'the peaceable citizen is not more to blame than the criminal' (Henderson 1939: 45) and whether perhaps the contemporary social world was 'partly by its restriction, and partly by its freedom and license and lack of understanding' responsible for 'manufacturing a good number of psychopaths':

> Their story is often not listened to, or if it is, it is not given a great deal of credence; and in any case, there is no provision, so why not lock him up in prison or hang him and be done with him? It is not to be wondered at that, under such circumstances, the aggressive psychopath becomes bitter, hates society and himself and attempts to square accounts by whatever impulse is, for the moment, in the ascendant.
> (Henderson 1939: 46)

The 'predominantly passive or inadequate' were viewed by Henderson as more consistently disordered, or even immoral, than the aggressive types (Henderson 1939: 78), and he suggests that a range of features and symptoms such as unstable lives, superficial engagement in relationships and a proneness to more obvious psychoneurotic or even psychotic symptoms might be characteristic. Some might appear to be quite good-natured, or even charming, but they were like 'flowers without perfume' since only when they had repeatedly let others down, and evidenced an 'absence of warmth and honor', would they be recognised as abnormal. They were also self-centred, narcissistic, exhibitionist and selfish, and prone to fantasies that were fairly 'obvious compensations for the failure to adapt to actual conditions' (Henderson 1939: 79–80). The 'predominantly creative' might be characterised by genius, stemming perhaps from 'an exaggerated sensitivity, an ability to receive, record, and express feelings and experiences which are foreign to the less gifted'. Despite these capabilities, such personalities were still at least 'uneven' and probably 'inadequate' (Henderson 1939: 118).

Although Henderson's book is often cited in reviews about the development of theories of psychopathy, there is some irony in the the fact that the reviews put emphasis on Henderson's classification, even while he himself was at pains to argue that the classification was not at all one of rigid nosology. Indeed, it is arguable that the most significant point about Henderson's work was the very clear argument he put forward that psychopathy had to be understood not simply as a problem for society; here were psychological states that could only be fully understood in terms of their social context. It was the relationship of the individual to the social order that was key to Henderson's understanding of the disorder. The psychopath 'is unable to fit into life of the herd, but tends to lead an independent, individualistic type of existence with no thought or feeling for his family, his friends, or his country' (Henderson 1939: 128).

Henderson is not simply restating here the asocial qualities that might be characteristic of the disorder; instead he is drawing an understanding of the relational nature of the disorder into the heart of the analysis. He sees these difficulties as emerging from the fabric of the social system of which they are a part. If the 'psychopath' is socially isolated, this has to be understood as a very unhappy human state. Henderson (with the help of Ian Suttie's 1935 critique of Freud) develops the theme that a sense of belonging is as innate a drive as hunger. A feeling of belonging and being part of 'the herd' protects people from feelings of fear, and promotes instead a sense of 'courage and happiness' without which the psychopath is left as 'an outcast', a differentiated individual prone to a

> lack of concentration, to a lessened sense of reality, to an inability to pursue a steady purpose, and on occasion to precipitate impulsive action . . . Such a state leads almost inevitably to fatalism and despair, the reaction to which may be either aggressive or submissive.
> 
> (Henderson 1939: 131)

In sketching the significance of a connection between the fear of isolation and violence, Henderson is prefiguring work on links between shame and violence (Gilligan 1997, 2003; Jones 2008). The solution to the problem of the psychopath, according to Henderson's scheme, lay not simply in the adjustment of the disordered individual, but instead was bound up with the social order itself. The problem of individual isolation could not simply be understood in terms of individual psychopathology but was instead a symptom of social organisation. In Henderson's own words, 'the successful readjustment of the psychopath is bound up with the practice of medicine as a social organization' (Henderson 1939: 138).

Henderson gestured towards plans for the development of state health and welfare services as a form of therapeutic social organisation. He pointed to the success of other health-related civic projects such as sewage disposal, vaccination programmes, slum removal and the provision of education. Henderson emphasised that his point was not the specific measures themselves '*but the spirit which they embody which means so much*' (Henderson 1939: 139–140). Henderson's book finishes with a plea for the adoption of nothing less than a full blown state-run health and social welfare system, which he admitted might worry some in Britain and many more in the USA. This plea was written just before the outbreak of the Second World War, which was to usher in social changes that were to give remarkable impetus to the issues that Henderson was raising. For one thing a great deal of government funding was then poured into the still developing disciplines of psychiatry and psychology (Rose 1979, 1985). As will be discussed in the following section, some of the experimentation (in terms of treatments that went on) was remarkable and was to have some lasting impact on perceptions of psychopathy and its treatment. More generally, by the end of the war there was sufficient political consensus to begin to put abstract ideas of welfare into practice. The landslide victory of the Labour Party in 1945 meant that funds to energise these grand projects were forthcoming and, most significantly, the National Health Service was born (Morgan 2001).

## 7.3 The Second World War and the rise of community therapy

Besides the influence on social policy, the impact of the war on the development of psychiatry itself should not be underestimated either. As Harrison and Clarke (1992) explain, before the war there were two groups of psychiatrists. There were those that worked in the psychiatric asylums, where they were mainly concerned with the daily management of what were considered to be chronic and perhaps incurable cases (often with such diagnoses as schizophrenia, but no doubt including many people who simply could not cope with the social world around them). Second, there was the small but growing group of psychoanalytically inclined clinicians who worked with a private clientele. The experiences of war brought these together in the military and put them all in contact with a much larger section of the population. These encounters with the large numbers of the population who were suffering from a variety of disorders (not only neurotic, but also what were to become classified as the personality disorders) had huge impact on the shape of the psychiatric and allied professions. As we will see in the next chapter, these encounters were to play a major role in the development of diagnostic categories within psychiatry – most notably through the development of the *Diagnostic and Statistical Manual* in the United States. The scale of the problem of psychological disorder that faced the armed forces appeared to be considerable. According to British government statistics, there were 118,000 discharges from the army due to psychiatric disorder between September 1939 and June 1944. This represented between one half and one third of all medical discharges, and half of medical discharges among men under the age of 28 (Privy Council 1947). Of those discharged, 64.3 per cent were described as suffering from 'Psychoneurosis and effort syndrome' (assumed to be related to combat stress or perhaps some other underlying problem) and 8.1 per cent were described as having a 'Psychopathic personality' (Privy Council 1947: 15). Recognition that warfare had highly psychological dimensions was fairly well established before the outbreak of the Second World War. As discussed in Chapter 5, experiences with shell shock during the First World War had demonstrated to many that not only was the individual psyche vulnerable to environmental trauma, but also the issues of group morale were crucial in determining the impact of such trauma (Stone 2004). The British government was certainly interested in understanding more about how people (whether combatants or civilians) were affected by war. It was understood that the morale of the whole population – and, of course, of troops in particular – would be crucial (Rose 1989). Energy and funding was thus directed towards services that promised to understand and treat the effects of combat. There was also interest in the use of psychological ideas in the selection and training of military personnel. There were two initiatives that were to have lasting impact: the Northfield experiments, which were to spark an interest in group therapy; and the Belmont initiative, which was to take this work with groups and apply it to issues of personality disorder, working with the British National Health Service.

### 7.3.1 The Northfield experiments

What became known as the 'Northfield experiments' took place in part of the Hollymoor Hospital in the Northfield area of Birmingham (Harrison and Clarke 1992; Whiteley 2004). This was a large psychiatric hospital given over to the treatment of psychiatric disorder among military personnel. Key staff in the unit were to go on to be influential members of the British psychiatric establishment in the post-war decades, and their work was marked by an interest in the significance of group work (Trist 2000). Wilfred Bion, who had some involvement with the ISTD and initiated some of the early work at Northfield, had been a young tank commander in the First World War, reaching the rank of major. By the time of the Second World War he was a psychiatrist and trained psychoanalyst. He only spent a short time at Northfield, but went to work as Director of the Tavistock Clinic. Another major figure was S. H. Foulkes, who fought in the German army in the First World War and then trained as a psychoanalyst in Vienna. He came to England as a refugee in 1933 and carried out innovative work with groups through his psychiatric practice in Devon. He developed this work at Northfield when posted there in 1942 and went on to found the Institute of Group Analysis in London. Other graduates of Northfield were John Rickman, who is considered to have been a major influence on psychoanalytic thought and practice in Britain, and Tom Main, who went on to do pioneering work at the Cassel Hospital in west London with families within a therapeutic community setting (Harrison 2000).

As the war went on the business of Northfield came to be increasingly taken up with treating the victims of the trauma brought about either by combat and or by the experience of being held as a prisoner of war. The earlier years of the war had brought forward large numbers of people who had not seen combat but who were having difficulties fitting in with military life and training. What were seen as 'inadequate selection procedures' were leading to the recruitment of people among whom there were high incidences of 'severe and incapacitating neurosis, personality disorders and psychosis' (Harrison and Clarke 1992: 118). Some of Bion's early war work was concerned with recruitment practices, in particular the selection of officers at the War Office Selection Boards (WOSBs). Bion's belief in the significance of the group can be seen here. His own experiences as tank commander in the First World War had brought him to believe that a very important dimension of good leadership was the capacity to encourage the development of feelings of respect and belonging among the group. Bion came to believe that a key leadership capacity was to be able demonstrably to consider the needs of others, even when under considerable strain oneself. His autobiographical writing (Bion 1982) gives moving testimony to his own reflections on the impact of trauma on the capacity of the mind to continue to take account of the feelings of others when under extreme stress. He seems to have been haunted throughout his life by feelings of guilt stemming from his own apparent inability to sustain, in highly stressful circumstances, an attitude of compassion for a young soldier under his command who had suffered terrible injury.

The first of the Northfield experiments was led by Bion and lasted only six weeks. He observed the high levels of disorganisation on the therapy wing that was put in his charge. Rather like Wills's Hawkspur experiment, Bion wanted the group to face what they were doing and to begin to take responsibility for organising themselves. As Bion described 'The Experiment', only a small number of formal regulations were applied: every man had to take one hour of physical exercise each day, and had to be a member of at least one group, which would have a particular task or activity (handicrafts, carpentry or map reading, for example). Anyone could start another group if they so wished. Any man who felt unable to attend his group would go to the rest room, where he could rest under the supervision of a nursing orderly. In addition all men were required to attend a 30 minute parade at 12.10 p.m. each day. This was to become the space that allowed for all to reflect on the activities of the entire group. It was these group meetings that Bion believed were crucial since they allowed the group to become aware of its own neurosis, to reflect upon it and act.

> With surprising rapidity the training wing became self-critical. The freedom of movement permitted by the original set-up allowed the characteristics of a neurotic community to show with painful clarity; within a few days men complained that the wards were dirty and could not be kept clean under system.
>
> (Bion 1961: 18)

It was also clear that most of the constructive activities and training that were available were not being taken up. The group was faced with the fact that it was not functioning well and the individuals had to work together to reflect upon why that was and what might be done. As Harold Bridger explains, the difficulties were not about rules and systems.

> [T]he problems of organization, of course, hinged on the problems of personal relationship. Lost tools in the handicraft section, defective cinema apparatus, permission to use the local swimming baths, the finding of a football pitch, all these matters came back to the same thing, the manipulation and harmonization of personal relationships.
> (Bridger 1985: 71)

Slowly, the group began to organise itself and basic cleaning tasks started to be carried out. Another crucial dimension to this work, occurring in the midst of war, was that it was concerned with fear and violence. Bion was keen to emphasise that what the unit was doing was preparing men to go back and fight, and risk death. Bion's own experiences as a tank commander in the First World War are surely germane to his attitude here (Bion 1982). He thought it important that medical staff were very clear about the role they were taking and that they should therefore not allow the guilt that they felt to interfere with the work they were doing (Bridger 1985: 72).

Despite the progress made in group functioning, the process had involved high levels of chaos and disruption as the group was faced with the consequences of its own inaction. It might be argued that this manifestation of group disorder did not go down well with the wider hospital authorities and Bion was moved on from the hospital, which Main (1983) later described as a 'secret sacking'. A second Northfield experiment carried on the thrust of the work after Bion's departure, led this time by Harold Bridger, who was joined by S. H. Foulkes.[5] Dalal (1998) has argued that to understand the significance of Foulkes's stance it is necessary to appreciate that not only was he a psychoanalyst working in a Freudian tradition, but also he was to some extent influenced by elements of the Frankfurt School of sociological thought (discussed in Chapter 6) or more particularly by the work of Norbert Elias, who himself was never actually a 'member' but was evidently influenced by his early studies alongside the group in Frankfurt. Elias was eventually to be hugely influential through his work *The Civilizing Process*, which argued that the assumptions we make about normal behaviour and consciousness are actually historically and culturally constructed. While Elias's work has many implications, the crucial one for Foulkes was the notion that an individual existing as if separate from their social context was a culturally constructed illusion. People, he argued, *always* had to be understood in terms of relationships with others. Meaningful psychotherapeutic endeavours, therefore, always had to be made at the level of the group.

According to Harold Bridger, who was brought in to command the training wing following Bion's departure and provided a first-hand account of this work (Bridger 1985), it was known from discussion with Bion that one of the key lessons learned from the early demise of the first experiment was that the whole of the hospital organisation had to be involved in the therapeutic endeavour.[6] It was at this point, therefore, that the phrase 'therapeutic community' first began to be used (Kennard 1998). A number of seminars and discussion groups were set up, all encouraging communication and reflection, and at the heart of the enterprise was an empty 'hospital club' or social club. This was 'with its deliberate emptiness, but space for potential development . . . an arena which represented the patient's own personality and social gaps' (Bridger 1985: 78). As an example of the group taking responsibility for itself Bridger described being summoned to a meeting which was organised to protest about such frivolous use of resources on a social club when there was a war going on. The group decided that they needed to put their energies into activities that would have some impact on the war effort. Bridger explains that in time the group 'began to share responsibility for those entering the admission ward and to care for those who might benefit from the empathy and experience of those who had been through it' (Bridger 1985: 79).

Harrison and Clarke (1992) suggest that the apparent success of the psychological techniques helped create a view at governmental levels that the professions of psychiatry and psychology did have a lot to offer. For, while the significance of wider political forces (notably of course the engagement of the US military in 1942) was no doubt huge, there was a feeling that the morale of the British population and of its front line combatants had made an important contribution to the war effort, and that

> [a] diverse society, in which individuals were encouraged to continue facing the unconscious conflicts stemming from childhood and explore reality based experiences, was able to survive more successfully than one in which the population avoided these anxieties and remained dependent on an idealised leader.
>
> (Harrison and Clarke 1992: 100)

Whether this is overstating the kudos given to psychological and psychoanalytic ideas in particular, it is certainly the case that the UK government did demonstrate confidence in therapeutic community ideas in the post-war decades, the best symbol of that being the funding of the Belmont Industrial Neurosis Unit.

### 7.3.2 Psychopathy, therapeutic communities and Belmont

The perception of the success of group and community work in the military prompted the Departments of Health, Labour and Pensions to set up a special unit at Belmont in April 1947 under the leadership of Maxwell Jones, devoted to the provision of therapy for the chronically unemployed, who were assumed to be suffering from some psychological disorder. Maxwell Jones had been mentored by David Henderson (hence his move to re-name the Unit as the Henderson Hospital in 1959) and had been involved in innovative practice at the 'effort syndrome unit' based in Mill Hill (north London) during the war. 'Effort syndrome' was the name given to the disorder suffered by those (very often troops who had experienced combat) who experienced intense exhaustion, breathlessness and giddiness with no obvious physical cause. Jones and colleagues initiated large group educational sessions and it was the observation of the significance of these meetings that led to further explorations in group work, particularly drama therapy (Jones 1952). This work with groups was continued at the Southern Hospital (Dartford unit) with ex-prisoners of war (Manning 1989) and an important objective had been the construction of good relationships with the surrounding community, with the aim of getting the men into steady employment. The extent to which Jones was directly influenced by the Northfield experiments is the source of some debate, but it is certainly true that the Henderson Hospital was run on principles that emerged from Northfield (Harrison and Clarke 1992; Vandevelde 1999).

As Jones (1952: 25) explained, the hard core of chronically unemployed who were of concern to the Ministry of Labour were also well known 'in every branch of medicine' as 'the chronic attenders' who, whatever their presenting complaint, were actually suffering from high levels of 'personality and social disorganization'. The unit took referrals from all over England and was admitting people 'usually considered unsuitable for treatment by psychotherapy or physical methods' who included 'inadequate and aggressive psychopaths, schizoid personalities, early schizophrenics, various drug addictions, sexual perversions and chronic forms of psychoneurosis' (Jones 1952: 26). Manning (1989: 10) identified five aims of the unit (from Jones 1952):

1 to study a sample of (hard core unemployed) and as far as possible to understand its clinical characteristics;
2 to give appropriate psychiatric treatment;
3 to decide on the most suitable job (for the patient);
4 to arrange resettlement, preferably while the patient is still in hospital;
5 to test the effect of those procedures by carrying out an adequate follow-up study.

The social purpose of the unit was very clear but over time its work became closely associated with the treatment of psychopathy and 'personality disorder' (Rapoport 1960). Shula Ramon argues that it was the apparent usefulness of these therapeutic methods that helped establish the diagnosis of psychopathy:

> In the forties and fifties it was confidently believed that poverty would soon be eradicated, and a new stereotype of the poor was developed. The poor were no longer viewed as irresponsible rascals; they were not the authors of their own misfortunes. On the contrary, they were victims of circumstances. Whilst, however, in the majority of cases, it was possible to accept that the poor were not to be blamed for their condition, there were those who appeared not to fit this analysis. Those who did not easily fall within the stereotype of passive victim had to be categorised in a different way. This is where the category of psychopath could be used.
>
> (Ramon 1986: 222)

Ramon is undoubtedly correct to an extent, but this analysis perhaps does not give full credit to the degree of therapeutic optimism there was in this British work on psychopathy, and in particular in the work of the therapeutic communities. Nor perhaps to the degree of social optimism that was apparent in some quarters as a whole new world of mental health was being envisaged. Rolph (1958), writing a response to the initial Percy Commission report that led to the 1959 Mental Health Act, could suggest (with some enthusiasm) that '[t]he whole new structure must inevitably depend on the personal attitudes of individual citizens'. A return to good mental health could come about by treatment in the community:

> [T]he companionship of one's fellows, the friendly good-morning in the street, the invitation to a lecture, a party, a game, the seeking of help by a neighbour in the garden – these are all of immense importance.... Unobtrusively, we must all become mental health practitioners.
>
> (Rolph 1958: 35)

### 7.3.3 Grendon and beyond: the therapeutic community in prison

While what became known as 'the Henderson Hospital' can probably claim to be the first democratic therapeutic community, it was to be followed by parallel innovations in other parts of the world. There is not the space to review these here, but some landmarks need to be noted. HM Prison Grendon deserves some mention for being an entire (albeit small) prison that has been organised on democratic therapeutic community lines, and was directly inspired by the Henderson. Despite some considerable lobbying for the creation of prisons that would treat psychopathy (East and Hubert 1939), it was only in 1962 that HMP Grendon was opened.[7] Grendon is a category B (medium secure) prison with a capacity of around 240 men, consisting of six wings, each of which functions as a separate therapeutic community (Stevens 2010). It should be noted that this is not a special hospital for those committed under the Mental Health Act. It takes men, most serving life sentences, who have often been found guilty of offences that involve violence (murder or manslaughter or other violent offences, often involving sexual transgression). The vast majority have been assessed as suffering from a personality disorder. In many respects the history of Grendon is marked by ambivalence. It has been subject to a number of research initiatives (Brookes 2011; Genders and Player 1995; Rawlings 1998; Shuker and Sullivan 2010) which report very favourably on the work. It is generally agreed that despite having an intake of men who are regarded as disruptive and difficult, the rates of violence and drug abuse are reported to be low. In contrast to many prison institutions, reports on Grendon have found good relationships between staff and inmates and thus the recourse to the use of force is also low. Despite this it remains conspicuously in a minority position in the British prison system. It is the only one of 140 prisons in England and Wales to be dedicated to work as a democratic therapeutic community. Overall, it is difficult to argue with Shuker's (2004: 55) comment that the influence of therapeutic communities over the past few decades has been 'fleeting and tenuous', although some specific initiatives have been funded under the UK government's 'dangerous and severe personality disorder' treatment initiative (discussed in Chapter 9).

Arguably, two distinct types of therapeutic community have subsequently developed: the 'democratic' and the 'concept' or 'hierarchical'. Opinion varies as to whether these are really very different or simply variations (Lees *et al.* 1999). In the USA there were a number of experiments made with therapeutic communities, which tended to be along the lines of more hierarchical models. As Rawlings (1998) suggests, they suffered badly from the Martinson 'nothing works' review in 1974. They have had something of a resurgence since that period and have been influential in promoting the use of 'drug-free' therapeutic communities in Europe. In Denmark, Herstedvester provided intensive treatment for offenders diagnosed with personality disorder. In Geneva the Pâquerette Sociotherapeutic Centre at Champ-Dollon prison was influenced by Grendon to organise along therapeutic community lines. Most famously, the Van der Hoeven Kliniek based in Utrecht (Netherlands) was created in 1955 to cater for forensic psychiatric patients (who very often will have diagnoses of personality disorder) and is run as a therapeutic community, although not explicitly on the lines of the democratic TCs; it has more in common with the US model of hierarchical TC for drug addiction (Feldbrugge and Haverkamp 1993).

## 7.4 Psychopathy as a legal category

The belief that what appeared to be individual psychological problems might be solved by social and community intervention is key to understanding how the category of 'psychopathy', as a form of moral insanity, came to have a place in the 1959 Mental Health Act. As already mentioned in the introduction to this chapter, the parliamentary debates on the legislation make it clear that the category was no minor afterthought. In addition to arguing that the inclusion of psychopathy was the most important aspect of the Act, Dr Summerskill MP argued that 'the whole problem of psychopathy' needed to be tackled 'with necessary conviction and firmness'. She noted the historical dimension of the story and observed that many prison officials and judges were beginning to appreciate that those afflicted with 'moral insanity' are after all 'distinctive types, emotionally and instinctively unstable, who have no more power to control their conduct than the epileptic can control his fit' (Hansard 1957: c52). Even Edith Summerskill, however, had concerns about the lack of a proposed definition in the Act and quoted approvingly David Henderson's definition:

> Dr Henderson describes psychopaths as those individuals who conform to a certain intellectual standard, sometimes high, sometimes approaching the realm of defect but not yet amounting to it, who, throughout their lives or from a comparatively early age, have exhibited disorders of conduct of an anti-social or asocial nature, usually of a recurrent or episodic type, which, in many instances, have proved difficult to influence by methods of social, penal and medical care . . . It is difficult to believe that a wide definition of that nature could create controversy in the psychiatric world.
>
> (Hansard 1957: c52)

There were more cautious voices, such as that of Christopher Mayhew (Woolwich East): 'What it comes down to is, plainly, that if we carry out the recommendations we shall create a new legal right to detain people – sometimes of high intelligence – who have committed no crime' (Hansard 1957).

Allied to the problem of detainment was that of definition, which

> leave[s] the matter far too wide open, because it is not only psychiatrists who have to decide who are psychopaths and who are not, but also in some cases the courts, and without any guidance from legislation, that may lead to undesirably wide variations in practice in different parts of the country.
>
> (Kenneth Robinson, MP for St Pancras North, Hansard 1957)

Walter Elliot (Glasgow Kelvingrove) was concerned that he would not like to trust his own liberty to 'even Professor Henderson's definition'. Dr Reginald Bennett (Gosport and Fareham; who had professional experience as a psychiatrist) also noted the frustration over the difficulty of definition, but he argued that it ought to be left to the medical profession. Bennett also argued that there ought to be more emphasis on preventive work, with interventions aimed to 'get them before they are criminals, and before they have been labelled with a far worse stigma than that of mental illness' (Hansard 1957: c75). Despite this he argued that it would be wrong to engage the medical profession in compulsory admission without magistrates' involvement and expressed concern over the practicalities: 'I am far from sure that the Royal Commission was itself sure of what it wanted to do about psychopaths' (Hansard 1957: c75).

Despite concerns about the definition, the legislation was passed and the diagnosis of 'psychopathy' achieved formal recognition in government legislation as 'a persistent disorder or disability of mind' which resulted in 'abnormally aggressive or seriously irresponsible conduct' that required or was 'susceptible to medical treatment' (DoH 1959: Part 1, Point 4). Some of the anxieties about the breadth and subjectivity of the definition were apparent in the following caveat, which observed that no one should be considered as suffering from a mental disorder 'by reason only of promiscuity or other immoral act' (DoH 1959: Part 1, Point 4).

Meanwhile, there was another strand of legislation that might potentially have had considerable impact on the treatment of psychopathy and personality disorder in the criminal justice system. This was the introduction of the charge of 'diminished responsibility' in the Homicide Act, largely as a response to widespread feeling that the M'Naghten rules were too restrictive in providing a definition of insanity that was of practical use.

### 7.4.1 Diminished responsibility and psychopathy in court

As previous chapters have explored, the M'Naghten rules had fixed a very narrow definition of insanity which, when applied in court, allowed for an insanity defence to be successful only in those cases where the defendant had very clearly lost their reason and had no real knowledge of what they had done. This was always at odds with many psychiatric definitions of insanity, but the development of thinking within psychiatry and beyond, fuelled by the experiences of the two world wars, was making such a narrow definition of insanity increasingly untenable. An important manifestation of this belief was in the formulation of the 1957 Homicide Act. Perhaps the most significant innovation of the Act was the introduction of 'diminished responsibility'. This allowed a defendant who was accused of homicide to plead and be found not guilty of murder, but instead guilty of manslaughter on the grounds of diminished responsibility. The manslaughter verdict allowed the mandatory sentence of execution, or life imprisonment, to be avoided. The Act laid out when a diminished responsibility verdict would be appropriate:

> Where a person kills or is a party to the killing of another, he shall not be convicted of murder if he was suffering from such abnormality of mind (whether arising from a condition of arrested or retarded development of mind or any inherent causes or induced by disease or injury) as substantially impaired his mental responsibility for his acts and omissions in doing or being a party to the killing.
> 
> (Home Office 1957: Part 1, Section 2 (1))

The issue of psychopathy was not directly addressed in the Homicide Act but of course it was formally recognised as an abnormality of mind in the MHA (DoH 1959). Even before that, the issues had been discussed during the construction of the Homicide Act, for example in the Gowers Commission (1949–1953) investigation into the death penalty. As Walker and McCabe (1973: 215) point out, much of this discussion was quite critical, despite the fact that David Henderson's evidence was taken seriously. However, the term, roughly as formulated by Henderson (and Hervey Cleckley in the United States), was beginning to appear in more general public discourse and in criminal trials. For example, in 1946 an attempt was made to use the notion of psychopathy and moral insanity to defend Neville Heath on a charge of murder after he had killed a woman (with what was assumed to be a sexual motivation). To both defence and prosecution, Heath was a 'psychopathic personality'; to the defence he was 'morally defective and certifiable as such'. The jury were persuaded that the issue was not about whether he was 'morally insane' but whether he was 'insane', and with the judge making strong reference to the wording of the M'Naghten rules, Heath was sentenced to death (*The Times* 27 September 1946: 8). Several years later in 1953 at the trial of John Wilkinson for murder both defence and prosecution were again agreed that the defendant had committed the acts and that he was 'a psychopath', and that it was not a disease but a defect of character. It was thus up to the jury to decide whether this was sufficient to avoid the straightforward verdict of 'murder'. The jury thought not and so returned a guilty verdict that was upheld on appeal (*The Times* 2 December 1953: 7).

According to *The Times* the first trial to consider the new 'diminished responsibility' verdict was that of Ronald Dunbar in May 1957, and it did feature psychopathy. Dunbar was accused of murdering an elderly widow in the course of a burglary and he was described as 'an inadequate psychopath' by the defence when they asked the jury to consider that he suffered from an abnormality of mind. The prosecution called medical witnesses who denied this claim, pointing out that he had an IQ of 112 (which suggests that recourse was still being made to concepts of feeblemindedness that were current some years earlier – discussed in Chapter 5). In words that were clearly referencing the new ruling on diminished responsibility, there was agreement in the court that psychopathy was an abnormality of personality which could be regarded as an abnormality of mind that might well impair 'mental responsibility'. The issue before the jury, according to the judge, was whether there was evidence of sufficient impairment of mental responsibility to issue the manslaughter verdict. The jury thought not, and Dunbar was sentenced to death (*The Times* 17 May 1957: 8).

Walker and McCabe (1973) note that the defence of diminished responsibility was actually used successfully in Yorkshire some days earlier than this. This was in the case of Shirley Campbell, who was accused of killing the baby of a friend of hers which had been left in her charge. Annoyed by its crying, and perhaps bearing a grudge as to an unpaid debt, she killed the baby and returned to her own home. The psychiatrists called by the defence drew attention to her 'low intelligence' but also described her as 'impulsive', 'aggressive' and with a 'gross personality defect ... a psychopathic personality' (Walker 1968: 152). The jury were strongly directed by the judge to use the new verdict, and they did so. The fact that this was a woman accused of child murder, where there is a long history of leniency, cannot be ignored (Kramar and Watson 2006; Ward 1999) and does suggest that the verdict was not entirely dependent upon acceptance of this new concept of psychopathy.

Walker and McCabe (1973: 216) suggest that the more significant case that seemed at the time to go some way to establishing the diagnosis of psychopathy in this context was that of Albert Matheson, whose defence of diminished responsibility was upheld by the Court of Appeal in terms that appeared to confirm that psychopathy could be used in this way. Matheson was tried for the murder of a 15-year-old following 'an unnatural association with the boy' (*Manchester Guardian* 31 January 1958). Matheson, perhaps following an argument about money, had killed him by battering him over the head with a bottle and burying his mutilated and disembowelled body under the boxing ring of a hall in Newcastle. At the original trial a number of psychiatric witnesses agreed that Matheson ought to be convicted of manslaughter rather than murder. Dr Pickering, senior medical officer at Durham prison, testified that Matheson had been diagnosed a 'psychopathic personality' in 1943, had a history of self-injury, had only an 'elementary' idea of right and wrong and had a mental age of less than 10. Agreeing with the diagnosis, Dr Cuthbert of the Newcastle Hospitals Board added that 'he had no feeling of remorse or of having done wrong, and the question of right or wrong hardly ever entered his mind' (*Manchester Guardian* 31 January 1958; Walker and McCabe 1973: 216*).* The judge, according to the *Manchester Guardian* account, summed up by indicating the new rule of diminished responsibility and suggesting that the jury must use the manslaughter verdict if they agreed that Matheson was suffering from 'an abnormality of the mind which substantially impaired his mental responsibility'. He went on to suggest, however, that sexual perversions were not abnormalities of the mind but an abnormality of morals. So directed, the jury returned a verdict of 'guilty of murder' and Matheson was sentenced to death. The case was taken to the Court of Appeal, and there the verdict of 'diminished responsibility' was applied on the grounds that the medical evidence given at the trial suggesting that Matheson was suffering from an abnormality of mind that had impacted on his moral responsibility had not actually been challenged. The verdict of 'guilty of murder' was in this case not 'in accordance with the evidence' (Walker and McCabe 1973: 216).

It is surely worth observing the prominence of crimes of a sexual nature among these cases. This mirrors the interest in 'sexual psychopaths' that was very visible and prominent in shaping legislation in the United States over a similar time period (as discussed in Chapter 6). Indeed, another notable case was that of Patrick Byrne, who was described in court as a 'sexual psychopath'. Patrick Byrne stood trial for the savage rape and murder of a young woman whose room he broke into at a YMCA hostel in Birmingham. He was not apprehended at the time, but gave himself up and made a full confession some weeks later (Walker 1968: 155). Since he had confessed to the act, the trial was really about testing his defence of diminished responsibility. At trial, three psychiatric witnesses for the defence all agreed that Byrne was a 'sexual psychopath' (*The Times* 5 July 1960: 19, column A). This meant, it was suggested, that he was prone to such strong perverse sexual feelings that he could not resist the impulse to act upon them. The judge directed the jury to find him guilty even if they agreed that he did suffer from abnormal sexual impulses, if they found that he was 'otherwise normal in every other respect'. So directed, the jury found him guilty of murder. The appeal was heard by Judges Hilberry and Diplock. They suggested that the facts of the case were not disputed: he had killed the woman and mutilated her body in 'revolting circumstances' and, put together with the history of sexual offending, 'the accused man was what would be described in ordinary language as on the borderline of insanity or partial insanity' (*The Times* 5 July 1960: 19, column A). In a ruling that seemed to reference Matthew Hale's seventeenth-century writing on partial insanity, they argued that it was 'up to the jury to decide' on the matter of whether the abnormality of mind was 'so great as to amount in their view to a substantial impairment of the accused's mental responsibility for the acts'. The appeal judges decided that this degree of judgment had effectively been withdrawn by the judge in the original trial, and therefore the appeal was upheld and so Byrne was found guilty of manslaughter and thus spared the death penalty.

Judgments such as this might have been expected to increase the number of insanity and diminished responsibility verdicts considerably, as a number of prominent commentators suggested (Baroness Wootton, for example, in 1960). As Walker points out, this did not happen: the overall numbers of successful defences using the various mechanisms (including the more familiar 'not guilty on the grounds of insanity' as well as the new 'diminished responsibility') did not increase over the period 1947 to 1963. Walker's figures suggest that this was largely because the new 'diminished responsibility' verdict was used in many cases instead of the 'guilty but insane' defence (Walker 1968: 158–159).

## Conclusion

The middle decades of the twentieth century, heavily influenced by the Second World War, were witness to a remarkable amount of work on the problem of 'psychopathy' in Britain which firmly distinguished itself from the biological models that had begun to dominate thinking in psychiatry at the end of the nineteenth century. Britain was much slower than the US to take interest in psychopathy at a policy level and thus when it did it was far more influenced by both psychoanalysis and the progressive social thinking born of the necessities of fighting a war involving the entire population.

Strong currents of thought framed the diagnosis of 'psychopathy' as a psychological state that could only be understood in terms of social context. It is important to acknowledge that other currents were around; as Schirmann (2014a, 2014b) notes, there was particular interest, in the 1940s and 1950s, in using the novel technology of electroencephalography (EEG) to identify the distinctive brain activities of 'psychopaths'. While such technological innovation gave the diagnosis a certain amount of respectability, it was a remarkably social understanding of the disorder that received a certain amount of official sanction, as manifest in the inclusion of 'psychopathy' in the 1959 Mental Health Act and the support of such initiatives as the Belmont (later the Henderson Hospital). The debate surrounding the bill that led to the enactment of the Mental Health Act makes it clear that the issue of psychopathy was not peripheral, but quite central to the new social perspective on mental health. In recognition of the importance of the topic, Walker and McCabe's final substantive chapter of the epic two volume work *Crime and Insanity in England* (Walker and McCabe 1973) was entitled 'Psychopathy in the Sixties'. The prominent presence of psychopathy perhaps says something of the assumed importance of the topic at that point in history. The inclusion of the diagnosis of psychopathy in the 1959 Mental Health Act and the challenge to the M'Naghten rules provided by the introduction of the diminished responsibility verdict in the 1957 Homicide Act meant that perhaps the issue was going to assume a central place in debate about the relationship between insanity and crime. Walker and McCabe observed, however, that research was suggesting very firmly that there had not been a marked increase in the use of the various 'insanity' verdicts, and they also noted that despite the fact that 'there has been no authoritative discussion of its exact meaning in a court of law, many psychiatrists have interpreted it in a curiously restrictive way' (Walker and McCabe 1973: 223). They speculate a little on the reluctance of psychiatrists to use the diagnosis as a legal category even in reference to patients who are undoubtedly 'abnormally aggressive' and whose difficulties 'clearly arise' from 'a persistent disorder of mind'. They suggest that the psychiatrists were viewing such people as outside the scope of the Mental Health Act because their condition was viewed as 'not responsive to treatment'. Walker and McCabe suggest this is a far too narrow, or even misleading, interpretation of the wording of the Act. They argue that in reality psychiatrists needed to take into account not only the issue of susceptibility to treatment, but also of the *requirement*. There are a great many people suffering from many different kinds of illness, whose condition is such that they are not 'responsive to treatment'. This does not mean that their condition, as in the case of various serious, and perhaps terminal, diseases, does not 'require' treatment. This rather angry observation was to be taken up near the end of the twentieth century by the then Home Secretary in the UK, Jack Straw. It will be discussed in some detail in Chapter

9, but it is worth noting here since it is perhaps very pertinent to an explanation of why the issue of 'psychopathy', so hotly debated, rather fell off governmental, criminological and penal agendas in Britain – despite the fact that there were government-sponsored reviews of provision for mentally abnormal offenders in 1975 (the Butler Committee report) and 1992 (the Reed report). Mainstream British psychiatric views on psychopathy were not entirely unreasonably summarised by Rollins (1976: 158), who suggested that although the Butler Committee report indicated that it would be beyond its remit to suggest that 'psychopathic disorder' be removed from the Mental Health Act, it did seem evident that this was what it was implying, and that '[t]here can be few practising psychiatrists who would not applaud the suggestion'. Nor would they, as a result of bitter experience, be in the least bit offended by the committee's categorical statement that 'psychopaths are not, in general, treatable in medical terms'. The later Reed report, which reviewed services for mentally disordered offenders, could only conclude that

> issues concerning the care and treatment of people with psychopathic (or personality) disorders are difficult and contentious. We have already given detailed consideration to these as a committee, but ministers have accepted our recommendation that they call for further, urgent work before it will be possible to offer any conclusions.
>
> (DoH 1992: 3)

The word 'psychopath' itself remained in the Mental Health Act until 2007, despite the move towards the more popular use of 'personality disorder', which was to be promoted by the *Diagnostic and Statistical Manual*, published by the American Psychiatric Association. Despite the radical thinking on the topic in Britain, it was to be American ideas that were to dominate debate in the second half of the twentieth century. The following chapter will explore those developments.

## Notes

1   In 1921 Maurice Hamblin Smith had given what Garland (1997: 37) argues to be 'the first university lectures in "criminology" delivered in Britain' to postgraduate medical students as part of a course entitled 'Medical Aspects of Crime and Punishment'.
2   This innovative community for delinquent and troubled children influenced A. S. Neill, who set up the famous Summerhill School in Suffolk, England.
3   William Hull gave a contemporary account:

> There is a vast amount of enthusiasm for everything American in this miniature Republic, and it is sought to direct this into channels of patriotism and love for the big Republic by elaborate ceremonies when raising and lowering the 'Stars and Stripes', by singing patriotic songs and declaiming patriotic addresses.
>
> (Hull 1897: 79)

4   Published in 1936, this was a series of lectures written for broadcast by the BBC on the relationship between psychoanalysis and social problems. The preface refers

to the difficulty of broadcasting on the topics of aggression, destructiveness and war on the eve of war in Britain. The key issue of the lectures was that all individuals have murderous and aggressive impulses, and that any society that tries to deny and repress these is likely to be storing up trouble. 'Psychologically regarded, the criminal is a scapegoat and so long as he performs the function of whipping boy for society, there is no great hope of radical change in criminal law or practice' (Glover 1936: 84).
5  S. H. Foulkes already had experience of working with a form of group therapy and brought this work to Northfield.
6  Bridger also records the influence of work at other places such as the Mill Hill 'effort syndrome' unit and the 'Peckham experiment'.
7  Specialist units have been run within HM Prisons Barlinnie and Gartree, for example (Rawlings 1998).

# Chapter 8
# DSM and the proliferation of personality disorders

## Introduction

The previous chapter discussed a number of developments that occurred in Britain in the middle decades of the twentieth century that led to official government acceptance of the concept of 'psychopathy' as a psychological state with crucial social dimensions. This recognition was carried so far that the category appeared in the 1959 Mental Health Act (DoH 1959), where it was to remain until 2007 (the debates around its replacement will be discussed in Chapters 9 and 10). In this same post-World War Two period there were moves across the Atlantic that have had far-reaching consequences for the acceptance and understanding of this psychological conceptualisation of psychopathy. Most notably, the term 'psychopathy' was to be partly displaced by a new nomenclature of personality disorder which was to include categories describing the kind of remorseless antisocial behaviour that had been included in the concept of psychopathy. The descriptions of the various categories of personality disorder were designed to cover a range of disorders apparently found in the general population far beyond the walls of the asylums and the prisons. The most prominent vehicle for the extension of this influence was the *Diagnostic and Statistical Manual of Mental Disorders* (DSM) published by the American Psychiatric Association, and the *International Classification of Diseases* (ICD) published by the World Health Organization. Increasingly differentiated notions of a wide variety of personality disorders have been introduced since the first edition of DSM was published in 1952, so that through the second half of the twentieth century there appeared to be an apparently ever expanding list of personality disorders appearing in the various versions of DSM (and ICD classifications). These developments can be understood in terms of contrasting perspectives. To the adherents of DSM the identification of the personality disorders was merely recognition of the widespread existence of psychological distress and misery throughout the population. Once properly identified, these disorders might be alleviated through the correct application of various strategies and interventions. To critics, the development of the personality disorder sections of DSM is nothing less than the apogee of a 'Foucaldian' nightmare as psychiatric expertise is allowed to capture, manage and control an ever wider range of more everyday aspects of human experience (Rimke and Brock 2012).

Despite the obvious shift towards the use of the name 'personality disorder', it would be wrong to say that the term has simply usurped that of 'psychopathy'. A major boost to the popularisation of the term came via the publication of Hervey Cleckley's book *The Mask of Sanity: An Attempt to Reinterpret the So-Called Psychopathic Personality* in 1941. Cleckley's very accessible account undoubtedly helped rescue psychopathy from its associations with theories about its hereditary nature which had led to discredited eugenical solutions (as discussed in Chapter 5). Nevertheless, there have been other areas where there is still little consensus to emerge from DSM as to the precise nature of the problem. Chief among those unresolved issues are the status and permanence of these disorders. Are they to be understood as disorders that can be defined simply by reference to the behaviour and overt symptomatology of an individual, or do they require a deeper understanding of their psychological makeup? Many, particularly those in the professions of clinical psychology, argue that the term 'psychopathy' ought to be reserved to describe an underlying psychological orientation that can manifest in various ways (including overt criminality). The view has received strong support and has had some success in steering practices in courts (DeMatteo and Edens 2006) and prison systems in the US and Britain (Cooke *et al.* 2005). Related to this is the debate on the permanence of these underlying psychological 'structures': are these better understood as 'states' that people will slip in and out of at different times in life, depending upon circumstances, or are they more like permanent dispositions of character? Another contentious question concerns the relationship between such disorders and the proximate and distal social conditions that surround an individual. As discussed in Chapter 7, work in the UK had strongly emphasised the social nature of psychopathy. The earliest edition of DSM (published in 1952) seemed to acknowledge very overtly the social dimension of the diagnosis with the specific category of 'sociopath'. As we will see, such overt reference to the social dimension was not continued through to later editions and there has, instead, arguably been a move to more individually based concepts.

This chapter will begin with a description and discussion of Hervey Cleckley's work, which has been so influential in popularising the concept of the psychopath that has in many ways gripped the popular imagination both in the US and in Europe (the growth in interest in the activities of 'sexual psychopaths' in the post-world war period in the USA was particularly notable and is discussed in Chapter 6). Cleckley's work was important in helping to establish the idea of 'the psychopath among us' in the twentieth century: someone who may be able to function well in many aspects of their life, but whose psychological difficulties would manifest themselves in highly disordered and destructive relationships often distressing to others. As discussed in previous chapters (particularly 6 and 7), it was the experiences of the First and Second World Wars that significantly shifted the attitudes of government, psychiatrists and the general population towards acceptance of the universality of 'psychological disorder'. War not only demonstrated the consequences of environmental trauma on an individual's psychological health but also generally encouraged the idea that the potential of great aggression and cruelty dwelt inside many, if not all, of us rather than simply in a minority of damaged or deficient individuals. The war had also led military psychiatrists to engage with a wider spectrum of the population and to be struck by the degree of psychological disturbance among them as they came into contact with a wider array of people through the mass mobilisation programmes.

The second, and main, part of the chapter moves on to describe the evolution of the 'antisocial personality disorder' diagnosis through the various editions of DSM.[1] The success of DSM has helped establish the terms in common culture and they have gained popularity and usage well beyond the courtroom and the mental health clinic. Indeed, in addition to the developing clinical literature, influential cultural analyses also began to focus on notions of personality and the significance of its 'disorders'. The idea that expectations of personality were now a significant aspect of the social order has been taken up in influential sociological analyses (Giddens 1991, for example). Christopher Lasch's thesis, published in 1979, suggesting that narcissistic personality disorders were now becoming the character dispositions of modern times in the United States, has had considerable impact on thought about western societies in general (Lasch 1979). The idea of narcissism has been taken up recently in relation to consumer culture and crime (Hall *et al.* 2008).

## 8.1 Hervey Cleckley and *The Mask of Sanity*

The publication by the American psychiatrist Hervey Cleckley of *The Mask of Sanity: An Attempt to Reinterpret the So-Called Psychopathic Personality* in 1941 was to have considerable popular influence. As we will see, it was ostensibly somewhat atheoretical and descriptive, but helped to establish a view of psychopathy as a psychological disposition that might well be associated with disorder and destructiveness and also might, in various manifestations, be found right across the population. One purpose of Cleckley's work was to move thinking away from the biological theories that had dominated thought in the US (and elsewhere) in the early decades of the twentieth century, towards a more clearly psychological domain. As we have seen in Chapter 5, policy and debate in the US had been focused on 'feeblemindedness', which had evolved from concepts of psychopathic inferiority and constitutional psychopathy developed largely within the German organic schools of psychiatry, with the assumption that such conditions were the result of 'congenital defect'. Cleckley was clear that he believed such assumptions were not warranted and were supported only by 'pure speculation'.

A substantial irony of Cleckley's influence was that he had a major role in propagating the use of the term 'psychopath', despite the fact that (as is clear in his use of the word 'so-called' in the subtitle of the book) he was rather doubtful about the utility of the term. In a brief review of various descriptions and schemes of 'psychopathy' drawn up by a largely German tradition of thought (through Meyer, Kraepelin, Kahn and Schneider), Cleckley drew attention to the problem created by the apparent lack of specificity in the use of the term 'psychopath' and suggested that 'semantic dementia' (1941: 268) might be a more useful term. In drawing up this diagnosis Cleckley was suggesting that such individuals have problems in understanding or formulating the meaning of the social world around them. It was the lack of insight that Cleckley found particularly striking:

> The patient seems to have little or no ability to feel the significance of his situation, to experience the real emotions of regret or shame, or determination to improve. . . . Such a deficiency of insight is harder to comprehend than the schizophrenic's deficiency; for it exists in the full presence of what might be thought of as the qualities by which insight is gained. . . . One is confronted by the spectacle of a person who uses all the words that would be used by one who understands and who could define all the words, but who is still blind to the meaning.
> (Cleckley 1941: 246)

The greater part of the *The Mask of Sanity* is taken up by description of the typical characteristic features (discussed below) and of case studies of individuals. These clinical profiles have been tremendously influential, in part perhaps because Cleckley wrote a very accessible, everyman account. In the first edition of the book Cleckley introduced a number of characteristics that he believed typified the psychopathic personality. These features were then developed over a number of editions over several decades. The list in Box 8.1 comes from the fifth edition.

Given the impact of this characterisation, it is worth dwelling a little on the features that Cleckley outlined. The first three characteristics are significant in emphasising the apparent normality of the presentation of the individual. As the title of Cleckley's work suggests, the appearance as a sane individual is a key feature. Such individuals often show superficial charm and good intelligence (1) – indeed, they may well be able to create a particularly good impression in social situations. They will be able to remain very calm and demonstrate an absence of 'nervousness' or psychoneurotic manifestations (3). Most crucially, of course, they have a perfectly rational understanding of the world and will not exhibit any sign of delusions or irrational thinking (2). These features are very much consistent with Prichard's description of 'moral insanity' from back in 1835 (as discussed in Chapter 2).

Despite the outward appearance of normality and even social competence, such individuals are likely to be unreliable (4), and be prone to outbreaks of very irresponsible behaviour. They are likely be untruthful and insincere

## Box 8.1 Cleckley's clinical profile

1. Superficial charm and good 'intelligence';
2. absence of delusions and other signs of irrational thinking;
3. absence of 'nervousness' or psychoneurotic manifestations;
4. unreliability;
5. untruthfulness and insincerity;
6. lack of remorse or shame;
7. inadequately motivated antisocial behavior;
8. poor judgment and failure to learn by experience;
9. pathologic egocentricity and incapacity for love;
10. general poverty in major affective reactions;
11. specific loss of insight;
12. unresponsiveness in general interpersonal relations;
13. fantastic and uninviting behavior, with drink and sometimes without;
14. suicide rarely carried out;
15. sex life impersonal, trivial, and poorly integrated;
16. failure to follow any life plan.

(This version based on the fifth edition of *The Mask of Sanity*)

(5) and be capable of very destructive and antisocial behaviour, even when they have no clear motivation (7). The quality of their intimate relationships is likely to be poor and Cleckley gives more space to sexual behaviour than any of the other characteristics. According to Cleckley, despite an appearance of being very motivated by sex, there seems little interest in mere pleasure, let alone in the sense of love and intimacy that might be expressed and achieved. Instead such individuals seem more interested in the potential for humiliating and destructive experiences (for themselves and others) and so their sex life is often impersonal, trivial and poorly integrated with the rest of their life (15). The path of their life will appear chaotic and unplanned (16), and despite the chaos and harm that they may cause, they will generally show a complete lack of remorse or shame (6); they do not seem to learn from experience (8) and they will continue to show poor judgment. They will be very egocentric and have no capacity for love (9), and will be generally unable to react with appropriate feelings to other people's situations (10). They are thus likely to be generally unresponsive within relationships (12), and to have no insight into their own behaviour (11). Cleckley gives some space to making the point that although very antisocial behaviour can be associated with alcohol intake (13), the drinking itself appears to be used as an excuse for allowing the expression of their antisocial inclinations and is not the cause of the antisocial behaviour in this group. Despite all the very destructive behaviour and risk taking, Cleckley argues, actual suicidal acts are rarely carried out (14).

As should be clear from the summary given here, Cleckley is, as Werlinder (1978: 165) puts it, 'distinctly clinical-descriptive' in his attempt to communicate his understanding of the core syndrome. In terms of understanding what underlies the condition, aside from being clear that he does not believe that there are biological causes he takes a fairly atheoretical stance, but does suggest that the psychopath 'has a serious and subtle abnormality or defect at deep levels disturbing the integration and normal appreciation of experience and resulting in a pathology that might . . . be described as semantic' (Cleckley 1988: 388).

Although the reference to 'deep levels' might suggest the assumptions of psychoanalysis (at the very least that the mind has to be understood in terms of depth and conflicting impulses), it becomes quite clear by the later editions that he distances himself from psychoanalytic theory. In the fifth edition (1988: 408), there is a particularly noteworthy section that mocks the 'healthy' American male response to a majorette with a 'Freudian' interpretation. More substantially, he also disputes the idea that such conditions resulted from emotionally deprived childhoods and argues that many of those he had studied came from backgrounds 'conducive to happy development and excellent adjustment' (1988: 410). Even by the fifth edition there is a reluctance to theorise the cause and he instead makes the plea that people should 'admit the incompleteness of our knowledge and modestly pursue our inquiry' (Cleckley 1988: 415).

Despite Cleckley's own scepticism towards the term 'psychopath', a number of clinicians and theorists, notably Robert Hare, have doggedly continued to argue that 'psychopathy' (largely as described by Cleckley) is an important psychological concept that is quite distinct from 'antisocial personality disorder' (the term which, as we shall see, came to be favoured in DSM). In subsequent years Hare and colleagues have taken the 16 factors described by Cleckley and used those to construct a number of versions of the 'Psychopathy Checklist'. This test is used as both a research and a clinical tool, both in the US and in the UK (PCL and PCL-R, as described, for example, by Schroeder et al. 1983). It has achieved a degree of popularity, with the measure being used in penal systems around the globe. This is not without controversy, however, as will be discussed further in Chapter 10.

The first edition of Cleckley's book appeared in 1941, on the eve of the United States becoming fully involved in the Second World War, which was already tearing Europe apart. This war, involving the military deployment in some form of over 16 million Americans, was to have a massive influence on culture in various ways. As early as 1941 Hervey Cleckley, in an address to the Medical Association of Georgia, suggested:

> In our efforts to prepare for national defence no problem which confronts the examining boards for selective service is more pressing or more subtle than that of the so-called psychopathic personality. . . . Not only will he fail regularly and in most vital crises, but he will prove a seriously disorganising influence and will demand time and energy from others.
> (quoted in Felthous and Sass 2007: 120)

The military did indeed turn to psychiatric concepts, not only to aid their understanding of selection processes, but also to help them with the treatment of battle stress. As described below, one of the key products of the increase of funding to US military psychiatry was the publication of the *Diagnostic and Statistical Manual* by the American Psychiatric Association in 1952. The identification of 'psychopathic' personalities was to be a critical driver of the development of DSM as it emerged and was shaped in the second half of the twentieth century.

## 8.2 Personality disorder and the *Diagnostic and Statistical Manual*

World War Two has loomed large in the story of the rapid escalation of interest in notions of psychopathy and it is especially prominent for its role in the development of the *Diagnostic and Statistical Manual*, which has been a factor in the promulgation of the various diagnoses of 'personality disorder'. It was the Second World War that prompted, not only a major revision of psychiatric categories, but also a belief that greater common agreement needed to be reached over their definitions. The first edition of DSM, published in 1952 (APA 1952), was created because the previous systems of classification based on the requirements of asylum administrators now appeared to be inadequate (Coolidge and Segal 1998; Grob 1991). As the military conscripted ever larger sections of the population, they felt the need to categorise in terms of the particular individual psychological problems they were seeing. As explained in the foreword of the first DSM, a much wider set of classification was needed as '[m]ilitary psychiatrists, induction station psychiatrists, and Veterans Administration psychiatrists, found themselves operating within the limits of a nomenclature specifically not designed for 90 per cent of the cases handled'. There needed to be alternative ways of classifying 'minor personality disturbances, which became of importance only in the military setting' other than simply as 'psychopathic personality'. The psychological impacts of combat were not medically classifiable at all. Overall the 'official system of nomenclature' had become 'untenable' (APA 1952: vi–vii). Thus, the Second World War represented a major broadening of the scope of psychiatry in the USA, as it had in the UK (discussed in Chapter 7). DSM sought to integrate the various systems of categorisation that different branches of the armed forces, the medical Veterans Administration and individual treatment and training centres had all advanced. The experiences of war had also drawn attention to the significance of the environment on psychological health and bolstered the credibility of those theories that assumed that individual psychology could be shaped by experience. It is not surprising that there was thus a surge of interest in psychoanalytic schools of thought, which had already been making major advances in mainstream psychiatry (as discussed in Chapter 6); these emphasised the significance of the environment and pointed out ways to rehabilitation and cure (Sanders 2010).

When introduced, DSM-I described 106 disorders, grouped under two principal categories: first, impairments 'caused by or associated' with impairments of the brain; and second, disorders of 'psychogenic origin', or at least where physical cause was not apparent (Sanders 2010: 397). One striking feature of the nomenclature is that the term 'psychopathy' is not employed; instead the term 'personality disorder' is used. Gurley (2009: 287) suggests the APA did not like the term 'psychopathy' because there was too much scope for confusion with the term 'psychotic'. It is perhaps also very likely that the APA was keen at this point to distance itself from hereditary ideas, which (particularly in the United States) had become so much associated with the terms 'psychopathy' and 'constitutional inferiority'. By this time there was widespread scepticism too about the sexual psychopath laws (described in Chapter 6). The personality disorders were described as

> characterized by developmental defects or pathological trends in the personality structure, with minimal subjective anxiety, and little or no sense of distress. In most instances, the disorder is manifested by a lifelong pattern of action or behavior, rather than by mental or emotional symptoms.
> (APA 1952: 34)

The handbook went on to describe various forms of personality disorder. It is worth noting the breadth of the conception of 'personality disorder' that is being introduced through these three categories (the third of which is of most consequence for this book).

i   personality pattern disturbance;
ii  personality trait disturbance;
iii sociopathic personality disturbance.

The first category is used to describe 'more or less cardinal personality types, which can rarely if ever be altered in their inherent structures by any form of therapy' (APA 1952: 35), whereas the second describes those 'who are unable to maintain their emotional equilibrium and independence under minor or major stress because of disturbances in emotional development' (APA 1952: 36). It is the third grouping which is of most relevance to the concerns of this book. Individuals who would fit into this diagnosis would be seen as being ill

> primarily in terms of society and of conformity with the prevailing cultural milieu, and not only in terms of personal discomfort and relations with other individuals. However, sociopathic reactions are very often symptomatic of severe underlying personality disorder, neurosis, or psychosis, or occur as the result of organic brain injury or disease. Before a definitive diagnosis in this group is employed, strict attention must be paid to the possibility

of the presence of a more primary personality disturbance; such underlying disturbance will be diagnosed when recognized.

(APA 1952: 38)

This category included the following descriptions of reactions: 'antisocial reaction', 'dysocial reaction', 'sexual deviation' and 'addiction'. The category of 'sexual deviation' signals some of the continuity with concerns about 'sexual psychopaths', and was to be reserved for those whose deviant behaviour was not symptomatic of some other disorder, but was to include 'cases formerly classed as "psychopathic personality with pathologic sexuality"' (APA 1952: 39). The strands of thinking that are constructing the overall definition of sociopathic personality disturbance are worth noting. The name 'sociopathy' directly draws attention to the social nature of the manifestation of the disorder. It is immediately apparent, however, that this is a diverse framework, since a range of factors including organic ones are thought to be possible causes. At the same time there is a nod towards psychodynamic traditions; the manual gives definitions of various *reactions*, starting with the 'antisocial reaction' (in which the influence of Cleckley's work on 'psychopathy' also seems clear). This

> refers to chronically antisocial individuals who are always in trouble, profiting neither from experience nor punishment, and maintaining no real loyalties to any person, group, or code. They are frequently callous and hedonistic, showing marked emotional immaturity, with lack of sense of responsibility, lack of judgment, and an ability to rationalize their behavior so that it appears warranted, reasonable, and justified.
>
> (APA 1952: 38)

The use of the term 'reaction' emphasises the influence of psychodynamic psychiatry. Adolf Meyer, himself with roots in a German tradition of psychiatry (discussed in Chapter 5) and American-inclined psychoanalysis (as discussed in Chapter 6), had prominently argued against the categorisation of mental disorders, preferring instead that individuals' difficulties be seen both in terms of their particular history and of their psychological defences and *reactions*. The category of 'dysocial reaction' was to be used to describe those who showed patterns of conflict with social norms, similar to the 'antisocial reaction', but only 'as the result of having lived all their lives in an abnormal moral environment'. They might be capable of maintaining strong loyalties within their disturbed group, and they 'do not show significant personality deviations other than those implied by adherence to the values or code of their own predatory, criminal, or other social group' (APA 1952: 38).

Overall, this very first version of DSM is notable for the influence of psychoanalytic ideas, which is fairly clear in the language being used. There is also strong reference to the significance of society, with the very existence of a disorder being open to question depending upon the social context. Thus some of the social thinking that had clearly strongly influenced British practice is evident here also. Despite the brevity of the descriptions and definitions given, DSM was 'a hit'. It was reprinted 20 times (Coolidge and Segal 1998) and widely used until it was superseded in 1968 by what became known as DSM-II.

### 8.2.1 DSM-II (1968): the rise of individual psychology

While this revision was not marked by any great public debate or conflict (Kirk and Kutchins 1992), there were significant revisions, notably in relation to 'personality disorders'. In DSM-II they were described as 'deeply ingrained maladaptive patterns of behaviour that are perceptibly different in quality from psychotic and neurotic symptoms . . . life long patterns, often recognisable by the time of adolescence or earlier' (APA 1968: 41). As Gurley (2009: 288) notes, the APA did not signal any significant changes to the categories that might relate to antisocial or criminal behaviour, and there were no changes even mentioned in Spitzer and Wilson's (1968) introduction to the new edition. It is surely striking, however, that a distinctly individualistic turn is detectable here. There was a shift away from the markedly social definition: the category of 'sociopathic' has disappeared and there is no equivalent of the 'dysocial reaction', which was all about belonging to an antisocial group. There was instead only reference to 'group delinquent' reaction to childhood, which is viewed as suggesting the diagnosis should not apply (as below). The important category to make its appearance was that of 'antisocial personality', which was consistently present right up to and including the fifth edition of DSM published in 2013.

> This term [antisocial personality disorder] is reserved for individuals who are basically unsocialized and whose behavior pattern brings them repeatedly into conflict with society. They are incapable of significant loyalty to individuals, groups, or social values. They are grossly selfish, callous, irresponsible, impulsive, and unable to feel guilt or to learn from experience and punishment. Frustration tolerance is low. They tend to blame others or offer plausible rationalizations for their behavior. A mere history of repeated legal or social offenses is not sufficient to justify this diagnosis. Group delinquent reaction of childhood (or adolescence) . . . and Social maladjustment without manifest psychiatric disorder . . . should be ruled out before making this diagnosis.
>
> (APA 1968: 43)

This is a narrower, more individualised, more 'psychological' definition. It is both less social and clearer in its distance from physiological disorder, since distinction was made between such disorders of personality and any 'malfunctioning of the brain'. If any such organic cause was found, then such cases should be classified under 'organic brain syndrome' (APA 1968: 42). Also important to note is the comment that the 'mere history' of offending is not sufficient for the diagnosis. There is thus some parallel with the concerns of those involved with drawing up the guidelines on the insanity defence, which was witnessing some considerable liberalisation away from the very tight criteria provided by the M'Naghten rules (as discussed in Chapter 9). In a precise mirroring of the American Law Institute's (ALI) model guidelines on insanity, there was anxiety to avoid the accusation that the personality disorder diagnosis was simply a rather 'circular' one that could be applied to people who behaved badly (see Chapter 9, pp. 217–218).

### 8.2.2 DSM-III (1980): the quantum leap

If the revisions made between DSM-I and DSM-II were relatively subtle, DSM-III represented, as Coolidge and Segal (1998: 591) put it, something of a 'quantum leap'. It achieved this by moving to a multi-axial approach (where the same person could be rated as suffering from different disorders) and a system of classification that was more narrowly based on the presence of particular overt symptoms. Both of these moves were to have considerable implications for the use of the term 'antisocial personality disorder' within psychiatry. The radical shifts came about through the powerful, and sometimes contradictory, criticisms and forces that psychiatry was facing. DSM-III certainly did continue the trend evident in DSM-II of shifting away from organic and medicalised perspectives on people's mental health problems. Pickersgill's (2012) detailed analysis of some of the discussions among the organising committee behind the DSM revisions stresses some of the conflict over the move away from the more social aspects of diagnosis and the significance of the Cleckley concept of psychopathy. Kirk and Kutchins (1992) argued that one reason DSM-III represented a break with the past was that psychoanalytic influences were expunged. I would suggest that Pickersgill (2010) is more accurate in suggesting that the various influences were interwoven as DSM developed and that psychoanalysis continued to play a role, albeit not in straightforward ways.

In many respects psychoanalytic ideas had by now come to have a very strong and directive role in the mental health field in North America. The direct influence of psychoanalysis on DSM was demonstrated through the inclusion of 'narcissistic personality disorder', which was so much dependent upon the psychoanalytic work of Kernberg and Kohut (Millon and Davis 1995, and as described in Chapter 6). The promotion of such psychodynamic approaches rooted in clinical practice created a major dilemma for the psychiatric profession as a branch of medicine, however. The logic of such understanding of psychiatric disorders was that they were treatable through psychotherapeutic means. What particular claim to expertise did medically trained psychiatrists have if social workers, psychologists, counsellors, psychotherapists and others could carry out the treatment? Kutchins and Kirk (1997) argue that one of the responses of the psychiatric profession to this very threatening question was to stake a claim to expertise through the elaboration of ever more detailed definitional criteria.

In addition, DSM-II had come under considerable criticism soon after its release in 1968. Born into an age marked by the social movements of the 1960s and 1970s, which were criticising the social mores and the status quo, DSM was exposed to strident criticism from 'antipsychiatry' perspectives. In the United States there were significant sociological critiques from the likes of Goffman (1961), Scheff (1963) and Szasz (1970), while in the UK, Laing (1965) was also mounting a popular assault on psychiatric orthodoxy. The work of Michel Foucault, who provided a radical historical analysis of psychiatric practice (Foucault 1967), was to have a lasting influence in giving intellectual bite to critiques of psychiatric practice across the world (see Sedgwick 1982 for a review of the various antipsychiatry positions in the 1960s and 1970s). Psychiatry was portrayed in these critiques as an oppressive tool of a capitalist and authoritarian system. As Farland (2002) argues, there was a groundswell of antipsychiatric sentiment evident in the popularity and acclaim of fictional literature that engaged with these themes. Sylvia Plath's *The Bell Jar* (originally published in Britain in 1963, and then in the US in 1971) and Joanne Greenberg's (1964) *I Never Promised you a Rose Garden* are notable examples. The critical and mainstream box office success of the film version of Ken Kesey's 1961 novel *One Flew Over the Cuckoo's Nest* in 1975 is testament to the widespread sympathy towards a discourse of antispsychiatry by the mid 1970s. On top of these very sweeping ontological attacks, there were more specific criticisms made, from within the profession, of the problems apparent in establishing the basic reliability of the diagnostic categories being used (Widiger 2001: 64). Reliability refers to the consistency with which different clinicians use the various categories. As Kirk and Kutchins (1992) observed, however, much of the criticism from outside the profession was really aimed at psychiatric practice as a whole and concerned issues of validity (that is, did the categories being used by psychiatrists reflect the reality of people's experiences?). The anxiety within the profession of psychiatry about the issue of the reliability (and validity) of their diagnostic categories was evident, Sanders argues, in the influence of what were to become known as 'Feighner's criteria' (Feighner *et al.* 1972). These were named after the lead author of a paper published in 1972 that spelled out a case for psychiatric diagnosis being made on the basis of the empirical observation of behaviour and symptoms, and not upon aetiological speculation and theoretical constructs. It became known as a 'neo-Kraepelin' model since it appeared to continue the work of Emil Kraepelin (see Chapter 5), and became one of the most cited articles to have been published in a psychiatric journal (Kendler *et al.* 2009). Robert Spitzer (1991), however, argued, from his direct involvement in the task force that produced DSM-III, that any assumed adherence to principles of empiricism was 'not true', and the group 'never believed that it was possible or desirable to limit diagnostic criteria to "attributes that could be readily observed"' (Spitzer 1991: 295). Instead, there was instead a strong reliance, Spitzer contended, on 'expert consensus' that drew upon the various clinical perspectives and experiences of working clinicians. One of the major clinical problems that psychiatrists were routinely encountering in everyday practice was that of 'co-morbidity'. Not only were mental disorders difficult to identify consistently but also they had a habit of not appearing as isolated disorders within individuals (Feinstein 1970). Instead, the same individual might appear to have two or more of these disorders. The chosen solution to this problem was the introduction of a multi-axial system so that individuals could be diagnosed with more than one type of disorder. Standard clinical syndromes (such as depression, panic disorder, schizophrenia) were located on Axis 1. The personality disorders were given their own Axis 2. Physical disorders could be considered on Axis 3, while Axis 4 was used to refer to particular stressors in people's lives. Axis 5 could be used to code individuals' general levels of functioning. All of this allowed physicians to consider the mental health of patients on a number of dimensions. Crucially, since the personality disorders had their very own axis, clinicians were quite explicitly invited to consider the categories of personality disorder.

This multi-axial solution to the problem of co-morbidity served to sidestep conceptual dilemmas raised by the issues that were debated in the period leading up to the publication of DSM-III (Krueger and Markon 2006). One understanding of the phenomenon of co-morbidity would be that psychiatric diagnoses are inaccurate and lack specificity. Less sweepingly, it might also be argued that the phenomenon is giving some insight into the fact that hidden propensities towards mental disorder may underlie more specific symptom patterns. Perhaps analysis of the underlying propensities might be the more fruitful approach compared with the effort put into trying to define particular 'disorders' based on symptom patterns. As we shall see, this particular point has been made in especially strong terms concerning the definitions of 'antisocial personality disorder' and whether they have become too descriptive of behaviour and less connected to the identification of an underlying psychological disorder (which some have characterised as 'psychopathy', as discussed in more detail in Chapter 10). Whatever debates there might be about the ideological influences on the evolution of DSM-III, it is clearly the case that the DSM definitions had become progressively more elaborate and detailed. As Kutchins and Kirk (1997) emphasise, the jump between DSM-II and DSM-III in terms of sheer volume of detail was indeed considerable. While DSM-II consisted of fewer than 150 pages in total and cost $3.50 to buy, DSM-III was over 500 pages long and cost more than $30 to buy.

There was arguably a concerted attempt to avoid the criticism psychiatry has faced over the validity of the diagnostic categories being described (that is, does the category actually reflect reality?) by concentrating on the issue of reliability (can the categories be shown to be consistently applied by different people in different situations?). As Kirk and Kutchins (1992: 30) say, 'solutions to reliability problems appeared to be closer at hand and required no firm knowledge about etiology, treatment, or prognosis'. They go on to explain how the introduction of the statistical test of reliability (*kappa*) was leapt upon as a technical fix to the problem of reliability:

> By introducing a modestly complex formula for *kappa*, by providing an additional statistical overlay for a weighted *kappa*, and by tying both to a relatively inaccessible computer technology, the reliability problem was removed from public prominence and ensconced in private laboratories of research psychiatrists.
>
> (Kirk and Kutchins 1992: 30)

Thus, the problem of reliability of psychiatric diagnosis, which had seemed to pose such a threat to the status of psychiatry, became 'embedded in a closely knit research community, which accepted responsibility for solving the problem, on its own terms and in its own territory' (Kirk and Kutchins 1992: 44). Additionally, the arguably much more significant problem of the very meaning (or validity) of psychiatric diagnoses could be avoided in the fog created by the dense statistical data on reliability. It is certainly notable that Robert Spitzer, who introduced the statistical technique, was to become influential on the subsequent development of DSM. He was, however, also a trained psychoanalyst and his inclusive style was held to be important to the success of DSM as an eclectic project (Sanders 2010).

Nevertheless, the emphasis on reliability has also encouraged users of DSM to be more concerned with the issue of the classification of symptoms than with analysis of the possible meaning, or causes, of those symptoms. Such an approach is at odds with psychoanalytic or cognitive models that suppose that particular behavioural symptoms are only clues as to the nature of the underlying difficulty. The emphasis on the classification of symptoms is evident in the lengthy criteria that are used, and DSM-III reached a high-water mark with its detailed behavioural criteria (Klonsky 2000). The details of the diagnosis of 'antisocial personality disorder' are perhaps instructive (see Box 8.2 below). This is a diagnosis that is to be applied to adults (over the age of 18), but there needs to have been evidence of antisocial behaviour ('conduct disorder') before the age of 15 (criteria A and B). The person's adult life then needs to be marked by at least four of the following factors: poor engagement with work life; the inability to adhere to social norms; irritable, aggressive and destructive behaviour; financial irresponsibility; impulsivity; lying; recklessness; and irresponsibility as a parent and partner (and the greatest detail is provided in relation to this final aspect).

Wulach (1983) pointed to the difficulty of the use of such wide and inclusive criteria and argued that the finding of higher reliability in DSM-III was simply owing to the use of these highly inclusive and extensive criteria. In other words they made it easy for diagnoses to be 'found' (false positives),

## Box 8.2 DSM-III (APA 1980) criteria for antisocial personality disorder[2]

A. Current age at least 18.
B. Evidence of Conduct Disorder with onset before age 15, as indicated by a history of three or more of the following:

   1. was often truant;
   2. ran away from home overnight at least twice while living in parental or parental surrogate home (or once without returning);
   3. often initiated physical fights;
   4. used a weapon in more than one fight;
   5. forced someone into sexual activity with him or her;
   6. was physically cruel to animals;
   7. was physically cruel to other people;
   8. deliberately destroyed others' property (other than by fire-setting);
   9. deliberately engaged in firesetting;
   10. often lied (other than to avoid physical or sexual abuse);
   11. has stolen without confrontation of a victim on more than one occasion (including forgery);
   12. has stolen with confrontation of a victim (e.g. mugging, purse-snatching, extortion, armed robbery).

C. A pattern of irresponsible and antisocial behaviour since the age of 15, as indicated by at least *four* of the following:

   1. is unable to sustain consistent work behaviour, as indicated by any of the following (including similar behaviour in academic settings if the person is a student);

      a. significant unemployment for six months or more within five years when expected to work and work was available;
      b. repeated absences from work unexplained by illness in self or family;
      c. abandonment of several jobs without realistic plans for others;

   2. fails to conform to social norms with respect to lawful behaviour, as indicated by repeatedly performing antisocial acts that are grounds for arrest (whether arrested or not) e.g. destroying property, harassing others, stealing, pursuing an illegal occupation;
   3. is irritable and aggressive, as indicated by repeated physical fights or assaults (not required by one's job or to defend someone or oneself), including spouse- or child-beating;

> 4. repeatedly fails to honour financial obligations, as indicated by defaulting on debts or failing to provide child support or support for other dependants on a regular basis;
> 5. fails to plan ahead, or is impulsive, as indicated by one or both of the following:
>    a. travelling from place to place without a prearranged job or clear goal for the period of travel or clear idea about when the travel will terminate;
>    b. lack of fixed address for a month or more;
> 6. has no regard for the truth, as indicated by repeated lying, use of aliases, or 'conning' others for personal profit or pleasure;
> 7. is reckless regarding his or her own or others' personal safety, as indicated by driving while intoxicated, or recurrent speeding;
> 8. if a parent or guardian, lacks ability to function as a responsible parent, as indicated by one or more of the following:
>    a. malnutrition of child;
>    b. child's illness resulting from lack of minimal hygiene;
>    c. failure to obtain medical care for a seriously ill child;
>    d. child's dependence on neighbours or non-resident relatives for food or shelter;
>    e. failure to arrange for a caretaker for young child when parent is away from home;
>    f. repeated squandering, on personal items, of money required for household necessities;
> 9. has never sustained a totally monogamous relationship for more than one year;
> 10. lacks remorse (feels justified in having hurt, mistreated, or stolen from another).
>
> D. Occurrence of antisocial behaviour not exclusively during the course of Schizophrenia or Manic Episodes.

which might not actually bear that much relation to the frequency of psychopathology. In regard to ASPD in particular, the concentration on antisocial and criminal behaviour led to larger numbers of the prison population being labelled with the disorder. The problem with this, Wulach (1983: 335) argued, was that despite the move away from a diagnosis based on the assumption of an underlying pathology, this was likely 'to magnify the stereotype of the criminal personality as one who is totally committed to crime, waiting to strike at the first opportunity . . . allowing the public to blame behaviour totally on inherent personality causes while ignoring any environmental influences'. Gurley (2009) also noted the shift towards behaviour and suggests that it looks as though the authors of DSM-III were trying to remove the diagnosis of psychopathy with its assumption that there were underlying personality traits and he argued: 'in doing so, the American Psychiatric Association created a new disorder, quite distinct from Cleckley's original personality construct of psychopathy. The American Psychiatric Association had created the diagnostic criteria for repeated criminal offending' (Gurley 2009: 292).

Gurley points to particular problems with the stability of the ASPD diagnosis and drew attention to findings from a number of pieces of research which suggested that individuals diagnosed with ASPD often did not meet the criteria when examined soon afterwards. Helzer *et al.* (1987), for example, suggested that 43 per cent of individuals diagnosed as ASPD no longer met the criteria 12 months later. Similarly, Vandiver and Sher (1991) found that one third of their sample no longer fulfilled the criteria for diagnosis after only six months. Of course, such findings are open to different interpretations and it might also be argued that this is evidence that such disorders are actually dynamic and open to change (rather as Henderson 1939 had argued some years earlier). To critics such as Wulach (1983), who were aligning themselves with a largely antipsychiatric stance, the move towards empirical respectability in DSM-III was a more sinister smokescreen, designed to disguise the fact that what was being created here was simply a more efficient way of denigrating the discontented poor and that it too deserved to be 'discarded' along with other such prejudicial terms as 'moral insanity, constitutional psychopathic inferiority, psychopathy, and sociopathy' (Wulach 1983: 338).[3]

### 8.2.3 DSM-IV (1994)

The introduction of the DSM-IV in 1994 did not bring in radical changes, despite growing criticism of the DSM project. While there was arguably a slight pruning of the number of personality disorders (Coolidge and Segal 1998), critics such as Klonsky (2000) were still able to claim that the categories of personality disorder were essentially led by clinical 'hunches' rather than empirical investigation. Like a number of critics they advocate a 'trait' approach, assuming that there is an underlying psychological disorder. As already noted, while this had been a long running dispute it reached a clamour in the period leading up to the publication of DSM-5 in 2013 (as will be discussed).

Some of the behavioural symptoms that were dropped from the DSM-IV criteria for ASPD were those concerned with relationships. Widiger *et al.* (1996: 13) report that field trials of the criteria of ASPD showed that the inability to sustain a monogamous relationship, and irresponsible parenting, could most easily be dropped since they provided little contribution to the reliability of the diagnosis. Researchers noted that interviewees would be very reluctant to

> **Box 8.3 APA (DSM-IV) criteria for antisocial personality disorder**[5]
>
> A.  There is a pervasive pattern of disregard for and violation of the rights of others occurring since age 15 years, as indicated by three (or more) of the following:
>
>     1.  failure to conform to social norms with respect to lawful behaviors as indicated by repeatedly performing acts that are grounds for arrest;
>     2.  deceitfulness, as indicated by repeated lying, use of aliases, or conning others for personal profit or pleasure;
>     3.  impulsivity or failure to plan ahead;
>     4.  irritability and aggressiveness, as indicated by repeated physical fights or assaults;
>     5.  reckless disregard for safety of self or others;
>     6.  consistent irresponsibility, as indicated by repeated failure to sustain consistent work behavior or honor financial obligations;
>     7.  lack of remorse, as indicated by being indifferent to or rationalizing having hurt, mistreated, or stolen from another.
>
> B.  The individual is at least 18 years.
> C.  There is evidence of Conduct Disorder (see criteria for CD) with onset before age 15 years.
> D.  The occurrence of antisocial behaviour is not exclusively during the course of Schizophrenia or a Manic Episode.

discuss their inability to care for children despite agreeing to discuss their criminal histories. The problem for the advocates of the trait approach was that field trials also found that the more psychological items (which would be more consistent with the diagnosis of 'psychopathy' as defined by PCL-R) were subject to lower inter-rater agreement. So instead the focus remained on more overt antisocial behaviour and criminality.[4]

There was acknowledgement of the social dimension of ASPD, with it being noted that it 'appears to be associated with low economic status and urban settings' and that there were concerns that such a diagnosis 'may be misapplied to individuals in settings in which seemingly antisocial behaviour may be part of a protective survival strategy'. Clinicians were encouraged to 'consider the social and economic context in which the behaviours occur' (APA 2000: 647). The tensions within and surrounding DSM concerning its clinical and empirical status were to become fully evident by the time of the publication of the fifth edition in 2013.

## 8.2.4 DSM-5 (2013)

The extensive discussions about the development of DSM-5 (dsm5.org; it was decided that Roman numerals would no longer be used for DSM editions at this stage), which was finally published in 2013, are described by Sanders (2010). The perception of the failure of the so-called 'neo-Kraepelin' system which had been adopted in DSM-III and continued into DSM-IV led to a sense of crisis that suggested that DSM-5 might look radically different. On the one hand there was a call for more reliance on biological markers of mental illness that might afford psychiatry greater medical respectability; on the other, criticism of the whole DSM enterprise also gained momentum. As Sanders notes, some of the most significant and heated debate took place around the proposals for changes in the definitions of the personality disorders. A ten person working group was set the task of reviewing the evidence in relation to personality disorders, and various debates crystallised into the one over whether the model should continue as a categorical one or whether the system should be dimensional (Trestman 2014). Generally, psychiatric clinicians were still comfortable with the categorical system favoured by the medical model; however, for some years a number of psychologists had advocated a dimensional approach which assumed that personality disorders were better seen in terms of individual differences in underlying personality factors (the five factor model being only one model advocated by some, e.g. Jackson and Richards 2007; Miller et al. 2001). A model that emphasised underlying traits rather than specific categories would also provide some relief to the problem of co-morbidity. A hybrid model was eventually proposed which was ultimately categorical and yet incorporated elements of dimensionality. Section B in the hybrid model referred directly to 'pathological personality traits' of 'antagonism' (characterised by manipulativeness, deceitfulness, callousness and hostility) and 'disinhibition' (characterised by irresponsibility, impulsivity and risk taking). A significant reduction in the number of categories of personality disorder to six was also proposed as part of the compromise. The process of debate, which extended over five years, 'was contentious enough to generate ongoing active and vociferous challenges to its implementation, and two of the committee members resigned in protest' (Trestman 2014: 142). Ultimately, the APA Board of Trustees took the decision to abandon the move to a dimensional approach and stuck with the ten disorders and definitions of DSM-IV.

The significant change that did come to the overall system was the fact that the multi-axial taxonomy was completely dropped so that the personality disorders no longer had their own dimension. The APA argued that this made sense and was in part a vote of confidence in the categories of personality disorder. One of the reasons for the creation of the separate axis had been the lack of 'clinical and research focus' formerly given to the personality disorders, but this, it was argued, was no longer the case (APA 2013). So, '[g]iven that there is no fundamental difference between disorders described on DSM-IV's

Axis I and Axis II, DSM-5 has shifted to a single axis system'. The literature review and secondary analyses carried out through the APA review suggested personality disorders, in general, were associated with distorted and maladaptive thinking about oneself and others. The crucial components of effective personality functioning were deemed to fall under the rubrics of *identity, self-direction, empathy* and *intimacy* (Bender et al. 2011; Morey et al. 2011).

DSM-IV had sold over a million copies, and it was fully anticipated that sales of DSM-5 would at least match that (*The Economist* 2013). Indeed, on one level the success of DSM could be judged by the fact that the launch of DSM-5 was a media event. Newspapers and television news channels carried stories on the launch. As Simon Wessely (who was elected to take up the Chair of the Royal College of Psychiatrists in 2014) noted in a blog describing a conference held at the Institute of Psychiatry to discuss the birth of DSM-5,

> We were surprised and then stunned by the increasing amount of coverage given to the forthcoming launch around the world. Editorials, features, commentaries, news items and interviews have appeared in most of the world's leading newspapers: the New York Times, Wall Street Journal, Washington Post, Der Zeit, the Guardian and Observer, Los Angeles Times, Daily Mail, New York Post, Toronto Globe and Star and so on. 'Specials' appeared on NBC, CBS, CNN, ABC, Fox news, Canadian Broadcasting Service and our own Radio 4 (several times). DSM appeared in . . . many of the key magazines and journals – the New York Review of Books, Economist, the London Review of Books, Prospect, Time, New Republic, the Atlantic and more, whilst new media such as Slate, Huffington Post (numerous times), BuzzFeed, The Conversation, and so on and so forth. It is easier to list the media outlets that have not covered DSM.
> 
> (Wessely 2013)

In other ways, however, the DSM could also be portrayed as being in something of a crisis. The media attention gave platforms to those offering swingeing criticism. Many of the salvoes were fired from familiar antipsychiatry territory (Callard 2014). The new version of DSM was again portrayed as an effort medically to colonise ever broader aspects of human life. Critics could point towards how the construction of DSM was being funded by the shady forces of the pharmaceutical industry, which would make vast fortunes from selling expensive medication to sufferers of ever more distinct psychiatric disorders (Cosgrove and Krimsky 2012). Some of the criticism was less familiar and was thus more damaging. The US-based National Institute of Mental Health (NIMH) announced just before the publication that it would withdraw support for research projects that used a diagnostic methodology based solely on DSM categorisations. In a remarkably sharply worded statement, it was argued that all DSM could claim to be was 'a dictionary' which created a series of labels and definitions (NIMH 2013). The statement drew critical distinction with the rest of medicine, which had, it argued, progressed from identifying diseases according to clusters of symptoms and moved to diagnosis of the underlying tissue or organ pathology. NIMH announced its own programme of research, which should not be constrained by DSM categories. While the 'antipsychiatric' critics might have been pleased the common enemy of DSM was being so brutally attacked, they would find little to cheer in NIMH's prescriptions. NIMH proposed a very clear biological orientation: it is simply stated that 'Mental disorders are biological disorders involving brain circuits that implicate specific domains of cognition, emotion, or behaviour'. There was no space at all here for understanding disorders as having roots in complex psychodynamic histories, let alone social distress.

## Conclusion

This chapter has reviewed the evolution of the formal concepts of psychopathy and antisocial personality disorder as they emerged in the latter half of the twentieth century. Cleckley's work was influential in the US and helped transform the meaning of the term 'psychopathy' from one associated with hereditarily endowed deficits to one that suggested a hidden psychological disorder marked by an individual failing to understand or act appropriately to the feelings of others. The diagnosis of antisocial personality disorder was created by the *Diagnostic and Statistical Manual*, itself a significant product of post-war American psychiatry. In many ways the story of the evolution of the *Diagnostic and Statistical Manual* itself is one of a highly successful project. The nomenclature and the definitions within the various editions have had enormous influence on the shape of psychiatric practice, policy and research. In addition much of the language and the categories have entered the public domain. The publication of DSM-5 in May 2013 was something of a media event.

However, despite the seemingly endless review and rumination, there have been trenchant criticisms of the DSM that have not gone away. Indeed, the publication of DSM-5 has been greeted by particularly high levels of scepticism. The views of many clinicians can be summed up by Dimaggio *et al.* (2005: 348), who suggest that the descriptions of personality disorders in the various editions of DSM are 'like a caricature . . . not in line with actual clinical experience'. Dimaggio *et al.* (2005) plead for more nuanced understanding of the internal worlds of individuals as being subject to change. In this their work fits in with a whole history of psychodynamic thought, including that of Meyer and Henderson (see Chapters 6 and 7). To those taking a more sociological and critical stance, DSM is still the most overt aspect of a machine involved in the process of labelling and incarcerating the poor and marginalised. Wulach, for example, recommended in the early 1980s that any psychologists using the diagnosis of antisocial personality disorder should append the statement 'the disorder is more common in lower class populations, partly because it is associated with impaired earning capacity' (Wulach 1983: 338).

Setting aside the methodological debates and the fundamental concerns about its premises, the DSM can claim to be have been a considerable success in propagating the use of psychiatric terminology. The next chapter looks specifically at how the diagnostic categories of 'antisocial personality disorder' and psychopathy were being used in practice in the criminal justice systems in the USA and the UK.

## Notes

1. The book will not deal separately with the *International Classification of Diseases* published by the World Health Organization. ICD-6 (1948) was the first edition to have a specific section on mental disorders – but there had been mental disorders in ICD-5 (1938) under 'Biology: Diseases of the Nervous System'. There was a strong biological orientation which made it unacceptable to US psychiatry. DSM-I included descriptions, albeit brief, of the disorders, making it of far more interest to clinicians. ICD-7 contained no revisions to the mental disorders, but ICD-8A (published in 1968) contained significant revisions following extensive efforts to include a range of opinion (Widiger 2001). DSM-II was published the same year and was designed to be compatible with ICD-8A.
2. Reprinted with permission from the *Diagnostic and Statistical Manual of Mental Disorders*, Third Edition (Copyright © 1980). American Psychiatric Association. All Rights Reserved.
3. As Gurley (2009) notes, 'Sociopathy' does appear in the index with a note saying 'See antisocial personality disorder'.
4. No real changes were made to the criteria for ASPD in the revised DSM-IV-R, produced in 2000 and reproduced here.
5. Reprinted with permission from the *Diagnostic and Statistical Manual of Mental Disorders*, Fourth Edition revised (Copyright © 2000). American Psychiatric Association. All Rights Reserved.

Chapter 9

# Shifting grounds

## The mass media and the insanity defence

### Introduction

As we have seen in the previous chapter, American psychiatry, mainly through the development of the *Diagnostic and Statistical Manual*, had considerably widened the scope of psychiatric diagnosis to include an even wider spectrum of the population. Some of these developments, particularly those concerned with the 'personality disorders', were to have marked impacts on the US legal system. During the immediate post-war period many states had enacted 'sexual psychopath' laws, with the later ones undoubtedly influenced by Cleckley's conception of the hidden disturbance of 'psychopathy' that could lurk behind a 'mask of sanity'. By the 1960s there was fairly widespread distrust of the notion of 'sexual psychopathy', and indeed the 'sexual psychopath' laws were being repealed. Instead, however, there was stronger interest in the personality disorders that were being described by DSM. This chapter charts the remarkable, and yet inconsistent, progress of these diagnoses in the courts in the following decades in the USA and UK. Deliberation on the meaning of the categories of personality disorder underlay a number of high profile criminal cases which led to significant policy changes in the UK and USA. On the surface at least, the fate of moral insanity in these criminal justice systems in the early decades of the twenty-first century appear very different. In the USA, personality disorder has all but disappeared as a defence, or even factor of mitigation. In the UK, concepts of personality disorder have informed important strands of justice and penal policy.

The first section of this chapter will focus on the US and will describe events surrounding the 'Durham rule' of 1954 and the introduction of the American Law Institute's (ALI) model insanity defence in 1962. In the USA the insanity defence rulings of most states had largely been governed by the M'Naghten rules until the middle of the twentieth century. In the post-Second World War period there was increasing dissatisfaction with this very narrow definition being used in courts. As documented in previous chapters, the development of psychiatry and psychology which took place during the war itself had created and popularised categories of 'personality disorder' and of 'psychopathy'. The post-war period saw these terms not only enter the professional lexicon but become an increasingly common part of everyday discourse. This latter process was particularly speedy as consumption of the mass media became an ever larger part of people's lives. The use of the diagnosis of personality disorder in a forensic context played a part in denting the M'Naghten conventions through the so-called 'Durham rule' of 1954. While this ruling, emerging from the Court of Appeals in the District of Columbia, did not in reality have great direct impact on legal practices in the US, it did, however, both rehearse old disputes on the link between guilt and rationality and herald debate on the legal implications of some of the refinements of the categories of personality disorder. The introduction of the ALI model for insanity (published in 1962) created a more significant shift in legal practice and the guidelines were widely accepted across the United States. The guidelines crucially loosened the criteria for the acceptance of insanity as a defence in court.

The second section of the chapter moves on to consider the case of John Hinckley in 1982, which became a significant landmark in shaping the consideration of insanity in US courts. A remarkable entwinement of psychiatry, criminal justice concerns with the insanity defence, debates about personality disorder and images of masculinity and insanity in popular culture occurred when Hinckley was found 'not guilty on the grounds of insanity' of the attempted assassination of the American President, Ronald Reagan. The trial of this would-be assassin was to carry remarkable echoes of the trial of Daniel M'Naghten, who tried to kill the British Prime Minister in 1843. Like M'Naghten, Hinckley was defended using the most modern psychiatric categories of the day. The prosecution case was that, although Hinckley might be eccentric and misguided, he was guilty because he had sufficient command of himself to go about his daily business and had very deliberately planned to kill the President. There were very modern twists in this case, however. A Hollywood film (*Taxi Driver*) was shown in court as evidence providing a window on Hinckley's mental state, and the very latest diagnostic categories featured in DSM were liberally used. The jury were ultimately swayed by the defence of insanity laid out by the psychiatrists, working in a court that operated within ALI guidelines. Just as after the M'Naghten trial, the press and public were very critical of the verdict, and the subsequent judicial review led to a substantial narrowing of the insanity defence in most of the United States.

The third and final section of the chapter will then discuss the Michael Stone case, which was to trigger considerable changes in aspects of penal and legal policy in Britain. As described in Chapter 7, the term 'psychopathy' had been included as a category in the 1959 Mental Health Act (MHA, England and Wales). While the category had been used in a number of cases in court, it was soon fairly clear that it was not being widely used on behalf of individuals as a means of avoiding criminal responsibility (Walker 1968). In many ways the diagnosis, and the associated ones of personality disorder, fell into a certain amount of disregard, at least within mainstream psychiatry in the UK (Lewis and Appleby 1988; Walker and McCabe 1973), until the very end of the twentieth century. It was the considerable public and government attention given to the prosecution of Michael Stone for the murder of Lin and Megan Russell in 1996 that gave fresh impetus to concern to engage with the problem. Again, the involvement of the mass media is striking in this case. The murder case itself was well publicised, involving as it did a horrific, motiveless attack on innocent victims, and it was a television appeal for information that eventually led a psychiatrist to come forward to identify a former psychiatric patient as a suspect. When it emerged that the man convicted had been diagnosed by psychiatrists as suffering from a personality disorder, the attention of the media prompted the government to put forward policies directed towards the treatment and confinement of those with personality disorder.

## 9.1 Liberalisation in the US: Durham, the ALI and the insanity defence

As is clear in the past two chapters, the events of the middle of the twentieth century were a stimulus for remarkable shifts in thinking and perspective on the problem of mental disorder. One very obvious manifestation of this was the move towards the publication of successive editions of DSM that began in 1952. A notable signal of the shift in thinking on insanity came through a significant legal ruling that occurred in the US Court of Appeals for the District of Columbia Circuit in 1954. This was to become known as the 'Durham rule' and concerns the case of a man who had acquired a diagnosis of personality disorder when he was discharged from the Navy in 1945.

In 1954 Monte Durham appealed against his conviction for housebreaking. His only defence at initial trial was that he was of unsound mind at the time of the offence. The grounds for appeal were that the court did not correctly apply the existing rules governing the burden of proof regarding the defence of insanity, but more substantially that the existing tests of criminal responsibility were obsolete and therefore needed to be updated in the light of contemporary knowledge of psychological disorders. Durham had a history of both imprisonment and hospitalisation. He had been discharged from the Navy at the age of 17 in 1945, diagnosed as suffering from 'a profound personality disorder which renders him unfit for naval service'. He received a number of convictions for motor theft and fraud and experienced prison sentences, hospitalisations and psychiatric examinations which led to diagnoses of 'psychosis with psychopathic personality' and 'psychopathic personality'. In July 1951 he was charged with housebreaking offences and again the defence of insanity was raised. The judge had concluded:

> I don't think it has been established that the defendant was of unsound mind as of July 13, 1951, in the sense that he didn't know the difference between right and wrong or that even if he did, he was subject to an irresistible impulse by reason of the derangement of mind.
> (US Court of Appeals, DC Circuit 1954)

What became known as the Durham rule actually emerged from a very long written deliberation by the Court of Appeals on the insanity defence. The thrust of the argument that emerged from the deliberation was to seek to broaden the definition of insanity, to allow for the advancements that were perceived to be occurring in the field of psychiatry and psychology. It was argued that courts needed to be able to consider a fuller understanding of mental disorder that went beyond the judgment of the ability to distinguish right from wrong (as demanded by the M'Naghten rules). This could be achieved by improving the relationship between professional expertise and the court system. It sought to allow psychiatric and psychological experts to explain their own concepts of mental disorder to courts, who would be invited to consider the pertinence of such reasoning. The evidence of the experts might well include aspects of the psychological history and assumed psychological makeup of defendants. One key aspect of the ruling concerned the possible hidden nature of mental disorder:

> The question will be simply whether the accused acted because of a mental disorder, and not whether he displayed particular symptoms which medical science has long recognized do not necessarily, or even typically, accompany even the most serious mental disorder.
> (US Court of Appeals, DC Circuit 1954: para 57)

Reference was made to the 'science of psychiatry', of which the advances were now assumed to have undermined the assumptions of the M'Naghten rules. Psychiatry, it was claimed,

> now recognizes that a man is an integrated personality and that reason, which is only one element in that personality, is not the sole determinant of his conduct. The right–wrong test, which considers knowledge or reason alone, is therefore an inadequate guide to mental responsibility for criminal behavior.
> (US Court of Appeals, DC Circuit 1954: para 39)

In the promotion of the new science of psychiatry there was, according to Arens (1967: 44), in the aftermath of the Durham rule, a recognisable bias towards psychoanalytic perspectives. The 'value of psychiatric testimony lay – in brief – in a mastery of the defendant's life history':

> The chief value of an expert's testimony in this field, as in all other fields, rests upon the material from which his opinion is fashioned and the reasoning by which he progresses from his material to his conclusion; in the explanation of the disease and its dynamics, that is, how it occurred, developed and affected the mental and emotional processes of the defendant.
> (*Carter v. United States* 1957, quoted in Arens 1967: 44)

Overall, the Durham rule was an ambitious attempt to promote the broad use of psychiatric expertise in the determination of insanity in the courts (Arens 1967). It would be a mistake, however, to believe that the ruling itself achieved its goals, since it did not bring about a major liberalisation of the insanity defence. For one thing, individuals who were successful in using this defence would find themselves confined to special hospital (St Elizabeths Hospital, in the case of Washington, DC, where the ruling was made) until they were deemed to be cured of the 'abnormality' that had rendered them dangerous. Also, while the Durham rule received some considerable publicity, and appeared to have some impact on court practice (Arens 1967) and the numbers of acquittals within the District of Columbia itself (Weiner 1980), it did not achieve wide acceptance and was only adopted as additional law by statute in the States of New Hampshire and Maine (Weiner 1980). The ruling was effectively dropped in 1972, even in the District of Columbia, in favour of what had become the more widely accepted model proposed by the American Law Institute.

### 9.1.1 The American Law Institute and the Model Penal Code

The American Law Institute was first organised in 1923 in response to a belief that the American legal system needed authoritative statements on the various challenges it was facing from seemingly unprecedented social changes (White 1997). The ALI Model Penal Code was published in 1962 and was adopted in many American jurisdictions. One of the most discussed and celebrated parts of the code was that concerning the insanity defence, and one of the drivers of the ALI guidelines here was concern about the status of personality disorder (Allen 1962; Lockey and Bloom 2007).

The Model Penal Code on insanity adopted a two prong approach to describing the grounds necessary for a defence of insanity to be successful:[1]

> (1) A person is not responsible for criminal conduct if at the time of such conduct as a result of mental disease or defect he lacks substantial capacity either to appreciate the criminality of his conduct or to conform his conduct to the requirements of law.

One prong accepted that an inability to control behaviour might be taken as a defence; the other prong was more cognitive and stressed the ability to distinguish between right and wrong. However, the latter was more liberal than the M'Naghten rule, which was narrowly based on judgment as to the presence or absence of knowledge of right or wrong. The ALI proposal was that a defence would only have to show the lack of 'substantial capacity ... to appreciate' the criminality of their act. So a defendant might know that they had committed an offence, but if they lacked an appreciation of the significance of the act, or the ability to control their behaviour, then they could be found not guilty. In addition there was a second clause which offered a substantial caveat: '(2) The terms "mental disease or defect" do not include an abnormality manifested only by repeated criminal or otherwise anti-social conduct.'

It can be argued that the latter statement was intended to 'deal with the difficult issue posed by the so-called sociopath or psychopathic personality' (Allen 1962), which had become somewhat discredited through the implementation of the 'sexual psychopath laws'. Thus Allen (1962) suggests the intention was to make it more difficult for the diagnoses to be used in defence. However, in other respects things are not so straightforward, and the clause might be better understood as an attempt to avoid the criticism that the definition was an entirely circular one which depended simply on the identification of immoral behaviour. Indeed, the caveat appears to echo the wording of the 1959 MHA (England and Wales, described in Chapter 7), which named 'psychopathic disorder' as a legitimate mental disorder but claimed that no individual should be identified as suffering from this disorder 'by reason only of promiscuity or other immoral conduct'. It is certainly worth noting that the committee that produced the guidelines on insanity included a number of members of the Group for the Advancement of Psychiatry (GAP), and so was unlikely to be hostile to the diagnoses so prominently acknowledged in the DSM, which was being formulated by the American Psychiatric Association. The ALI model was to become widely accepted so that by the beginning of the 1980s a majority of states, like the District of Columbia, had adopted some version of the Model Penal Code, with only 16 states still using a version of the M'Naghten test. While practice varied and there might be some debate about the overall impact on acquittal rates (Lockey and Bloom 2007), the code gave considerable scope for a range of assumptions about insanity to be allowed into the court and for professional judgment to hold some sway. The weight that might be given to professional opinion was certainly apparent in the trial of John Hinckley in 1982, the aftermath of which was to have major implications for the defence of insanity across the USA (Kim 2012).

## 9.2 The trial of John Hinckley (1982): the end of the insanity defence in the US?

In 1982 John Hinckley was put on trial for the attempted murder of President Ronald Reagan and three of his entourage. Hinckley had shot the President, his Press Secretary James Brady, a secret service agent named Timothy McCarthy and a police officer called Thomas Delahanty outside a Washington, DC hotel. There are a number of remarkable aspects to this trial. The trial and the verdict of 'not guilty, on the grounds of insanity' sparked a major debate about the legal basis of the insanity defence. Events surrounding the trial were played out in a highly public realm and the boundaries between representations of the crime itself in the media, fictionalised accounts of assassination and debates about the psychological state of the perpetrator became very blurred. The crime was an attempt on the life of the President, which, as we have seen in previous chapters, is an event that might well lead to public debate and changes in legal practice towards the mentally disordered (Chapter 2 has dealt with the trials of Hadfield, Oxford and M'Naghten, for example). Hinckley's attempt to kill President Reagan was captured by television cameras and this was shown repeatedly on prime time television. The trial itself was a huge news story. Of course, because Hinckley was filmed shooting at Reagan it was uncontested that Hinckley had fired the shots that injured the four men. The trial itself came to be concerned more or less entirely with debate over Hinckley's mental state. The debate ranged into discussion about the nature of personality disorder and of psychosis, and it explored the details of Hinckley's life and fantasies. Images of insanity and disordered personalities from popular culture were brought directly into the courtroom, since an important plank of the defence case was that Hinckley's mental disorder was manifest in an irrational identification with the arguably 'psychopathic' (Yates 2011: 108) and certainly seriously disturbed anti-hero of the film *Taxi Driver*.[2] The film focuses on the psychological disintegration of the character 'Travis Bickle', a lonely, isolated New York cab driver who is increasingly angry at the world he sees around him, which not only appears depraved and immoral but takes no notice of him at all. At the time the film was made and released New York City was widely regarded as 'in crisis', the City itself was on the point of official bankruptcy and order was generally perceived as having broken down almost entirely (Gotham and Greenberg 2014). Bickle's attention is drawn to the corruption apparent in the political system through his romantic interest in a young political activist ('Betsy'). His social misapprehensions lead to him being rejected by her, and then, more alienated, he begins to plot to assassinate the presidential candidate whom she supports. Bickle meanwhile becomes interested in the welfare of 'Iris', a 12-year-old girl who works as a prostitute, played by Jodie Foster. To Bickle, her fate seems to represent his own alienation from a corrupt and heartless world, and he can enjoy his own protective feelings towards her. He begins to plot and fantasise an attack on the corrupt world he sees around him, as he accumulates an armoury of weapons and practises his violent performances alone and in front of the mirror. Perhaps the most famous scene of the film comes when he rehearses the question he means as a menacing taunt which would be a prelude to violence: 'You talkin' to me? You talkin' to me?' This scene is later acted out in court by one of the defence psychiatric witnesses (Caplan 1987) and of course can be seen as not only a menacing taunt but also a poignant, and narcissistic, plea for attention. Bickle's attempt to kill the presidential candidate is thwarted by security guards who spot his 'oddness' and warn him away from the area. In the final scenes of the film he initiates a bloodbath as he takes out his violent impulses on the men at the the sleazy hotel where Iris entertains her clients. Collapsing, seriously injured, amidst the carnage, Bickle tries to shoot himself, but he fails as the gun clicks impotently, empty of bullets. He is left to make a suicidal gesture, grinning and pretending to shoot himself with his empty hand as the police arrive. As the screenplay has it:

> The slaughter is the moment Travis has been heading for all his life, and where this screenplay has been heading for over 100 pages. It is the release of all that cumulative pressure; it is a reality unto itself. It is the psychopath's Second Coming.
>
> (quoted in Fairbairn 1995: 228)

The camera lifts itself away from this slaughter and the very final scenes consist of what looks like a fantasy ending as Bickle is shown recovered and still driving a cab. He is now considered a hero by the press and Iris's family, who write to thank him for 'rescuing' her from her desperate situation. He picks up Betsy in his cab, who is now blatantly admiring and suggests that Bickle might keep in touch with her.

Overall, Bickle, who is portrayed in the film as of distinctly modest means and education, seems an unlikely role model for Hinckley, whose father ran a small, but highly lucrative, oil company. He was born in Oklahoma, but moved several times in his childhood before the family settled in the largely white, middle class suburban town of Evergreen, in Colorado. Hinckley seemed to be on track to follow his siblings towards graduation through high school and university, until he began to live as a loner before finishing high school. He attempted to engage with a college education on a number of occasions but was unable to complete his studies. Instead, he moved to Los Angeles in order to pursue his dream of becoming a songwriter. It was during this period that he repeatedly watched the film *Taxi Driver*, over 15 times, it was suggested at the trial. The film had apparently become very meaningful to Hinckley. He began to dress and behave like the central character. He adopted Bickle's interest in the young prostitute character by becoming obsessed with the actor Jodie Foster, who played the part. The obsession grew to the extent that he enrolled on a writing programme at Yale University when he knew that she was a student there. In a strange emulation of the film Hinckley seemed to adopt the belief that, in the build-up to the 1980 presidential election, he could win Foster's attention and love if he assassinated either President Carter or the presidential candidate (and later President) Reagan. This belief persisted and it led Hinckley to leave his Washington, DC motel room on 30 March 1981 with the intention of shooting Ronald Reagan, who was due to give a talk at another hotel that morning. Before Hinckley left, he wrote a letter to Foster in which he made it quite clear that he was setting out to 'get Reagan' in order to 'impress' her (Caplan 1987: 21).

The essence of the prosecution case bore much resemblance to the trial of Daniel M'Naghten in 1843 (as described in some detail in Chapter 2). The prosecution team pointed to the fact that Hinckley had planned the attack and had been managing the affairs of his life. On the morning itself, Dr Park Elliott

Dietz stated, he had gone for breakfast, had a shower and bought a newspaper.[3] Dietz went on to argue that Hinckley made knowing decisions to choose the bullets and load the gun. He chose to write to Jodie Foster, making his intentions clear. He left the motel, concealed the gun and waited outside the conference centre while he chose the best time to get near to the President. He kept his cool until the best moment to shoot, at which point he adopted a 'combat crouch', held the gun in a firm two handed grip and aimed all six rounds in the President's direction. Dietz argued that 'These are not disorganized random motions. These are specifically designed, organized acts'.

The prosecution team commissioned a lengthy psychiatric assessment of Hinckley (Caplan 1987) which was not submitted in evidence but was used as the basis for an attempt to pre-empt the defence case. The influence of DSM-III diagnostic categories, published just two years earlier, is very clear. Hinckley was diagnosed as 'suffering from dysthemic disorder, or depressive neurosis, and from three types of personality disorder – schizoid, narcissistic and mixed – the last with borderline and passive-aggressive features' (Caplan 1987: 90). The prosecution argued that the narcissistic disorder provided the motive (and not the excuse) since it manifested in 'a grandiose sense of self-importance or uniqueness (with exaggerations of achievements and talents); preoccupation with fantasies of unlimited success and ideal love; the search for constant attention' (the theoretical underpinnings of psychoanalytic work on narcissism are discussed in Chapter 8). There were also feelings of 'cool indifference, and marked feelings of inferiority, shame, and emptiness in response to perceptions of defeat and failure' (Caplan 1987: 91). As Caplan emphasised, an important passage of the report that informed Dietz's prosecution testimony drew attention to Hinckley's psychological predicament and acknowledged that his acts were those of a troubled individual. It was accepted that he had been a 'failure in his social, educational and occupational efforts' and that he was driven by desire for notoriety and fame and the pursuit of Jodie Foster. His efforts to get help from psychiatry had not been successful, and 'his identification with literary characters' had not produced personal satisfaction. He was not, the prosecution acknowledged, 'a completely rational individual' (Caplan 1987: 91). The prosecution report still concluded, however, that Hinckley was responsible and they returned to the notion that not only did he *know* that he had done wrong, but – as was crucial to rebutting the ALI insanity defence – he could also *appreciate* it and control his behaviour:

> Mr Hinckley's history is clearly indicative of a person who did not function in a usual, reasonable manner. However, there is no evidence that he was so impaired that he could not appreciate the wrongfulness of his conduct or conform his conduct to the requirements of the law.
>
> (quoted in Caplan 1987: 93)

The defence team also pointed to the story of an ever more wayward and disordered life. He had become increasingly lonely and reclusive in school, described by a fellow student as a 'non-guy'. Dr William Carpenter was one of the key expert witnesses for the defence. His testimony in front of the jury followed a detailed discussion between the judge and attorneys on the nature of this expert psychiatric evidence. Carpenter was directed by Hinckley's attorney to give direct evidence on the issue of his client's capacity to *appreciate* the wrongfulness of an act. Carpenter then engaged with lengthy, detailed and sophisticated arguments in court about the nature of reason. He argued that there were two chief grounds for the belief that Hinckley 'lacked substantial capacity to appreciate the wrongfulness of his conduct'. First, although there was reasoning behind his acts, this reasoning was based on his aims to 'terminate his own existence' and 'accomplish this union with Jodie Foster through death'. Second, he had constructed an 'inner world' in which the effect of his actions on the victims was simply 'trivial' because his mind was dominated by the fantastical wish to achieve his goal of 'ending his own life' and thus establishing his relationship with Foster. This rather complex and phenomenological approach to the understanding of the nature of reason and emotion, coupled with a rather psychodynamic understanding of Hinckley's inclination to suicide (see Bell 2001, for example), was supplemented by David Bear's more 'traditional' psychiatric testimony. He argued that Hinckley was suffering from a progressive form of schizophrenia (Caplan 1987). The trial, as Caplan describes, included an extraordinary interlude as Bear went to some lengths to insist that the court should consider CAT scan images of Hinckley's brain. These, he argued, showed enlarged 'sulci' (folds in the brain) which, he suggested, were often associated with the presence of schizophrenia. Caplan observed that this evidence was not at all convincing, since the scans

> were projected on a small screen set up across the large room from the jury. The performance had the impact of a poorly rehearsed, and annoying farce. In washed out colours, the scans looked like slices of bruised and misshapen fruit.
>
> (Caplan 1987: 109)

Bear also paid considerable attention to the significance of *Taxi Driver* and Hinckley's apparent identification with the character Travis Bickle. Such was the attention paid to the film that the judge requested that Bear give a summary of the plot in some detail, which he did, giving attention to the degree of parallel and association between Bickle's story and Hinckley's. At the close of the defence case, the court was shown the entire film *Taxi Driver* and they were invited to understand how the film might have influenced Hinckley: 'The television sets were moved back into position and, in the light of the courtroom, the movie's colours were dark and brooding. The feature's blue jazz and monologues by a sleepless Robert De Niro sounded close, intimate, unnerving' (Caplan 1987: 114).

The prosecution then called Sally Johnson, a young psychiatrist who had spent more time with Hinckley than other witnesses and who agreed that the elements of 'personality disorder' were strong in Hinckley's life, notably the narcissism. Her testimony implied that he was now

> pleased that his name had gone from 'totally nothing' to publication in thousands of newspapers; how he had a swollen sense of self-importance; and how he suffered from personality disorders, with narcissistic and mixed (schizoid, borderline, and passive aggressive) features.
>
> (Caplan 1987: 113)

So while the reality of personality disorder, and indeed its presence in Hinckley, was not disputed, the prosecution's contention was that a personality disorder did not prevent Hinckley from being responsible for his actions. In his summing up for the prosecution, Adelman acknowledged that Hinckley might be suffering from a mental disorder, but that this was not severe, and he mocked the concept of 'personality disorder' in this context:

> These disorders that the Government doctors testified they found in Mr Hinckley [are] personality disorders. Are they severe mental disorders? They could be. Were they severe in Mr Hinckley? No, they were not. What are personality disorders? They don't make you out of contact with reality. Not delusional. [They are] things that hundreds of thousands of people have. I think we all had a laugh when Dr Dietz said that this narcissistic personality even applies to some doctors. We didn't count noses on that one, but I think we could all put it on some of the psychiatrists.[4]

In summing up the case, Judge Parker reminded the jury of the criteria for 'insanity' as laid down by the ALI guidelines: the term 'insanity' does not

> require a showing that the defendant was disoriented at the time or place. 'Mental disease or defect' includes any abnormal condition of the mind, regardless of its medical label, which substantially affects mental or emotional processes and substantially impairs his behavior controls.[5]

Perhaps not surprisingly, given the judge's reference to the ALI guidelines, the jury returned a verdict of 'not guilty by reason of insanity' and Hinckley was committed to St Elizabeths Hospital. There followed a storm of protest, powerfully echoing that following the case of Daniel M'Naghten (Freedman 1983). In this case there was a racialised inflection rather than nationalism (M'Naghten believed his Scottish nationalism had led to his persecution). The trial had taken place in what many Americans saw as a 'black town' and indeed the judge and all but one of the jury were black. Some white Americans protested that the verdict said more about black people's feelings towards a white, right wing President than anything else (Caplan 1987). Just as in the M'Naghten case, government also became involved. Congress moved quickly to 'stem the hysteria' unleashed by very hostile reporting of the Hinckley trial and there followed a series of Congress hearings over nearly two years, leading to the Insanity Defense Reform Act (Kim 2012). Reagan himself went to the Senate Judiciary Committee to argue for the restriction of the insanity defence (Kim 2012). The trial jurors were questioned by the Senate committee (Freedman 1983) and it was reported that several of them had felt 'compelled' to find the defendant not guilty because of the criteria of proof of sanity in the Model Penal Code (Stoll 2009). Statements from the American Psychiatric Association and the American Bar Association supported a view that personality disorder should not be used as an insanity defence (Sparr 2009). The resulting reforms represented a radical narrowing of the criteria for a defence.

### 9.2.1 The Insanity Defense Reform Act (1984)

In 1984 Congress enacted the IDRA (Insanity Defense Reform Act), which shifted the burden of proof on to the defence to argue on the following grounds for a person to be found not guilty by reason of insanity:

> It is an affirmative defense to a prosecution under any federal statute that, at the time of the commission of the acts constituting the offense, the defendant as a result of a severe mental disease or defect, was unable to appreciate the nature and quality or the wrongfulness of his acts. Mental disease or defect does not otherwise constitute a defense.
> (18 U.S.CA 17 (a), e.g. Scheb 2008)

Here the defence now have to show that the accused is unable to appreciate that what they have done is wrong owing to severe mental disease or defect. It effectively means a reversion to the 'knowledge of right and wrong' test, and the second prong introduced by the ALI guidelines, the ability to control conduct, has gone entirely. The resulting reforms of the insanity defence have generally seen a reversion to something at least as narrow as the M'Naghten criteria across the United States. Freedman (1983) puts this into the political context of a sharp turn towards a right wing, neo-liberal agenda well represented by the Reagan presidency in the US and Thatcher's government in the UK through the 1980s. It was an era marked by high levels of anxiety about crime and a return to punitive attitudes to crime control.

Sherrill (1984), in the immediate wake of the IDRA, was led to protest angrily that in the State of Florida, such was the zeal of the criminal justice system to put the guilty to the electric chair, that insanity was no longer any defence at all. One example that Sherrill reports is of Arthur Frederick Goode, who had been frankly and brazenly dangerous and disturbed since childhood and was put on trial for the rape and murder of an 11-year-old boy. Goode was considered by the court to be sufficiently competent not only to stand trial but to conduct his own defence (having fallen out with his attorney). There is little doubt that Goode was best considered, by anyone's standards, to be a vicious, sadistic killer. Indeed he evidently enjoyed describing to the court what he had done 'in such intimate detail that many spectators wanted to throw up'. Despite such evidence of disorder he was not found to be insane and was sentenced to death. This case was to become particularly notorious, Goode's own behaviour and the lurid detail of the murders ensuring plenty of publicity even years after his execution in the electric chair.[6]

Such early signals have been proven valid since many of the interpretations of IDRA that followed in subsequent years do appear to have virtually ruled out the insanity defence (Rolf 2006). Most states followed swiftly to enact laws along the IDRA model, and a small number of states (Montana, Utah, Idaho and Kansas) eliminated the insanity defence altogether (Stoll 2009: 1777). A number of notorious cases suggest that some states ignore even quite overt cases of psychosis. In 2003, Michael Clark was found guilty of first degree murder (of a police officer) in an Arizona court despite strong evidence that he was suffering delusions, hallucinations characteristic of schizophrenia. For some years his behaviour had become increasingly bizarre as he became withdrawn, self-neglecting and fearful that he was in danger from aliens. He refused to eat at home because of his fear of poison, and carried a bird in his car to warn of poison gas (but came to believe that aliens had replaced its lungs with robotics). Despite substantial evidence of behaviour being driven by psychotic beliefs, the judge concluded that Clark's mental disease did not distort his perceptions of reality so as to interfere with his understanding of the fact that he shot a police officer and knew that it was wrong to do so. Despite considerable effort to challenge the decision at Supreme Court level, the verdict was allowed to stand (Kim 2012).

The case of Andrea Yates, occurring a year later in Texas (Rolf 2006), caught popular attention; she was a mother found guilty of murdering three of her own children by drowning them in a bath tub. Despite a substantial history of insanity and episodes of post-partum depression, she was still found guilty because she had known what she had done (she had immediately phoned the police and confessed). It is fair to say that both she and Clark would probably have been found not guilty under ALI model rules, and the M'Naghten rules (as they have generally been interpreted). On the very narrow criteria of the IDRA she was found guilty, however.

Legal practice towards the treatment and disposal of those deemed to suffer mental disorders in the United States has undoubtedly lurched towards the draconian since the trial of John Hinckley. A number of states have effectively dropped the insanity defence. Even those who are frankly psychotic are finding that there is no defence when the most strict application of M'Naghten rule logic is applied. If an individual knows what they have done, and knows it is wrong, then they are guilty. It is therefore of little surprise that in this climate there has been little sign of a move towards greater consideration of the issue of the criminal culpability, and treatment potential, of individuals with 'personality disorder'. The issue of personality disorder and the insanity defence was subject to specific debate in Oregon (Lockey and Bloom 2007) and, not surprisingly in the context of the general application of such narrow criteria, the state did not see fit to allow the diagnosis to be used as a defence. Strikingly, however, in what appears to be a turn back towards the 'sexual psychopath laws' of the middle of the twentieth century (discussed in Chapter 6), a number of states began in 1997 to introduce 'Sexually Violent Predator' laws, which aim to increase levels of surveillance and incarceration for those individuals convicted of sexual offences who are also deemed to suffer from mental disorder and personality disorder (Simon 1998). Thus far, this appears to be simply another layer of surveillance that has no implications for the attribution of responsibility.

In the UK, the debate on the relationship between crime and personality disorder has been highly animated since the end of the 1990s. Indeed there has been considerable interest at government levels in the criminological significance of personality disorder. This interest was sparked by one particular case that stimulated a great deal of publicity since it involved a notably brutal murder that evoked widespread horror. The subsequent trial and inquiry then created significant debate about the status of personality disorder, which led to a number of practice and legislative initiatives that are internationally quite unique (Sparr 2009). Some detail on this case and the responses are worth dwelling upon. The potent mix of press attention, government concern and professional interest has arguably led to important readjustment of official responses to the link between personality disorder and crime (Pickersgill 2013).

## 9.3 The invention of 'dangerous and severe personality disorder' in the UK

On 9 July 1996 Lin Russell and both her daughters, aged 6 and 9 years old, were walking home along a country lane in Kent, England. They were savagely attacked, their heads battered with an object that was never found, but might well have been a hammer. Lin and her eldest daughter, Megan, were killed. Meanwhile 6-year-old Josie was so badly injured that it was certain she had been 'left for dead'. The murder was a major news story for days afterwards. The popular tabloid the *Daily Mirror* ran a story on Saturday 12 July under the headline 'PICTURES OF HAPPINESS SHATTERED BY CRAZED HAMMER MANIAC' and a photograph of a happy smiling family. The lead detective was quoted as saying: 'This is the most horrific, terrible murder I have had the misfortune to come across. . . . [T]his attack was utterly, utterly frenzied. The post mortem was the worst I have ever attended. This man could strike again.'

As details of the forensic examination emerged in the following months the emphasis shifted away from the 'frenzied' and 'deranged' nature of the attack and instead focused on the cooler viciousness of the assault. As the *Daily Mail* (6 March 1997) explained, the victims had been rather time-consumingly bound and gagged. Meanwhile, the police had no real leads at all and so they used the anniversary of the attack to appeal for witnesses on the popular BBC television programme *Crimewatch*, which involves the police presenting information about real unsolved crimes and appealing to the public for information. The psychiatrist who had treated Michael Stone watched the programme and became concerned that Stone was the individual being sought by the police. After discussion with colleagues, the psychiatrist contacted the police. It was this information that led to Stone's arrest,[7] and he was eventually tried and convicted twice. The first conviction in October 1998 was quashed at appeal in February 2001. The appeal was successful mainly because a prosecution witnesses confessed to having lied in evidence given at the initial trial. Stone was then tried again in September 2001, was found guilty on two counts of murder and one of attempted murder and received three life sentences. Perhaps, given the absence of forensic evidence or witness accounts that could directly associate Stone with the crime, or indeed the apparent lack of any ostensible motive, it is not surprising that Stone's conviction has been contested.[8] Stone was only arrested following information from one of his psychiatrists and it might be argued that some of the strongest evidence against him, apart from the circumstantial evidence concerning his familiarity with the area, was his psychiatric profile. What emerged during the trial was that Stone had a long history of violence and of contact with an array of state and welfare services including prisons and psychiatric hospitals. He had been discharged from psychiatric hospital in January 1995 (the year before the attacks), in spite of psychiatrists' awareness that he was psychologically disturbed and prone to violence. It was believed, however, that he was suffering from an untreatable personality disorder, which meant that he should not therefore be detained in hospital. As discussed in Chapter 7, although the Mental Health Act in England and Wales had since 1959 included 'psychopathic disorder', it also had the additional clause that the disorder should 'require' or be 'susceptible to treatment'.

The issue caught the attention of politicians and the media and the government of the day were drawn into response. An opposition MP, Alan Beith, asked the Home Secretary a question in Parliament on 26 October 1998:

> Does the Home Secretary believe that further measures will be needed to deal with offenders who are deemed to be extremely violent because of mental illness or personality disorder, but whom psychiatrists diagnose as not likely to respond to treatment? Is he aware that this concern has arisen not simply following the conviction of Michael Stone for those two brutal and horrible murders, but because there has been a tendency in recent years for psychiatrists to diagnose a number of violent people as not likely to respond to treatment?
>
> (Hansard 1998: c9)

The then Home Secretary, Jack Straw, replied in full agreement, making it clear that he was certainly engaging with what the media had to say since he had been listening to what Louis Blom-Cooper (a distinguished judge) had said on the radio about changes in the practices of the psychiatric profession,

> which, 20 years ago, adopted what I would call a common-sense approach to serious and dangerous persistent offenders, but these days goes for a much narrower interpretation of the law. *Quite extraordinarily for a medical profession, the psychiatric profession has said that it will take on only patients whom it regards as treatable. If that philosophy applied anywhere else in medicine, no progress would be made in medicine. It is time that the psychiatric profession seriously examined its own practices and tried to modernise them in a way that it has so far failed to do.*
> (Hansard 1998: c9; see also Warden 1998: 1270, my emphasis)

The immediate response was the proposal 'Managing Dangerous People with Severe Personality Disorder' (Home Office/DoH, 1999). The most controversial element of the proposal was that those individuals suffering from severe personality disorder who were considered dangerous might receive indeterminate sentences (Seddon 2008). The formal inquiry into Stone's treatment and detention confirmed that Stone had been considered unsuitable for hospital treatment. The report into Stone's care, treatment and detention quotes from a psychiatric assessment made in January 1995, some 18 months before the killings:

> A tough minded man . . . [who] . . . at no point displayed any features of a psychotic illness. He had credible explanations for apparently psychotic episodes . . . [and] . . . denied ever hearing voices. The most striking abnormality was his extremely callous attitude towards victims and anger and contempt towards several professionals involved with him. . . . My impression is that he has committed major violent crimes in the past and is likely to do so in the future. . . . He fulfils the criteria for anti-social personality disorder and there may also be a paranoid mental illness.
> (South East Coast Strategic Health Authority 2006: 196)

Despite identifying 'antisocial personality disorder' and linking this to likely future violence, the psychiatrist suggested that Stone's detention under the MHA was 'highly inappropriate' and that therefore it would not appear to be 'appropriate to offer [Mr. Stone] a bed as firstly he is no longer mentally ill and secondly he is unlikely to respond to a graded rehabilitation package'. This issue had been picked up by the press in Britain, and some of the coverage did simply spell out the dilemma that might face professionals. The *Evening Standard* (23 October 2001), for example, described the problem of 'Antisocial personality disorder' and the destruction it might bring, but noted that it 'may not be considered treatable' and so its sufferers, even if diagnosed, 'mostly end up in court and prison'. The journalist Melanie Phillips, writing in the *Sunday Times* on 25 October, was less measured in her tone. Writing under the headline 'Forget psychiatry, stop psychopaths', Phillips was uncompromising in expressing her view that the psychiatric profession had failed everyone by adopting the stance that Stone was 'Not our problem, guv!'. She raged at psychiatry's attitude to personality disorder, declaring it 'the black hole' at the very 'heart' of the profession. To psychiatrists, she argued, it was only a label that they used when they knew that something was wrong with someone, but did not know what was wrong. They did not 'bother to find out' what was wrong, since 'If it doesn't fit any of the categories of illness they can treat with drugs, they say it's merely a problem of containment and shunt the (non-)patient in the direction of the prison system' (*Sunday Times* 25 October 2001).

The government of the day responded to the furore by pressing forward with a series of initiatives that aimed to push both the National Health Service and the criminal justice system to engage with the problem of personality disorder. Maden (2007) suggests that the drama surrounding the Stone case was only the catalyst to action following many years of frustration that so little was being done with serious offenders with personality disorder in the prison system. The most prominent government response was to set up an initiative called the DSPD (Dangerous and Severe Personality Disorder) programme. This initiative brought together elements of the Home Office, the Department of Health and the Prison Service in order to explore and provide viable forms of treatment (Home Office 2005; Taylor 2011). The strong intent to press the National Health Service itself to build capacity to treat personality disorder was signalled by the 2003 document *Personality Disorder: No Longer a Diagnosis of Exclusion* (DoH 2003). The government response was further informed by other data suggesting that personality disorders were linked to a whole range of social difficulties, from severe and violent offending to drug abuse, homelessness, antisocial behaviour and general heavy use of the welfare and social services (e.g. Cabinet Office 2006). Government interest in the importance of 'personality disorder' was to be an important driver to the drafting of a new Mental Health Act in England and Wales, as will be discussed in more detail in the following section.

### 9.3.1 Personality disorder and Mental Health Act reform

In 1998 the British government announced the intention to revise the 1983 MHA (Gostin 1985) and to introduce a new Act, and charged the Richardson Committee with a review of the Act. As the process of review continued it became clear, as Wright notes, that there were two central drivers of the reform. There was first the intention to 'break the link between detention in hospital and compulsory treatment' (Wright 2002: Summary). This was designed to alleviate anxiety about the relatively large numbers of people who were viewed as suffering from mental disorder who, in an era of community care, were living independently, yet were not compliant with medication regimes. The second motivation came from government anxiety about severe personality disorder; the aim was to ensure that personality disorders were unambiguously included within the Act with just as much status as any other mental disorder. Both issues were to prove highly contentious. The most obvious source of discontent was that expressed by the many different groups and individuals who were very concerned about the threat to civil liberties posed by attempts to allow for compulsory treatment for individuals who were not necessarily hospitalised (Mental Health Alliance 2012). The issue of the definition of 'personality disorder' was to compound the problem, however. The government was very keen to make sure that personality disorders were entirely included in the Act and that mental health services engaged with individuals with such problems. It was felt that the separate categorisation of 'psychopathy' in the 1983 Act, alongside the caveat about treatability, had allowed psychiatry to avoid engagement (Peay 2011). The solution was to propose a very general and all-encompassing definition: 'any disability or disorder of mind or brain, whether permanent or temporary, which results in an impairment or disturbance of mental functioning' (Wright 2002: 24). The inclusive and rather circular nature of this definition, coupled with civil liberty concerns raised by 'community treatment orders', focused the anxieties of groups of professionals and other interested organisations. Also, despite being defended by the Richardson Report, the notion of treatability as one of the criteria for compulsory treatment and detention was removed from the government draft bills (Pickersgill 2013). The plans galvanised an alliance of professional organisations and civil libertarian groups who could agree that the combination of vague and inclusive definitions of mental disorder (which did not include a caveat on treatability) alongside considerable power to treat and detain represented dangerous levels of state power. Eventually, despite years of negotiation, the government failed to get sufficient agreement on a new Mental Health Act and instead the original Act was simply amended. The 2007 MHA (Amendment Act), when it was passed, did introduce this very general definition of mental disorder and removed the 'treatability test' (DoH 2006). Sen and Irons (2010: 330) argue that although it might appear that the treatability test has been removed, in reality it is 'alive and well in practice' since anyone applying to use the powers of the Act to detain or treat still has to demonstrate that appropriate treatment will be of benefit to the patient (anything else would be contrary to Department of Health codes of practice, and even Human Rights legislation).

Overall, despite the degree of dispute and opposition to these changes, the terrain of mental health practice, particularly in relation to personality disorders, was being significantly altered by a series of connected initiatives. Building on the intention set by the announcement of Dangerous and Severe Personality Disorder programmes, the UK government has poured considerable sums of money into research and practice programmes. As Pickersgill (2013: 39) highlights, the availability of funding for initiatives seems to have the effect of turning the tide of opinion in the professions of psychiatry and psychology towards the idea that 'personality disorders' are perhaps amenable to treatment. There were many benefits to be gained through this switch in attitude; 'acceptance by their peers, as well as increased funding, jobs and support' (Pickersgill 2013: 45). Support for the argument in favour of the treatability of personality disorders was found in a number of reviews (Dolan and Coid 1993; Warren *et al.* 2003). What became gradually clearer was that a number of treatment options were being favoured. Programmes that strove for the treatment of individuals using particular psychological methods appeared to be favoured in the early decades of the twenty-first century. The assumption that psychiatry, with its strong roots and allegiance to organic models, is not necessarily favoured, has led some to claim something of a crisis for the profession (Bracken *et al.* 2012; Craddock *et al.* 2008). On the other hand, the social treatments which had been such important planks in the argument for the inclusion of psychopathy in the 1959 MHA appear to be out of favour. The Henderson Hospital, a pioneer in the treatment of personality disorder through democratic therapeutic community treatment (see Chapter 7), for example, was closed down in 2008. The Cassel Hospital, which used therapeutic community methods to treat families, also faced closure in 2011. Instead a range of psychological techniques, notably cognitive behaviour therapy, DBT (dialectical behaviour therapy) and mentalisation, appear to be much more in favour. While there is some diversity in the theoretical approaches there (CBT has roots in behaviourism, and mentalisation in psychodynamic psychotherapy), the assumption that these are disorders of individual psychology appears to be strong. Nevertheless, as Sparr (2009) emphasises, the UK is in many ways relatively unusual in its quite direct and overt engagement with the issue of personality disorder in its crime and justice system.

## Conclusion

By the turn of the century the issue of personality disorder in the criminal justice system continued in a state of some flux. In the USA, where the diagnosis has been most successfully promoted by the American Psychiatric Association through the DSM, it enjoyed a high profile and some apparent utility in courts, notably in the trial of John Hinckley in 1982. This trial made the interaction between systems of justice, media, psychiatry and the public very clear. A stylish Hollywood film portraying a cultish character who was arguably morally insane roaming the streets was shown in the courtroom as part explanation for the murderous personality of the accused. Despite the success of Hinckley's defence, the public furore following the verdict, with so many echoes of the trial of Daniel M'Naghten 140 years earlier, led to the US government narrowing the possible defence of insanity so that 'personality disorder' as a defence was all but ruled out. Nevertheless, as will be discussed in the following chapter, the diagnosis is commonly used in the criminal justice system; however, it is arguable that here it is often used as a measure of risk rather than as a factor of mitigation (Seddon 2008).

In the UK the diagnosis of psychopathy had been officially recognised for some decades, since its inclusion in the Mental Health Act (England and Wales) in 1959. Its status remained ambiguous, however. The fact that it was named as a separate category in the Act perhaps reinforced the belief it was not *really* a proper mental disorder. At the end of the twentieth century the high profile case of Michael Stone appeared to help galvanise government to try to ensure that health and welfare services were geared up to engage with the issue of personality disorder. The category of 'dangerous and severe personality disorder' was proposed as a description of individuals who might receive particular penal and treatment attention. There was also interest in the broader categories of personality disorder, and there was a series of initiatives from the Department of Health, notably the policy document *Personality Disorder: No Longer a Diagnosis of Exclusion* (DoH 2003). As the title suggests, this aimed to press the health services to engage with and attempt to treat the large numbers of people who might receive one of various diagnoses of personality disorder. Connected to this there was also a wider set of initiatives which attempted to limit the damage of what become known as 'social exclusion'. For example, the Sure Start initiative (Eisenstadt 2011) was driven by research that showed the poor, and often criminal, outcomes for those with difficult childhoods (Utting *et al.* 1993).

Despite the publicity of the Stone case and the evident agitation of press and government, the years following the Stone trial were not marked by a notable increase in the apparent acceptability of personality disorder as a defence in court. The trial of Brian Blackwell at Liverpool Crown Court in 2005 saw the successful use of the diagnosis of 'narcissistic personality disorder' as defence against the charge of murder on the grounds of diminished responsibility. This case remains something of a curiosity rather than a signal of a major shift (Cohen 2005; Jones 2008). Instead we are more likely to see cases like that of Stephen Farrow, whose trial in 2012 introduced the book (see Introduction, p.1). As discussion following the trial indicated, Farrow's vicious and violent behaviour seemed inexplicable, other than by recourse to a disorder that demands help or prevention and yet still does not constitute an 'excuse'.

The concluding chapter will provide an overview of the findings of the book and an analysis of the direction in which we might be heading.

## Notes

1  Article 4: Responsibility, Section 4.01: Mental Disease or Defect, Excluding Responsibility (in Morris 1961: 423).

2  This film, directed by Martin Scorsese, was first released in 1976. It went on to be regarded as a classic and has attracted academic attention from a number of perspectives, with its psychological and cultural significance being noted (Rafter 2011; Yates 2007).
3  Accounts and transcripts of the trial are available here: http://law2.umkc.edu/faculty/projects/ftrials/hinckley/hinckleytranscript.htm#Dr.%20Park, accessed 7 January 2015.
4  Trial transcript available at: http://law2.umkc.edu/faculty/projects/ftrials/hinckley/hinckleytranscript.htm (accessed 26 June 2015).
5  Trial transcript available at: http://law2.umkc.edu/faculty/projects/ftrials/hinckley/hinckleytranscript.htm (accessed 26 June 2015).
6  http://charlotte.floridaweekly.com/news/2009-11-19/Top_News/THE_ULTIMATE_PERSONIFICATION_OF_EVIL.html (accessed 26 April 2015).
7  See *Joint Agencies' Response to the Recommendations of the Independent Inquiry Report into the Care and Treatment of Michael Stone*, South East Coast Strategic Health Authority, Kent County Council, Kent Probation Area, Medway Primary Care Trust, Kent and Medway NHS and Social Care Partnership Trust and Medway Council.
8  Wagenaar *et al.* (1993) argue that courts often make verdicts on the basis of the strength of the competing narratives presented by defence and prosecution. Those crimes where good forensic or witness evidence is lacking and which appear to be without motive may well be very difficult to prosecute in the absence of a clear narrative that would include the attacker's motivation.

Chapter 10

# Concluding discussion
## The contemporary debates: policy, theory and treatment

### Introduction

The previous chapters have outlined a history of the diagnosis of moral insanity through its diverse manifestations since the beginning of the nineteenth century.

What emerges from this historical analysis is that the diagnosis can be viewed as a creation of the modern state, most evidently constructed at the junction of the legal system and the welfare services. Less obviously, but also crucially, it is a diagnosis of what Habermas described as the 'public sphere'. In this it is shaped by the concerns of that public, one that is as much plebeian as bourgeois (Calhoun 1992). The development of the public sphere not only allowed for debate and discussion about psychological and psychiatric disorders alongside a whole range of social and human issues, but it also created the conditions that demanded a better understanding of how individuals acted in this public realm. As rigid socially determined roles fell away, so the need for individuals to manage and manoeuvre in this public sphere grew. Thus interest in understanding the capacity of individuals to manoeuvre and relate in this public sphere became more significant. This curiosity to know more about ourselves and others encouraged interest in notions of interiority and the exploration of hidden forms of insanity such as moral insanity and monomania. Alongside curiosity there has always been anxiety, and public anxieties about violence and sexuality loom large in this story. In its bleaker forms, moral insanity has been, as Federman *et al.* (2009) suggest, part of 'a cultural matrix' connected to 'the public's sense of fear of criminality, the fear of the unknown, the fear of the unfamiliar and the fear of cultural pollution'. At different times curiosity and anxiety have had varying degrees of influence. Anxiety about the threat posed by dangerous 'others' has led to the need to label and control. Curiosity has been more likely to lead to exploration and reflection.

At times moral insanity has been perceived as a psychological disorder that might be understood as arising within the mind of an individual and manifesting in abnormally antisocial or even violent behaviour. This psychological disorder has been construed as caused by external and internal factors. At other times moral insanity has been understood as a wholly hereditarily endowed physiological deficiency which afflicts particular individuals. At other times, perhaps quite particularly during the middle of the twentieth century, it was understood as a disturbance of relationships among the social group. One notable constancy detectable through all its various manifestations is the fact that the diagnosis has always had its trenchant critics. It has been consistently criticised within criminal justice systems and the medical and psychological professions (Ellard 1996; Lewis and Appleby 1988). The absence of a solid definition, one that avoided dependence on an apparently circular process of labelling cruel or immoral behaviour, has provided the critics with a strong evidential case that this is not a 'real' disorder at all (Pilgrim 2001). To such critics this is not a psychological, psychiatric or medical disorder; it is simply a fictional category, created through an unholy alliance of the medical and the criminal justice systems of the modern state. It is applied to individuals whom 'the state' would wish to see labelled, locked up or otherwise controlled. The longevity of the diagnosis, surviving in its various forms for over two centuries in the face of professional ambivalence, suggests that an unreserved dismissal of the concept as an agent of policing and control is not necessarily warranted. The argument has been made throughout this book that the story of moral insanity not only involves interaction between agencies of criminal justice and health, but also involves the beliefs, hopes and fears of the wider public.

It is argued in Chapter 1 that in the eighteenth century there were evident traces in London's central criminal court of what was later to be called moral insanity as rather different ways of understanding the relationship between individual conduct, emotions and relationships were being forged. The emerging mass urban spaces, of which London was the epitome at this time, required different ways of understanding individuals and of controlling disorder. The issue of masculinity and its relationship to violence and to others seemed to emerge as an issue at this point. Indeed, the diagnoses have generally been applied to men and the association with the control of masculine deviance and violence has been fairly consistent. Verdicts concerning otherwise inexplicable acts of violence were inextricably linked to anxieties about the capacity of the community to notice, let alone intervene in, disturbing situations, and to the question of what to do with individuals who might have such hidden forms of dangerousness and disorder. Although a new sensitivity towards insanity is apparent in the late eighteenth century, it was the nineteenth that was to witness the birth of psychiatry, and debate about moral insanity was a key driver of its development (as discussed in Chapter 2). It is surely no coincidence that so many of the important cases since the early nineteenth century which have had impacts on policy have been acts of very public violence: the attempted or actual assassinations of monarchs and politicians. The public trials of Oxford, Hadfield and M'Naghten in London in the first half of the nineteenth century appeared to establish the nascent psychiatric profession's claim to expertise. By the 1840s, in Britain and France, forms of moral insanity or monomania appeared to have become somewhat established in the courts, indeed rather well accepted in Britain. It was the highly public furore over the M'Naghten verdict in 1843 that was eventually to lead to a very noticeable retreat of the British psychiatric profession away from the promotion of moral insanity in the courtroom. Meanwhile, moral insanity was taken up enthusiastically by a wider, perhaps more bourgeois, literary culture, and it was to have a life outside the clinic and the courts. As discussed in Chapter 4, it appeared in various forms, such as monomania, in the works of some of the giants of nineteenth-century English literature, such as George Eliot, Emily Brontë and Joseph Conrad. The idea that individuals were psychologically complex and could therefore incorporate good, bad, kind or violent hidden facets became mainstream and helped legitimate a perspective on the human world that was to become a feature of western culture and emphasised a psychological dimension to human experience (Rieff 1966; Rose 1989). At the same time the perception that the urban spaces of the nineteenth century were filled with dangerous criminal classes helped to spur the urge to find solutions to this danger. The budding psychiatric profession was keen to contribute to this search, yet, chastened by the reversal of the post-M'Naghten decades, psychiatry turned to biological models of moral insanity that might be used to investigate and classify the criminal classes (as discussed in Chapter 3). At the same time those in the medical professions and beyond became enthralled by the popular interest in Darwinian ideas. In the hands of some writers theories of evolution raised the spectres of the primitive ancestral beings that might be a part of all of us, but others made the rather different suggestion that there were only some individuals who were tainted by earlier forms of the human species and were thus themselves primitive and dangerous. To the eugenicists, directly inspired by the work of Francis Galton (but deeply influenced as well by the gloomy predictions of theories of degeneracy), the human race was imperilled by the threat of bad genes proliferating and leading to the *degeneration* of the race. Thus moral insanity was elided with moral imbecility and feeblemindedness. While eugenical theories were 'invented in Britain' they were put into practice in a remarkably systematic way in the United States. The super-charged growth of urban areas was no longer to be found in Paris or London, but instead in the new cities of the United States, most famously and notably Chicago. Across the United States, people who were viewed as feebleminded (or who were identified as carrying the genes of feeblemindedness) were sterilised and incarcerated on a remarkable scale. As described in Chapter 5, the Municipal Court in Chicago had the power to divert young offenders away from the system of justice and instead towards psychological assessment, which could lead to incarceration. The interaction between American psychiatry's interest in degeneration and the 'scientific' authors of Hitler's final solution is startling. Of course, in many respects that eugenical story ran into a calamitous dead end in Hitler's Germany. The full horror of what happens when groups of people come to be seen as wholly bad, and the fault is assumed to be simply inherent, became all too clear.

Besides the horror of the Holocaust, the prominence of war, particularly the First and Second World Wars, deserves some reflection in the story of the evolution of moral insanity. As discussed in Chapters 5, 6 and 7, the experience of war had major, sometimes paradoxical, impacts on the understanding of insanity and dangerousness. The impact of trauma on the psychological health of otherwise healthy young men had become very apparent during the First World War. The idea that insanity was caused by genetically determined degeneracy became unsustainable as the fittest and bravest men came home bearing the symptoms of psychological damage. At the same time governments on both sides of the Atlantic poured money into psychiatry for a number of reasons. Not only were they interested in the role that psychiatry might play in the treatment of battle stress and the selection of personnel for military roles, but there was also more general interest in ideas that would help to understand and promote the morale of the population. Military service brought psychiatrists into contact with a wider range of the population compared with their work in the asylums. They found that the concept of psychopathy became a useful one at this time, and definitions were applied that were much broader than those confined to matters of criminal justice (in keeping with Prichard's nineteenth-century formulation of 'moral insanity'). It might have been simply the increase in government funding and the contact that psychiatrists had with a wider range of the public that led to the attention given to personality disorder. In addition, perhaps, there was also something about wartime and the experience and understanding of the violence that followed. Perhaps, amidst the dusty ruins of cities and towns flattened by war, it was all too clear that violence and destructiveness was a part of all of us and not something that existed only in 'other people'. If violence was a problem, it had its roots in 'us' rather than 'them'. This perspective was taken up most obviously in the development of the theory and practices of group and community therapy that became popular during, and in the aftermath of, World War Two (as discussed in Chapter 7). Experiments in community therapy in the UK, which assumed that 'psychopathic states' (to use David Henderson's phrase) were disorders that did not simply exist within individuals, but had to be understood and treated at a community level, became popular and achieved a degree of official sanction through the Mental Health Act in 1959 (in England and Wales).

In subsequent decades the diagnostic categories of personality disorder were to proliferate, thanks in considerable part to the success of the *Diagnostic and Statistical Manual* (DSM), published by the American Psychiatric Association. Many of the categories, such as the narcissistic and antisocial personality disorders, were to enter everyday language, and the clinical concepts have formed part of wider social and cultural analyses (as discussed below). Courts in the US and UK were to witness notable moves towards the liberalisation of the rules around the various forms of the 'insanity defence' in the post-war decades as they moved away from the strictures of the M'Naghten rules. Discussion of personality disorder loomed large in many of the debates in the USA, in relation to the Durham rule and the ALI guidelines which widened the criteria for legal insanity. The issue of personality disorder and its relationship to criminal culpability was also at the heart of the debate that followed the controversial and dramatic trial of John Hinckley who was found not guilty on the grounds of insanity of the attempted murder of President Reagan (all discussed in Chapter 9) that led to a narrowing of the definition. The rather different, but nonetheless high profile, case of Michael Stone in the UK led to great government attention being paid to the issue of personality disorder. Conflict emerged between government enthusiasm for the health services doing more to engage and treat personality disorders and the various professions and service user groups, who were often concerned about the catch-all definitions and the degree of power that might be wielded over individuals caught up with those definitions.

Before moving on to discuss the possible future of moral insanity it is worth noting that despite the long running debate about the precision and efficacy of the diagnoses, the language of the clinical concepts has become part of common cultural parlance and the sociological landscape. In 1979, for example, Christopher Lasch used the clinical concept of 'narcissistic personality disorder' as a basis for his wide-ranging, and highly influential, cultural critique of post-industrial American society. He argued, from the perspective of North America in the late 1970s, that 'narcissistic personalities' were becoming the disorders of modern times and that contemporary social conditions were creating a culture of narcissism. The fragmentation of communities and families meant that many people were growing up without any sense of solid identity or worth (which might have been fostered through consistent relationships with others and playing valued roles in those families and communities). Those relationships were being replaced by the promises of consumerism carried by mass media increasingly dominated by commercial interests. While this was to become known as cultural critique, as Lasch (1979) was at pains to point out, it was strongly rooted in the psychoanalytic theorisation of narcissism propounded by Kohut and Kernberg (Jones 2013). Lasch was well aware of the interaction between the wider culture and the world of clinical psychiatry. Many of the disorders of personality that he was writing about were being 'discovered' in the clinic. He presents evidence from a number of writers who argued that the complaints that patients were bringing to psychoanalysts were changing in the second half of the twentieth century. They were no longer bringing their symptoms of neurosis and repression but their 'vague, ill defined complaints', their feelings of emptiness, their disorders of character (Lasch 1979: 43). The dangers posed by a culture that was creating individuals with diminished and disordered selves was a staple of a whole genre of cultural critique that emanated from the Frankfurt School, which featured such diverse writers as Erich Fromm, Herbert Marcuse and Max Horkheimer (Jay 1973). It is certainly the case that such disorders appear to be commonly detectable, as seen in the evidence provided by a number of community surveys. Torgersen *et al.* (2001), for example, using DSM-III criteria, found an overall prevalence of any type of personality disorder in the city of Oslo to be 13.1 per cent. Coid *et al.* (2006)

found a prevalence rate of 4.4 per cent of DSM-IV personality disorders in their community sample in London. Surveys of users of general medical services find much higher rates (Cabinet Office 2006). Surveys of prison populations suggest that the prevalence of 'antisocial personality disorder' is as high as 60–70 per cent (DoH 2011). While figures like these can be used to reinforce the significance of the discovery and propagation of knowledge about these disorders, it is also possible to view such evidence as proving how far psychiatric concepts now shape individual experience and our very perceptions of ourselves. Back in the 1970s Lasch also argued that the language, concepts and practices of psychiatry had themselves become part of the social fabric which was damaging individuals' capacities to strive and function. In argument that prefigured later work on the significance of 'risk' to later modern societies (e.g. Beck 1992), Lasch noted how modern medical science 'had conquered the plagues and epidemics that once made life so precarious' but had instead prepared the ground for new and constant anxieties:

> Medicine and psychiatry – more generally, the therapeutic outlook and sensibility that pervade modern society – reinforce the pattern created by other social influences, in which the individual endlessly examines himself for signs of aging and ill health, for tell tale signs [and] symptoms of psychic stress, for blemishes and flaws that diminish his attractiveness.
> (Lasch 1979: 49)

The significance of the management of risk has been argued by Ulrich Beck (1992) and others (e.g. Giddens 1999) to be a key driver of governmental attention and social change. Of course, elements of risk management have arguably been immanent in the story of moral insanity since at least the middle of the nineteenth century. The promise of crime reduction through the assessment of prison populations and the subsequent categories of constitutional psychopathy and feeblemindedness ended in the moral disarray of eugenics and final solutions (as described in Chapter 5). The language of risk management has now become a very prominent part of the story again in the beginning of the twenty-first century. The argument that there are underlying, scientifically measurable, psychological constructs (whether termed 'antisocial personality disorder' or 'psychopathy') that can be used to inform decisions about care, confinement and rehabilitation has again gained some ascendance.

## 10.1 What is the future for moral insanity?

The diagnosis has survived, albeit understood in very different ways, for over two centuries. At some points it has appeared alongside attempts to understand ourselves and others better. At other times the diagnosis has been used in quite cruel and catastrophic ways, so it might well be worth thinking about what might be happening now and in the future. If we can assume that this is a diagnosis of the public sphere, then perhaps it would be useful to think about the voices and forces that might be shaping our understanding of moral insanity and directing practices in the future. The first thing to note is that the diagnosis is unlikely to disappear. Empirical evidence has arguably been gathering for some time to suggest that there is an issue here that will continue to attract attention and demands for action. There appears to be a considerable degree of popular appetite for the topic, with books such as *The Psychopath Test* (Ronson 2012) and *The Sociopath Next Door* (Stout 2005) appearing in popular formats and achieving considerable sales. In addition to this there are large numbers of people in prisons across the world who have already been given a diagnosis of 'antisocial personality disorder', and there are even larger numbers whose behaviour suggests that they might well have the diagnosis applied (Fazel and Danesh 2002). While such figures are open to the not unreasonable challenge that this is simply a teleological and vacant process of labelling 'antisocial' behaviour, a volume of evidence has also been gathering for some years that suggests there are patterns of behaviour and criminality which do significantly point to the existence of something that does look very much like 'moral insanity'. Since the middle of the last century longitudinal studies, carried out in a number of countries (e.g. McCord 1990; Moffitt 1993; West 1982), have been producing data that suggest there may be some meaning to these categories. These studies have involved the collection of data on young children and their lives, and following them up over time as they achieve adulthood and beyond. The data demonstrate that the most serious offending tends to be carried out by relatively small numbers of people. These same people tend also to have various health and social problems. They are more likely than their peers to have problems with drug and alcohol misuse and addiction and to have achieved a diagnosis of antisocial personality disorder. They are more likely to have come from troubled families living amidst troubled communities. Their childhoods are more likely to be marked by disruption, inconsistency and even abuse and neglect. Their schooling is likely to have been disrupted, and to have led to very few qualifications. They are less likely than most to have a stable record of conventional employment and more likely to have a history of problems in relationships with others (see Jones 2008 for a review of this material). For all this, they do not suffer from any conventionally recognised form of insanity that manifests in delusion and hallucination. Clearly, the description of such difficulties echoes that of nineteenth-century fears of the 'criminal classes'. The problem, then as now, is how such observations might be most helpfully interpreted. What the review of the history of the various manifestations of moral insanity presented in this book emphasises is that such interpretations are highly contingent and shaped within the public sphere, which can be full of fear and anxiety. It might therefore be helpful to think about the cultural climate in the early decades of the twenty-first century and where things might be going. What is being said in the public sphere about this group and to whom do the voices belong? There is no doubt that the voices of official government have been prominent, most notably in the UK since the late 1990s, and they have been concerned to see higher levels of intervention into the problem (as discussed in Chapter 9). Responding to these prompts, professional groups have also been keen to have their say and stake new claims for expertise as they have done over the past two centuries.

Looking at wider cultural factors, perhaps the most obvious social and cultural influences that might shape the debate are those of neo-liberalism (Harvey 2005), marked by an increasing emphasis on the individual as a site of action and of reaction. The individual is considered to be responsible for the management of their own life-project and encouraged to enjoy the rewards and endure the punishments of success and failure. Consistent with this cultural climate, there are two very notable currents that seek to locate 'moral insanity' within the individual. We are seeing a growing interest in biological and psychological explanations, which both locate the disturbance within some presumed inner organic or psychological realm. Both of these explanations are potentially problematic since they may both ignore the social dimensions of this disorder, which are very clear when the history is taken into account. A third rather different force will then be considered: the voices of those who have had experience of diagnosis themselves. Public discussion of issues of mental health has been influenced for some decades by the inclusion of the views of those individuals who have been diagnosed (Wallcraft and Bryant 2003, for example). We are starting to hear more from those diagnosed with personality disorders, and it may well be that this will have a significant impact on future understanding.

### 10.1.1 Biology and the reductionist drift: the neural basis of psychopathy?

Strong claims are being made about the power of contemporary techniques in neuroscience and genome analysis to understand and predict serious criminality (Rose 2010). A serious attempt to reinvigorate the field of biological criminology has been prominently made by Adrian Raine (2013) through his effort (which has received a great deal of media attention) to launch the new field of 'neurocriminology'. Not only has the book received reviews in the popular and serious press, but the American media company CBS has expressed interest in making a television series (*Daily Pennsylvanian* 25 March 2013). Raine acknowledges that there might be good reason for scepticism about his line of argument, but suggests that the impetus for this 'return' to biological explanation comes from two factors. First, he suggests, there are advances in molecular and behavioural genetics, and second, 'revolutionary advances in brain imaging':

> Together these two advances are prodding us to redefine our sense of self. They have jointly placed us on the threshold of the new discipline that I call neurocriminology – the neural basis to crime – which involves the

application of the principles and techniques of neuroscience to understand the origins of antisocial behaviour.

(Raine 2013: 9)

I would argue that this line of argument is problematic for a number of reasons. First, as discussed in previous chapters, there may be grave danger in attempting to pinpoint sources of crime and violence within individuals and, as will be discussed a little more, the claims being made for genetics and neuroscience do not stand up to scrutiny, even when taken on their own terms. Second, there is a philosophical problem here which is raised and sidestepped. The preceding chapters have illustrated that the phenomena of moral insanity have been highly contingent upon social and cultural circumstances. The term has clearly meant rather different things at different times; its form over time has been shaped by social anxieties and the needs of professional groups. There have been times when a crude biological reductionism has triumphed over other perspectives and the consequences have been catastrophic. It would be interesting to speculate why there is so much pressure towards such biological reductionism.

It is instructive that, while Raine (2013) acknowledges that social factors have their part to play, there is no doubt that this is a bit part in Raine's greater drama, as foreshadowed by the book's title: *The Anatomy of Violence: the Biological Roots of Crime*. Similarly, despite the more measured tone taken by James Blair in his review of literature, 'Psychopathy: Cognitive and Neural Dysfunction', it is very striking how the problem of psychopathy is assumed to exist entirely within the individual. Not one of Blair's four levels of analysis involves the social or cultural context of the individual. Instead, he argues that we need to describe the

> behavioural profile (i.e. its clinical description), the functional impairments that give rise to this behavioral profile (i.e. cognitive psychology), the neural systems that mediate these functions (i.e. systems neuroscience), the molecular-level factors that are impacting on the neural systems (i.e. molecular neuroscience), and the genetic bases of these molecular-level factors.
>
> (Blair 2013: 181)

Blair goes on to argue that evidence from neuroscience has moved on to such an extent that with 'appropriate biomarkers' identified it becomes possible to 'determine treatment efficacy' and that with the field at such an exciting juncture: 'Now we need to identify effective treatments' (Blair 2013: 189). It is difficult not to feel some unease at the expression of such levels of enthusiasm about the possibility of being able to identify dangerous individuals, however well meaning the wish to 'identify effective treatments'. Closer examination of the literature on which such strong claims are being made makes it clear that the empirical foundations for such assertions are weak. A serious dent in the credibility of the project of behavioural neuroscience was made by Button and colleagues (Button et al. 2013). They reviewed a large sample of published research in neuroscience and emphasised a number of severe problems, but focused their conclusions on the low statistical power of the studies. The problem is complex but can be summarised by the argument that there are a large number of studies, all with small sample sizes, that use a wide range of variables. The publishing bias in academic journals towards interesting findings, combined with the pressure on researchers to publish, means that the chances of positive findings being published are much higher than those for negative or inconclusive findings. Button et al. conclude that the average statistical power of studies in the field of neuroscience is between 8 per cent and 31 per cent; they emphasise the implication of this finding 'is that the likelihood that any nominally significant finding actually reflects a true effect is small' (Button et al. 2013: 371).

Analysis of studies reviewed by Anderson and Kiehl (2012), who laud the progress being made to identify the neurological basis of 'psychopathy', reinforces the points made by Button et al. Sample sizes are indeed small, and the location of the supposed neurological site of psychopathy often varies from study to study (a point made by Koenigs et al., 2010 in their review). Pujol et al. (2012), for example, point to the fact that there appeared to be less activity in a neural network (which included the medial frontal cortex, the posterior cingulate cortex and the angular gyrus, viewed bilaterally) among their study group of 22 psychopaths when confronted with moral dilemmas. Meanwhile, Müller et al. (2008: 146) argue that 'the fronto-temporal brain structure and function' show signs of impairment among their study group of 10 'criminal psychopaths'. Yang et al. (2011: 108) examined the related regions of the 'the basal forebrain-hypothalamus, frontal and temporal poles, STS and OFC' in their study of 27 'psychopaths'. Boccardi et al. (2011: 86) used brain imaging techniques to suggest that there were enlarged central and lateral nuclei in those studied who were categorised as 'psychopathic' (N = 22), compared to non-psychopaths among offender populations.

Another weakness of these studies on psychopathy, not explored by Button and colleagues, is the variety of definitions used and the choice of control groups. An analysis of definitions and control groups in the studies points towards major difficulties in this area. The study by Boccardi et al. (2011: 86), for example, involved comparing the brain activity of 'psychopathic' offenders who had been 'charged with violent offences (2 murders, 10 manslaughters, 4 attempted murders or manslaughters, 1 assisting manslaughter, 6 assaults and 3 armed robberies)', who had a history of recurrent violent acts, (including previous convictions for violence), with 'healthy volunteers' who were identified as 'students, hospital staff and skilled workers' (Boccardi et al. 2011: 86). No details about the lives, circumstances and occupational status of either group are given, but we know from other work that it is likely that their life histories would be very different from one another (Jones 2008). The lives of the offending group would be very likely to be marked by serious disruption and difficulties from early years (Moffitt 1993). The sole focus of the study on controlling for substance abuse is something that other studies do as well, and is an issue that will be returned to. Other examples of using healthy controls come from studies already mentioned. Pujol *et al.* (2012) also used a control group that consisted of healthy volunteers who were matched on age, sex and IQ scores with a 'psychopathic group' (N = 22) who were all convicted of severe offences and who scored a mean of 27.8 on the PCL-R. Müller *et al.* (2008) used healthy male volunteers (N = 12) with low scores on the PCL-R (less than 10) as a control group in their comparison with 10 'criminal psychopaths' recruited from a forensic psychiatric unit; all of these had a score of greater than 28. Harenski *et al.* (2010) provide an example of study that used an offending control group. In this case the control group have lower non-case scores on the PCL-R, while the subject group have high scores. No effort was made to control for other factors. Yang *et al.* (2011) adopted a slightly different strategy and identified a sample of 'psychopaths' (N = 27) from a non-offending population (recruited from temporary employment agencies in Los Angeles). The PCL-R was used with evidence from self-reports of crime and violence, and criminal history, to identify the high scores. The control group (N = 32) had low scores on the PCL-R and was matched for age, gender, ethnicity, handedness and substance dependence. However, no other effort was made to document differences in their lives, other than substance abuse. This issue of the control of substance abuse points to what might be described as a major epistemological problem. The premise appears to be that only a chemical substance can have a serious influence on the 'mind'. This idea that the 'mind' can simply be reduced to a physical substance is certainly worth questioning. There seems to be a much reduced and simplified model of the person operating here. It is very likely that individuals in the control groups will have very different lives, contexts and histories from experimental groups. Despite the major shortcomings of the research, Anderson and Kiehl (2012) still provide an enthusiastic review of a number of studies that have endeavoured to pin down the presence of psychopathy in the brain. They concede that the studies they review 'ultimately describe correlation relationships between behaviour, neural structure and functional activity', and that the determination 'of causal relationship between biology and behaviour or personality is more elusive'. They still go on to suggest that emerging research that determines 'path models of connectivity' in the brain, together with 'genetic analyses', form 'a promising enterprise' in tracking down the distinctive brains of psychopaths (Anderson and Kiehl 2012: 58–59). As Anderson and Kiehl imply, claims for the neurological bases of psychopathy tend to be made alongside similarly enthusiastic promotion of genetic research in this area. Despite the fact that strong, so far unfounded, claims for the genetic basis of psychopathy have been made for around 150 years, new advances in the analysis and understanding of genetic processes have given a fresh confidence to those seeking explanation in genetics (Hunter 2010). As the sober review of the evidence by Viding *et al.* (2008) concerning genetic influences on antisocial behaviour suggests, those claims should be stated far more modestly than they often are. The fundamental problem of twin and adoption studies, frequently referred to in studies of human genetics, is that the power of the environment is not being tested, since the selection of adoptive families means that children are (quite understandably) not being placed in very negative, poorly functioning and abusive family environments. The failure to test the significance of negative family environment is routinely ignored by proponents of genetic research (Beaver 2011). More recently efforts have been made to utilise genome and genetic marker research to try to pin down the genetics of antisocial behaviour at a biochemical level. Tielbeek *et al.* (2012) carried out a search for genetic markers of 'adult antisocial behavior' among a group of 1,649 twins and 3,167 adults in a community sample. It is worth emphasising that they found no significant association between any of the genome-wide genetic polymorphisms and antisocial behaviour.

Overall, despite the claims being made for the existence of a neural, genetically determined basis for antisocial behaviour (Carrido 2012), the evidence is very scanty. The historical perspective taken in this book can help us understand the strength of feeling that may lead people to try to identify the source of violence and antisocial behaviour within particular identifiable individuals. Arguments being made for the 'moral bioenhancement' of the human species (e.g. DeGrazia 2014) are fresh evidence of this impulse to try to reduce complex human phenomena to identifiable human types.

### 10.1.2 Psychology and the reductionist drift: psychopathy as an underlying disorder?

Another effort to locate the existence of violence within particular individuals has been made through attempts to construct the diagnosis of psychopathy as a psychological disorder which exists only within the psyche of particular individuals. This conceptualisation of psychopathy as a distinct psychological disorder was put most influentially by Cleckley, as discussed in Chapter 8, in the various editions of *The Mask of Sanity* (first published in 1941). In recent decades we have seen the Psychopathy Checklist (the PCL-R) developed and promoted, chiefly by the Canadian psychologist Robert Hare, as a psychometric tool that claims to measure individual levels of psychopathy (Schroeder *et al.* 1983). These tools have become popular and widespread and are being used extensively within the prison systems of a number of countries, including the United States and the UK. In addition to portraying psychopathy as a distinct psychological construct that is detectable and measurable, Hare has been keen to emphasise the 'enormity of the problem' and estimated that there were at least two million psychopaths in North America, and 100,000 in New York City alone (Hare 1993: 2). Some of them are violent and dangerous criminals but far more, according to Hare, are not in prison but are 'using their charm and chameleonlike abilities to cut a swath through society and leaving a wake of ruined lives behind [them]' (Hare 1993: 2). Hare and colleagues have promoted various adaptations of Cleckley's checklist as empirically sound measures of psychopathy. The PCL-R is a clinical tool that involves the assessment of individuals, partly through interview, but also using the known records of individuals. It is argued that those who score highly on these measures of psychopathy form a distinct group making up only a minority of offenders. Those in the psychopathic group are, however, more likely to present longer term and more serious problems. As described in Chapter 8, the essence of the disorder is taken not to be the destructive and antisocial behaviour that is often in evidence, but instead the assumed underlying failure of capacity to empathise and experience remorse. Yet again, as we have seen over the past 150 years, strong claims are made about professional expertise and the ability to identify the disorder (Buzina 2012). Questions may be asked about how well such claims stand up to critical analysis. As has emerged from discussion of the evolution of DSM (in Chapter 8), the distinction that might be made between 'psychopathy' and 'ASPD' has captured some of the debate about whether the problem is most fittingly seen as emerging from a specific psychological disorder.

*10.1.2.1 Psychopathy versus antisocial personality disorder*

The consistent refrain from those who advocate for the distinction between ASPD and psychopathy is that there are some very important differences between the two concepts and that a great deal is being lost if we do not pay attention to this. Robert Hare (1996, for example) suggests that the distinction emerged when more behavioural criteria were used to define 'antisocial personality disorder' in DSM-III (APA 1980). As discussed previously, this occurred through a belief that the reliability of the criteria would be strengthened by focusing more on measurable behaviour. A side-effect of this strategy was to move away from an understanding of the psychological constructs that might underlie antisocial behaviour.[1] The model of 'psychopathy' understood as consisting of a series of underlying personality traits has been propagated through the development of Cleckley's model of psychopathy (Andrade 2008, for example). A series of checklist style research tools has been developed in order to derive a score reflecting the degree of psychopathy that is argued to exist within the individual. The overall rating is derived by the assessor allocating a score to each of the factors. The scoring method is simply that if the particular characteristic is not present the rating is '0' and if the description applies 'somewhat' then the score is '1', while the score is '2' if the characteristic clearly applies to the individual. Ogloff (2006: 522, as shown in Table 10.1) presents an analysis of the PCL-R (adapted from Hare's *Manual for the Hare Psychopathy Checklist*, 2003) as consisting of two factors, each of which can be broken down into two different facets, with each facet portrayed as consisting of several characteristics.

Table 10.1 The Psychopathy Checklist – Revised

| Factor 1 Interpersonal/Affective | | Factor 2 Social Deviance | |
|---|---|---|---|
| Facet 1 Interpersonal | Facet 2 Affective | Facet 3 Lifestyle | Facet 4 Antisocial |
| • Glibness/ superficial charm<br>• Grandiosity<br>• Pathological lying<br>• Cunning and/or manipulative | • Lack of remorse or guilt<br>• Shallow affect<br>• Callousness and lack of empathy<br>• Failure to accept responsibility | • Need for stimulation and prone to boredom<br>• Parasitic lifestyle<br>• Lack of realistic, long term goals<br>• Impulsive<br>• Irresponsible | • Poor impulse/ behavioural control<br>• Evidence of behaviour problems early in life<br>• Juvenile delinquency<br>• Infringement of prison release conditions<br>• Criminal versatility |

(adapted from Ogloff 2006)

Those characteristics included in factor 1 are conceived to be reflective of some underlying psychological construct, while those in factor 2 are understood to be more behavioural. Hare and colleagues argue that use of PCL-R can thus provide accurate detection and measurement of deep levels of personality construct. This understanding still leaves some potential questions, however. On the one hand, of course, it supposes that there are some deep and relatively stable personality structures to be measured; on the other hand there is the obvious methodological challenge of being able to measure those structures. In reality the professionals using the scales are often reliant on the self-reports of the individuals themselves and their own subjective view of these, and their own, perhaps limited, knowledge of the personal history of the individual. One significant argument marshalled in favour of the psychopathy construct is that it has been consistently found that a smaller percentage of the prison population is rated as 'psychopathic' compared with those reaching diagnostic criteria for 'antisocial personality disorder' (Ogloff 2006). Supporters of the psychopathy concept cite such findings as evidence of the finer specificity of the construction and suggest that the reliance of the DSM criteria on behavioural characteristics means that the antisocial personality disorder diagnosis is rather a circular exercise in the description of people who offend. Studies have found that higher psychopathy scores do correlate well with more serious offending and higher rates of recidivism (e.g. Laurell and Daderman 2005). Strong claims have also been made that PCL-R is efficient at measuring the risk posed by individual offenders (Dolan and Doyle 2000).

There are serious problems with some of these claims, however. Tyrer et al. (2007) document evidence that questions the stable and fixed nature of the psychopathy construct and point to evidence that suggests that typical measures are not that stable over time. A meta-analysis of nine commonly used risk assessment measures carried out by Singh *et al.* (2011) found that the PCL-R had the lowest rate of predictive validity despite the strong claims often made for it. Similarly negative findings emerged from a systematic literature review carried out by Farrington *et al.* (2008), who found that the PCL-R appeared to be less predictive in the UK than in North America, and that it seemed to be becoming less predictive over time. Allan and Dawson (2002) draw attention to problems with the use of the PCL-R across different cultures.

Willemsen and Verhaeghe (2012) use their own analysis of questionnaire data to question the utility of the general concept of 'psychopathy' as constructed by the PCL-R. Instead they note that it would be more meaningful to focus on the particular facets. They find, for example, that the lifestyle and antisocial facets are 'more relevant when it comes to forensic issues such as impulsive behaviour and risk assessment' (Willemsen and Verhaeghe 2012: 274). Walters (2012) also questioned the construct of psychopathy through statistical analyses of responses to the PCL-R. He found that a three facet model of psychopathy (interpersonal, affective and lifestyle) worked better than the four facet model (which included the 'antisocial' facet). A major potential problem for the proponents of the significance of the psychopathy construct to the criminal justice system is that Walters (2012: 409) also found that *without* the antisocial facet then 'the PCL-R may not be particularly effective in predicting general and violent recidivism'. Simple measures such as age and criminal history were at least as effective at predicting poor outcomes.

Despite the major conceptual questions and concerns about the accuracy of the PCL-R it is being commonly promoted and used as part of risk assessment among prison populations. One signal of its ubiquity is the appearance of a book called *Pass the PCL-R* by Abraham Gentry. This self-published book aims to provide advice for those who have recently been convicted of a felony and may well be assessed using the PCL-R: 'The stakes of passing this test can literally mean spending additional decades in prison and in some cases a recommendation for the death penalty' (Gentry 2011: 7). The book provides advice on how to approach the questions that the test administrator will ask, in order to obtain a lower score. The publication of this book is not only a sign of how common the PCL-R has become but also signals more active engagement with the issue of diagnosis on the part of those who might be receiving it. It is this latter factor that might be an important one in providing some resistance to the attempts simply to locate 'psychopathy' within individuals.

### 10.1.3 The voices of experience

An important source of voices who might have an influence on shaping ideas and practices is the group of individuals who are having the diagnosis applied to them, or who might be more actively engaged in using the diagnosis. Callard

(2014: 526) observed that the very public debates about DSM-5 had 'reanimated earlier 20th century disputes about the effects of psychiatric diagnosis', and that 'it felt as though the debates over DSM-5 had plunged us back into the 1960s and 1970s, the era of intense disagreements between representatives of the psychiatric orthodoxy and those positioned as "antipsychiatrists"'. Callard (2014) goes on to make a plea for understanding diagnoses less as definitive categories or labels and more as process. As medical sociologists have noted for some time the reality of the application of a diagnosis tends to occur more through a process of negotiation between professionals, individual patients and their families rather than through a simple one way process (e.g. Mishler 1981). Over the past several decades the terrain of mental illness has been altered by the presence of various kinds of service user groups and disability lobbies (Barnes and Cotterell 2011). Even when the process of diagnosis appears to occur in a straightforward fashion, it is never unmediated, as Callard suggests:

> a person commonly receives, interprets and forms a relationship with a psychiatric diagnosis via multiple, fragmented routes, many of which do not involve direct encounters with a clinician. The routes often entail complex engagements with various kinds of paperwork, with forms of media (including newspapers, internet fora, social media, etc) and through discussions with a wide variety of people embedded in different frameworks through which they understand 'diagnosis'.
>
> (Callard 2014: 528)

It is reasonable to argue that these factors are particularly powerful when we are thinking about a diagnosis like 'antisocial personality disorder', which is subject to so much media attention and anxiety. The world wide web is arguably a major additional dimension that has been added to the public sphere since the end of the twentieth century. This has not only extended the scale and scope of the public sphere, but has also perhaps made major strides towards its democratisation (Gerhards and Schäfer 2010). There is a number of very well used websites that provide support and advice for people who themselves have diagnoses, or think they might suffer from a particular disorder, or who have friends or relatives who either have the diagnosis or whose behaviour they suspect fits with that diagnosis. Out of the Fog,[2] for example, is a US-based site that aims to provide support and advice for relatives of people who are perceived as suffering from a personality disorder. Psychopathfree[3] is a website aimed at providing support and information for those who feel they are in relationships with 'psychopaths'. Psychforums[4] is another US-based site containing a range of forums, one for those who self-identify as suffering from a range of psychiatric disorders, including personality disorders. In addition to these internet-based informal networks there are several service user groups (Wallcraft and Bryant 2003) for people who have had experience of personality disorder diagnosis. Prominent among these is Emergence[5] in the UK, which aims to provide support, advice and education for people affected by personality disorders. This user-led organisation has been involved in putting forward a manual co-written with practitioners that aims for better support for those 'with personality disorder in the community' (Bolton *et al.* 2014).

As the definitions and ideas of disordered personalities enter the popular lexicon within the public sphere, it appears ever more likely that the concept of something like moral insanity is going to be with us for the foreseeable future. It is difficult to conclude that the diagnoses of personality disorder are simply being imposed by professionals upon entirely unwitting members of the public. There are certainly strong interactions here with a wider public. It is to be hoped that the voices of experience will help balance some of the debate so that some of the excessive and damaging 'bullying or scapegoating tendencies' so prominent in former decades may be avoided (Scanlon and Adlam 2011: 251).

## Notes

1 The five factor model of personality is one model advocated to have relevance (e.g. Miller *et al.* 2001).
2 http://outofthefog.net/ (accessed 25 January 2015). 'Information and support for those with a family member or loved one who suffers from personality disorder.'
3 www.psychopathfree.com/ (accessed 25 January 2015).
4 www.psychforums.com/personality-disorders/ (accessed 25 January 2015).
5 www.emergenceplus.org.uk/ (accessed 25 January 2015). 'Emergence is a service user-led organisation supporting all people affected by personality disorder including service users, carers, family and friends and professionals.'

# References

Adams, M. B., Allen, G. E. and Weiss, S. F. (2005) 'Human Heredity and Politics: A Comparative Institutional Study of the Eugenics Record Office at Cold Spring Harbor (United States), the Kaiser Wilhelm Institute for Anthropology, Human Heredity, and Eugenics (Germany), and the Maxim Gorky Medical Genetics Institute (USSR)', *Osiris*, 2nd Series, 20, 232–262.

Adler, H. M. (1917) 'Organization of Psychopathic Work in the Criminal Courts', *Journal of the American Institute of Criminal Law and Criminology*, 8(3), 362–374.

Adorno, T. W. (1950) 'Types and Syndromes', in T. W. Adorno, E. Frenkel-Brunswik, D. Levinson and R. Sanford, *The Authoritarian Personality* (Studies in Prejudice, Vol. 1), Chapter 19, p. 744. New York: Harper.

Aichhorn, A. (1935) *Wayward Youth*. New York: Viking.

Ainsley, J. N. (2000) 'Some Mysterious Agency': Women, Violent Crime, and the Insanity Acquittal in the Victorian Courtroom', *Canadian Journal of History*, 35(1), 37–55.

Alford, C. F. (1987) 'Habermas, Post-Freudian Psychoanalysis, and the End of the Individual', *Theory, Culture & Society*, 4(1), 3–29.

Allan, A. and Dawson, D. (2002) *Developing a Unique Risk of Violence Tool for Australian Indigenous Offenders* (CRC6/00–01). Australian Institute for Criminology: Canberra.

Allderidge, P. H. (1974) 'Criminal Insanity: Bethlem to Broadmoor', *Proceedings of the Royal Society of Medicine*, 67(9), 897–904.

Allen, F. A. (1962) 'The Rule of the American Law Institute's Model Penal Code', *Marquette Law Review*, 45(4), 494–505.

Allen, G. E. (1986) 'The Eugenics Record Office at Cold Spring Harbor, 1910–1940: An Essay in Institutional History', *Osiris*, 2nd Series, 2, 225–264.

*American Law Register* (1856) 'The Plea of Insanity', 4(12), 705–716.

*American Law Register* (1864) 'Mental Unsoundness as Affecting Testamentary Capacity. Being Remarks on an Essay in the American Law Register for November 1863', 12(7), 385–399.

American Psychiatric Association (1952) *Diagnostic and Statistical Manual of Mental Disorders*, (DSM-I). APA: Washington.

American Psychiatric Association (1968) *Diagnostic and Statistical Manual of Mental Disorders*, 2nd edn (DSM-II). APA: Washington.

American Psychiatric Association (1980) *Diagnostic and Statistical Manual of Mental Disorders*, 3rd edn (DSM-III). APA: Washington.

American Psychiatric Association (1987) *Diagnostic and Statistical Manual of Mental Disorders*, 3rd edn rev. (DSM-III-R). APA: Washington.

American Psychiatric Association (1994) *Diagnostic and Statistical Manual of Mental Disorders*, 4th edn (DSM-IV). APA: Washington.

American Psychiatric Association (2000) *Diagnostic and Statistical Manual of Mental Disorders*, 4th edn rev. (DSM-IV-R). APA: Washington.

American Psychiatric Association (2013) *Diagnostic and Statistical Manual of Mental Disorders*, 5th edn (DSM-5). APA: Washington.

Anderson, K. (1981) *Wartime Women: Sex Roles, Family Relations, and the Status of Women during World War II*. Greenwood Press: Westport, CT.

Anderson, N. E. and Kiehl, K. (2012) 'The Psychopath Magnetized: Insights from Brain Imaging', *Trends in Cognitive Sciences*, 16(1), 52–60.

Andrade, J. T. (2008) 'The Inclusion of Antisocial Behavior in the Construct of Psychopathy: A Review of the Research', *Aggression and Violent Behavior*, 13(4), 328–335.

Andrews, J. (1990) 'A Respectable Mad-Doctor? Dr. Richard Hale, F.R.S. (1670–1728)', *Notes and Records of the Royal Society of London*, 44(2), 169–204.

Anonymous (1800) *The Trial of James Hadfield for High Treason. The Whole of the Evidence*. W. I. Clement: London.

Anonymous (1864) *The Trial and Respite of George Victor Townley for Wilful Murder. With Original Documents and Correspondence*. Bemrose and Sons: Derby.

Appignanesi, L. (2009) *Mad, Bad and Sad: A History of Women and the Mind Doctors from 1800 to the Present*. Virago: London.

Arata, S. (1996) *Fictions of Loss in the Victorian Fin de Siècle: Identity and Empire*. Cambridge University Press: Cambridge.

Arditi, J. (1994) 'Hegemony and Etiquette: An Exploration on the Transformation of Practice and Power in Eighteenth-Century England', *The British Journal of Sociology*, 45(2), 177–193.

Arens, R. (1967) 'The Durham Rule in Action: Judicial Psychiatry and Psychiatric Justice', *Law & Society Review*, 1(2), 41–80.

Arlow, J. A. (1990) 'Psychoanalysis and Character Development', *Psychoanalytic Review*, 77, 1–10.

Arnold, T. (1786) *Observations on the Nature, Kinds, Causes and Prevention of Insanity, Lunacy or Madness*, Vol. 2. Richard Philips: London.

Arrigo, B. A. and Shipley, S. (2001) 'The Confusion Over Psychopathy (1): Historical Considerations', *International Journal of Offender Therapy and Comparative Criminology*, 45(3), 325–344.

Augstein, H. F. (1996) 'J. C. Prichard's Concept of Moral Insanity: A Medical Theory of the Corruption of Human Nature', *Medical History*, 40(3), 311–343.

Baars, J. and Scheepers, P. (1993) 'Theoretical and Methodological Foundations of the Authoritarian Personality', *Journal of the History of the Behavioral Sciences*, 29(4), 345–353.

Bailey, V. (1997) 'English Prisons. Penal Culture, and the Abatement of Imprisonment, 1895–1922', *Journal of British Studies*, 36(3), 285–324.

Barnes, M. and Cotterell, P. (2011) *Critical Perspectives on User Involvement*. Policy Press: Bristol.

Barrett, B. and Byford, S. (2012) 'Costs and Outcomes of an Intervention Programme for Offenders with Personality Disorders', *British Journal of Psychiatry*, 200(4), 336–341.

Bean, P. (2008) *Madness and Crime*. Willan: Cullompton.
Beaver, K. (2011) 'Genetic Influences on Being Processed Through the Criminal Justice System: Results from a Sample of Adoptees', *Biological Psychiatry*, 69(3), 282–287.
Beck, T. R. and Beck, J. B. (1860) *Elements of Medical Jurisprudence*. J. B. Lippincott: Philadelphia.
Beck, U. (1992) *Risk Society: Towards a New Modernity*, (first published in German in 1986). Sage: London.
Behrendt, S. (1994) 'Questioning the Romantic Novel', *Studies in the Novel*, 26(1/2), 5–25.
Bell, D. (2001) 'Who is Killing What or Whom? Some Notes on the Internal Phenomenology of Suicide', *Psychoanalytic Psychotherapy*, 15(1), 21–37.
Bell, M. (2005) *The German Tradition of Psychology in Literature and Thought, 1700–1840*. Cambridge University Press: Cambridge.
Bender, D. S., Morey, L. C. and Skodol, A. E. (2011) 'Toward a Model for Assessing Level of Personality Functioning in DSM-5, Part I: A Review of Theory and Methods', *Journal of Personality Assessment*, 93(4), 332–346.
Berg, M. (2005) *Luxury and Pleasure in Eighteenth-Century Britain*. Oxford University Press: Oxford.
Berman, M. (1982) *All that is Solid Melts into Air*. Verso: New York.
Berrios, G. E. (1993) 'European Views on Personality Disorders: A Conceptual History', *Comprehensive Psychiatry*, 34(1), 14–30.
Bion, W. R. (1952) 'Group Dynamics: A Review', *International Journal of Psycho-Analysis*, 33(2), 235–248.
Bion, W. R. (1961) *Experiences in Groups and Other Papers*. Tavistock: London.
Bion, W. R. (1982) *The Long Week-End 1897–1919: Part of a Life*. Karnac Books: London.
Bisch, L. E. (1916) 'A Police Psychopathic Laboratory', *Journal of the American Institute of Criminal Law and Criminology*, 7(1), 79–88.
Black, J. (1987) *The English Press in the Eighteenth Century*. University of Pennsylvania Press: Philadelphia.
Blackman, L. (2008) *The Body: The Key Concepts*. Berg: Oxford.
Blair, R. J. (2013) 'Psychopathy: Cognitive and Neural Dysfunction', *Dialogues in Clinical Neuroscience*, 15(2), 181–190.
Boccardi, M., Frisoni, G., Hare, R., Cavedo, E., Najt, P., Pievani, M., Rasser, P., Laakso, M., Aronen, H., Repo-Tiihonen, E., Vaurio, O., Thompson, P. and Tiihonen, J. (2011) 'Cortex and Amygdala Morphology in Psychopathy', *Psychiatry Research*, 193(2), 85–92.
Bock, M. (2002) *Joseph Conrad and Psychological Medicine*. Texas Tech University Press: Lubbock, TX.
Bogacz, T. (1989) 'War Neurosis and Cultural Change in England, 1914–22: The Work of the War Office Committee of Enquiry into "Shell-Shock"', *Journal of Contemporary History*, 24(2), 227–256.
Boime, A. (1991) 'Portraying Monomaniacs to Service the Alienist's Monomania: Géricault and Georget', *Oxford Art Journal*, 14(1), 79–91.
Bolton, W., Lovell, K., Morgan, L. and Wood, H. (2014) *Meeting the Challenge, Making a Difference: Working Effectively to Support People with Personality Disorder in the Community*. Department of Health: London.

Booth, C. (1903) *Life and Labour of the People in London*, Vol. 17: 'Notes on Social Influences and Conclusion'. Macmillan: London.
Booth, W. (1890) *In Darkest England and the Way Out*. Salvation Army: London.
Boyes, P. S. (2001) *The Oxford Handbook to United States History*. Oxford University Press: Oxford.
Bracken, P. et al. (2012) 'Psychiatry beyond the Current Paradigm', *British Journal of Psychiatry*, 201(6), 430–434.
Bracton, H. (c.1250) *On the Laws and Customs of England*. Published online by Harvard University: http://bracton.law.harvard.edu/ (accessed 3 May 2015).
Braggins, J. and South, N. (1998): 'ISTD: Where Theory Meets Practice', *Criminal Justice Matters*, 34(1), 6–8.
Breggin, P. R. (1993) 'Psychiatry's Role in the Holocaust', *International Journal of Risk and Safety in Medicine*, 4(2), 133–148.
Bridger, H. (1985) 'The Discovery of the Therapeutic Community: The Northfield Experiments', in E. Trist and H. Murray (eds) (1990), *The Social Engagement of Social Science* (A Tavistock Anthology, Vol. 1: The Socio-Psychological Perspective). Free Association Books: London.
Brontë, E. (1870) [1847] *Wuthering Heights*. Smith, Elder: London.
Brookes, M. (2011) 'Therapeutic Communities, the Treatment Regime at HMP Grendon and Some Ethical Considerations', Counselling in Prisons Network: Fourth Annual Conference: Celebrating Therapy in the Custodial Setting: Slides.
Brown, P. (2006) 'Risk versus Need in Revising the 1983 Mental Health Act: Conflicting Claims, Muddled Policy', *Health, Risk & Society*, 8(4), 343–358.
Browne, J. (2004) 'Darwin and the Face of Madness', in W. F. Bynum, R. Porter and M. Shepherd (eds), *The Anatomy of Madness: Essays in the History of Psychiatry*, Vol. 1, People and Ideas. Routledge: London.
Brundage, A. (2002) *The English Poor Laws, 1700–1930*. Palgrave: Basingstoke.
Brüne, M. (2007) 'On Human Self-Domestication, Psychiatry, and Eugenics', *Philosophy, Ethics, and Humanities in Medicine*, 2, 21.
Bucknill, J. C. (1857) 'Plea of Insanity – the Trial of William Dove', *The Asylum Journal of Mental Science*, 125–134.
Bulmer, M. (1984) *The Chicago School of Sociology: Institutionalization, Diversity, and the Rise of Sociological Research*. University of Chicago Press: Chicago.
Burnham, J. (2012) *After Freud Left: A Century of Psychoanalysis in America*. University of Chicago Press: Chicago.
Burns, L. C. (1954) 'A Forgotten Psychiatrist – Baron Ernst von Feuchtersleben', *Proceedings of the Royal Society of Medicine*, 47(3), 190–194.
Burton, R. (1638) *The Anatomy of Melancholy: What it Is, with All the Kinds, Causes, Symptomes, Prognostickes, and Severall Cures of it*. Henry Cripps: Oxford.
Button, K. S., Ioannidis, J. P., Mokrysz, C., Nosek, B. A., Flint, J., Robinson, E. S. and Munafò, M. R. (2013) 'Power Failure: Why Small Sample Size Undermines the Reliability of Neuroscience', *Nature Reviews Neuroscience*, 14(5), 365–376.
Buzina, N. (2012) 'Psychopathy – Historical Controversies and New Diagnostic Approach', *Psychiatria Danubina*, 24(2), 134–142.
Bynum, W. F. (1964) 'Rationales for Therapy in British Psychiatry: 1780–1835', *Medical History*, 18(4), 317–344.
Cabinet Office (2006) Reaching Out: An Action Plan on Social Exclusion. HM Government Cabinet Office: London.

Calhoun, C. (1992) *Habermas and the Public Sphere*. MIT Press: Cambridge, MA.
Callard, F. (2014) 'Psychiatric Diagnosis: The Indispensability of Ambivalence', *Journal of Medical Ethics*, 40(8), 526–530.
Caplan, L. (1987) *The Insanity Defense and the Trial of John W. Hinckley, Jr*. Dell Publishing: New York.
Carlson E. T. and Dain, N. (1962) 'The Meaning of Moral Insanity', *Bulletin of the History of Medicine*, 36, 130–140.
Carrido, (2012) 'Revisiting the Insanity Defense: A Case for Resurrecting the Volitional Prong of the Insanity Defense in Light of Neuroscientific Advances', *Southwestern Law Review*, 41, 309–330.
Cartwright, D. (2002) *Psychoanalysis, Violence and Rage-Type Murder: Murdering Minds*. Routledge: London.
Castel, R. (1988) *The Regulation of Madness: The Origins of Incarceration in France*, trans. W. D. Halls. Polity Press: Cambridge.
Chamberlin, J. E. and Gilman, S. L. (eds) (1985) *Degeneration: The Dark Side of Progress*. Columbia University Press: New York.
Chaperon, S. (2010) 'The Foundations of 19th-Century Psychiatric Approaches to Sexual Deviance', *Recherches en Psychanalyse*, 2(10), 276a–285a.
Chauncey, G. (1993) 'The Postwar Sex Crime Panic', in W. Graebner (ed.) *True Stories from the American Past*, 160–178.
Chenier, E. (2003) 'The Criminal Sexual Psychopath in Canada: Sex, Psychiatry and the Law at Mid-Century', *Canadian Bulletin of Medical History*, 20(1), 75–101.
Claydon, T. (1996) 'William III's *Declaration of Reasons* and the Glorious Revolution', *The Historical Journal*, 39(1), 87–108.
Cleckley, H. (1941) *The Mask of Sanity: An Attempt to Reintepret the So-Called Psychopathic Personality*. Mosby: St Louis.
Cleckley, H. (1988) *The Mask of Sanity: An Attempt to Clarify Some Issues about the So-Called Psychopathic Personality*, 5th edn. Harry Kimpton: London.
Cohan, S. M. (1976) '*Clarissa* and the Individuation of Character', *English Literary History*, 43(2), 163–183.
Cohen, D. (2012) *The Escape of Sigmund Freud*. Overlook: New York.
Cohen, N. (2005) 'We All Have Personality Disorders Now', *New Statesman*, 11 July.
Cohen, W. A. (2003) 'Material Interiority in Charlotte Brontë's *The Professor*', *Nineteenth-Century Literature*, 57(4), 443–476.
Coid, J. and Ullrich, S. (2010) 'Antisocial Personality Disorder is on a Continuum with Psychopathy', *Comprehensive Psychiatry*, 51(4), 426–433.
Coid, J., Yang, M., Tyrer, P., Roberts, A. and Ullrich, S. (2006) 'Prevalence and Correlates of Personality Disorder in Great Britain', *British Journal of Psychiatry*, 188(5), 423–431.
Combe, G. (1828) *The Constitution of Man Considered in Relation to External Objects*. Fowler & Wells: New York.
Comte, A. (1855) *The Positive Philosophy*, trans. H. Martineau. Calvin Blanchard: New York.
Conrad, J. (1907) *The Secret Agent. A Simple Tale*. Methuen: London.
Conrad, J. (1933) [1899] *The Heart of Darkness*. The Golden Book: New York.
Cooke, D. J., Michie, C., Hart, S. D. and Clark, D. (2005) 'Assessing Psychopathy in the UK: Concerns about Cross-Cultural Generalisability', *British Journal of Psychiatry*, 186, 335–341.

Coolidge, F. L. and Segal, D. L. (1998) 'Evolution of Personality Disorder Diagnosis in the *Diagnostic and Statistical Manual of Mental Disorders*', *Clinical Psychology Review*, 18(5), 585–599.

Cosgrove, L. and Krimsky, S. (2012) 'A Comparison of DSM-IV and DSM-5 Panel Members' Financial Associations with Industry: A Pernicious Problem Persists', *PLOS Medicine*, 9(3), www.plosmedicine.org/article/info%3Adoi%2F10.1371%2Fjournal.pmed.1001190 (accessed 7 August 2014).

Costello, J. (1986) *Love, Sex and War: Changing Values, 1939–45*. Pan: London.

Covey, R. D. (2009) 'Criminal Madness: Cultural Iconography and Insanity', *Stanford Law Review*, 61(6), 1375–1428.

Craddock, N. et al. (2008) 'Wake-Up Call for British Psychiatry', *British Journal of Psychiatry*, 193(1), 6–9.

Cromartie, A. (1995) *Sir Matthew Hale, 1609–1676: Law, Religion and Natural Philosophy*. Cambridge University Press: Cambridge.

Dalal, F. (1998) *Taking the Group Seriously: Towards a Post-Foulkesian Group Analytic Theory*. Jessica Kingsley: London.

Dames, N. (1996) 'The Clinical Novel: Phrenology and *Villette*', *NOVEL: A Forum on Fiction*, 29(3), 367–390.

Darwin, L. (1921) 'The Aims and Methods of Eugenical Societies', *Science, New Series*, 54(1397), 313–323.

Dauge-Roth, K. (2005) 'Textual Performance: Imprinting the Criminal Body', in F. Beasley and K. Wine (eds), *Intersections*. Narr: Tübingen, Germany.

David, S. (1995) *Mutiny at Salerno, 1943: An Injustice Exposed*. Chrysalis Books: London.

Davie, N. (2010a) 'The Impact of Criminal Anthropology in Britain (1880–1918)', *Histoire de la Criminologie*, 4: 'L'Anthropologie Criminelle en Europe'. Available online: http://criminocorpus.revues.org/319 (accessed 12 November 2012).

Davie, N. (2010b) 'The Role of Medico-Legal Expertise in the Emergence of Criminology in Britain (1870–1918)', *Histoire de la Criminologie*, 3: 'Criminologie et Droit Pénal'. Available online: http://criminocorpus.revues.org/316 (accessed 12 November 2012).

Davies, O. (2005) *Murder, Magic, Madness: The Victorian Trials of Dove and the Wizard*. Pearson Education: Harlow.

Davison, C. M. (1997) *Bram Stoker's* Dracula: *Sucking Through the Century, 1897–1997*. Dundurn Press: Toronto.

DeGrazia, D. (2014) 'Moral Enhancement, Freedom, and what we (Should) Value in Moral Behaviour', *Journal of Medical Ethics*, 40(6), 361–368.

DeMatteo, D. and Edens, J. F. (2006) 'The Role and Relevance of the Psychopathy Checklist – Revised in Court. A Case Law Survey of U.S. Courts (1991–2004)', *Psychology, Public Policy, and Law*, 12(2), 214–241.

Denno, D. (1998) 'Life Before the Modern Sex Offender Statutes', *Northwestern University Law Review*, 92(4), 1317–1387.

Department of Health (1959) 'The Mental Health Act 1959', c. 72 (Regnal. 7 and 8 Eliz 2). HMSO: London.

Department of Health (1992) *Review of Health and Social Services for Mentally Disordered Offenders and Others Requiring Similar Services: Final Summary Report*, (Reed Report), Cm 2088. HMSO: London.

Department of Health (2003) *Personality Disorder: No Longer a Diagnosis of Exclusion.* HMSO: London.
Department of Health (2006) 'Mental Health Bill 2006'. HMSO: London.
Department of Health (2007) 'The Mental Health Act 2007', c. 12. HMSO: London.
Department of Health (2011) *Consultation on the Offender Personality Disorder Pathway Implementation Plan.* HMSO: London.
Devereaux, S. (2003) 'The Fall of the Sessions Paper: The Criminal Trial and the Popular Press in Late Eighteenth-Century London', in L. A. Knafla (ed.), *Crime, Punishment and Reform in Europe.* Praeger: Westport, CT.
Dicks, H. (1972) *Licensed Mass Murder: A Socio-Psychological Study of Some SS Killers.* Chatto: London.
Dikötter, F. (1998) 'Race Culture: Recent Perspectives on the History of Eugenics', *The American Historical Review*, 103(2), 467–478.
Dimaggio, G., Carcione, A., Petrilli, D., Procacci, M., Semerari, A. and Nicolò, G. (2005) 'State of Mind Organization in Personality Disorders. Typical States and Triggering of Inter-State Shifts', *Clinical Psychology and Psychotherapy*, 12(5), 346–359.
Dixon, T. (2001) 'The Psychology of the Emotions in Britain and America in the Nineteenth Century: The Role of Religious and Antireligious Commitments', *Osiris*, 2nd Series, 16, 288–320.
Dolan, B. and Coid, J. (1993) *Psychopathic and Antisocial Personality Disorders: Treatment and Research Issues.* Gaskell: London.
Dolan, M. and Doyle, M. (2000) 'Violence Risk Prediction. Clinical and Actuarial Measures and the Role of the Psychopathy Checklist', *British Journal of Psychiatry*, 177, 303–311.
Dollimore, J. (1998) *Death, Desire, and Loss in Western Culture.* Routledge: New York.
Donovan, J. (1991) 'Women and the Rise of the Novel: A Feminist-Marxist Theory', *Signs*, 16(3), 441–462.
Donovan, K. A. (2009) 'Lost in London; or, A Study of Early Urban Gothic Literature', thesis submitted in partial fulfilment of Ph.D., Department of English, Tufts University, MA.
Donzelot, J. (1979) *The Policing of Families.* Doubleday: New York.
Dörner, K. (1981) *Madmen and the Bourgeoisie: A Social History of Insanity and Psychiatry.* Blackwell: Oxford.
Dowbiggin, I. (2004) 'Degeneration and Hereditarianism in French Mental Medicine 1840–90: Psychiatric Theory as Ideological Adaptation', in W. F. Bynum, R. Porter and M. Shepherd (eds), *The Anatomy of Madness: Essays in the History of Psychiatry*, Vol. 1, People and Ideas. Routledge: London.
Doyle, P. (2012) *First World War Britain.* Shire: Colchester.
Dugaw, D. (1998) 'High Change in "Change Alley": Popular Ballads and Emergent Capitalism in the Eighteenth Century', *Eighteenth-Century Life*, 22(2), 43–58.
Dugdale, R. (1877) *'The Jukes': A Study in Crime, Pauperism, Disease and Heredity.* Putnam's: New York.
Duggan, C. (2011) 'Dangerous and Severe Personality Disorder', *British Journal of Psychiatry*, 198(6), 431–433.
Dunham, H. W. (1942) 'War and Personality Disorganization', *American Journal of Sociology*, 48(3), 387–397.

During, S. (1988) 'The Strange Case of Monomania: Patriarchy in Literature, Murder in *Middlemarch*, Drowning in *Daniel Deronda*', *Representations*, 23, 86–104.

Durkheim, É. (1982) [1895] *The Rules of Sociological Method*, trans. W. D. Halls. Macmillan: New York.

Durkheim, É. (1984) [1893] *The Division of Labour in Society*, trans. W. D. Halls. The Free Press: New York.

East, W. N. and Hubert, W. H. (1939) *Report on the Psychological Treatment of Crime*. HMSO: London.

*The Economist* (2013) 'DSM-5: By the Book: The American Psychiatric Association's Latest Diagnostic Manual Remains a Flawed Attempt to Categorise Mental Illness', 18 May.

Editors (1864) *Insanity and Crime: A Medico-Legal Commentary on the Case of George Victor Townley*. John Churchill and Sons: London.

Eigen, J. P. (1991) 'Delusion in the Courtroom: The Role of Partial Insanity in Early Forensic Testimony', *Medical History*, 35(1), 25–49.

Eigen, J. P. (1995) *Witnessing Insanity: Madness and Mad-Doctors in the English Court*. Yale University Press: New Haven, CT.

Eigen, J. P. (1998) 'Criminal Lunacy in Early Modern England. Did Gender Make a Difference?', *International Journal of Law and Psychiatry*, 21(4), 409–419.

Eigen, J. P. (1999) 'Lesion of the Will: Medical Resolve and Criminal Responsibility in Victorian Insanity Trials' *Law & Society Review*, 33(2), 425–459.

Eigen, J. P. (2003) *Unconscious Crime: Mental Absence and Criminal Responsibility in Victorian London*. Johns Hopkins University Press: Baltimore, MD.

Eigen, J. P. (2004) 'Intentionality and Insanity: What the Eighteenth-Century Juror Heard', in W. F. Bynum, R. Porter and M. Shepherd (eds), *The Anatomy of Madness: Essays in the History of Psychiatry*, Vol. 2, *Institutions and Society*. Routledge: London.

Eigen, J. P. (2010) 'Diagnosing Homicidal Mania: Forensic Psychiatry and the Purposeless Murder', *Medical History*, 54(4), 433–456.

Eigen, J. P. and Andoll, G. (1986) 'From Mad-Doctor to Forensic Witness: The Evolution of Early English Court Psychiatry', *International Journal of Law and Psychiatry*, 9(2), 159–169.

Eisenstadt, N. (2011) *Providing a Sure Start: How Government Discovered Early Childhood*. The Policy Press: Bristol.

Elias, N. (1994) [1939] *The Civilizing Process: Sociogenetic and Psychogenetic Investigations*, trans. E. Jephcott. Blackwell: Oxford.

Eliot, G. (1874) *Middlemarch: A Study of Provincial Life*. William Blackwood: Edinburgh.

Eliot, G. (2013) [1876] *Daniel Deronda*. Northen Grove Publishing Project: Manchester.

Ellard, J. (1996) 'Personality Disorder or the Snark Still at Large', *Australasian Psychiatry*, 4(2), 58–65.

Elliott, C. and Gillett, G. (1992) 'Moral Insanity and Practical Reason', *Philosophical Psychology*, 5(1), 53–68.

Ellis, H. (1890) *The Criminal*. Scribner's: New York.

Esquirol, E. (1845) *Mental Maladies: A Treatise on Insanity*, trans. E. K. Hunt (French edition 1835). Lea and Blanchard: Philadelphia.

Estabrook, A. H. (1916) *The Jukes in 1915*. Carnegie Institution: Washington.

Evans, F. (1981) 'Roads, Railways, and Canals: Technical Choices in 19th-Century Britain', *Technology and Culture*, 22(1), 1–3.

Faas, E. (1988) *Retreat into the Mind: Victorian Poetry and the Rise of Psychiatry*. Princeton University Press: Princeton, NJ.

Fairbairn, M. (1995) 'Cinema as Secular Church: A Phenomenological and Hermeneutics', thesis submitted in partial fulfilment of the requirements for the degree of Doctor of Philosophy, McMaster University, Hamilton, Ontario.

Faller, L. B. (1987) *Turned to Account: The Forms and Functions of Criminal Biography in Late Seventeenth- and Early Eighteenth-Century England*. Cambridge University Press: Cambridge.

Farland, M. (2002) 'Sylvia Plath's Anti-Psychiatry', *The Minnesota Review*, n.s. 55–57, 245–256.

Farrington, D. P., Jolliffe, D. and Johnstone, L. (2008) 'Assessing Violence Risk: A Framework for Practice'. Available online: www.rmascotland.gov.uk/files/2112/7263/5786/Assessing%20Violence%20Risk%20-%20A%20Framework%20for%20Practice.pdf (accessed 5 August 2014).

Fazel, S. and Danesh, J. (2002) 'Serious Mental Disorder in 23,000 Prisoners: A Systematic Review of 62 Surveys', *Lancet*, 359(9306), 545–550.

Federman, C., Holmes, D. and Jacob, J. D. (2009) 'Deconstructing the Psychopath: A Critical Discursive Analysis', *Cultural Critique*, 72, 36–65.

Feeley, M. and Little, D. L. (1991) 'The Vanishing Female: The Decline of Women in the Criminal Process, 1687–1912', *Law and Society Review*, 25(4), 719–757.

Feighner, J. P., Robins, E., Guze, S. B., Woodruff, R. A., Winokur, G. and Munoz, R. (1972) 'Diagnostic Criteria for Use in Psychiatric Research', *Archives of General Psychiatry*, 26(1), 57–63.

Feinstein, A. R. (1970) 'The Pre-Therapeutic Classification of Co-Morbidity in Chronic Disease', *Journal of Chronic Diseases*, 23(7), 455–468.

Feldbrugge, J. T. and Haverkamp, A. D. (1993) 'Identity and Development: The Dr. Henri van der Hoeven Kliniek in the Nineties', *International Journal of Law and Psychiatry*, 16(1–2), 241–246.

Felthous, A. and Sass, H. (2007) *International Handbook on Psychopathic Disorders and the Law*, Vol. 1. Wiley: Chichester.

Fenning, F. A. (1914) 'Sterilization Laws from a Legal Standpoint', *Journal of the American Institute of Criminal Law and Criminology*, 4(6), 804–814.

Feuchtersleben, E. von (1847) *The Principles of Medical Psychology*, trans. H. Evans Lloyd. Sydenham Society: London.

Field, J. A. (1911) 'The Progress of Eugenics', *The Quarterly Journal of Economics*, 26(1), 1–67.

Fielding, H. (1749) *The History of Tom Jones: a Foundling*. Andrew Millar: London.

Fielding, H. (1751) *An Enquiry into the Causes of the Late Increase of Robbers, &c. With Some Proposals for Remedying This Growing Evil, in which the Present Reigning Vices are Impartially Exposed*. A. Millar: London.

Fine, R. E. (1969) 'Lockwood's Dreams and the Key to *Wuthering Heights*', *Nineteenth-Century Fiction*, 24(1), 16–30.

Flyvbjerg, B. (1998) 'Habermas and Foucault: Thinkers for Civil Society?', *The British Journal of Sociology*, 49(2), 210–233.

Forshaw, D. (2008) 'The Origins and Early Development of Forensic Mental Health', in Keith Soothill, Paul Rogers and Mairead Dolan (eds) *Handbook of Forensic Mental Health*. Willan: Cullompton.

Foucault, M. (1967) *Madness and Civilization: A History of Insanity in the Age of Reason*, trans. Richard Howard. Tavistock: London.
Foucault, M. (1974) *The Order of Things: Archaeology of the Human Sciences*. Tavistock: London.
Foucault, M. (1977) *Discipline and Punish: The Birth of the Prison*, trans. Alan Sheridan. Penguin: London.
Foucault, M. (1979) *The History of Sexuality*, Vol. 1, trans. R. Hurley. Penguin: Harmondsworth.
Foucault, M. (1980) *Power/Knowledge: Selected Interviews and Other Writings 1972–1977*, ed. C. Gordon. Harvester: Brighton.
Foucault, M. (2003) *Abnormal: Lectures at the Collège de France 1974–1975*, trans. G. Burchell. Verso: London.
Foucault, M. (2006) *Psychiatric Power: Lectures at the Collège de France 1973–1974*, trans. G. Burchell. Palgrave Macmillan: Basingstoke.
Foulkes, S. H. (1946) 'On Group Analysis', *International Journal of Psycho-analysis*, 27, 46–51.
Fountain, N. (comp. and ed.) (2014) *When the Lamps Went Out: From Home Front to Battle Front: Reporting the Great War 1914–1918*. Guardian Books: London.
Franklin, M. (1966) 'Introductory, Including Notes on the Origin and Inception of the Work, in M. Franklin (ed.), *Q Camp: An Epitome of Experiences at Hawkspur Camp (1936 to 1940) for Young Men Aged 16 1/2 to 25*, first published in 1943. Planned Environment Therapy Trust London.
Freedman, E. B. (1987) '"Uncontrolled Desires": The Response to the Sexual Psychopath, 1920–1960', *The Journal of American History*, 74(1), 83–106.
Freedman, L. Z. (1983) 'The Politics of Insanity: Law, Crime, and Human Responsibility', *Political Psychology*, 4(1), 171–179.
Freud, S. (1917) 'On Mourning and Melancholia', in The Penguin Freud Library, Vol. 11, *Papers on Metapsychology*. Penguin: Harmondsworth.
Freud, S. (1991a) [1930] 'Civilization and Its Discontents', in The Penguin Freud Library, Vol. 12, *Civilization, Society and Religion*. Penguin: Harmondsworth.
Freud, S. (1991b) [1915] 'Instincts and Their Vicissitudes', in The Penguin Freud Library, Volume 11, *Papers on Metapsychology*. Penguin: Harmondsworth.
Freud, S. (1991c) [1914] 'On Narcissism: An Introduction', in The Penguin Freud Library, Vol. 11, *Papers on Metapsychology*. Penguin: Harmondsworth.
Freud, S. (1991d) [1915] 'Thoughts for the Times on War and Death', in The Penguin Freud Library, Vol. 12, *Civilization, Society and Religion*. Penguin: Harmondsworth.
Fromm, E. (1942) *The Fear of Freedom*. Routledge and Kegan Paul: London.
Frosh, S. (1987) *The Politics of Psychoanalysis: An Introduction to Freudian and Post-Freudian Theory*. Macmillan: Basingstoke.
Frosh, S. (2013) 'Transdisciplinary Tensions and Psychosocial Studies', *Enquire*, 6(1), 1–15.
Galton, F. (1865) 'Hereditary Talent and Character', *Macmillan's Magazine*, 12, 157–166, 318–327.
Galton, F. (1904) 'Eugenics: Its Definition, Scope, and Aims', *The American Journal of Sociology*, X(1).
Gardiner, J. (2010) *The Blitz: The British under Attack*. Headline: London.

Garland, D. (1985) *Punishment and Welfare: A History of Penal Strategies*. Gower: Aldershot.
Garland, D. (1997) 'Of Crimes and Criminals: The Development of Criminology in Britain', in M. Maguire, R. Morgan and R. Reiner (eds), *The Oxford Handbook of Criminology*, 2nd edn. Oxford University Press: Oxford.
Genders, E. and Player, E. (1995) *Grendon: A Study of a Therapeutic Prison*. Clarendon Press: Oxford.
Gentry, A. (2011) *Pass the PCL-R: Your Guide to Passing the Hare Psychopathy Checklist – Revised AKA the Psychopath Test*. Self Published, printed by Createspace: Charleston, SC.
George, W. R. (1910) *The Junior Republic: Its History and Ideals*. Appleton: New York and London.
Georget, J. E. (1820) *De la Folie: Considérations sur Cette Maladie*. Crevot: Paris.
Georget, J. E. (1826) *Discussion Médico-Légale sur la Folie ou Aliénation Mentale, Suivie de l'Examen du Procès Criminel d'Henriette Cornier*. Migneret: Paris.
Georget, J. E. (1827) *Des Maladies Mentales, Considérées dans Leurs Rapports avec la Législation Civile et Criminelle*. Cosson: Paris.
Gerard, D. L. (1997) 'Chiarugi and Pinel Considered: Soul's Brain/Person's Mind', *Journal of the History of the Behavioral Sciences*, 33(4), 381–403.
Gerhards, J. and Schäfer, M. (2010) 'Is the Internet a Better Public Sphere? Comparing Old and New Media in the US and Germany', *New Media & Society*, 12(1), 143–160.
Gibbens, T. C. (1951-2) 'Recent Trends in the Management of Psychopathic Offenders', *British Journal of Delinquency*, 1951-2, 103–116.
Giddens, A. (1990) *The Consequences of Modernity*. Stanford University Press: Stanford, CA.
Giddens, A. (1991) *Modernity and Self-Identity: Self and Society in the Late Modern Age*. Polity: Cambridge.
Giddens, A. (1999) 'Risk and Responsibility', *Modern Law Review*, 62(1), 1–10.
Gidley, B. (2000) *The Proletarian Other: Charles Booth and the Politics of Representation*. Centre for Urban and Community Research, Goldmiths College: London.
Gilbert, M. (2009) 'Churchill and Eugenics'. Published online: www.winstonchurchill.org/resources/reference/related-websites/uncategorised/finest-hour-online/churchill-and-eugenics-1 (accessed 3 May 2015).
Gilligan, J. (1997) *Violence: Reflections on a National Epidemic*. Vintage: New York.
Gilligan, J. (2003) 'Shame, Guilt, and Violence', *Social Research*, 70(4), 1149–1180.
Gladfelder, H. (2001) *Criminality and Narrative in Eighteenth-Century England: Beyond the Law*. Johns Hopkins University Press: Baltimore, MD.
Glannon, W. (1997) 'Psychopathy and Responsibility', *Journal of Applied Philosophy*, 14(3), 263–275.
Glover, E. (1936) *The Dangers of Being Human*. Unwin Brothers: Woking.
Glover, E. (1947) 'The Investigation and Treatment of Delinquency', *British Medical Journal*, 29 March, 421.
Glover, E. (1955) 'Delinquency Work in Britain: A Survey of Current Trends', *The Journal of Criminal Law, Criminology and Police Science*, 46, 172–177.
Glover, E. (1957) 'Denis Carroll', *International Journal of Psycho-Analysis*, 38(3–4), 277–279.

Goddard, H. (1911) 'The Elimination of Feeble-mindedness', *Annals of the American Academy of Political and Social Science*, 37(2), 261–272.
Goddard, H. (1912) *The Kallikak Family: A Study in the Heredity of Feeble-Mindedness*. Macmillan: New York.
Goddard, H. (1913) *Sterilization and Segregation*. Russell Sage Foundation: New York.
Goddard, H. (1920) *Feeble-mindedness: Its Causes and Consequences*. Macmillan: New York.
Goddard, H. (1921) *Juvenile Delinquency*. Dodd, Mead: New York.
Goddard, K. S. (2004) 'A Case of Injustice? The Trial of John Bellingham', *The American Journal of Legal History*, 46(1), 1–25.
Godfrey, B. and Lawrence, P. (2005) *Crime and Justice 1750–1950*. Willan: Cullompton.
Goffman, E. (1961) *Asylums*. Penguin: Harmondsworth.
Goldstein, J. (1987) *Console and Classify: The French Psychiatric Profession in the Nineteenth Century*. Cambridge University Press: Cambridge.
Goldstein, J. (1998) 'Professional Knowledge and Professional Self-Interest: The Rise and Fall of Monomania in 19th-Century France', *International Journal of Law and Psychiatry*, 21(4), 385–396.
Goring, C. (1913). *The English Convict: A Statistical Study*. His Majesty's Stationery Office: London.
Gostin, L. (1985) *Secure Provision: A Review of Special Services for the Mentally Ill and Mentally Handicapped in England and Wales*. Tavistock: London.
Gotham, K. F. and Greenberg, M. (2014) *Crisis Cities: Disaster and Redevelopment in New York and New Orleans*. Oxford University Press: Oxford.
Grannuchi, A. and Grannucchi, S. J. (1969) 'Indiana's Sexual Psychopath Act in Operation', *Indiana Law Journal*, 44(4), 555–594.
Green, J. B. (2003) 'Science, Religion and the Mind-Brain Problem – the Case of Thomas Willis 1621–1675', *Science and Christian Belief*, 15(2), 165–185.
Greene, J. K. (1910) 'The Municipal Court of Chicago', *University of Pennsylvania Law Review and American Law Register*, 58(6), 335–346.
Greenslade, W. (1994) *Degeneration, Culture and the Novel 1880–1940*. Cambridge University Press: Cambridge.
Grob, G. (1991) *From Asylum to Community: Mental Health Policy in Modern America*. Princeton University Press: Princeton, NJ.
Grogan, S. (2014) *Shell Shocked Britain: The First World War's Legacy for Britain's Mental Health*. Pen and Sword: Barnsley.
Gurley, J. (2009) 'A History of Changes to the Criminal Personality in the DSM', *History of Psychology*, 12(4), 285–304.
Guttmacher, M. and Weihofen, H. (1952) 'Sex Offenses', *The Journal of Criminal Law, Criminology, and Police Science*, 43(2), 153–175.
Guy, W. A. (1869) 'On Insanity and Crime; and On The Plea of Insanity in Criminal Cases', *Journal of the Statistical Society of London*, 32(2), 159–191.
Habermas, J. (1989) [1962] *The Structural Transformation of the Public Sphere: An Inquiry into a Category of Bourgeois Society*, trans. T. Burger with the assistance of F. Lawrence. Polity Press: Cambridge.
Hacking, I. (1998) *Mad Travelers: Reflections on the Reality of Transient Mental Illnesses*. University Press of Virginia: Charlottesville and London.

Haldane, D. (2006) 'Vignette: a Doyen of "Psychological Medicine": Sir David Henderson', *Summons*, Autumn 2006, 23. MDDMUS: Edinburgh.

Hale, M. (1736) *The History of the Pleas of the Crown*. Gyles: London.

Hale, Nathan G. (1971) *Freud and the Americans: The Beginnings of Psychoanalysis in the United States, 1876–1917*. Oxford University Press: New York.

Hall, S., Winlow, S. and Ancrum, C. (2008) *Criminal Identities and Consumer Culture: Crime, Exclusion and the New Culture of Narcissism*. Willan: Cullompton.

Haney, C. (1982) 'Criminal Justice and the Nineteenth-Century Paradigm: The Triumph of Psychological Individualism in the "Formative Era"', *Law and Human Behavior*, 6(3/4), 191–235.

Hansard (1957) HC Deb 8 July, Vol. 573, cc35–103.

Hansard (1998) HC Deb 26 October, Vol. 318, cc8–10.

Hansen, Lee Ann (1998) 'Metaphors of Mind and Society: The Origins of German Psychiatry in the Revolutionary Era', *Isis*, 89(3), 387–409.

Hare, R. (1993) *Without Conscience: The Disturbing World of the Psychopaths Amongst Us*. Guilford Press: New York.

Hare, R. (1996) 'Psychopathy and Antisocial Personality Disorder: A Case of Diagnostic Confusion', *Psychiatric Times*, 13(2), 39–40.

Harenski, C., Harenski, K., Shane, M. and Kiehl, K. (2010) 'Aberrant Neural Processing of Moral Violations in Criminal Psychopaths', *Journal of Abnormal Psychology*, 119(4), 863–874.

Harper, Andrew (1789) *A Treatise on the Real Cause and Cure of INSANITY*. C. Stalker: London.

Harris, R. (1989) *Murders and Madness: Medicine, Law and Society in the Fin de Siècle*. Clarendon Press: Oxford.

Harrison, T. (2000) *Bion, Rickman, Foulkes and the Northfield Experiments: Advancing on a Different Front*. Jessica Kingsley: London.

Harrison, T. and Clarke, D. (1992) 'The Northfield Experiments', *British Journal of Psychiatry*, 160, 698–708.

Hartley, D. (1749) *Observations on Man, His Frame, His Duty, and His Expectations: in 2 parts*. Hitch and Austen (booksellers): London.

Harvey, D. (2005) *A Brief History of Neo-Liberalism*. Oxford University Press: Oxford.

Hawkins, M. (1999): 'Durkheim's Sociology and Theories of Degeneration', *Economy and Society*, 28(1), 118–137.

Hay, D. (1980) 'Crime and Justice in Eighteenth- and Nineteenth-Century England', *Crime and Justice*, 2, 45–84.

Heidensohn, F. (1996) *Women and Crime*. Palgrave: Basingstoke.

Helzer, J. E., Spitznagel, E. L. and McEvoy, L. (1987) 'The Predictive Validity of Lay Diagnostic Interview Schedule Diagnoses in the General Population. A Comparison with Physician Examiners', *Archives of General Psychiatry*, 44(12), 1069–1077.

Henderson, D. K. (1939) *Psychopathic States*. Norton: New York.

Higonnet, M. R. (1987) *Behind the Lines: Gender and the Two World Wars*. Yale University Press: New Haven, CT.

Hitchman, J. (1864) 'An Interview with George Victor Townley, and reflections thereon', *The Journal of Mental Science*, 10, 21–34.

Hobbes, T. (1651) *Leviathan*. Andrew Crooke: London.

Hoffman, L. (1992) 'American Psychologists and Wartime Research on Germany, 1941–1945', *American Psychologist*, 47(2), 264–273.
Hoffman, L. (2010) 'One Hundred Years after Sigmund Freud's Lectures in America: Towards an Integration of Psychoanalytic Theories and Techniques within Psychiatry', *History of Psychiatry*, 21(4), 455–470.
Holmes, G. (ed.) (1969) *Britain after the Glorious Revolution, 1689–1714*. Macmillan: London.
Home Office (1957) 'The Homicide Act, 1957', c. 11 (Regnal. 5 and 6 Eliz 2). HMSO: London.
Home Office (2005) *Dangerous and Severe Personality Disorder (DSPD) Programme – Key Points*. Home Office: London.
Horney, K. (1939) *New Ways in Psychoanalysis*. Norton: New York.
Houston, R. A. (2001) 'Professions and the Identification of Mental Capacity in Eighteenth-Century Scotland', *Journal of Historical Sociology*, 14(4), 441–466.
Houston, R. A. (2002) 'Madness and Gender in the Long Eighteenth Century', *Social History*, 27(3), 309–326.
Houston, R. A. (2004) 'Clergy and the Care of the Insane in Eighteenth-Century Britain', *Church History*, 73(1), 114–138.
Howard League (2014) 'The History of the Prison System'. Available online: www.howardleague.org/history-of-prison-system/ (accessed 25 January 2014).
Howorth, P. W. (2000) 'The Treatment of Shell-Shock: Cognitive Therapy before Its Time', *The Psychiatric Bulletin*, 24, 225–227.
Hulbert, H. S. (1939) 'Constitutional Psychopathic Inferiority in Relation to Delinquency', *Journal of Criminal Law and Criminology*, 30(1), 3–21.
Hull, W. (1897) 'The George Junior Republic', *Annals of the American Academy of Political and Social Science*, 10, 73–86.
Hume, D. (1738) *A Treatise of Human Nature: Being an Attempt to Introduce the Experimental Method of Reasoning into Moral Subjects*. John Noon: London.
Hundert, E. J. (1994) *The Enlightenment's Fable: Bernard Mandeville and the Discovery of Society*. Cambridge University Press: Cambridge.
Hunter, A. (1983) *Joseph Conrad and the Ethics of Darwinism: The Challenges of Science*. Routledge: London.
Hunter, J. D. (1914) 'Sterilization of Criminals (Report of Committee H of the Institute)', *Journal of the American Institute of Criminal Law and Criminology*, Vol. 5(4), 514–539.
Hunter, P. (2010) 'The Psycho Gene', *EMBO Reports*, 11(9), 667–669.
Hurley, K. (1996) *The Gothic Body: Sexuality, Materialism, and Degeneration at the Fin de Siècle*. Cambridge University Press: Cambridge.
Hurtado Prieto, J. (2004) 'Bernard Mandeville's Heir: Adam Smith or Jean-Jacques Rousseau on the Possibility of Economic Analysis', *The European Journal of the History of Economic Thought*, 11(1), 1–31.
Hutcheson, F. (1725) *An Enquiry into the Original of Our Ideas of Beauty and Virtue: in Two Treatises*. W. and J. Smith: London.
Jackson, E. (1992) 'Catharine MacKinnon and Feminist Jurisprudence: A Critical Appraisal', *Journal of Law and Society*, 19(2), 195–213.
Jackson, M. (2000) *The Borderland of Imbecility: Medicine, Society and the Fabrication of the Feebleminded in Late Victorian and Edwardian England*. Manchester University Press: Manchester.

Jackson, R. L. and Richards, H. J. (2007) 'Psychopathy and the Five Factor Model: Self and Therapist Perceptions of Psychopathic Personality', *Personality and Individual Differences*, 43, 1711–1721.

Jackson, S. (1983) 'Melancholia and Partial Insanity', *Journal of the History of the Behavioral Sciences*, 19(2), 173–184.

Jacoby, R. (1978) *The Repression of Psychoanalysis*. University of Chicago Press: Chicago.

James, N., Thomas, K. and Foley, C. (2008) *Civil Commitment of Sexually Dangerous Persons*. Nova Science: New York.

Jay, M. (1973) *The Dialectical Imagination: A History of the Frankfurt School and the Institute of Social Research, 1923–1950*. University of California Press: Berkeley, CA.

Jones, D. W. (2002) 'Madness, the Family and Psychiatry', *Critical Social Policy: A Journal of Theory and Practice in Social Welfare*, 22(2), 247–272.

Jones, D. W. (2008) *Understanding Criminal Behaviour: Psychosocial Approaches to Criminality*. Willan: Cullompton.

Jones, D. W. (2013) 'Putting the Psyche into 'Cultural Criminology': A Psychosocial Understanding of Looting, Masculinity, Shame and Violence', *Journal of Psycho-Social Studies*, 7(1), 6–30.

Jones, G. (1971) *Outcast London: A Study in the Relationship between the Classes in Victorian Society*. Oxford University Press: Oxford.

Jones, K. (1972) *A History of the Mental Health Services*. Routledge and Kegan Paul: London.

Jones, L. (1996) 'George III and Changing Views of Madness', in T. Heller, J. Reynolds, R. Gomm, R. Muston and S. Pattison, *Mental Health Matters*. Palgrave: Basingstoke.

Jones, M. (1952) *Social Psychiatry: A Study of Therapeutic Communities*. Tavistock: London.

Junius, J. (1812) *Bellingham: The Defence Defended, or The Trial Re-Tried*. M. Jones: London.

Karpman, B. (1949) 'Criminality, Insanity and the Law', *Journal of Criminal Law and Criminology*, 39(5), 584–605.

Kātz, B. M. (1987) 'The Criticism of Arms: The Frankfurt School Goes to War', *The Journal of Modern History*, 59(3), 439–478.

Kaye, H. (1993) 'Why Freud Hated America', *The Wilson Quarterly*, 17(2), 118–125.

Kearns, M. S. (1987) *Metaphors of Mind in Fiction and Psychology*. University of Kentucky Press: Lexington, KY.

Keller, T. (1995) 'Railway Spine Revisited: Traumatic Neurosis or Neurotrauma?', *Journal of the History of Medicine and Allied Sciences*, 50(4), 507–524.

Kendler, K. S., Muñoz, R. A and Murphy, G. (2009) 'The Development of the Feighner Criteria: A Historical Perspective', *American Journal of Psychiatry*, 167(2), 134–142.

Kennard, D. (1998) *An Introduction to Therapeutic Communities*. Jessica Kingsley: London.

Kernberg, O. (1975) *Borderline Conditions and Pathological Narcissism*. Jason Aronson: Northvale, NJ.

Kernberg, O. (1989) 'The Temptations of Conventionality', in Arnold M. Cooper, Otto Kernberg and Ethel Spector Person (eds), *Psychoanalysis: Towards the Second Century*, pp. 12–34. Yale University Press: New Haven, CT.

Kernberg, O. (1995) *Love Relations: Normality and Pathology*. Yale University Press: New Haven, CT.

Kernberg, O. (2004) *Aggressivity, Narcissism and Self-Destructiveness in the Psychotherapeutic Relationship: New Developments in the Psychopathology and Psychotherapy of Severe Personality Disorders*. Yale University Press: New Haven, CT.

Kim, J. K. (2012) 'The Story of *Clark v. Arizona*: The Incredible Shrinking Insanity Defence', in R. Weisberg and D. Coker (eds), *Criminal Law Stories*. Foundation Press.

King, D. (2002) *In the Name of Liberalism: Illiberal Social Policy in the United States and Britain*. Oxford University Press: Oxford.

King. E. (1990) 'Reconciling Democracy and the Crowd in Turn-of-the-Century American Social-Psychological Thought', *Journal of the History of the Behavioral Sciences*, 26(4), 334–346.

King, P. (1830) *The Life of John Locke, with Extracts from His Correspondence, Journals and Common-Place Books*, Vol. 2. Henry Colburn: London.

King, P. (1989) 'Activities of British Psychoanalysts during the Second World War and the Influence of Their Inter-Disciplinary Collaboration on the Development of Psychoanalysis in Great Britain', *International Journal of Psycho-Analysis*, 16, 15–32.

King, P. (2007) 'Newspaper Reporting and Attitudes to Crime and Justice in Late-Eighteenth- and Early-Nineteenth-Century London', *Continuity and Change*, 22(01), 73–112.

King, P. (2009) 'Making Crime News: Newspapers, Violent Crime and the Selective Reporting of Old Bailey Trials in the Late Eighteenth Century', *Crime, History and Societies*, 13(1), 91–116.

Kirk, S. and Kutchins, H. (1992) *The Selling of DSM: The Rhetoric of Science in Psychiatry*. Aldine De Gruyter: New York.

Klonsky, E. D. (2000) 'The DSM Classification of Personality Disorder: Clinical Wisdom or Empirical Truth? A Response to Alvin R. Mahrer's Problem 11', *Journal of Clinical Psychology*, 56(12), 1615–1621.

Koch, J. L. A. (1891) *The Psychopathic Inferiorities*. Dorn: Ravensburg, Germany.

Koenigs, M., Baskin-Sommers, A., Zeier, J. and Newman, J. P. (2011) 'Investigating the Neural Correlates of Psychopathy: A Critical Review', *Molecular Psychiatry*, 16(8), 792–799.

Kohut, H. (1966) 'Forms and Transformations of Narcissism', *Journal of the American Psychoanalytic Association*, 14, 243–272.

Konrath, S. K. (2007) 'Egos Inflating over Time: Rising Narcissism and Its Implications for Self-Construal, Cognitive Style, and Behavior', dissertation submitted in partial fulfilment of the requirements for the degree of Ph.D., the University of Michigan.

Kraemer, S. (2011) '"The Danger of This Atmosphere": A Quaker Connection in the Tavistock Clinic's Development', *History of the Human Sciences*, 24(2), 82–102.

Kramar, J. K. and Watson, W. D. (2006) 'Medico-Legal Knowledge and the Development of Infanticide Law', *Social and Legal Studies*, 15(2), 237–255.

Krueger, R. and Markon, K. (2006) 'Reinterpreting Comorbidity: A Model-Based Approach to Understanding and Classifying Psychopathology', *Annual Review of Clinical Psychology*, 2, 111–133.

Kuriloff, E. A. (2014) *Contemporary Psychoanalysis and the Legacy of the Third Reich: History, Memory, Tradition*. Routledge: New York.

Kutchins, H. and Kirk, S. (1997) *Making US Crazy: DSM: The Psychiatric Bible and the Creation of Mental Disorders*. Constable: London.

Lacey, N. (2009) 'Psychologising Jekyll, Demonising Hyde: The Strange Case of Criminal Responsibility', *LSE Law, Society and Economy Working Papers*, 18.
Lacour, A. (2001) 'Faces of Violence Revisited. A typology of Violence in Early Modern Rural Germany', *Journal of Social History*, 34(3), 649–667.
Laing, R. D. (1965) *The Divided Self*. Penguin: Harmondsworth.
Landsman, S. (1998) 'One Hundred Years of Rectitude: Medical Witnesses at the Old Bailey, 1717–1817', *Law and History Review*, 16(3), 464–494.
Langbein, J. H. (1978) 'The Criminal Trial before the Lawyers', *The University of Chicago Law Review*, 45(2), 263–316.
Langbein, J. H. (1983) 'Shaping the Eighteenth-Century Criminal Trial: A View from the Ryder Sources', *The University of Chicago Law Review*, 50(1), 1–136.
Lasch, C. (1979) *The Culture of Narcissism: American Life in an Age of Diminishing Expectations*. Norton: New York.
Laughlin, H. L. (1922) *Eugenical Sterilization in the United States*. Psychopathic Laboratory of the Municipal Court of Chicago: Chicago, IL.
Laurell, J. and Daderman, A. (2005) 'Recidivism is Related to Psychopathy (PCL-R) in a Group of Men Convicted of Homicide', *International Journal of Law and Psychiatry*, 28(3), 255–268.
Lave, T. R. (2009), 'Only Yesterday: The Rise and Fall of Twentieth Century Sexual Psychopath Laws.' *Louisiana Law Review*, 69(3), 549–591.
Laycock, T. (1868) 'Suggestions for Rendering Medico-Mental Science Available to the Better Administration of Justice and the More Effectual Prevention of Lunacy and Crime', *Journal of Mental Science*, 67(XV), 334–345.
Lees, J., Manning, N. and Rawlings, B. (1999) *Therapeutic Community Effectiveness: A Systematic International Review of Therapeutic Community Treatment for People with Personality Disorders and Mentally Disordered Offenders*, CRD Report 17. NHS Centre for Reviews and Dissemination, University of York: York.
Lemmings, D. (2012) *Crime, Courtrooms and the Public Sphere in Britain, 1700–1850*. Ashgate: Farnham.
Levy, E. (1996) 'The Psychology of Loneliness in *Wuthering Heights*', *Studies in the Novel*, 28(2), 158–177.
Lewes, G. H. (1879) *Problems of Life and Mind: Third Series: The Study of Psychology, Its Object, Scope and Method*. The Riverside Press: Cambridge.
Lewis, G. and Appleby, L. (1988) 'Personality Disorder: The Patients Psychiatrists Dislike', *British Journal of Psychiatry*, 153(1), 44–49.
Liddle, A. M. (1996) 'State, Masculinities and Law: Some Comments on Gender and English State-Formation', *British Journal of Criminology*, 36(3), 361–380.
Limentani, A. (1989) 'The Psychoanalytic Movement during the Years of the War (1939–1945)', *International Review of Psycho-Analysis*, 16, 3–13.
Lindsey, E. (1925) 'Historical Sketch of the Indeterminate Sentence and Parole System', *Journal of Criminal Law and Criminology*, 16(1), 9–69.
Lipton, H. R. (1950) 'The Psychopath', *Journal of Criminal Law and Criminology*, Vol. 40(5), 584–596.
Livesley, W. J. (2000) 'Introduction to Special Feature', *Journal of Personality Disorders*, 14(1), 1–2.
Livesley, W. J. (2001) *Handbook of Personality Disorders: Theory, Research, and Treatment*. Guilford Press: New York.

Lockey, C. J. and Bloom, J. (2007) 'The Evolution of the American Law Institute Test for Insanity in Oregon: Focus on Diagnosis', *Journal of the American Academy of Psychiatry and the Law*, 35(3), 325–329.

Lombardo, P. (2008) *Three Generations, No Imbeciles: Eugenics, the Supreme Court, and Buck v. Bell*. The Johns Hopkins University Press: Baltimore, MD.

Lombroso, C. (2006) [1876] *Criminal Man*, trans. and ed. M. Gibson and N. H. Rafter. Duke University Press: Chesham.

Loughnan, A. (2007) '"Manifest Madness": Towards a New Understanding of the Insanity Defence', *Modern Law Review*, 70(3), 379–401.

Loughnan, A. (2012) *Manifest Madness: Mental Incapacity in Criminal Law*. Oxford University Press: Oxford.

Lunbeck, E. (2014) *The Americanization of Narcissism*. Harvard University Press: Cambridge, MA.

McCallum, D. (2001) *Personality and Dangerousness: Genealogies of Antisocial Personality Disorder*. Cambridge University Press: Cambridge.

McCord, J. (1990) 'Long term perspective on parental absence', in L. Robins and M. Rutter (eds), *Straight and Devious Pathways from Childhood to Adulthood*. Cambridge University Press: Cambridge.

McCord, W. and McCord, J. (1964) *The Psychopath: An Essay on the Criminal Mind*. Van Nostrand: Princeton, NJ.

MacDonald, M. (1981) *Mystical Bedlam: Madness, Anxiety, and Healing in Seventeenth-Century England*. Cambridge University Press: Cambridge.

MacDonald, M. (1988) 'Suicide and the Rise of the Popular Press in England', *Representations*, 22, 36–55.

MacDonald, M. (1989) The Medicalization of Suicide in England: Laymen, Physicians, and Cultural Change, 1500–1870', *The Milbank Quarterly*, 67(Suppl 1), 69–91.

McGowen, R. (2005) '"Making Examples" and the Crisis of Punishment in Mid-Eighteenth-Century England', in D. Lemmings (ed.), *The British and Their Laws in the Eighteenth Century*, pp. 182–205. The Boydell Press: Rochester, NY.

McKenzie, A. (2005) 'From True Confessions to True Reporting? The Decline and Fall of the Ordinary's Account', *The London Journal*, 30(1), 55–70.

MacKenzie, C. (1992) *Psychiatry for the Rich: A History of Ticehurst Private Asylum, 1792–1917*. Routledge: London.

McKeon, M. (1985) 'Generic Transformation and Social Change: Rethinking the Rise of the Novel', *Cultural Critique*, 1, 159–181.

McLaughlin, N. (1999) 'Origin Myths in the Social Sciences: Fromm, the Frankfurt School and the Emergence of Critical Theory', *Canadian Journal of Sociology*, 24(1), 109–139.

Maden, A. (2007) 'Dangerous and Severe Personality Disorder: Antecedents and Origins', *British Journal of Psychiatry*, 190(Suppl 49), s8–s11.

Main, T. (1983) 'The Concept of the Therapeutic Community', in M. Pines, *The Evolution of Group Analysis*. Routledge and Kegan Paul: London.

Mandeville, B. (1705) *The Grumbling Hive*. Sam Ballard: London.

Mandeville, B. (1725) *An Enquiry into the Causes of the Frequent Executions at Tyburn*. Roberts: London.

Mandeville, B. (1732) *The Fable of the Bees: or, Private Vices, Publick Benefits*, 6th edn. Edmund Parker: London.

Mannheim, H. (1955) *Group Problems in Crime and Punishment*. Routledge and Kegan Paul: London.
Manning, N. (1989) *The Therapeutic Community Movement: Charisma and Routinization*. Routledge: London.
Marshall, G. (2007) *The Cambridge Companion to the Fin de Siècle*. Cambridge University Press: Cambridge.
Marx, O. M. (1970) 'Nineteenth-Century Medical Psychology: Theoretical Problems in the Work of Griesinger, Meynert, and Wernicke', *Isis*, 61(3), 355–370.
Maudsley, H. (1868) 'Ilustrations of a Variety of Insanity', *Journal of Mental Science*, 66(XIV), 149–162.
Maudsley, H. (1874) *Responsibility in Mental Disease*. Appleton: New York.
May, A. (2003) *The Bar and the Old Bailey, 1750–1850*. University of North Carolina Press: Chapel Hill, NC.
Mayhew, H. and Binny, J. (1862) *The Criminal Prisons of London and Scenes of Prison Life*. Griffin, Bohn: London.
Meiers, J. I. (1945) 'Origins and Development of Group Psychotherapy: A Historical Survey, 1930–1945', *Sociometry*, 8(3/4), 261–296.
Melville, H. (1892) [1851] *Moby-Dick, or The White Whale*. Botolph Society: Boston.
Memon, R. (2006) 'Legal Theory and Case Law Defining the Insanity Defence in English and Welsh Law', *Journal of Forensic Psychiatry & Psychology*, 17(2), 230–252.
Mental Health Alliance (2012) *The Mental Health Act 2007: A Review of Its Implementation*. Mental Health Alliance: London.
Merriam, C. E. (1915) 'Findings and Recommendations of the Chicago Council Committee on Crime', *Journal of the American Institute of Criminal Law and Criminology*, 6(3), 345–362.
Messerschmidt, J. W. (1993) *Masculinities and Crime: A Critique and Reconceptualization of Theory*. Rowman and Littlefield: Lanham, MD.
Midelfort, H. C. E. (1981) 'Madness and the Problems of Psychological History in the Sixteenth Century', *The Sixteenth Century Journal*, 12(1), 5–12.
Mighall, R. (1999) *A Geography of Victorian Gothic Fiction: Mapping History's Nightmares*. Oxford University Press: Oxford.
Miller, J. (1983) *The Glorious Revolution*. Longman: London.
Miller, J., Lynam, D. R., Widiger, T. A. and Leukefeld, C. (2001) 'Personality Disorders as Extreme Variants of Common Personality Dimensions: Can the Five-Factor Model Adequately Represent Psychopathy?', *Journal of Personality*, 69(2), 253–276.
Millon, T. (1981) *Disorders of Personality: DSM-III, Axis II*. John Wiley and Sons: New York.
Millon, T. with Davis, R. D. (1995) *Disorders of Personality: DSM-IV and Beyond*. Wiley Interscience: New York.
Millon, T., Simonsen, E., Birket-Smith, M. and Davis, R. D. (eds) (1998) *Psychopathy: Antisocial, Criminal and Violent Behavior*. Guilford Press: New York.
Mishler, E. G. (1981) 'The Social Construction of Illness', in E. G. Mishler, L. R. Amarasingham, S. D. Osherson, S. T. Hauser, N. E. Waxler and R. Liem (eds), *Social Contexts of Health, Illness and Patient Care*. Cambridge University Press: Cambridge.

Moffitt, T. (1993) 'Adolescence-Limited and Life-Course-Persistent Antisocial Behavior: A Developmental Taxonomy', *Psychological Review*, 100(4), 674–701.

Moran, R. (1981) *Knowing Right from Wrong: The Insanity Defense of Daniel McNaughtan*. Free Press: New York.

Moran, R. (1985) 'The Origin of Insanity as a Special Verdict: The Trial for Treason of James Hadfield (1800)', *Law & Society Review*, 19(3), 487–519.

Morel, B. (1857) *Traité des Dégénérescences Physiques, Intellectuelles et Morales de l'Espèce Humaine et des Causes qui Produisent Ces Variétés Maladives*. Baillière: Paris.

Morey, L. C., Berghuis, H., Bender, D. S., Verheul, R., Krueger, R. F. and Skodol, A. E. (2011) 'Toward a Model for Assessing Level of Personality Functioning in DSM-5, Part II: Empirical Articulation of a Core Dimension of Personality Pathology', *Journal of Personality Assessment*, 93(4), 347–353.

Morgan, K. O. (2001) *Britain Since 1945: The People's Peace*. Oxford University Press: Oxford.

Morison, A. (1843) *The Physiognomy of Mental Diseases*. Longman: London.

Morris, C. E. (2002) 'Pink Herring and the Fourth Persona: J. Edgar Hoover's Sex Crime Panic' *Quarterly Journal of Speech*, 88, 228–244.

Morris, H. (1961) *Freedom and Responsibility: Readings in Philosophy and Law*. Stanford University Press: Stanford, CA.

Morris, N. (1950) 'A Prison for Psychopaths, and Other Recent European Penal Developments', delivered at a meeting of the Medico-Legal Society held on Saturday 2 December, 1950, at British Medical Association Hall, Albert Street, East Melbourne. The Medico-Legal Society of Victoria: Melbourne.

Morrow, W. R. (1950) 'Criminality and Antidemocratic Trends: A Study of Prison Inmates', in T. W. Adorno, E. Frenkel-Brunswik, D. Levinson and R. Sanford, *The Authoritarian Personality*, (Studies in Prejudice, Vol. 1). Harper: New York.

Müller, J. L., Sommer, M., Döhnel, K., Weber, T., Schmidt-Wilcke, T. and Hajak, G. (2008) 'Disturbed Prefrontal and Temporal Brain Function during Emotion and Cognition Interaction in Criminal Psychopathy', *Behavioral Sciences & the Law*, 26(1), 131–150.

Munday, M. (1982) 'The Novel and Its Critics in the Early Nineteenth Century', *Studies in Philology*, 79(2), 205–227.

National Institute of Mental Health (NIMH) (2013) 'Director's Blog: Transforming Diagnosis', 29 April. Available online: www.nimh.nih.gov (accessed 14 January 2014).

Newell, T. and Healy, B. (2006) 'The Historical Development of the UK Democratic Therapeutic Community', in M. Parker (ed.), *Dynamic Security: The Democratic Therapeutic Community in Prison*. Jessica Kingsley: London.

Nordau, M. (1895) [1892] *Degeneration*. William Heinemann: London.

Nourse, V. F. (2004) 'Rethinking Crime Legislation: History and Harshness', *Tulsa Law Review*, 39(4), 925–940.

Nye, R. (1985) 'Sociology and Degeneration: The Irony of Progress', in J. E. Chamberlin and S. L. Gilman (eds), *Degeneration: The Dark Side of Progress*. Columbia University Press: New York.

O'Connor, J. P. B. (2003) 'Thomas Willis and the Background to *Cerebri Anatome*', *Journal of the Royal Society of Medicine*, Mar 96(3), 139–143.

Ogborn, M. (1998) *Spaces of Modernity: London's Geographies 1680–1780*. Guilford Press: New York.

Ogloff, J. R. P. (2006) 'Psychopathy/Antisocial Personality Disorder Conundrum', *Australian and New Zealand Journal of Psychiatry*, 40(6–7), 519–528.

Oliveira-Souza, R., Hare, R., Bramatic, I., Garrido, G., Azevedo Ignácio, F., Tovar-Moll, F. and Moll, J. (2007) 'Psychopathy as a Disorder of the Moral Brain: Fronto-Temporo-Limbic Grey Matter Reductions Demonstrated by Voxel-Based Morphometry', *Neuroimage*, 40(3), 1202–1213.

Olson, H. (1915) 'The Psychopathic Laboratory Idea', *Journal of the American Institute of Criminal Law and Criminology*, 6(1), 59–64.

Olson, H. (1920) 'The Psychopathic Laboratory', *Journal of the American Judicature Society*, 1920–1921, 24.

Olson, H. (1923) 'Crime and Heredity', *Journal of the American Judicature Society*, 23(2), 37–78.

O'Malley, P. (1987) 'Marxist Theory and Marxist Criminology', *Crime and Social Justice*, 29, 70–87.

O'Reilly-Fleming, T. (1992) 'From Beasts to Bedlam: Hadfield, the Regency Crisis, M'Naghten and the "Mad" Business in Britain, 1788–1843', *The Journal of Psychiatry & Law*, 20(2), 167–190.

Overholser, W. (1959) 'Shakespeare's Psychiatry – and After', *Shakespeare Quarterly*, 10(3), 335–352.

Owen, D. (2005) *Murder, Magic, Madness: The Victorian Trials of Dove and the Wizard*. Routledge: Abingdon.

Pailthorpe, G. (1932) *Studies in the Psychology of Delinquency*, (Medical Research Council, Special Report Series, 170). HMSO: London.

Parkin, A. (1975) 'Feuchtersleben: A Forgotten Forerunner to Freud', *Canadian Psychiatric Association Journal*, 20(6), 477–481.

Paštar, Z., Petrov, B., Križaj, A., Bagarić, A. and Jukić, V. (2010) 'Diagnoses of Personality Disorders between 1879 and 1929 in the Largest Croatian Psychiatric Hospital', *Croatian Medical Journal*, 51(5), 461–467.

Pearce, J. M. S. (2002) 'Historical Note: Thomas Laycock (1812–1876)', *Journal of Neurology, Neurosurgery & Psychiatry*, 73, 303.

Peay, J. (2011) 'Personality Disorder and the Law: Some Awkward Questions', *Philosophy, Psychiatry & Psychology*, 18(3), 231–244.

Pepper, A. (2011) 'Early Crime Writing and the State: Jonathan Wild, Daniel Defoe and Bernard Mandeville in 1720s London', *Textual Practice*, 25(3), 473–491.

Perfect, W. (1787) *Select Cases in the Different Species of Insanity, Lunacy, or Madness; with the Modes of Practice as Adopted in the Treatment of each*. W. Gillman: Rochester.

Perkin, H. (1969) *The Origins of Modern English Society, 1780–1880*. Routledge: London.

Persky, J. (1997) 'Retrospectives: Classical Family Values: Ending the Poor Laws as they Knew them', *The Journal of Economic Perspectives*, 11(1), 179–189.

Peters, O. (ed.) (2014) *Degenerate Art: The Attack on Modern Art in Nazi Germany, 1937*. Prestel: Munich.

Pick, D. (1989) *Faces of Degeneration: A European Disorder, c.1848–1918*. Cambridge University Press: Cambridge.

Pick, D. (2009) '"In Pursuit of the Nazi Mind?" The Deployment of Psychoanalysis in the Allied Struggle against Germany', *Psychoanalysis and History*, 11(2), 137–157.

Pickersgill, M. (2010) 'From Psyche to Soma? Changing Accounts of Antisocial Personality Disorders in the American Journal of Psychiatry', *History of Psychiatry*, 21(3), 294–311.

Pickersgill, M. (2012) 'Standardising Antisocial Personality Disorder: The Social Shaping of a Psychiatric Technology', *Sociology of Health and Illness*, 34(4), 544–559.

Pickersgill, M. (2013) 'How Personality Became Treatable: The Mutual Constitution of Clinical Knowledge and Mental Health Law' *Social Studies of Science*, 43(1), 30–53.

Pilgrim, D. (2001) 'Disordered Personalities and Disordered Concepts', *Journal of Mental Health*, 10(3), 253–265.

Pilgrim, D. (2008) 'The Eugenic Legacy in Psychology and Psychiatry', *International Journal of Social Psychiatry*, 54(3), 272–284.

Pinel, P. (1806) *A Treatise on Insanity: In which are Contained the Principles of a New and More Practical Nosology of Maniacal Disorders Than Has Yet Been Offered to the Public*, trans. D. D. Davis. Cadell and Davies: London.

Polk, K. (1994) *Why Men Kill*. Cambridge University Press: Cambridge.

Poovey, M. (1995) *Making A Social Body: British Cultural Transformation 1830–1864*. The University of Chicago Press: Chicago.

Porter, R. (1983) 'The Rage of Party: A Glorious Revolution in English Psychiatry?', *Medical History*, 27, 35–50.

Porter, R. (1987) *Mind-Forg'd Manacles: A History of Madness in England from the Restoration to the Regency*. Athlone Press: London.

Porter, R. (2000) *Enlightenment: Britain and the Creation of the Modern World*. Allen Lane: London.

Porter, R. (2002) *Madness: A Brief History*. Oxford University Press: Oxford.

Porter, R. (2004) *Madmen: A Social History of Madhouses, Mad-Doctors and Lunatics*. Tempus Publishing: Stroud.

Pratt, J. (1998) *Governing the Dangerous: Dangerousness, Law and Social Change*. The Federation Press: Sydney.

Prichard, James Cowles (1835a) *A Treatise on Insanity and Other Disorders Affecting the Mind*. Sherwood, Gilbert and Piper: London.

Prichard, James Cowles (1835b) 'Soundness and Unsoundness of Mind', in *The Cyclopaedia of Practical Medicine*, Vol. 4. Sherwood, Gilbert and Piper: London.

Prins, H. (1980) *Offenders, Deviants, or Patients? An Introduction to the Study of Socio-Forensic Problems*. Tavistock: London.

Privy Council (1947) *Report of an Expert Committee on the Work of Psychologists and Psychiatrists in the Services*. HMSO: London.

Pujol, J. et al. (2012) 'Breakdown in the Brain Network Subserving Moral Judgment in Criminal Psychopathy', *Social Cognitive and Affective Neuroscience*, 7(8), 917–923.

Quakers in the World (2014) 'Quakers in Action: David Wills'. Available online: www.quakersintheworld.org/quakers-in-action/182 (accessed 17 June 2014).

Rafter, N. (1997) *Creating Born Criminals*. University of Illinois Press: Urbana, IL.

Rafter, N. (2004) 'The Unrepentant Horse-Slasher: Moral Insanity and the Origins of Criminological Thought', *Criminology*, 42(4), 979–1008.

Rafter, N. (2009) *The Origins of Criminology: A Reader*. Routledge: London.

Rafter, N. (2011) *Criminology Goes to the Movies: Crime Theory and Popular Culture*. New York University Press: New York.

Rafter, N. and Ystehede, P. (2010) 'Here Be Dragons: Lombroso, the Gothic, and Social Control', in Mathieu Deflem (ed.), *Popular Culture, Crime and Social Control*, pp. 263–284. Emerald Group: Bingley.

Raine, A. (2013) *The Anatomy of Violence: The Biological Roots of Crime*. Allen Lane: New York.

Ramon, S. (1986) 'The Category of Psychopathy: Its Professional and Social Context in Britain', in P. Miller and N. Rose (eds), *The Power of Psychiatry*. Routledge: London.

Rapoport, R. N. (1960) *The Community as Doctor*. Routledge and Kegan Paul: London.

Rawlings, B. (1998) *Research on Therapeutic Communities in Prisons: A Review of the Literature*. Report for the Prison Service: UK.

Ray, I. (1853) *A Treatise on the Medical Jurisprudence of Insanity*, 3rd edn (first published in 1838). Little, Brown: Boston, MA.

Ray, L. J. (1983) 'Eugenics, Mental Deficiency and Fabian Socialism between the Wars', *Oxford Review of Education*, 9(3), 213–222.

Reed, E. (1997) *From Soul to Mind: The Emergence of Psychology from Erasmus Darwin to William James*. Yale University Press: New Haven, CT.

Regan, S. (2001) *The Nineteenth-Century Novel: A Critical Reader*. Routledge: London.

Reich, W. (1972) [1933] *Character Analysis*, 3rd edn, trans. V. Carfagno, ed. M. Higgins and C. M. Raphael. Farrar, Straus and Giroux: New York.

Rembis, M. A. (2002) 'Breeding up the Human Herd: Gender, Power, and the Creation of the Country's First Eugenic Commitment Law', *Journal of Illinois History*, 5(4), 283–308.

Rembis, M. A. (2003) *Breeding Up the Human Herd: Gender, Power, and Eugenics in Illinois 1890–1940*. University of Arizona Press: Tucson, AZ.

Rembis, M. A. (2011) *Defining Deviance: Sex, Science, and Delinquent Girls, 1890–1960*. University of Illinois Press: Urbana, IL.

Reumann, M. G. (2005) *American Sexual Character: Sex, Gender, and National Identity in the Kinsey Reports*. University of California Press: Berkeley, CA.

Richards, R. J. (1998) 'Rhapsodies on a Cat-Piano, or Johann Christian Reil and the Foundations of Romantic Psychiatry', *Critical Inquiry*, 24(3), 700–736.

Rieff, P. (1966) *The Triumph of the Therapeutic: Uses of Faith after Freud*. Chatto and Windus: London.

Rimke, H. and Hunt, A. (2002) 'From Sinners to Degenerates: The Medicalization of Morality in the 19th Century', *History of the Human Sciences*, 15(1), 59–88.

Rimke, H. and Brock, D. (2012) 'The Culture of Therapy: Psychocentrism in Everyday Life', in M. Thomas, R. Raby and D. Brock (eds), *Power and Everyday Practices*. Nelson: Toronto.

Rivers, W. H. R. (1918) 'The Repression of War Experience', *Proceedings of the Royal Society of Medicine*, 11(Sect Psych), 1–20.

Roback, A. (1927) *The Psychology of Character*. Routledge and Kegan Paul: London.

Robertson, C. L. and Maudsley, H. (eds of the *Journal of Mental Science*) (1864) *Insanity and Crime: A Medico-Legal Commentary on the Case of George Victor Townley*. John Churchill and Sons: London.

Robinson, R. (1971) 'Plato's Separation of Reason from Desire', *Pronesis*, 16(1), 38–48.

Rodensky, L. (2003) *The Crime in Mind: Criminal Responsibility and the Victorian Novel*. Oxford University Press: Oxford.

Rolf, C. A. (2006) 'From M'Naghten to Yates – Transformation of the Insanity Defense in the United States – Is it Still Viable?', *Rivier College Online Academic Journal*, 2(1), 1–18.

Rollins, H. (1976) 'Focus: Current Issues in Medical Ethics', *Journal of Medical Ethics*, 2, 157–162.

Rolph, C. (1958) *Mental Disorder: A Brief Examination of the Report of the Royal Commission on the Law Relating to Mental Illness and Mental Deficiency 1954–1957*. National Association for Mental Health: London.

Ronson, J. (2012) *The Psychopath Test*. Picador: Basingstoke.

Roper, M. (2010) *The Secret Battle: Emotional Survival in the Great War*. Manchester University Press: Manchester.

Rose, G. (1958) 'Trends in the Development of Criminology in Britain', *The British Journal of Sociology*, 9(1), 53–65.

Rose, N. (1979) 'The Psychological Complex: Mental Measurement and Social Administration', *Ideology and Consciousness*, 5, 5–68. Available online: http://eprints.lse.ac.uk/622/1/NikRose_I_C_5.pdf (accessed 3 May 2015).

Rose, N. (1985) *The Psychological Complex: Psychology, Politics and Society in England, 1869–1939*. Routledge and Kegan Paul: London.

Rose, N. (1989) *Governing the Soul*. Routledge: London.

Rose, N. (2010) '"Screen and Intervene": Governing Risky Brains', *History of the Human Sciences*, 23(1), 79–105.

Rothman, D. (1971) *The Discovery of the Asylum*. Little, Brown: Toronto.

Rousseau, G. S. (1969) 'Science and the Discovery of the Imagination in Enlightened England', *Eighteenth-Century Studies*, 3(1), 108–135.

Rousseau, G. S. (1991) '*Retreat into the Mind: Victorian Poetry and the Rise of Psychiatry* by Ekbert Faas [Book Review]', *Isis*, 82(3), 581–582.

Royal Commission on the Care and Control of the Feeble-Minded (1908) *Report*. HMSO: London.

Royal Commission on the Law Relating to Mental Illness and Mental Deficiency (1957) *Minutes of Evidence*. HMSO: London.

Rubinstein, W. D. (1998) *Britain's Century: A Political and Social History 1815–1905*. Oxford University Press: Oxford.

Rush, B. (1793) *Medical Inquiries and Observations*, Vol. 2. Dobson: Philadelphia, PA.

Sanders, J. L. (2010) 'A Distinct Language and a Historic Pendulum: The Evolution of the Diagnostic and Statistical Manual of Mental Disorders', *Archives of Psychiatric Nursing*, 25(6), 394–403.

Scanlon, C. and Adlam, J. (2008) 'Refusal, Social Exclusion and the Cycle of Rejection: A Cynical Analysis?', *Critical Social Policy*, 28(4), 529–549.

Scanlon, C. and Adlam, J. (2011) 'Cosmopolitan Minds and Metropolitan Societies: Social Exclusion and Social Refusal Revisited', *Psychodynamic Practice*, 17(3), 235–239.

Scheb, J. M. (2008) *Criminal Law and Procedure*. Wadsworth: Belmont, CA.

Scheff, T. (1963) *Being Mentally Ill: A Sociological Theory*. Weidenfeld: London.

Schirmann, F. (2014a) 'The Good, the Bad, and the Brain: Theory and History of the Neuroscience of Morality', thesis submitted to obtain the degree of Ph.D. at the University of Groningen, Netherlands.

Schirmann, F. (2014b) 'The Wondrous Eyes of a New Technology – A History of the Early Electroencephalography (EEG) of Psychopathy, Delinquency, and Immorality', *Frontiers in Human Neuroscience*, 8(232), 1–10.

Schmidt, J. (2004) 'Melancholy and the Therapeutic Language of Moral Philosophy in Seventeenth-Century Thought', *Journal of the History of Ideas*, 65(4), 583–560.

Schroeder, M., Schroeder, K. and Hare, R. D. (1983) 'Generalizability of a Checklist for Assessment of Psychopathy', *Journal of Consulting and Clinical Psychology*, 51(4), 511–516.

Scull, A. (1979a) 'Moral Treatment Reconsidered: Some Sociological Comments on an Episode in the History of British Psychiatry', *Psychological Medicine*, 9(3), 421–428.

Scull, A. (1979b) *Museums of Madness: The Social Organization of Insanity in Nineteenth-Century England*. Allen Lane: London.

Scull, A. (1984) 'A Brilliant Career? John Conolly and Victorian Psychiatry', *Victorian Studies*, 27(2), 203–235.

Seddon, T. (2008) 'Dangerous Liaisons: Personality Disorder and the Politics of Risk', *Punishment and Society*, 10(3), 301–317.

Sedgwick, P. (1982) *Psychopolitics*. Pluto Press: London.

Sen, P. and Irons, A. (2010) 'Personality Disorder and the Mental Health Act 1983 (amended)', *Advances in Psychiatric Treatment*, 16(5), 329–335.

Seneca (1928) *Moral Essays*, in 3 vols, with an English trans. by J. Basore (*Seneca*, Vol. 1). Heinemann: London.

Shapira, M. (2013) *The War Inside: Psychoanalysis, Total War, and the Making of the Democratic Self in Postwar Britain*. Cambridge University Press: Cambridge.

Sharp, H. C. (1908) *The Sterilization of Degenerates*. Indiana Reformatory Hospital: Jeffersonville, IN.

Sheppard, F. (1998) *London: A History*. Oxford University Press: Oxford.

Sherrill, R. (1984) 'In Florida, Insanity Is No Defense', *Nation*, 239(17), 537–556.

Shoemaker, R. (2001) 'Male Honour and the Decline of Public Violence in Eighteenth-Century London', *Social History*, 26(2), 190–208.

Shoemaker, R. (2008) 'The Old Bailey Proceedings and the Representation of Crime and Criminal Justice in Eighteenth-Century London', *Journal of British Studies*, 47(3), 559–580.

Shuker, R. (2004) 'Changing People with Programmes', in D. Jones, *Working with Dangerous People: The Psychotherapy of Violence*. Radcliffe Medical Press: Oxford.

Shuker, R. and Sullivan, E. (eds) (2010) *Grendon and the Emergence of Forensic Therapeutic Communities: Developments in Research and Practice*. Wiley-Blackwell: Chichester.

Shuttleworth, S. (1996) *Charlotte Brontë and Victorian Psychology*. Cambridge University Press: Cambridge.

Simon, J. (1998) 'Managing the Monstrous: Sex Offenders and the New Penology', *Psychology, Public Policy and Law*, 4(1/2), 452–467.

Simpson, D. (2005) 'Phrenology and the Neurosciences: Contributions of F. J. Gall and J. G. Spurzheim', *ANZ Journal of Surgery*, 75(6), 475–482.

Singh, J. P., Grann, M. and Fazel, S. (2011) 'A Comparative Study of Violence Risk Assessment Tools: A Systematic Review and Metaregression Analysis of 68 Studies Involving 25,980 Participants', *Clinical Psychology Review*, 31(3), 499–513.

Small, H. (1996) *Love's Madness: Medicine, the Novel, and Female Insanity, 1800–1865*. Clarendon Press: Oxford.

Smith, A. (1759) *The Theory of Moral Sentiments*. A. Millar: London.
Smith, H. N. (2007) 'The Madness of Ahab', in H. Bloom (ed.), *Herman Melville's Moby-Dick*. InfoBase: New York.
Smith, R. (1981) *Trial by Medicine: Insanity and Responsibility in Victorian Trials*. Edinburgh University Press: Edinburgh.
South East Coast Strategic Health Authority (2006) *Joint Agencies' Response to the Recommendations of the Independent Inquiry Report into the Care, Treatment and Supervision of Michael Stone*. South East Coast Strategic Health Authority: Horley.
Sparr, L. (2009) 'Personality Disorders and Criminal Law: An International Perspective', *Journal of the American Academy of Psychiatry and the Law*, 37(2), 168–181.
Spencer, K. L. (1992) 'Purity and Danger: *Dracula*, the Urban Gothic, and the Late Victorian Degeneracy Crisis', *English Literary History*, 59(1), 197–225.
Spiro, J. (2009) *Defending the Master Race: Conservation, Eugenics, and the Legacy of Madison Grant*. University of Vermont Press: Lebanon, NH.
Spitzer, R. (1991) 'An Outsider-Insider's Views about Revising the DSMs', *Journal of Abnormal Psychology*, 100(1), 294–296.
Spitzer, R. and Wilson, P. (1968) 'An Introduction to the American Psychiatric Association's New Diagnostic Nomenclature for New York State Department of Mental Hygiene Personnel', *Psychiatric Quarterly*, 42(3), 487–503.
Sprinkle, R. H. (1994) *Profession of Conscience: The Making and Meaning of Life-Sciences Liberalism*. Princeton University Press: Princeton, NJ.
Stevens, A. (2010) 'Introducing Forensic Democratic Therapeutic Communities', in R. Shuker and E. Sullivan (eds), *Grendon and the Emergence of Forensic Therapeutic Communities: Developments in Research and Practice*. Wiley-Blackwell: Chichester.
Stevens, H. C. (1915) 'Eugenics and Feeblemindedness', *Journal of the American Institute of Criminal Law and Criminology*, 6(2), 190–197.
Stevenson, R. L. (1886) *The Strange Case of Dr Jekyll and Mr Hyde*. Longmans, Green: London.
Stoker, B. (2009) [1897] *Dracula*. Puffin Classics: London.
Stoll, M. (2009) 'Miles to Go Before We Sleep: Arizona's "Guilty Except Insane" Approach to the Insanity Defense and Its Unrealized Promise', *The Georgetown Law Journal*, 97(6), 1767–1799.
Stone, L. (1969) 'Literacy and Education in England 1640–1900', *Past and Present*, 42, 69–139.
Stone, L. (1990) *The Family, Sex and Marriage in England 1500–1800*. Penguin: Harmondsworth.
Stone, M. (2004) 'Shellshock and the Psychologists', in W. F. Bynum, R. Porter and M. Shepherd, (eds), *The Anatomy of Madness: Essays in the History of Psychiatry*, Vol. 2, *Institutions and Society*. Routledge: London.
Stout, M. (2005) *The Sociopath Next Door*. Broadway Books: New York.
Stubblefield, A. (2007) '"Beyond the Pale": Tainted Whiteness, Cognitive Disability, and Eugenic Sterilization', *Hypatia*, 22(2), 162–181.
Sulloway, F. J. (1979) *Freud, Biologist of the Mind: Beyond the Psychoanalytic Legend*. Basic Books: New York.
Summers, J. (2011) *When the Children Came Home: Stories of Wartime Evacuees*. Simon and Schuster: London.

Sutherland, E. P. (1950) 'The Sexual Psychopath Laws', *Journal of Criminal Law and Criminology*, 40(5), 543–554.
Suttie, I. (1935) *The Origins of Love and Hate*. Kegan Paul, Trench, Trubner: London.
Swanson, A. H. (1960) 'Sexual Psychopath Statutes: Summary and Analysis', *The Journal of Criminal Law, Criminology, and Police Science*, 51(2), 215–235.
Symington, N. (1980) 'The Response Aroused by the Psychopath', *International Review of Psychoanalysis*, 7, 291–298.
Szasz, T. (1970) *The Manufacture of Madness*. Harper and Row: New York.
Taylor, C. (2011) 'Nothing Left to Lose? Freedom and Compulsion in the Treatment of Dangerous Offenders', *Psychodynamic Practice*, 17(3), 291–306.
Thomson, J. B. (1869) 'The Hereditary Nature of Crime', *Journal of Mental Science*, 15, 487–498.
Thomson, J. B. (1870) 'The Psychology of Criminals', *Journal of Mental Science*, 16, 321–350.
Thomson, M. (1998) *The Problem of Mental Deficiency: Eugenics, Democracy, and Social Policy in Britain, c.1870–1959*. Clarendon Press: Oxford.
Thurston, H. W. (1910) 'Book Review: *The Junior Republic: Its History and Ideals* by William R. George', *The School Review*, 18(8), 566–567.
Tielbeek, J., Medland, S., Benyamin, B., Byrne, E., Heath, A., Madden, P., Martin, N., Wray, N. and Verweij, K. (2012) 'Unraveling the Genetic Etiology of Adult Antisocial Behavior: A Genome-Wide Association Study', *PLoS One*, 7(10), e45086.
Tomes, N. (1994) *The Art of Asylum-Keeping: Thomas Story Kirkbride and the Origins of American Psychiatry*. University of Pennsylvania Press: Philadelphia, PA.
Tomlinson, S. (1997) 'Phrenology, Education and the Politics of Human Nature: The Thought and Influence of George Combe', *History of Education*, 26(1), 1–22.
Toms, J. (2013) *Mental Hygiene and Psychiatry in Modern Britain*. Palgrave: Basingstoke.
Torgersen, S., Kringlen, E. and Cramer, V. (2001) 'The Prevalence of Personality Disorders in a Community Sample', *Archives of General Psychiatry*, 58(6), 590–596.
Trestman, R. L. (2014) 'DSM-5 and Personality Disorders: Where Did Axis II Go?', *Journal of the American Academy of Psychiatry and the Law*, 42(2), 141–145.
Trist, E. (2000) 'Working with Bion in the 1940s: The Group Decade', in M. Pines (ed.), *Bion and Group Psychotherapy*. Jessica Kingsley: London.
Tucker, E. B. (1978) 'James Jackson Putnam: An American Perspective on the Social Uses of Psychoanalysis, 1895–1918', *The New England Quarterly*, 51(4), 527–546.
Tuke, D. H. (1885) 'Moral or Emotional Insanity', *Journal of Mental Science*, 31(134), 174–191.
Tuke, H. (1867) 'On Monomania, and Its Relation to the Civil and Criminal Law', *British Journal of Psychiatry*, 13, 306–314.
Tuke, S. (1813) *Description of The Retreat, an Institution near York for Insane Persons of the Society of Friends*. W. Alexander: York.
Turner, B. and Rennell, T. (1995) *When Daddy Came Home: How Family Life Changed for Ever in 1945*. Hutchinson: London.
Tyrer, P., Coombs, N., Ibrahimi, F., Mathilakath, A., Bajaj, P., Ranger, M., Rao, B. and Din, R. (2007) 'Critical Developments in the Assessment of Personality Disorder', *British Journal of Psychiatry*, 190(Suppl 49), s51–s59.

United States Court of Appeals, District of Columbia Circuit (1954) *Durham v. United States* 214 F.2d 862. Available online: http://law.justia.com/cases/federal/appellate-courts/F2/214/862/314341/ (accessed 3 May 2015).

Utting, D., Bright, J. and Henricson, C. (1993) *Crime and the Family: Improving Child-Rearing and Preventing Delinquency*. Family Policy Studies Centre: London.

Valier, C. (1995) 'Psychoanalysis and Crime during the Inter-War Years', in Jon Vagg and Tim Newburn (eds), *The British Criminology Conferences: Selected Proceedings*, Vol. 1. British Society of Criminology: Loughborough.

Vandevelde, S. (1999) 'Maxwell Jones and His Work in the Therapeutic Community', thesis submitted to obtain the degree of Master in Educational Sciences (Orthopedagogics) at the University of Ghent, Belgium.

Vandiver, T. and Sher, K. J. (1991) 'Temporal Stability of the Diagnostic Interview Schedule', *Psychological Assessment: A Journal of Consulting and Clinical Psychology*, 3(2), 277–281.

Verplaetse, J. (2002) 'Prosper Despine's *Psychologie Naturelle* and the Discovery of the Remorseless Criminal in Nineteenth-Century France', *History of Psychiatry*, 13(50), 153–175.

Verwey, G. (1985) *Psychiatry in an Anthropological and Biomedical Context*, (Studies in the History of Modern Science, 15). D. Reidel: Dordrecht, Netherlands.

Viding, E., Larsson, H. and Jones, A. P. (2008) 'Quantitative Genetic Studies of Antisocial Behaviour', *Philosophical Transactions of the Royal Society of London B*, 363(1503), 2519–2527.

Vogt, S. (2009) 'Diagnosing Defectives: Disability, Gender and Eugenics in the United States, 1910–1924', *Hektoen International: A Journal of Medical Humanities*, 1(3), 1.

Wagenaar, W. A., van Koppen, P. J. and Crombag, H. F. M. (1993) *Anchored Narratives: The Psychology of Criminal Evidence*. Harvester Wheatsheaf: New York.

Walcutt, C. C. (1968) *Man's Changing Mask: Modes and Methods of Characterization in Fiction*. University of Minnesota Press: Minneapolis, MN.

Waldinger, R. J. (1979) 'Sleep of Reason: John P. Gray and the Challenge of Moral Insanity', *Journal of the History of Medicine and Allied Sciences*, 34(2), 163–179.

Walker, N. (1968) *Crime and Insanity in England*, Vol. 1, *The Historical Perspective*. Edinburgh University Press: Edinburgh.

Walker, N. and McCabe, S. (1973) *Crime and Insanity in England*, Vol. 2, *New Solutions and New Problems*. Edinburgh University Press: Edinburgh.

Wallcraft, J. and Bryant, M. (2003) *The Mental Health Service User Movement in England*. Sainsbury Centre for Mental Health: London.

Walters, G. D. (2012) 'Psychopathy and Crime: Testing the Incremental Validity of PCL-R-Measured Psychopathy as a Predictor of General and Violent Recidivism', *Law and Human Behavior*, 36(5), 404–412.

Wanke, P. (1999) 'American Military Psychiatry and Its Role among Ground Forces in World War II', *Journal of Military History*, 63(1), 127–146.

Ward, T. (1999) 'The Sad Subject of Infanticide: Law, Medicine and Child Murder, 1860–1938', *Social and Legal Studies*, 8(2), 163–180.

Warden, J. (1998) 'Psychiatrists Hit Back at Home Secretary', *British Medical Journal*, 317(10), 1270.

Warren F., Preedy-Fayers, K., McGauley, G., Pickering, A., Norton, K., Geddes, J. R. and Dolan, B. (2003) *Review of Treatments for Severe Personality Disorder*, Home Office Report, 30 March. Home Office: London.

Watt, I. (1979) *Conrad in the Nineteenth Century*. University of California Press: Berkeley, CA.
Watt, I. (1987) [1957] *The Rise of the Novel*. The Hogarth Press: London.
Weber, M. (1996) 'Ernst Rüdin, 1874–1952: A German Psychiatrist and Geneticist', *American Journal of Medical Genetics*, 67(4), 323–331.
Weiner, B. A. (1980) 'Not Guilty by Reason of Insanity: A Sane Approach', *Chicago-Kent Law Review*, 56(4), 1057–1085.
Werlinder, H. (1978) *Psychopathy: A History of the Concepts: Analysis of the Origin and Development of a Family of Concepts in Psychopathology*. University of Uppsala: Uppsala, Sweden.
Wessely, S. (2013) 'DSM-5 at the IoP', South London and Maudsley NHS Foundation Trust blog: www.slam.nhs.uk/our-blog/brcu/dsm-5-at-the-iop (accessed 13 July 2014).
West, D. J. (1982) *Delinquency: Its Roots, Careers and Prospects*. Heinemann: London.
White, G. E. (1997) 'The American Law Institute and the Triumph of Modernist Jurisprudence', *Law and History Review*, 15(1), 1–47.
Whiteley, S. (2004) 'The Evolution of the Therapeutic Community', *Psychiatric Quarterly*, 75(3), 233–248.
Widiger, T. A. (1993)'The DSM-III-R Categorical Personality Disorder Diagnoses: A Critique and an Alternative', *Psychological Inquiry*, 4(2), 75–90.
Widiger, T. A. (2001) 'Official Classification Systems', in W. J. Livesley, *Handbook of Personality Disorders: Theory, Research, and Treatment*. Guilford Press: New York.
Widiger, T. A., Cadoret, R., Hare, R., Robins, L., Rutherford, M., Zanarini, M., Alterman, A., Apple, M., Corbitt, E., Forth, A., Hart, S., Kultermann, J., Woody, G. and Frances, A. (1996) 'DSM-IV Antisocial Personality Field Trial', *Journal of Abnormal Psychology*, 105(1), 3–16.
Wiener, M. J. (1999) 'Judges v. Jurors: Courtroom Tensions in Murder Trials and the Law of Criminal Responsibility in Nineteenth-Century England', *Law and History Review*, 17(3), 467–506.
Wiener, M. J. (2001) 'Alice Arden to Bill Sikes: Changing Nightmares of Intimate Violence in England, 1558–1869', *Journal of British Studies*, 40(2), 184–212.
Willemsen, J. and Verhaeghe, P. (2012) 'Psychopathy and Internalizing Psychopathology', *International Journal of Law and Psychiatry*, 35(4), 269–275.
Williams, C. (1856) *Observations on the Criminal Responsibility of the Insane: Founded on the Trials of James Hill and of William Dove*. John Churchill: London.
Willrich, M. (1998) 'The Two Percent Solution: Eugenic Jurisprudence and the Socialization of American Law, 1900–1930', *Law and History Review*, 16(1), 63–111.
Willrich, M. (2003) *City of Courts: Socializing Justice in Progressive Era Chicago*. Cambridge University Press: Cambridge.
Wills, W. D. (1941) *The Hawkspur Experiment: An Informal Account of the Training of Wayward Adolescents*. Allen & Unwin: London.
Winslow, F. (1843) *The Plea of Insanity in Criminal Cases*. Little and Brown: Boston.
Wolfgang, M. E. (1961) 'Pioneers in Criminology: Cesare Lombroso (1825–1909)', *Journal of Criminal Law, Criminology, and Police Science*, 52(4), 361–391.
Woodfine, P. (2006) 'Debtors, Prisons and Petitions in Eighteenth-Century England', *Eighteenth-Century Life*, 30(2), 1–31.

Wootton, (1960) 'Diminished Responsibility: A Layman's View', *Law Quarterly Review*, 76, 224–239.
Worrell, M. P. (2008) *Dialectics of Solidarity: Labor, Antisemitism, and the Frankfurt School*. Brill: Leiden, Netherlands.
Wouters, C. and Mennell, S. (2013) 'Discussing Civilisation and Informalisation: Criteriology', *Politica y Sociedad*, 50(2), 553–579.
Wright, K. (2002) *Reform of the Mental Health Act 1983: The Draft Mental Health Bill*, Research Paper 02/80. House of Commons Library: London.
Wright, T. R. (1982) 'From Bumps to Morals: The Phrenological Background to George Eliot's Moral Framework', *The Review of English Studies, New Series*, 33(129), 34–46.
Wulach, J. S. (1983) 'Diagnosing the DSM-III Antisocial Personality Disorder', *Professional Psychology: Research and Practice*, 14(3), 330–340.
Yakeley, J. (2009) 'Individual Psychoanalytic Psychotherapy for Violent Patients', in A. Yakeley, *Working with Violence: A Contemporary Psychoanalytic Approach*, (Basic Texts in Counselling and Psychotherapy). Palgrave Macmillan: New York.
Yang, Y., Raine, A., Colletti, P., Toga, A. and Narr, K. (2011) 'Abnormal Structural Correlates of Response Perseveration in Individuals with Psychopathy', *Journal of Neuropsychiatry and Clinical Neurosciences*, 23(1), 107–110.
Yates, C. (2007) *Masculine Jealousy and Contemporary Cinema*. Palgrave Macmillan: London.
Yates, C. (2011) 'Reviews and Their Uses as Affective Texts: Viewing and Re-Viewing *Taxi Driver* (M. Scorsese, US 1976)', *Free Associations*, 61, 96–115.
Zalampas, S. O. (1990) *Adolf Hitler: A Psychological Interpretation of His Views on Architecture, Art and Music*. Bowling Green State University Popular Press: Bowling Green, OH.
Zaretsky, E. (2004) *Secrets of the Soul: A Social and Cultural History of Psychoanalysis*. Knopf: New York.
Zedner, L. (1991) *Women, Crime and Custody*. Clarendon: Oxford.
Zenderland. L. (1998) *Measuring Minds: Henry Herbert Goddard and the Origins of American Intelligence Testing*. Cambridge University Press: Cambridge.

# Subject index

Bold refers to substantial discussion on a topic

Act for the Better Government of Convict Prisoners (Great Britain, 1850) 93
Albert Matheson (tried for murder, Newcastle 1958) 186
alcohol 110, 111, 112, 195, 241
ALI *see* American Law Institute
American Law Institute (ALI) vi, vii: guidelines on insanity defence vi, 19, 201, 213, 214, 215, **217–218**, 221, 223, 224, 225 238
American Psychiatric Association (APA) 4, 5, 19, 81, 163, 166, 189, 191, 197, 207, 218, 224, 231, 238
Andrea Yates (tried for murder, Texas 2004) 225
Annales Médico-Psychologiques 81
antisocial personality disorder vii, 2–3, 7, 161, 163, 193, 196, 200, 201, 203, **204–208**, 211–212, 228, 238, 240, 241, 247–249, 250
APA *see* American Psychiatric Association
Arthur F. Goode (tried for murder, Florida 1984) 225
Association of Medical Officers of Asylums and Hospitals for the Insane (Great Britain) 81
Association of Medical Superintendents of American Institutions for the Insane 81
asylum (institution) 40, 50–53, 54, 77, 81–83, 124, 129, 131, 175; Bethlem Hospital 41, 65, 70, 72, 73, 74, 77, 88, 94, 111; Bicêtre (Paris) 52, 56, 82; Hanwell 69; Royal Lunatic Asylum Glasgow 73; York Retreat 52, 53, 83, 124
Asylum Act (1845, England) 81
*Asylum Journal see Journal of Mental Science, The*
atavism 94; *see also* criminal anthropology
authoritarian personality *see* psychology of fascism

Baron Eyre (Judge) 29; *see also* Old Bailey trials: William Walker and John Simpson
barrister *see* counsel
Belmont (Belmont Industrial Unit, Belmont Hospital) vi, 176, 179–181, 188; *see also* Henderson Hospital
Bethlem Hospital (London) *see* asylum
Bicêtre *see* asylum
Binet intelligence test 131
borderline personality disorder 162, 221, 223
Bracton (Henry de Bratton, c.1210–1268) 42–43
Brian Blackwell (tried for murder, Liverpool 2005) 232
Broadmoor Hospital 65, 70, 89
*Buck v. Bell* (the case of Carrie Buck) 135–136

## Subject index

Cassel Hospital (London) 176
chaplain 32; *see also* Ordinary
Chiarugi, Vincenzo 52
Chicago Municipal Court vi, 17, 122, 130, **136–140**, 151, 237
Cleckley psychopathy profile vii, 4, 185, 192, **193–197**, 199, 201, 207, 246–247
cognitive (model of psychology) 204, 213, 243
combat stress 175; *see also* shell shock
co-morbidity 203, 209
Conolly, John (British psychiatrist 1794–1868) 67, 69–70, 77, 79, 81, 83
constable 25, 31
coroner 12, 69, 89
counsel (defence and prosecution) 29, 35, 62, 68, 71, 73; *see also* Erskine, Thomas (barrister)
Creighton, Dr 64
criminal anthropology 80, 93–95, 96, 114–115; *see also* Lombroso, Cesare
criminal lunacy (Criminal Lunatics Act) 65–66

Dangerous and Severe Personality Disorder (DSPD) 3, 228–230
Daniel M'Naghten (tried for murder in 1843) vi, 16, 50, 62, 66, **71–75**, 79, 80, 84, 86, 90, 101, 145, 214, 220, 223, 231, 236; *see also* M'Naghten ruling
defence counsel *see* counsel
degenerate art (Nazi exhibition, Munich 1937) 116
degeneration (theory, degeneracy, *dégénérescence*), vi, 18, 80, 96, 100, **109–119**, 121, 127 134, 150, 237
delusion 54, 62, 64, 68, 72–74, 86, 241
DGPPN *see* German Association for Psychiatry and Psychotherapy
*Diagnostic and Statistical Manual* (DSM) 5, 19, 161, **191–212**, 214, 221, 238, 240, 247, 250
diminished responsibility (and homicide) 167, **184–187**, 188, 232
domestic violence *see* violence against women

*Dracula* (Bram Stoker) 112, 114–115; *see also* novels depicting monomania and moral insanity
DSM *see* Diagnostic and Statistical Manual
DSPD *see* Dangerous and Severe Personality Disorder
drug abuse *see* substance abuse
Duesbury, Dr. Frederick (London) 83
Durham rule 19, 213, 215–217, 238

Edward Oxford: the trial of v, 50, 67–71, 72, 74, 76, 86, 219, 236
EEG *see* electroencephalography
effort syndrome 174, 180, 190; *see also* battle stress; shell shock
electroencephalography (EEG) 188
Emergence (organisation, UK) 250
Erskine, Thomas (barrister) (1750–1823) 63–66
etiquette 13–14, 19
Eugenical Record Office (ERO) **130–136**, sterilization acts,
eugenics, vi, 84, 95, 116, **121–146**, 240; Brock Commission (Great Britain 1932) 145; 'Commitment and Care for the Feeble-Minded Person' Bill (Illinois 1915) 139; Eugenics Education Society (later renamed Eugenics Society) 93; 'Law for the Prevention of Hereditarily Diseased Offspring' (Germany 1933) 130

Fanny Adams (killed by Frederick Baker) 89–90
Farrow, Stephen (tried for murder 2012) 1–2, 3, 232
fascism *see* psychology of fascism
feeblemindedness 2, 7, 147, 149. **121–146**, 193, 237, 240
Ferrers, Earl (tried for murder, London 1760) 41
Fielding, Henry (novelist and magistrate) 13, 14, 29, 36
First World War 123, 140, 142, 153, 154, 166, 167, 168, 176, 177, 178, 238
Forbes Winslow, Dr 73, 84, 85, 86, 97, 88, 89, 97

French psychiatry 5, 8, 17; *dégénérescence* vi, 18, 80, 96, 100; Esquirol and monomania 55–59; Pinel 52–55
Frankfurt school (Institut für Sozialforchung) 157–158, 163, 178, 239
Frederick Baker (tried for murder, Winchester 1867) 89–90

gender and violence 37–39; *see also* violence against women
George III (King) 63
Géricault, Théodore (painter) 55–56
George Victor Townley (tried for murder, Derby 1863) **84–91**
German psychiatry vi, 4, 8, 17, 54, 59, 60, 80, 81, 97, 122, 123–128, 139, 145, 146, 148, 154
German Association for Psychiatry and Psychotherapy (DGPPN) 81
Gothic (literature) 17, 94, 112–115
Grendon (HMP) 181–182

Hale, Sir Mathew (1609–1676) 213, **43–44**, 63, 154, 187
Hawkspur (Q-camp) vi, 168, 169–171, 177
Heathcliff (*Wuthering Heights*) 103
Henderson Hospital 180, 181, 231; *see also* Belmont
Henriette Cornier (tried for murder, France 1885) 56–59, 73, 77, 104
Herstedvester Hospital (Denmark) 182
Home Secretary (UK): George Gray 88; Jack Straw 188, 227–228; Winston Churchill 141–142
Homicide Act (Great Britain 1975) 167, 184–185, 188

IDRA *see* Insanity Defence Reform Act
Illinois Juvenile Psychopathic Institute 138
imagination (as a capacity of mind) **10–11**, 17, 27, 28, 60; public imagination 17, 38, 50, 52, 100, 192
infanticide 22, 24, 77, 90

insanity defence: not guilty by reason of insanity 65, 223–224; special Verdict 62, 74, 70; *see also* diminished responsibility; M'Naghten rules
Insanity Defence Reform Act (IDRA) (1984) 224–226
Institute for Group Analysis (London) 176
Institute for the Study and Treatment of Delinquency (ISTD) 167–169, 170, 171, 176

James Hadfield (tried for treason, London 1840) 40, 50, **62–67**, 77, 86, 219
jealousy 24, 28, 44, 80, 86
John Bellingham (tried for murder, London 1812) 66
John Hinckley (tried for attempted murder, Washington DC 1982) 15, 19, 214, **218–224**, 225, 231, 239
John Wilkinson (tried for murder, London 1953) 185
*Journal of Mental Science, The* 84, 89, 90, 93, 94; *Asylum Journal* 81, 82, 84

King's Bench 63
Kinsey Report 150

lesion of will 70
Lombroso, Cesare 70, 93, 94, 114, 115–116
London 12–13, 14, 34–35, 36, 63, 109, 113, 114; 116; 141, 157, 167, 236, 240; City of London 8, 22; *see also* Bethlem Hospital (London); Ludgate (Debtors' Prison); Newgate Prison; Old Bailey; Tyburn (London gallows)
Ludgate (Debtors' Prison) 23

magistrate 14, 32, 40, 69
male violence: confrontational homicide 37, 44; state formation 37–39; marital, domestic violence 38; Old Bailey cases 22–33
M'Murdo, Gilbert (surgeon at Newgate Prison) 73

manslaughter 46, 167, 182, 184, 185, 186, 187, 244
*manie sans délire* 3, 28, 32, 54, 55, 58, 62
masculinity 52, 53, 156, 163, 164, 172, 228
Medico-Psychological Association of Great Britain and Ireland 81
melancholia (melancholy) 42–44, 57, 110, 156,
Mental Deficiency Act (Great Britain 1913) 141, 166; *see also* Radnor Commission
Mental Health Act (MHA): 1959 MHA 18, 163, 165, 166, 171, 181, 182, 185, 188–189, 191, 214, 218, 231, 232, 238; 1983 MHA; 227, 228, 229; 2007 Mental Health Amendment; vi, 3, 229, 230
Michael Clark (tried for murder, Arizona 2003) 225
Michael Stone (tried for murder, Nottingham 1998) 214–215, **226–229**, 232, 233, 239
military psychiatry 167, 170, 176, 177, 179, 193, 196, 197, 238; *see also* Northfield (Hollymoor Hospital)
M'Naghten rules (ruling) **75**, 82–83, 87–88, 90–92, 96, 99, 141, 167, 184–185, 188, 201, 213, 216, 217, 218, 224, 225, 238; *see also* Daniel M'Naghten
monomania 5, 6, 16, 21, 55–56, 58, 59, 61–62, 72–73, 76 82, 89–90, 96, 102, 108, 110, 118, 121, 123, 125, 145, 235, 236, 237; affective monomania 58; *Daniel Deronda* 104–105; homicidal monomania 58; *Middlemarch* 104–105; *Moby Dick* 103–104; portraits of monomania *see* Géricault, Théodore (painter)
Monro, Edward Thomas (doctor at Bethlem Hospital) 72, 73
moral imbecility 80, 95, **121–146**, 237
moral insanity: as defined by James Prichard 59–61; in relation to moral treatment 51

moral treatment v, 50, **51–53**, 54, 76, 81–82, 100; in relation to German psychiatry 124, 169
moron 131–132; *see also* feeblemindedness
murder *see* homicide; manslaughter

National Institute for Mental Health (NIMH) 210–211
narcissism vi, 18, 156, 159, **160–162**; culture 193, 239; narcissistic personality disorder (in court) 246; trial of John Hinckley 221, 223;
National Health Service (NHS) 168, 233
neurocriminology 242–246
neurology: neurological investigation 43, 124, 128, 139, 155, 244, 245
Neville Heath (tried for murder, London 1946)
Newgate Prison 27, 29, 45, 46, 69, 72, 73
NHS *see* National Health Service
NIMH *see* National Institute for Mental Health
nom compos mentis 12
Northfield (Hollymoor Hospital) vi, 170
Northfield experiments with community therapy 176–180
novels depicting monomania and moral insanity: *Daniel Deronda* (Eliot) 104; *Dracula* 112, 113–114; (Stoker) *Heart of Darkness* (Conrad) 107–108, 113–114; *Jekyll and Hyde* (Stevenson) 112–113; *Middlemarch* (Eliot) 104–105; *Moby Dick* (Melville) 103–104; *Secret Agent, The* (Conrad) 108, 114; *Wuthering Heights* (Brontë) 103

object relations 103, 157, 162, 167; Melanie Klein 157, 162; *see also* psychoanalysis
Old Bailey v, 15, 21, 44,
Old Bailey session papers **22–23**, 41
Old Bailey trials: James Carse (tried for murder 1787) 46–47; John Simpson (tried for murder 1786) 32–33;

Richard Parrott (tried for murder 1761) 25–29; Robert Finch (tried for murder 1754) 23–25; Thomas Bowler (tried for murder 1812) 66; William Allnutt (tried for murder 1847) 83; William Walker (tried for murder 1884) 29–32; *see also* Daniel M'Naghten; Edward Oxford
Ordinary (Chaplain of Newgate) 24–25, 27, 45, 46
Overseer 29, 30, 32, 45, 46; *see also* Poor Laws
Oxford, Edward *see* Edward Oxford

partial insanity xi, 6, 16, 21, **42–44**, 59, 62, 76, 89, 118, 125, 145, 187; in relation to the trial of Daniel M'Naghten 72–74
passion 10, 24, 38, 41, 42, 44, 51, 57, 103
Patrick Byrne (tried for murder, Birmingham 1960) 187
Pâquerette Sociotherapeutic Centre (Switzerland) 182
PCL *see* Psychopathy Checklist
PCL-R *see* Psychopathy Checklist-Revised
Percy Commission 181; *see also* Mental Health Act 1959
phrenology 53–54, 77, 103, 106, 146
Poor Laws 46; vagrancy 40, 149; workhouse 29; *see also* asylum; Overseer; pauper lunacy
Portman Clinic (Psychopathic Clinic) 168
poverty 10, 13, 109, 111, 117, 138, 142, 181
prison psychiatry 93–94, 121
prostitution 46, 109, 132, 135, 219, 220
psychoanalysis vi, 18, 38, 96, 100, 114, 123, 143, 147, 148; 'Civilization and Its Discontents' 153; Freud and personality theory 155–156; in the US 152–155; Kernberg, Otto 159, 160, 161–162, 163, 201, 239; Kohut, Heinz 161, 163, 201, 239

psychology of fascism vi, 156–160
Psychopath Clinic (London) *see* Portman Clinic
Psychopathic Laboratory *see* Chicago Municipal Court
Psychopathy Checklist (PCL) 196, 208, 245, 246, 247, 248–249
Psychopathy Checklist-Revised (PCL-R) 196, 208, 245, 246, 247, 248–249
public sphere v, xi, 7–9, 11–12, 22–23, 35, 92, 99–101, 109, 144–145, 150, 235, 241, 250–251

Q Camps *see* Hawkspur
Quaker 53, 124

Radnor Commission (Royal Commission on the Care and Control of the Feeble-Minded), 1913 141
rape 187, 143, 224
Report of the War Office Committee of Enquiry in 'Shell Shock' (Great Britain 1922)
Ronald Dunbar (tried for murder, Newcastle 1957)
Royal College of Psychiatry (UK) 97, 210

sadomasochistic 158
Salpêtrière *see* asylum
schizophrenia 175, 180, 194, 203, 206, 208, 222, 225
scrofula 83, 93
Second World War 153, 156, 157, 159, 162, 165, 166, 167, 187, 196, 213; and community therapy 175–179
sexual perversion 180
sexual psychopath laws 148–152
shell shock **142–145**; *see also* combat stress; effort syndrome
Shirley Campbell (tried for murder, Newcastle 1957) 185
sociopath (sociopathy, sociopathic reactions) 2, 4, 19, 192, 198, 199, 200, 207, 212, 218, 241
special verdict: not guilty by reason of insanity v, 62–67, 70, 74

substance abuse 182, 229, 245
suicide 12, 42, 72, 90, 97, 142, 195, 222; self-murder 12
syphilis 127, 134

Tavistock Clinic (London) 159, 168, 176
*Taxi Driver* (film) 214, 219–223
temporary insanity 32, 33
therapeutic communities **165–190**, 231
treason 44, 63, 66, 67, 71
Tyburn (London gallows) 25, 29
Vagrancy Act (1744, Great Britain) 40
Van der Hoeven Kliniek (Netherlands) 182

Vineland Training School 122, 131, 132–135, 139
violence against women 22–33, 37–39

war *see* First World War; Second World War
wild beast test of insanity 42–43
William Allnuttt (tried for murder, London Old Bailey 1847) 83–84
William Dove (tried for murder, York 1856) 83–84
workhouse *see* Poor Laws

York Retreat *see* asylum

# Author index

Adams, M. B. 128
Adlam, J. 251
Adler, H. M. 138–139
Adorno, T. W. 158–159
Ainsley, J. N. 90
Alford, C. F. 157
Allan, A. 249
Allderidge, P. H. 65
Allen, F. A. 217–218
Allen, G. E. 130
Ancrum, C. 193
Anderson, K. 150
Anderson, N. E. 244, 245
Andoll, G. 21
Andrade, J. T. 247
Andrews, 246
Appignanesi, L. 56
Appleby, L. 214, 236
Arata, S. 108
Arditi, J. 13–14
Arens, R. 216–217
Arlow, J. A. 156
Arnold, T. 42
Arrigo, B. A. 4
Augstein, H. F. 54, 60, 77

Baars, J. 158
Bailey, V. 93
Barnes, M. 250
Bean, P. 2–3
Beaver, K. 246
Beck, J. B. 56
Beck, T. R. 56
Beck, U. 240
Behrendt, S. 102

Bell, D. 222
Bell, M. 124–125
Berg, M. 8
Berman, M. 101
Berrios, G. E. 5
Binny, J. 109
Bion, W. R. 168, 176, 177–179
Bisch, L. E. 137
Black, J. 12
Blackman, L. 119
Blair, J. 243–244
Bloom, J. 217, 218, 226
Boccardi, M. 244
Bock, M. 107
Bogacz, T. 143–144
Boime, A. 50, 55–56
Bolton, W. 251
Booth, C. 117
Booth, W. 114
Boyes, P. S. 137
Bracken, P. 231
Bracton, H. 42, 43
Braggins, J. 168
Breggin, P. R. 145
Bridger, H. 178–179, 190
Bright, J. 232
Brock, D. 192
Brontë, E. 237
Brookes, M. 182
Brown, P. 3
Browne, J. 55–56
Brundage, A. 29
Brüne, M. 127
Bryant, M. 242
Bucknill, J. C. 84, 98

Bulmer, M. 137
Burnham, J. 154
Burns, L. C. 82
Burton, R. 42, 43
Button, K. S. 244
Buzina, N. 247
Bynum, T. F. 39, 40, 62, 76–77

Calhoum, C. 12, 235
Callard, F. 210, 249–250
Caplan, L. 219–224
Carlson E. T. 4
Carrido, M. 256
Cartwright, D. 161
Castel, R. 40
Chamberlin, J. E. 109
Chaperon, S. 112
Chauncey, G. 151
Chenier, E. n 148 n 163
Clark, D. 175–177, 179–180
Claydon, T. 63
Cleckley, H. 4, 185, 192, **193–197,** 199, 201, 207, 211, 213, 246–7
Cohan, S. M. 13, 19
Cohen, D. 157
Cohen, N. 232
Cohen, W. A. 103
Coid, J and Ullrich, S
Coid, J. 231, 239
Combe, G. 53
Comte, A. 106, 117
Conrad, J. 107–108,113–114, 237
Cook, D. J. 192
Coolidge, F. L. 197, 200, 201, 207
Cosgrove, L. 210
Costello, J. 150
Cotterell, P. 250
Covey, R, D. 149, 152, 163
Craddock, N. 231
Cromartie, A. 43

Daderman, A. 248
Dain, N. 4
Dalal, F. 178
Darwin, L. 142
Davie, N. 93, 94, 95
Davies, O. 83
Davison, C. M. 115

Dawson, D. 249
DeGrazia, D. 246
DeMatteo, D. 192
Denno, D. 149, 151, 152
Devereaux, S. 22, 23
Dicks, H. 159
Dikötter, F. 128
Dimaggio, G. 211
Dixon, T. 11
Dolan B. 231
Dolan, M. 249
Dollimore, J. 108
Donovan, J. 101,
Donovan, K. A. 113
Dorner, K. 40
Dowbiggin, I. 110
Doyle, M. 248
Doyle, P. 166
Dugaw, D. 8
Dugdale, R. 130–131
Duggan, C. 3
Dunham, W. W. 156
During, S. 56, 73, 104, 121
Durkheim, E. 117

East, N. 181
Edens, J. F 192
Eigen, J. P. 21,24, 40,41, 62, 64, 66, 68, 73, 79, 81, 92, 94, 97
Eisenstatdt, N. 232
Elias, N. 9, 19, 178
Eliot, G. 16, 100, 102, 104–106, 107, 121
Ellard, J. 236
Elliott, C. 5
Esquirol, E. 4, 50, 55–59, 60, 61, 100, 109–110, 121
Estabrook, A. H. 131
Evans, F. 101

Faas, E. 102,
Faller, L. B. 36
Farland, M. 202
Farrington, D. P. 249
Fazel, S. 249
Federman, C. 235
Feeley, M. 37
Feighner JP, 202

Feinstein A. R. 203
Feldbrugge, J. T. 182
Felthous, A. 196
Fenning, F. A. 138
Feuchtersleben, E. von 82, 97
Field, J. A. 121, 130
Fielding, H. 13, 14, 29, 36
Fine, R. F. 103
Flyvbjerg, B. 19
Foley, C. 149
Forbes Winslow, H. 73, 84, 85, 86, 87, 88, 89, 97
Forshaw, D. 84
Foucault, M. 3, 6–7, 19, 29, 38, 52, 56, 58, 152, 202

Foulkes, S. H. 176, 178
Fountain, N. 166
Franklin, M. 169
Freedman, E. B. 149, 150, 151
Freedman, L. Z. 223, 224
Freud, S. 82, 105, 119, 123, 128, 148, 152–156, 157, 158, 160, 174, 178, 196
Fromm, E. 158, 239
Frosh, S. 6, 158

Galton, F. 84, 93, 116, 140, 237
Gardiner, J. 166
Garland, D. 92, 93, 168, 189,
Genders, E. 182
Gentry, A. 249
George, W. R. 170
Georget, J. E. 55, 56, 57, 58, 59, 60
Gerard, D. L. 52
Gerhards, J. 250
Gibbens, T. C. 152
Giddens, A. 101, 109, 193, 240
Gidley, B. 117
Gilbert, M. 142
Gillet, G. 5
Gilligan, J. 161, 174
Gilman, S. L. 109
Gladfelder, H. 36
Glannon, W. 5
Glover, E. 18, 157, 168–169, 170, 171, 172–173, 190

Goddard, H. 66, 122, 131–136, 139, 140, 145
Godfrey, B. 35, 46
Goffman, E. 202
Goldstein, J. 5, 55, 56, 58, 61, 81, 109
Goring, C. 94
Gostin, L. 229
Grann, M. 249
Granucchi, S. J. 163
Grannuchi, A. 163
Green, J. B. 10
Greenberg, M. 219
Greene, J. K. 137
Greene, J. K. 137
Greenslade, W. 114
Grob, G. 197
Grogan, S. 144
Gurley, J. 198, 200, 207, 212
Guttmacher, M. 150
Guy, W. A. 93

Habermas, J. 7–8, 11, 19, 23, 235
Hack Tuke, D. 95
Hacking, I. 2
Haldane, D. 171
Hale, M. 21, 43–44, 63, 187
Hale, N. G. Jr. 154
Hall, S. 193
Haney, C. 129, 166
Hansen, L. A. 54, 61, 124
Hare, R. 196, 246–248
Harenski, C. 245
Harenski, K. 245
Harris, R. 109, 111
Harrison, T. 168, 175, 176, 177, 179, 180
Harvey, D. 242
Havelock, E. 95
Haverkamp, A, D. 182
Hawkins, M. 117
Hay, D. 34, 35
Heidensohn, F. 37
Henderson, D. K. 171–175, 180, 183, 185, 207, 211, 238
Henricson, C. 232
Higonnet, M. R. 150
Hitchman, J. 89, 98
Hoffman, L 153, 156

Holmes, D. 235
Holmes, G. 8
Horney, K. 160
Houston, R. A. 7
Howard League 92
Howorth, P. W. 142, 143
Hubert, W. H. 181
Hulbert, H. S. 133, 140
Hull, W. 189
Hume, D. 10
Hundert, E, J. 9
Hunt, A. 51, 82
Hunter, A. 108
Hunter, J. T. 135
Hunter, P. 245
Hurley, K. 112
Hutcheson, F. 9

Irons, A. 230

Jackson, M. 142
Jackson, R. L. 209
Jackson, S. 42
Jacob, J. D. 235
Jacoby, R. 163
James, N. 149
Jay, M. 157, 239
Johnstone, L. 249
Jolloffe, D. 249
Jones, D. W. 152, 174, 232, 239, 241, 244
Jones, G. 109
Jones, K. 40
Jones, L. 63
Junius, J. 66

Karpman, B. 147
K?tz, B. M. 159
Kaye, H. 154
Kearns, M. S. 101, 102–103, 105, 106
Keller, T. 119
Kendler, K. S 202
Kennard, D. 179
Kernberg, O. 159, 160, 161, 162, 163, 201, 239
Kiehl, K. 244, 245
Kim, J. K. 218, 224, 225

King P. 101
King, D. 145
King, P. 10
King, P. H. 157
King. E. 101
Kirk, S. 200, 201, 202, 203, 204
Klonsky, E. D. 204, 207
Koch J. L. A. 4, 125, 126
Koenigs, M. 244
Kohut, H. 161, 163, 201, 239
Konrath, S. K
Kraemer, S. 169
Kramar, J. K. 22, 186
Krimsky, S. 210
Krueger, R. 203
Kuriloff, E. A. 160
Kutchins, H. 200. 201, 202, 203, 204

Lacey, N. 113
Lacour, A. 37
Laing, R. D. 202
Landsman, S. 40, 41
Langbein, J. H. 22, 27, 29, 34
Larsson, H. 245
Lasch, C. 193, 239, 240
Laughlin, H. L. 130, 136, 146
Laurell, J. 248
Lave, T. 151, 162–163
Lawrence, P. 35, 46
Laycock, T. 91, 94
Lees, J. 182
Lemmings, D. 23, 35
Levy, E. 103
Lewes, G. H. 106
Lewis G. 214, 236
Liddle, A. M. 38, 49
Limentani, A. 157
Lindsey, E. 129
Lipton, H. R. 147
Little, D. L. 37
Livesley, J. 5
Lockey, C. J. 217, 218n, 226
Lombardo, P. 130, 135, 136
Lombroso, C. 80, 93, 114, 115
Loughnan, A. 27, 20, 25, 45
Lovell, K. 251
Lunbeck, E. 162

MacDonald, M. 8, 11, 12, 42
Maden, A. 229
Main, T. 176
Mandeville, B. 9–10, 29
Mannheim, H. 167, 168, 169–170
Manning, N. 180, 182
Markon, K. 203
Marshall, G. 107
Marx, O. M. 126
Maudsley, H. 4, 90, 92, 96, 100, 112, 118
May, A. 12, 35–36
Mayhew, H. 109
McCabe, S. 65, 71, 185, 186, 188, 214
McCallum, D. 148
McCord, J. 169, 241
McCord, W. 169
McGowen, R. 36
McKenzie, A. 27, 46
McKeon, M. 8, 22
McLaughlin, N. 157
Melville, H. 102, 103–104
Memon, R. 71
Mennell, S. 9
Merriam, C. E. 139–140
Messerschmidt, J. W. 38
Midelfort, H. C. E. 39
Mighal, R. 113
Miller, J. 8
Miller, J. (with Lynam, D. B. Widiger, T. A and Leukefeld) 209
Millon. T. 126, 154, 155, 160, 161, 281
Mishler E. G. 250
Moffitt, T. 241, 245
Moran, R. 63, 64, 65, 71
Morel, B. 67, 100, 109, 110–111
Morgan, K. O. 175
Morgan, L. 251
Morison, A. 73
Morris, C.E. 151
Morris, H. 232
Morrow, W. R. 159
Müller, J. L. 244, 245
Munday, M. 102,

Nordau, M. 108, 115–116, 119
Nourse, V. 149
Nye, R. 111

O'Connor, J. P. B. 10
Ogborn, M. 8, 22, 35
Ogloff, J. R. P. 247, 248
Oliveira–Souza, R.
Olson, H. 122, 130, 136, 137, 138, 139
O'Malley, P. 34
O'Reilly–Fleming, T. 63, 77
Overholser, W. 39

Pailthorpe, G. 160, 168, 169
Parkin, A. 82
Pa?tar, Z. 126
Pearce, J. M. S 91
Peay, J. 230
Pepper, A. 36
Perfect, W. 42
Perkin, H. 101
Peters, O. 116
Pick, D. 108, 110, 115, 117, 157, 158, 159
Pickersgill, M. 5, 201, 226, 230, 231
Pilgrim, D. 146, 236
Pinel, P. 3–4, 28, 52–55, 62, 81, 124, 172
Player, E. 182
Polk, K. 37
Poovey, M. 108
Porter, R. 8, 21, 22, 39, 40, 50
Pratt, J. 109, 128, 148
Prichard, J. C. 5, 50, 58, 59–61, 70, 77, 83, 89, 95, 103, 118, 125, 172, 194, 238
Prins, H. 172
Pujol, J. l. 244, 245

Rafter, N. 5, 93, 94, 114, 115, 129, 136, 233
Raine, A. 242–243
Ramon, S. 5, 172, 180–181
Rapoport, R. N. 180
Rawlings, B. 182, 190
Ray, I. 56, 58, 61
Reed, E. 106
Regan, S. 102
Reich, W. 160
Rembis, M. A. 140
Rennell, T. 150
Reumann, M. G. 150

Richards, H. J. 209
Richards, R. J. 124, 125
Rieff, P. 237
Rimke, H. 51, 82, 192
Rivers, W. H. R. 142
Roback, A. 126
Robertson, C. L. 96
Robinson. R. 25
Rodensky, L. 105
Rolf, C. A. 225
Rollins, H. 189
Rolph, C. 181
Ronson, J. 241
Roper, M. 166
Rose, G. 167
Rose, N. 156, 175, 176, 237
Rothman, D. 40
Rousseau, G. S. 10–11, 27, 119
Rubinstein, W. D. 101
Rush, B. 4, 51, 54, 77

Sanders, J. L. 197, 198, 202, 204, 209
Sass, H. 196
Scanlon, C. 251
Schäfer, M. 250
Scheb, J. M. 224
Scheeper, P. 158
Scheff, T. 202
Schirmann, F. 188
Schmidt, J. 52
Schroeder, M. 196, 246
Schroeder. K. 196, 246
Scull, A. 7, 39, 40, 42, 50, 57, 67, 69
Seddon, T. 228. 232
Segal, D, L. 192, 200, 201, 207
Sen, P. 230
Shapira, M. 157
Sharp, H. C. 129
Sheppard, F. 8
Sherrill, R. 224
Shipley, S. 4
Shoemaker, R. 23, 24, 37, 44, 49
Shoemaker, R. 23, 24, 37. 44, 49
Shuker, R. 182
Shuttleworth, S. 100, 101, 102, 103, 104
Simon, J. 226
Simpson, D. 53
Singh, J. P. 249

Small, H. 103
Smith, A. 10
Smith, R. 21, 50, 61, 79, 89
Smith, N. H. 103
Sparr, L. 224, 226, 231
Spencer, K. L. 113, 115
Spiro, J. 209
Spitzer, R. 200, 202–203, 204
Sprinkle, R. H. 136
Stevens, A. 181
Stevens, H. C. 133, 140
Stevenson, R. L. 112–113, 114
Stoll, M. 224, 225
Stone, L. 12, 38, 101
Stone, M. 142–143, 176
Stout, M. 241
Stubblefield, A. 131, 135, 136
Sullivan, E. 182
Sulloway, F. J. 128
Summers, J. 166
Sutherland, E. P. 150
Suttie, I. 174
Swanson, A. H. 148
Symington, N. 103
Szasz, T. 202

Taylor, C. 229
Thomas, K. 149
Thomson, J. B. 92, 93, 94, 112, 117
Thomson, M. 142
Thurston, H. W. 170
Tielbeek, J. 246
Tomes, N. 40
Tomlinson, S. 53
Toms, J. 169, 170, 171
Torgersen, S. 239
Trestman, R. L. 209
Trist, E. 176
Tucker, E. B. 154
Tuke, D. H. 95
Tuke, S. 53
Turner, B. 150
Tyrer, P. 248

Utting, D. 232

Valier, C. 167
Vandevelde, S. 180

Verplaetse, J. 93
Verwey, G. 155
Viding, E. 245
Vogt, S. 133

Wagenaar, W. A. 233
Walcutt. C. C. 108
Walker, N. 22, 29, 41, 43, 44, 46, 49, 62, 64, 65, 66, 71, 73, 74, 75, 77, 84, 89, 185, 186, 187,188, 214
Wallcraft, J. 242, 250
Walters, G. D. 249
Wanke, P. 156
Ward, T. 22, 186
Warden, J. 228
Warren F. 231
Watson, W. D. 22, 186
Watt, I. 12–13, 19, 100, 101, 107
Weber, M. 128
Werlinder, H. 4, 6, 52, 54, 55, 76, 77, 97, 110, 112, 123, 125, 126, 127, 154, 172, 196
Wessely, S. 13, 210
White, G. E. 217
Whitelye, S. 169, 176
Widiger, T. A. 202, 207, 212
Wiener, B. A. 15, 38, 46, 49, 50, 79, 90

Williams, C. 83, 84
Willrich, M. 131, 136, 137, 138, 139, 140
Wills, D. 169, 170, 171, 177
Wilson, P. 200
Winlow, S. 193
Winslow, F. 73, 84, 85, 86, 87, 88, 89, 97
Wolfgang, M. E. 115
Wood, H. 251
Woodfine, P. 24
Wootton, B. 187
Worrell, M. P.158
Wouters, C. 9
Wright, K. 229, 230
Wright, T. R. 106
Wulach, J. S. 204, 206, 207, 211

Yakeley, J. 168
Yang, Y. 244, 245
Yates, C. 219, 233
Ystehede, P. 94, 114, 115

Zalampas, S. 116
Zaretsky, E. 154, 155
Zedner, L. 22
Zenderland, L. 135

# eBooks
## from Taylor & Francis

Helping you to choose the right eBooks for your Library

Add to your library's digital collection today with Taylor & Francis eBooks. We have over 50,000 eBooks in the Humanities, Social Sciences, Behavioural Sciences, Built Environment and Law, from leading imprints, including Routledge, Focal Press and Psychology Press.

**Choose from a range of subject packages or create your own!**

**Benefits for you**
- Free MARC records
- COUNTER-compliant usage statistics
- Flexible purchase and pricing options
- All titles DRM-free.

**Benefits for your user**
- Off-site, anytime access via Athens or referring URL
- Print or copy pages or chapters
- Full content search
- Bookmark, highlight and annotate text
- Access to thousands of pages of quality research at the click of a button.

**REQUEST YOUR FREE INSTITUTIONAL TRIAL TODAY**

**Free Trials Available**
We offer free trials to qualifying academic, corporate and government customers.

## eCollections

Choose from over 30 subject eCollections, including:

| | |
|---|---|
| Archaeology | Language Learning |
| Architecture | Law |
| Asian Studies | Literature |
| Business & Management | Media & Communication |
| Classical Studies | Middle East Studies |
| Construction | Music |
| Creative & Media Arts | Philosophy |
| Criminology & Criminal Justice | Planning |
| Economics | Politics |
| Education | Psychology & Mental Health |
| Energy | Religion |
| Engineering | Security |
| English Language & Linguistics | Social Work |
| Environment & Sustainability | Sociology |
| Geography | Sport |
| Health Studies | Theatre & Performance |
| History | Tourism, Hospitality & Events |

For more information, pricing enquiries or to order a free trial, please contact your local sales team:
www.tandfebooks.com/page/sales

**www.tandfebooks.com**